THE WORLD'S MOST NOTORIOUS WOMEN

CHANCELLOR
PRESS

This 2001 edition published by
Chancellor Press, an imprint of Bounty Books,
a division of Octopus Publishing Group Ltd,
2-4 Heron Quays, London E14 4JP

Reprinted 2002, 2003 (twice)

The material in this book has previously appeared in
The World's Wickedest Women
(Hamlyn, Octopus Publishing Group Ltd, 1995)
The World's Wealthiest Losers
(Hamlyn, Octopus Publishing Group Ltd, 1999)
The World's Greatest Crooks & Conmen
(Hamlyn, Octopus Publishing Group Ltd, 1997)
The World's Greatest Trials
(Hamlyn, Octopus Publishing Group Ltd, 1997)
The World's Greatest Cults
(Hamlyn, Octopus Publishing Group Ltd, 1999)
The World's Greatest Secrets
(Hamlyn, Octopus Publishing Group Ltd, 1991)
The World's Greatest Spies & Spymasters
(Hamlyn, Octopus Publishing Group Ltd, 1985)
The World's Greatest Lovers
(Bounty, Octopus Publishing Group Ltd, 1985)
The World's Worst Murders
(Bounty, Octopus Publishing Group Ltd, 2001)
The World's Greatest Sex and Scandals
(Bounty, Octopus Publishing Group Ltd, 2001)

ISBN 0-7537-0465-X

Produced by Omnipress, Eastbourne

Printed in Great Britain

Front cover picture acknowledgements:
Corbis

Contents

Mistresses and Lovers

Cora Pearl

By the mid-1860s a red-haired English siren called Cora Pearl was the most famous courtesan in Paris – and the most costly. She was so rich that her jewels alone were valued at a million francs. She had three houses furnished regardless of cost, a platoon of servants and a magnificent stable of 60 horses. Her passion for luxury became a mania.

When one lover panicked at her spending she would simply move on to another until in the end she had gone through five or six great fortunes. She seldom had one lover at a time and coolly played them off, one against another, keeping a note of her wealthy admirers in a special book with a column for adding up what or how much they had given her. A young man called Duval, whose father had made millions out of hotels and restaurants, pleaded with her in a letter: 'Will you let me prove my devotion. Command me and I will die . . .' She replied briefly and tartly: 'I would rather you lived and paid my bills!'

One wild extravagance followed another. She bathed in a rose marble bathroom with her initials inlaid in gold at the bottom of the bath and indulged charming little whims like serving her guests with hothouse peaches and grapes on a bed of Parma violets, the violets alone costing 1,500 francs. Her dinners, masked balls and banquets were legendary. She seldom had fewer than 15 people to dine, so her chef insisted that he could not buy less than a side of beef at a time. One night she wagered her guests that she would give them some meat which they would not dare to cut. They waited impatiently for dinner and for the *pièce de résistance* to arrive. When it did, it took their breath away. Cora had had herself served up on a huge silver salver borne by four footmen. She was stark naked with a tasteful sprinkling of parsley!

Her extravagance seemed to spark off a streak of madness in her lovers. One presented her with a vast box of marron glacés, each marron wrapped in a 1,000-franc note. Another sent her a model of a silver horse, so heavy that it had to be carried in by two porters and was discovered to be full of gold and jewels. Prince Napoleon gave her a carriage full of rare orchids which she strewed on the floor, and an Irish lover, James Whelpley, gave her his entire fortune which she spent in eight weeks.

She was certainly not born to luxury, nor with the name Cora Pearl. Her real name was Eliza Emma Crouch and she was the daughter of a Plymouth music teacher, Frederick Crouch, who became famous on his own account. He wrote the beautiful ballad 'Kathleen Mavourneen' in 1835, the year of her birth, and she was educated on the profit from its sales.

Several years at a convent school in Boulogne gave Cora a taste for the French way of life. By the time she returned home to live with her grandmother in London, she was a captivating young woman with rose-petal skin and glorious auburn hair, only too well aware of her effect on men. She began to get bored with the steady, sober life she was expected to lead and decided she wanted to become an actress. She began to pay secret visits to the theatre. On one of these excursions she was approached by a charming, distinguished-looking stranger, who told her he was a diamond merchant. Naïvely accepting his invitation to dine, the inevitable happened. Rather than go back home she picked up the £5 he had left by her bedside and took a room near Covent Garden.

A theatrical speculator called Robert Bignell engaged her to sing and dance, though she had talent for neither, at the Argyll Rooms, a notorious pleasure haunt. She probably became his mistress for, when he offered to take her to Paris, they travelled as husband and wife. Once in

France, however, she lost no time in getting rid of him. She had plans of her own.

First she changed her name to Cora Pearl. Then she began to haunt the smart little cafés where singers were required. Managers hired her because they could see that her looks alone would attract customers. She was not particularly beautiful but had a perfect figure, glorious colouring and a kind of piquancy that made her wildly attractive.

At first she had to live in quite humble lodgings and her lovers were of no distinction. But when they became richer she squeezed every penny out of them to buy dresses from Worth and jewels from Cartier. She was a firm believer in the idea that to look successful was half the battle towards being successful. Her policy soon began to pay off.

Her first important lover was the Duc de Rivoli who not only bought her fabulous clothes and jewels but moved her into a delightful house where he paid her servants, her enormous food bills and her gambling debts. Gambling soon became an obsession and she lost money at an appalling rate. At the same time as the Duc was keeping her in luxury Cora was also giving her favours to the 17-year-old Prince Achille Murat. He could refuse Cora nothing. He gave her her first horse and she was so pleased with it that nothing would content her until she had a magnificent stable, tended by English grooms in yellow livery.

From 1862 Cora Pearl set the pace for the gay and elegant Paris of the Second Empire. She had started what she called her 'golden chain' of lovers. After the Duc de Rivoli and Prince Murat she added the Prince of Orange, heir to the Netherlands throne, the Duc de Morny, half-brother of the Emperor, and then Prince Napoleon, the Emperor's cousin. All of them spent fortunes on her.

Her rivals were green with envy. Some maintained that

she was downright coarse and had no looks to speak of, but she retorted by asking what did it matter as she found it perfectly easy to seduce the husbands of the most beautiful women in Paris.

She would drive out in a sky-blue *calèche,* lined with yellow satin and drawn by a team of *café au lait* coloured horses. Sometimes she dyed her hair yellow or blue to match. She used face powders tinted with silver and pearl and in summer stayed out in the sun to brown her skin, an almost unbelievable idea in those days of pale complexions and parasols. Her bottles of toilet water and her creams and powders were all specially sent from London, though she admitted her finest beauty treatment was sponging all over with cold water every day.

The last five years of the Second Empire – from 1865 to 1870 – were dazzling ones for Cora. She had been introduced to the Emperor's cousin, the 42-year-old libertine, Prince Napoleon, who was married to the intensely devout Princess Clothilde. He fell in love with her and she soon began to demolish his bank balance. The Prince bought her a house in the Rue de Chaillot, said to be the finest residence in Paris and rumoured to have cost two million francs to furnish. By now Cora behaved as though money ruled everything and everybody and could procure everything she desired, but Prince Napoleon seems to have genuinely wanted to please her. She had a longer relationship with him than with any other man and he was always loyal to her. On one of the nights she entertained him in her bed with its black satin sheets monogrammed in gold, she persuaded him to buy her a second house in the Rue des Bassins and to pay her gambling debts at Monte Carlo where she had lost 70,000 francs in eight months.

On 26 January 1867 she created a sensation when she appeared on the Paris stage as Cupid in Offenbach's comic opera *Orphee aux Enfers*. For one thing she was half-naked, for another she wore boots on which the buttons were huge diamonds and the soles were a solid mass of diamonds. After the performance an anonymous Count offered 50,000 francs for the boots, double that if Cora was inside them.

Suddenly everything changed. In July 1870 the Franco-Prussian War began. Although it was brief it brought the overthrow of the Second Empire and the scattering of all those who had in the past decade paid, and paid dearly, to maintain her wildly extravagant way of life.

Surprisingly, Cora rose to the occasion during the siege of Paris. The pampered courtesan turned her house in the rue de Chaillot into a hospital. She tore up her fine linen for bandages and shrouds, tied an apron over her fine dresses and worked among the wounded for 16 hours at a stretch.

Prince Napoleon, in exile, remained constant, but Cora had to have someone to take his place. Among those who paid their court to her was a young man, ten years her junior, called Alexandre Duval. He was besotted by her now mature charms and begged her to let him prove his love. Smiling indulgently she agreed. First he could pay off all her debts. And perhaps he would pick up the bill for a banquet she was planning to give . . . Although Duval belonged to a very rich family owning a chain of hotels and restaurants, 12 months of Cora's demands brought the young man to his knees. When he confessed he could no longer keep up with her insane spending and that he had reached the end of his resources, she turned her back on him.

One day he followed her home and asked to speak with her. When she refused he took out a gun and shot himself. With his body sprawled on her front doorstep all that seemed to worry Cora Pearl was how society would react to this appalling business. She thought him dead and afterwards everyone remembered her lack of pity for

Duval, her complete lack of compassion. Although she did not realize it at the time, her treatment of him helped to bring about her downfall.

Duval recovered from the gunshot wound but things were never to be the same again for Cora. One night when she drove to the theatre she was hissed and felt the fury of the Paris mob at her heels. Her treatment of young Duval had been too callous even for the French *demi-monde*. The affair caused such an uproar, in fact, that she decided it would be tactful to go on a world tour.

London did not receive her well. She had booked a suite on the first floor of the Grosvenor Hotel and paid for a month in advance. But no sooner had her mountain of luggage been deposited in the foyer than the manager, suddenly realizing who she was, quietly informed her that she must leave. It was a bitter humiliation and she had to rent a house in Mayfair at a very high price. Nevertheless, she enjoyed some triumphs in England.

She wandered about Europe for a time – Monte Carlo, Nice, Milan – making a tour of the chief casinos where she hoped to boost her flagging bank account with luck at the tables. To her fury she met with fresh humiliation at Baden where she was refused admission to the tables. Fortunately one of her admirers, a cousin of the Kaiser, saw what had happened, offered her his arm and led her in.

When she felt she had been away long enough to let the Duval affair fade in public memory, she returned to Paris and for a time continued to give dinners and receptions paid for by admirers. But from 1874, when Prince Napoleon decided to break off his relationship with her, her life began to disintegrate.

First she had to sell off the house in the rue de Chaillot. Her jewels went to pay her gambling debts. All her fabulous possessions were auctioned to provide money to keep her afloat. She was able to hold her own for nearly ten years but then her slide down the social ladder was rapid. She ended her career in a cheap boarding-house in the back streets of Paris, her looks ravaged, her admirers gone.

On 8 July 1886, she died of cancer. Not a single newspaper recorded the fact, the cheapest of coffins was ordered for her and a local undertaker received instructions to bury her as a pauper. Before he could carry out his orders he received a visit from a distinguished man of aristocratic bearing. 'What will the best funeral for Madame Cora Pearl cost?' he asked. Holding out a sheaf of notes he said: 'The lady must have the finest funeral.' Just before he turned to go, he added: 'I warn you an agent of mine will be present to see you fulfil your part of the bargain.' The stranger never identified himself but Cora was buried in the cemetery at Batignolles in the style to which she was once accustomed.

Lola Montez

In her time, Lola Montez was probably the most outrageous woman in the world. She caused a King to lose his throne, set off rebellions and riots, mesmerized men both famous and infamous and stung French writer Alexandre Dumas into saying: 'She is fatal to any man who dares to love her.'

She was a fabulous liar, a meddler in politics, mistress to more men than she could remember and very beautiful. Her life was so crammed with adventure and disaster that one wonders how she managed to fit it all in.

Her real name was not Maria Dolores Porres Montez. It was Eliza Gilbert. Nor was she, as she so often claimed, the daughter of Lord Byron and an Irish washerwoman or, alternatively, a child of noble Spanish birth stolen by gypsies. Her background was far more sedate than she cared to admit.

Lola was born not in Spain but in Limerick, Ireland, in 1818. Her mother was a milliner from Dublin and her father a captain in the British East Indian Army. She was brought up in Calcutta and proved to be a wild young thing, spoiled by the attention of too many servants. When her father died of cholera her mother married her best friend, a staunch young Scotsman called Captain Craigie, who was to become Sir Patrick Edmonstone Craigie, Adjutant-General of the Army in Bengal. Lola was sent home to his Calvinist relations in Montrose, then to schools in England and Paris so that she could be properly educated and taught some manners.

When it was time for her to return and join the Calcutta set, Mrs Craigie herself came to fetch her. It was not through fondness. She had no affection for Lola. But she did have ambitions. The rich 60-year-old Judge of the Supreme Court in India, Sir Abraham Lumley, had asked her to find him a wife. When she saw that her rebellious child had turned into a young beauty with clouds of black hair and gentian-blue eyes, she felt her problems were over. But Lola thwarted her by eloping with a young officer called Captain James who had travelled over with Mrs Craigie, warned Lola what was going on, and took her back to India himself.

The charming Captain James turned out to be more interested in other men's wives and horses and soon deserted her, by which time Mrs Craigie had given up her daughter for good. She refused her financial help and thought the best thing she could do would be to go back to the good Calvinists in Montrose. But her stepfather, a kind man who liked her spirit, put a cheque for £1,000 into her hand before she sailed.

Nothing would make her go back to the pious Scots, so she found herself alone in the world. She would have to earn her living. An American who befriended her on the passage over suggested she should go on the stage. It was the turning point in her life. She couldn't act so decided to become a dancer – a Spanish dancer. Probably the fact that her mother had sometimes boasted of a drop of Spanish blood in the family, in order to make herself more 'interesting', gave her the idea. She hired an Andalusian dancing master and when he had taught her all he knew she went to Spain for six months to absorb the atmosphere, learn the language and acquire a new persona.

When she stepped onto the stage at Her Majesty's Theatre in London, she was Lola Montez. She was not a very good dancer. She had little sense of rhythm and timing. But, dressed in black lace and red roses, she looked stunning and the management relied on her looks to bring in the crowds. But her first and only appearance on the London stage was a total disaster. To start with she was recognized by some young blade who called out 'Why, it's Betty James'. Then her exotic and highly provocative Tarantula dance, in which she conducted a frenzied search of her body for a lost spider, had to be brought to a swift end as the whole house erupted in hisses and catcalls.

Her mother, hearing of the shocking display her daughter was making of herself, decided that from that moment she no longer existed. She went into mourning and had her stationery edged with black.

For a few years Lola drifted about Europe taking engagements where she could. To make herself interesting she swore at one point she had been reduced to singing in the streets of Brussels to keep herself from starving. She also told a fanciful tale about being engaged as a spy by the Tsar of Russia. She certainly *almost* met the Tsar. He was the guest of Frederick of Prussia at a Grand Fête where Lola had been engaged to dance. The following day a military tattoo was held in his honour. As the grand parade ended there was a sudden commotion among the onlookers. Lola appeared on horseback. Suddenly her mount, excited by the glitter and noise – or perhaps by a sharp jab of spurs – headed straight for the royal box. Lola was on the point of being thrown into the Tsar's lap when a guard dashed forward and caught the reins. She rewarded him by raising her riding whip and bringing it down across his face.

Lola also gave a highly coloured version of her visit to Warsaw where her name first became involved in politics. She had been engaged to dance there and the Viceroy of Poland, a very rich old man, fell desperately in love with her. According to Lola he offered her a splendid country estate and handfuls of diamonds if she would become his mistress. He was, apparently, such a short, grotesque looking man that she respectfully declined.

The Viceroy was deeply insulted by the refusal. Next day the director of the theatre where she was appearing called on her and urged her to reconsider the offer. He started by being persuasive, then, seeing that he was getting nowhere, threatened her. Fiery little Lola threw him out.

That night when she appeared on stage she was hissed and booed by a claque stationed in the gallery. It had obviously been arranged. The third night it happened Lola stamped up to the footlights in a rage, told the rest of the audience why she was being harassed and to her delight was overwhelmed by cheering and applause.

An immense crowd escorted her back to the hotel where she was staying. What she did not know was that both the Viceroy and the theatre manager were suspected of being traitors and the hatred the Polish people felt for their Tsarist-dominated government and its agents had suddenly found an outlet. The crowds did not go home. Rioting started in the streets and within 24 hours Warsaw was on the brink of revolution.

Told that her arrest had been ordered, she barricaded herself in her hotel room and informed the police when they arrived that she had a gun and would use it. The

French Consul gallantly came forward and offered her his protection until the city quietened down. She was then asked to leave.

People were beginning to talk about Lola but not, she felt, quite enough. While in Dresden she met the Hungarian composer and pianist, Franz Liszt, who had half the women in Europe swooning over his profile and demonic playing. She gazed into his eyes, and he was trapped. For a while they enjoyed a consuming passion, travelling everywhere together, quarrelling and making up interminably. They were a magnetic pair. But Liszt was a showman as well as a musician and it gradually dawned on him that Lola was stealing his thunder. His fears became certainty after a solemn occasion in Bonn at which he unveiled a statue to Beethoven. Lola, who had not been invited, gatecrashed the banquet that followed and before royalty and heads of state leaped onto a table and danced among the dishes.

After this Liszt realized he must get rid of her. One morning, while she was still asleep, he gathered his belongings together and crept out of their apartment, making sure to lock the door behind him. Passers-by were later astonished at the sight of furniture being thrown through a window by an enraged and beautiful woman.

She flounced off to Paris where her growing notoriety helped her to get an engagement at the Port Saint Martin Theatre. But nothing could cover the fact that her dancing was still second-rate and that she couldn't pick up her feet in time to the music. She was hissed and this time answered her critics with a firework display of temper and a gesture for which she became famous. She took off her garters and flung them into the audience.

One night, intrigued by the stories he had heard about her, Henri Dujarier, literary critic and part-owner of *La Presse*, went to see her dance. They were introduced backstage after her performance and found each other fascinating. Lola became his mistress and he began to show her a world she had never entered before. He took her to the salon of Georges Sand, Chopin's mistress. She met literary giants like Dumas, Victor Hugo, Balzac and Gautier. She amazed them by her intelligence and, always interested in politics, she became an ardent republican like Dujarier. He asked her to marry him. But the idyll was not to last.

At a party one night Dujarier became involved in a argument with Jean de Beauvallon of *Le Globe*, a rival newspaperman he cordially disliked. The party ended with de Beauvallon challenging Dujarier to a duel. Lola was distraught. She knew her lover had never handled a duelling pistol in his life. De Beauvallon was a crack shot. She tried to persuade him not to take part but the duel took place at dawn and Dujarier was shot through the heart.

Lola grieved deeply and was the focus of all eyes at the sensational murder trial that followed. Swathed in black silk and lace she cried out: 'I could handle a pistol more accurately than poor Dujarier. I would have been quite willing to have gone out with M. de Beauvallon myself!'

But it was too late. The tragedy left her at the age of 27 quite comfortably off but in an emotional vacuum. There was nothing to do but go on dancing. She made up her mind to arrange a tour of Bavaria. It was the most important decision of her life and led to her greatest love affair, with King Ludwig I of Bavaria.

For King Ludwig nothing in the world mattered as much as art, sculpture, architecture and beauty. He lived in a cloud-cuckoo land of Greek columns and classical verse, showing complete indifference to the ordinary, everyday needs of his country. He created modern Munich and made it the art centre of Germany but allowed his government to be dominated by reactionary elements and Jesuit priests.

He collected beautiful women in much the same way as

he collected fine statues and it is highly likely that Lola, knowing his weakness, planned to take advantage of it. When she reached Munich the manager of the state theatre, after seeing her dance, explained ruefully that she was not good enough and took her name off the bill. Lola exploded and said she would appeal to Ludwig himself for help.

Having been kept waiting in Ludwig's ante-room for rather a long time she became impatient and decided to enter the royal presence without introduction. Just as she opened the door to Ludwig's private apartment a guard rushed forward to grab her and in the struggle tore the bodice of her dress. Lola swished through the door, slammed it behind her and was left facing an astounded Ludwig. His eyes became fixed on the torn bodice. Capriciously she snatched a pair of scissors from his desk and slashed it to the waist exposing her splendid bosom. Ludwig dismissed his *aide de camp* and before she left the palace she had been promised an engagement at the Munich Theatre.

The King went to see her dance three nights in succession and became completely infatuated. Five days later he presented her at court and astounded his ministers by introducing her as 'my best friend'.

At first not a voice was raised against her. Ludwig's Queen was used to his infidelities and did not realize that Lola was different from the rest. But it soon became clear that 'the Spanish dancer' was more than a mistress. She had political ambitions. Her first aim was to show the King how, while he had been busy collecting Greek statues and reading classic verse, his government had become riddled with corruption and Jesuits had infiltrated everywhere. Within weeks she had exposed his Jesuit Prime Minister as a villain. She wanted above all to steer him towards republicanism and the whole country watched, appalled, as he hung on her every word. The

Jesuits called her an 'emissary of Satan' and an 'Apocalyptic whore' and tried hard to 'bring the King to his senses'. But the minority Protestants in Bavaria regarded her as a heroine and a champion of liberty.

The relationship between Lola and Ludwig was complex. He undoubtedly loved her. He built her a small palace, then, feeling it was not grand enough, added two wings of white marble, gilded and lavishly decorated, one of which housed an amazing glass staircase. He designed a marble fountain for the courtyard which sprayed delicately perfumed water. Lola felt she could not live in such splendour without a title so he created her Countess of Landsfeld and Baroness Rosenthal and gave her a gold-trimmed coach lined with ermine to drive about in. People were beginning to say: 'What Lola wants, Lola gets.'

Her temper was as fiery as ever. She had thrown priceless vases at her interior decorators; the chief of police had had his ears boxed and she had thrown champagne at Ludwig's ministers during a state banquet. She became obsessed with a hatred of Jesuits and complained that they followed her everywhere. She bought a bulldog and taught it to snarl at the black-robed priests, even to bite them if necessary. She carried a whip and people learned to keep out of the way.

Realizing her influence over the King, even the most powerful ministers tried to win her favour. But the matter of her titles brought their real feelings into the open. Most ministers said she could not be ennobled unless she was naturalized – and they would never consent to nationalization. Ludwig, furious, not only raised her to Countess but also granted her an allowance from the treasury. The ruling ministry resigned and a new one was formed from advanced liberals. It became known as the 'Lola Ministry'. The bitter politicians said they had been driven from power by 'a strolling dancer of ill fame'.

Although she was young and full of idealistic fervour,

she did not carry the students with her. And, to her cost, she did not realize soon enough the importance of student opinion.

One unpleasant incident brought about by this mistake contributed to her downfall. While she was out walking one day she ran into a Jesuit professor whom she hated because she suspected him of criticizing her at the university. She set her bulldog on him. The deeply offended professor called a meeting of his colleagues to denounce Lola and her influence. Ludwig was told of the meeting and dismissed him. When they heard what had happened crowds of students gathered outside her palace shouting insults. She appeared defiantly on a balcony and stood there mockingly nibbling marzipan and sipping champagne. When she lifted her glass in a mock toast bricks began to fly through her window. The King, on being told what was happening, rushed to join her. For the first time in his life, he had to be provided with a military escort.

After this incident about 20 students who still supported her ideas rallied to her, forming a guard which became known as the *Alemannia*. They became very unpopular with their fellow students and soon the Press was full of stories and lampoons about the Countess of Landsfeld and her male harem.

In the streets riots continued spasmodically, Lola's windows were protected with iron bars and everywhere she went she had to be escorted by members of the *Alemannia*, as showers of abuse and insult were hurled at her. Students frequently confronted her in the streets. On one of these occasions, flexing the whip she always carried, she said in an icy voice: 'I will close down the university.' Nothing could have been worse.

Friends, advisers and members of his own family were by this time appealing to the distraught Ludwig to get rid of her. But he still loved her and he was stubborn. On 8 February 1848, to satisfy Lola he gave the order for the university to be closed. Hundreds rioted. Lola, by now feeling that nothing was beyond her, went out into the streets certain she could quell the violence, but as soon as she was recognized she was jostled and jeered. She tried to seek refuge at the Austrian Legation but no one would open the door for her. Eventually it was necessary to send for a detachment of soldiers to make sure she got back to her palace alive.

The King at last seemed to wake from his dream and realize that revolution was in the air. He was persuaded to take up a pen and with a shaking hand signed a document banishing Lola Montez from Bavaria. The mob was heading for her palace as she escaped through the back entrance and took to her carriage. Ludwig went to face the mob with great courage. Hatless, the strain showing on his face, he shouted: 'Scoundrels. The house is empty. She is gone.' At least, he thought she had. But Lola couldn't quite accept what had happened to her and kept turning up in disguise, for one last farewell. Ludwig was asked to abdicate in favour of his son.

The rest of his life was devoted to a harmless study of architecture, painting and beautiful things, but he wrote long letters to the mistress who had cost him his crown and supported her with a pension for many years to come.

She arrived in London looking stunning in black velvet with a red rose in her hair. All the young women copied her and the fashionable young men tried to get to her parties so that they could say that they had met Lola Montez. One of these young blades was a Lifeguards officer called George Heald who was 20 years younger than her and due one day to inherit a fortune. She agreed to marry him only to find herself confronted with an army of aged relatives who had no intention of their money going to keep an adventuress. One of them, a rigid spinster who had brought up George, took time to dig into Lola's past and came up with her husband, Captain James, and the fact that since they parted in India they had never been legally divorced. Lola found herself on a bigamy charge at Marlborough Street Court. The besotted George stood bail for her and when nobody was looking they quietly left the country.

They managed to stay together for about three years but Lola's temper was getting worse and one day, after a terrible row, she stabbed him. He left her but, as he had done many times before, returned because he couldn't live without her. They were seen together in Spain at the Casino in Perpignan. Lola, wearing a flaming red gown, rubies flashing on her fingers, was the centre of attention. George Heald stood behind her chair. She kept putting her hand over her shoulder for more gold pieces. He ran out of funds. Next time the croupier called 'Faites vos jeux' she turned to her lover impatiently: 'Come, money, quick, money.' Flushing, he replied: 'You have played enough, come away. I have no more money.' Lola rose and struck him across the face. 'Learn,' she hissed, 'that he who accompanies Lola must always have money at his command.'

She left him and their two children, and he began to drink his life away. Paris was her next hunting ground. Her income had dwindled so she appealed to Ludwig for funds which he provided and she was soon to be seen at the Café Royale looking exquisite in white silk and camellias and escorted by Prince Jung Bahadoor, the handsome Nepalese ambassador.

But Europe was finished for Lola. She was looking for a new life and decided that the Americans would appreciate a dancer who was also a real-life Countess. Barnum, the great showman, made her an offer, but she did not see herself as 'Lola, the Notorious Montez' exhibited along with his freaks. Instead she signed with an American agent called Edward Willis who considered her a lady and felt sure she could conquer the New World.

Lola made a spectacular arrival in New York in 1852 dressed in perfect gents' suiting with spurred, polished boots and a riding whip. One over-familiar American who dared to grab hold of her coat tails received a cut across the face for his pains.

Her progress across America was accompanied all the way by stories of her violent temper. She would rage at her critics and sometimes lash out with the whip so that managers began to ask themselves if she was worth the money. On reaching San Francisco she found herself without an agent. He had just been told that back in New Orleans she had kicked the prompter and he had kicked her back; worn out with trying to smooth her path after such episodes, he handed in his notice.

While in California, she met and married a newspaperman called Patrick Hull, who reminded her of her old love Dujarier, and they set off on a tour of the gold-rush towns, Lola taking with her 50 trunks containing silk draperies, gilt mirrors and exquisite *objets d'arts* as well as a stupendous wardrobe.

Her spider dance had become vulgar beyond words and it was said the miners would leave gold in the ground to see her perform it.

Patrick Hull lasted only a few weeks. Though charming he turned out to have an Irish will as fierce as her own. One night she threw his belongings out of the window and he went back to his newspaper.

When she wasn't touring she lived in a white-painted house in Grass Valley and came near to settling there for good. She loved the scenery and became devoted to her menagerie of animals, including a grizzly bear which she took for walks. But her huge expenditure on entertaining, even when she was supposed to be living simply, made it necessary for her to keep on dancing.

She became attracted to a small-time theatrical manager called Ned Fellin, who obviously saw Lola as a means of making his name. He suggested a world tour in 1855 to include Australia, Paris and New York. They became lovers and set out to storm the antipodes.

Lola shocked Australia. After what she considered a tasteful version of 'Tarantula' in Sydney she was found to be 'suggestive' and 'indelicate'. She moved on to Melbourne where a local editor called her performance 'immoral'. She went after him armed with a whip. At Geelong the audience called upon the mayor to stop her act and at Ballarat, where at least the miners cheered her, she attacked the editor of the local paper, only to be given a taste of her own medicine. Eventually they had to admit that the Australian tour was a failure and they agreed to go home to America.

Fellin had become tiresome as far as Lola was concerned – far too sensitive about her little flirtations. Afterwards Lola said little of the mysterious incident that ended their relationship, but it was obviously traumatic.

On the night of 18 July 1856 they were on board ship, heading for home. They had reached Fiji and Fellin apparently asked Lola for some money she had in reserve. She went to her cabin to fetch it. Suddenly there was a terrible scream. People rushed on deck to find Lola lying in a dead faint. Fellin was nowhere to be seen. A thorough search was made but to no avail. He had simply disappeared. When questioned about precisely what happened that night, Lola would never discuss details but would say 'I have been wild and wayward, but never wicked', implying that Fellin had not met his death at her hands but had fallen overboard.

Back in America she was a different woman. Her temper seemed under control, she never again carried a whip and she turned to religion. She disappeared at the end of 1856 and did not appear on the scene again for a year. It was rumoured she had married again, though when asked the name of her husband she would laugh and dismiss the matter. Years later in the records of the royal family of Bavaria was found a record of a morganatic marriage between Lola Montez and Ludwig. He was then 72. If so, then means must have been found to dissolve her marriage with Captain James.

By 1859 she was thinner, her hair came out in handfuls and her dress became slovenly. She was desperately ill and she knew it. She sought consolation more and more in religion and spiritualism, boarding at a Methodist hotel where she rented two furnished, pleasant rooms. After suffering a slight stroke she was taken under the wing of a so-called fervent Christian called Mrs Buchanan, who persuaded her to go and live with her and her husband.

News of Lola's illness reached her mother, now Lady Craigie, and the avaricious woman travelled to America on the pretext of seeing her daughter for the last time, but in fact to ascertain whether Lola still had Ludwig's jewels. What she did not know was that the cunning Mrs Buchanan had persuaded the sick woman to hand over the few pieces she had left, including a diamond necklace, with the promise that she would look after her till the end.

Disappointed, Lady Craigie went home, leaving 10 dollars towards the care of her dying daughter. The evil Mrs Buchanan moved Lola to a wretched hovel of a boarding-house and left her there in the care of a filthy old hag.

The Protestant Minister who visited her at the end thought naïvely that she had chosen this place as a penitence for all the bad years. He stayed with her and gave her comfort as she died like a pauper on a pile of rags.

Barbara Villiers

There came a point in the reign of Charles II when people began to wonder who really ruled England; the amiable, amoral King or his mistress, Barbara Villiers. Her power over him was absolute, her avarice insatiable and her temper formidable.

Through the corrupt practices of the beautiful Barbara, the whole administration was tainted. Lord Clarendon, the great Chancellor she brought to ruin, could not bring himself to utter her name – he always called her 'That Lady' – and diarist, John Evelyn, fuming about her morals, called her 'the curse of our nation'.

Her greed was never satisfied. When Charles had given her all he could, she plundered public funds for money to buy houses and jewels. She dominated the Keeper of the Privy Purse to such an extent that he gave her thousands of pounds that should have been spent on the royal household. Soon it became known that the only way to advance a career in government or at court was to apply to the King's mistress for a place or preferment – and to pay her accordingly. The King would eventually agree to anything to avoid Barbara's wrath.

No one is quite certain how they met. It was probably just before his return from exile when she and her husband, as true Royalists, went to the Continent to offer him their support on regaining the throne. She was then at the height of her beauty, tall, with a glorious figure, midnight black hair and flashing, imperious blue eyes. She became his mistress and his obsession. Her great hold on him, it was believed, was her incredible sexual prowess, for the King was a very sensual man.

On the momentous day when Charles returned from exile to a tumultuous welcome in the city of London and retired to what contemporary historians called 'his sweet and sedate repose', it was Barbara Villiers, in all her glory, who waited to greet him in the royal bed.

The Villiers family, from which she sprang, had produced some of the most successful and powerful courtiers since the time of the Norman Conquest. They had a long history of intimacy with Kings. Barbara was born in 1641 in the parish of St Margaret's, Westminster. Her father, William Villiers, Viscount Grandison, fought for the Royalists at the Battle of Edgehill and died of his wounds at the siege of Bristol when she was only three. Her mother then married a cousin, Charles Villiers, a decent but relatively poor man, and Barbara was brought up in the country without luxury.

Taken to London at the age of 16 she soon showed her true mettle and became involved with one of the most notorious rakes in town, the 23-year-old Earl of Chesterfield, who admitted he would sleep with any woman provided she was not old or ugly. He had the upper hand where Barbara was concerned and she suffered agonies of jealousy. The experience made her vow that in future affairs she would be dominant.

When she was 18 she married Roger Palmer, son of a wealthy and respected country knight who was studying law. Scholarly and quiet he hardly seemed the partner for Barbara Villiers. But, having fallen in love with her, nothing would do but marriage and her own family encouraged the match.

Their wedding took place on 14 April 1659 and the minute it was over Roger whisked his bride away to the country. He hoped to be able to keep her from temptation, but his efforts were futile. Half-crazy with boredom, she wrote passionate letters to Chesterfield and slipped away to see him whenever she could. The affair ended when the Earl killed a man in a duel, fled to the Continent and, to her fury, married someone else.

But, if Palmer thought his worries were over with

Chesterfield's departure, he had no idea of what was to come. Once his wife had met the King, Palmer ceased to exist as far as she was concerned – except to play the role of father to her offspring.

He seems to have had no idea what was going on at first, but when he suddenly gained the title Earl of Castlemaine shortly after the birth of Barbara's first royal child he had to face the truth. Public sympathy was very much for Roger Palmer who had served the Stuarts well and suffered great injustice. Although he lived to a great age he never took his seat in the House of Lords and hardly ever used his title.

There was no doubt that the King's mistress was the most dazzling figure at court. By 1662 her power over the monarch was growing daily. He dined with her nearly every night, hardly ever appeared in public without her and was plainly influenced by her opinions. Her very presence at court seemed to create an atmosphere of tension and unease. Her manner was so imperious and arrogant that many of the great nobles became hostile towards her. Lord Clarendon was particularly aware of the danger in her growing influence and did everything he could to curb it. Nor did it go unnoticed that her Ladyship now dressed in clothes and jewels of great splendour and extravagance.

Just as she was at her zenith, Barbara was brought down to earth with a shock. The King told her he was to be married and implied that her position would be somewhat changed by the arrival of his bride. 'The whole affair,' Samuel Pepys noted gleefully in his diary, 'will put Madame Castlemaine's nose out of Joynt.'

Charles travelled to Portsmouth to meet the ship bringing Catherine of Braganza, Infanta of Portugal, to be his Queen. Himself gloriously tailored in velvet and lace, he was somewhat surprised by the frumpy appearance of his bride and her equally dowdy ladies-in-waiting. Short, plain, swarthy-complexioned, the Portuguese Princess was nothing like the women Charles found attractive. But it was a political marriage and the King had enough good in him to recognize her qualities. He found her sweet and pious and her conversation proved most agreeable.

While the royal pair made a magnificent progress to Hampton Court, Barbara, eight months pregnant, was impatiently kicking her heels. She was eventually delivered of a son. Her husband, a recent convert to Rome, had the boy baptized by a priest. He was only playing the part expected of him, but when his wife heard the news she exploded with rage, packed her bags and went to live in her brother's house in Richmond, swearing that she would never again live with Lord Castlemaine. Her reaction was calculated. In one stroke she had managed to rid herself of her husband and move nearer to the King.

For a short time after the arrival of Catherine, Lady Castlemaine stayed out of sight. But then Charles himself precipitated a scene which profoundly shocked the court. He was horrified by the unattractive, prudish women his Queen had brought with her as ladies-in-waiting. He thought it time to appoint a few English beauties to the Queen's bedchamber in the hope that his wife would be influenced by their taste and refinement. Barbara begged and pleaded with him to allow her to be one of them as a public demonstration of his loyalty to her.

When the Queen saw Lady Castlemaine's name at the top of the list Charles presented to her, she fainted with shock. She refused even to set eyes on the woman of whom she had heard so much. Her mother had told her never to allow her name to be mentioned in her presence. The King withdrew, murmuring apologies but Barbara pestered him so much that he decided to try once more. This time he led her into the Queen's presence without warning and asked to be allowed to present her. Catherine, face to face with the dreaded mistress, fell down in a fit, blood pouring from her nose, and the court scattered in confusion.

Clarendon, who had supported the Queen all along, was called to issue an ultimatum. Either Catherine accepted Lady Castlemaine or the King would feel free to have as many mistresses as he chose. The Queen gave in for, though she had been cruelly humiliated, she had grown to love Charles. In fact the row marked a turning point in their relationship. The King discovered he had grown fond of his plain little wife, although he had a poor way of showing it.

Her success over the business of the bedchamber made Barbara even more demanding and arrogant. She travelled in the royal coach with the King and even persuaded him to break his solemn promise to Catherine not to allow her to live under the royal roof. She was given an apartment next to the King so they could live together almost as man and wife. At this point her influence over him was quite sinister. She knew his weaknesses better than anyone and enslaved him with her passion, often when he should have been attending to affairs of state.

Meddling in politics was one of her worst faults. She had no particular allegiance but just wanted to get rid of those who opposed her or who objected to the fortune she made out of selling important posts. She talked Charles into getting rid of many of his elder statesmen so that she could replace them with her own favourites. Lord Clarendon, whom she still hated and feared, once remarked bitterly: 'That woman would sell every place if she could.' The words were reported to her and she replied tartly that his Lordship could rest easy for his place was already contracted for and the bargain near completion!

Money was her god. She raided the privy purse to pay her ever-increasing debts and squandered thousands of pounds in gambling or in reckless spending. The King dared not cross her. Sometimes when she was displeased, she would summon him from some important meeting and berate him like a fishwife.

The first sign of a crack in her Ladyship's power came with the arrival from France of a new lady-in-waiting for the Queen. Although she was only 15 and a distant relation, the King was captivated the moment he set eyes on her. Her name was Frances Stuart though her porcelain prettiness had earned her the title La Belle Stuart. She was the opposite of the King's voluptuous mistress in every way. Fresh and sweet-natured, she knew how to flirt deliciously while keeping him at arm's length. She had no interest in politics or intrigue. Barbara watched her rival flitting about the court like some exquisite butterfly and treated everyone to bouts of her foul temper. The fact that she was heavily pregnant with yet another of the King's children, and needed to rest, made his dalliance all the easier. But, though the ardent Charles wooed Frances Stuart with all the charm he possessed, he did not win her. She was in love with the young Duke of Richmond and one night eloped with him. The court was startled by the King's jealous anger and not too happy to see Lady Castlemaine back again, all-powerful.

With Frances Stuart out of the way, the King's mistress now turned her venom on her old enemy, Clarendon.

Politically and economically England had been through a difficult time both at home and abroad. Lord Clarendon, as the King's chief minister and one of the few experienced politicians left, was blamed for a good deal of it. Talk against him was inflamed by Barbara and her associates until in the end even Charles, who owed him so much, felt he must go. What really irritated the King was his Chancellor's puritanical attitude and obvious distaste for the libertine court. In the interview that took place between them, Clarendon was unwise enough to speak out against Lady Castlemaine and her meddling in state affairs. The

King was furious and told him to hand in his seal of office and never return. As Clarendon left, devastated, the King's mistress was seen on a balcony in her nightclothes laughing and jeering him on his way.

The fall of Clarendon convinced Barbara that she could do anything with the King. He was clay in her hands. Once she forced him to beg her forgiveness on his knees while the court looked on appalled at his weakness and her power.

During their affair neither had been faithful to the other. So profligate was the court of Charles II that infidelity was regarded as a trifle. Barbara became infatuated with a world-famous rope dancer, a handsome fellow called Jacob Hall, and it was said she gave him a pension from money intended for national defence. Another lover was a back-stairs page, who later became an actor. Then there was a young footman who accompanied her coach and whom, malicious tongues said, was forced to take a bath with her.

When she became pregnant for the sixth time, Charles knew the child was not his. When he accused her of infidelity and suggested the notorious rake, Henry Jermyn, was more likely to be the father, she threatened to publish his letters if he did not accept paternity. For once Charles stood firm. In a dreadful scene she swore that if he did not acknowledge the child she would bring it to court and dash out its brains in front of everybody. 'God damn you! But you *shall* own it!' she screeched. She had gone too far.

His wisest councillors began to advise the King to dismiss Barbara – and he listened to them. It was time for a change. He took Moll Davies, a common actress, as his mistress and set her up in a splendid house in Suffolk Street. But she was soon eclipsed by another who was to delight Charles for the rest of his life. Her name was Nell Gwynne and she was a match for Lady Castlemaine as well as a salve for Charles's battered ego.

Though their days as lovers were over, Barbara now began to take advantage of her new status. For it was while Charles was making the effort to rid himself of her that she cost him most. To keep her quiet he bestowed yet more titles upon her, so that in 1670 she became Duchess of Cleveland, Countess Nonsuch and Countess of Southampton. These favours of course meant yet more money from the privy purse so that she could live the life of a Duchess. People thought that with the bestowal of the title and the lands that went with it she would be satisfied. They did not know she was also receiving £30,000 a year, money to settle her debts and enormous sums from the Customs and Excise and Post Office revenues.

Although her affair with the King had virtually come to an end she still had enough beauty at the age of 30 to raise men's blood pressure when she chose. The great Duke of Marlborough, then a handsome young man of 21 newly arrived from Devon, became her lover and she bore his child. The King was said not to mind in the least but he wished her, if she was having an affair, 'not to make such a damned show of it'. Her influence at court was now entirely eclipsed by the King's latest favourite, a beautiful Breton girl called Louise de Kerouallle.

Charles dipped into public funds once more in 1674 for lavish weddings for two of Barbara's daughters, Charlotte, who became Countess of Litchfield, and Anne, who became Countess of Sussex. But this time people came out into the streets and demonstrated against this latest extravagance of 'the King's whore'.

Two years later Barbara Villiers, new Duchess of Cleveland, took herself off to Paris where she took as many lovers as she pleased and managed to bring about the downfall of the British ambassador.

Throughout her life abroad she and the King exchanged letters and when she returned to London in 1685 the diarist John Evelyn recorded that she was graciously received by him. She was certainly one of a group playing cards with the King a few nights before he had the seizure which brought about his death.

Years passed and the days when she dominated the court with her arrogance and beauty must have seemed a long way off. Her gambling debts were huge and the money she had accumulated had slipped away, largely falling into the hands of rogues.

In 1705, when she was 64, she allowed herself to be talked into marriage with a reprobate called Beau Fielding who had been married twice and had already squandered two fortunes. The match was the talk of the season and the subject of some cruel satires. Fielding, discovering that the Duchess of Cleveland was not as wealthy as he had supposed, beat her so violently that she thought she would die. Fortunately evidence was produced to show that the rogue had never been divorced from his first wife and he was marched off to court for bigamy.

After the shame of this episode she spent her last years in her house in Chiswick Mall near the Thames, known today as Walpole House. Her once glorious body swelled with dropsy and she died there on 9 October 1709. But her spirit, always restless and unsatisfied in life, would not rest and she is said to haunt the Mall to this day.

Eliza Lynch

By the muddy bank of the river Aquidaban in Paraguay, only a stone's throw from the Bolivian border, a beautiful Irish woman knelt to dig a grave with her bare hands. She had asked to be allowed to bury the body of her lover, and the son who died with him, at the end of what was one of the bloodiest and most futile wars ever fought in South America.

The horror of the scene was one she could not have

envisaged in all the years through which she, and the man whose corpse she now covered with stones, had dreamed and schemed to make Paraguay a dominant power and themselves Emperor and Empress of the South American states.

The woman's name was Eliza Lynch. For 16 years she had been the mistress of Francisco Solano López, a vain, ruthless megalomaniac who succeeded his father as President of Paraguay. Together they had precipitated a war against the combined forces of Brazil, Argentina and Uruguay which ended with cities in ruins, the economy destroyed and half the population dead.

They first came together in a totally different world.

In the year 1854 Eliza Alicia Lynch from County Cork had never even heard of Paraguay. She was just another pretty courtesan who had set herself up in Paris hoping to make her fortune. Her family had fled from Ireland in the great famine with hopes of making a new life in France. Eliza was married at 15 to a French officer, Xavier Quatrefages, but, as being his wife condemned her to live in a hot, dusty Algerian outpost, she soon thought better of it. By 18 she was back in Paris and ready for a different kind of life.

She became a courtesan because she could think of no other way for a girl like her to live in wealth and luxury. Through a few fortunate introductions she got herself into the elite circle around Princess Mathilde and soon she was seen at every great occasion.

Her Junoesque figure, golden hair and provocative smile attracted men by the dozen, but she didn't want a dozen. She wanted only one who was prepared to commit himself and his money to a long liaison and become not only her lover but also her protector. The French had proved too fickle so she decided it must be a foreigner. She told her servants to leave her card at the best hotels and foreign embassies. On it she had printed 'Madame Lynch,

Instructress in languages'. She obviously preferred to forget her husband Quatrefages.

Before long it became the fashionable thing to call on Madame Lynch, exchange a few words (she spoke Spanish and French as well as English) and play a few cards. One day, staring across the room at her, she saw an ugly little man with a pear-shaped head, a negroid nose and a mouthful of dark brown teeth, the front ones missing. His teeth were clenched on a huge cigar. 'Who on earth is that?' she asked someone. Told that it was Francisco López, the immensely rich eldest son of the dictator-President of Paraguay, she became very interested.

By the following morning they were lovers and López, totally infatuated, asked Eliza to return with him to South America. She had listened to his egotistical talk and to his grandiose plans for becoming Emperor. She realized that if she linked her destiny to his she would have to encourage him in his mad ambitions, continually reassure him that he was a fascinating man and turn a blind eye to his coarse nature. She did not even know where Paraguay was but he made it sound like an earthly paradise. Her answer was yes.

They went off on a European honeymoon, López buying his new mistress all the diamonds, furs and beautiful gowns she wanted. On visiting Napoleon's tomb he made note that he would order one exactly the same for himself. But his aging father had been bombarding him with pleas to come home and on the morning of 11 November 1854 they sailed.

Eliza took with her a vast wardrobe of Paris gowns, trunks full of household linen, an elaborate table service and cases and cases of Sèvres porcelain as well as opulent furniture and a Pleyel piano. López took a large number of ornate uniforms. She had a vision of herself bringing European culture, refinement and style to the Paraguayans and felt sure they would love her. If she had a model in mind, it was probably the Empress Eugenie.

Her reception was not quite what she expected. The 1,000-mile journey upriver to the capital, Asunción, was made in terrible heat and humidity. It was a colourful world she looked out on – floating islands of water lilies, crocodiles and orange trees – but she was pregnant and felt sick. The 'First Family' was waiting to greet them on the quay, lined up in their separate carriages.

The President himself, Carlos Antonio, answered her smile with a few grunts. The López women – Francisco's mother and two sisters – frumpily dressed in black – stared with hostility at the figure in pale lilac silk and drove off without a word. She did not know that, while his family had no objection to him womanizing at home, they would not tolerate a foreigner. She was known before she arrived as 'the Irish strumpet' and the women had tried hard to get the old President to forbid her entry.

Eliza was appalled at the sight of Francisco's 'paradise', for when the dust settled Asunción showed itself to be a dilapidated and dismal place. She decided there and then that it must be rebuilt, whatever the cost.

Francisco did his best to get his family to accept Eliza, without success. But here, on his home ground, she began to learn what he was really like. His only real interest, apart from women, was in power for himself and war. He considered himself a military genius like Napoleon. He was a cruel profligate who considered any virgin to be fair game. Many of the noblest families in Paraguay sent their daughters abroad rather than risk having them raped by López. One girl threatened that she would commit suicide if he touched her and another, about to marry, was presented with her bridegroom's body as a wedding present after refusing to submit.

Eliza knew all this. She knew about his visits to brothels, too. She decided to accept his appetites but told him that if he was going to have concubines she would choose them for him. She had already given birth to his son and he built her a pink and white palace, a *quinta*, the first two-storey habitation in Paraguay. She was to have six more children before she was 32.

The old aristocratic families treated her as a whore and their womenfolk averted their eyes as she passed. Many of the foreign wives also went out of their way to snub her. She put up with it for seven years, shrugging her white shoulders and concealing her bitterness with smiles. Then came the moment she had been waiting for. The old President died. Francisco told her she was now First Lady of Paraguay. He made it clear to everyone that his mistress was to be accorded the courtesy and honour due to any consort. She was ready to play the part to the hilt. When the time was ripe she would repay ruthlessly those who had insulted her.

Within a month of his succession, López had imprisoned or exiled more than 1,000 prominent men whose loyalty he suspected. Those who left quietly through the back door had made a shrewd assessment of the new President and his lady and smelt danger.

The old dictator's dying words to his son had been to settle troubles with the pen rather than the sword. He had come to realize that his son was of such an explosive nature that leaving him in command of the powerful military force he had built up in Paraguay was like leaving a lunatic in a fireworks factory.

But Eliza encouraged him in his vanity and illusions of military grandeur. She had come into her own. Anyone who failed in paying due respect was humiliated. The newly appointed British Minister was rash enough to say he had no intention of recognizing the 'Paraguayan Pompadour'. She suggested to López that he should be made to present his credentials walking the length of Asunción instead of arriving in state. The proud ladies of the capital soon got the message. They began to call on the First Lady in droves, full of sweet compliments, only to tear her to bits when they were out of hearing.

Eliza then had her position threatened in a way she had never dreamed of. López, who swore to her he would never marry anyone else, asked Dom Pedro of Brazil for his daughter's hand. It was a terrible shock to her. Alan Brodsky, who served with the US Embassy at Asunción in 1955 and who has written a detailed account of the Lynch-López relationship, explains: 'The dream they shared – a not entirely unrealistic one, given the circumstances of the time – was to convert Paraguay into the capital of an empire that would embrace the entire Rio de la Plata region: Paraguay itself, the Argentine Confederation, Uruguay and Brazil . . .' Of course, she saw herself as Empress of this great vision and never thought it would be otherwise.

But Eliza had nothing to worry about. The Emperor of Brazil considered López to be 'licentious, dissolute and cruel' and, as Madame Lynch had such an influence over him, she was probably just the same. Nothing would induce him to give his daughter to such a man. By this reply Dom Pedro made himself a bitter enemy.

Somehow López had to make amends to Eliza, fuming in her pink and white *quinta*. He arranged for her to have enough funds to give a dazzling succession of balls, fêtes and suppers, showing the 'provincial' ladies of Asunción how it was done in Paris. But it was not enough. She wanted more say in the affairs of state and assumed the title of Minister Without Portfolio.

She could sense something in the air. The whole continent was in a state of unrest, the two giants, Brazil and Argentina, beginning to rumble like unquiet volcanoes and Uruguay, the small country between them, fearing for her independence. She turned to Paraguay as an ally. Scenting trouble, López put his country on a war footing.

For the next few weeks all the South American

countries engaged in brinkmanship that could only lead to disaster. López, after one successful diplomatic effort regarding Argentina, imagined himself as a go-between, but he only succeeded in making things worse. He continually sent bombastic notes to everybody, demanding to know what was going on. Thanks to his statesmanship, Uruguay and Brazil were soon at war with each other. His only contribution as the former's ally seems to have been a complaint that he was being ignored!

Behind it all Eliza schemed and conferred with the few men who were her close confidantes and admirers. She wanted war. She was convinced now that the only way Paraguay could gain consequence was by taking up arms against one of the major South American powers. Thornton, the British Minister, advised his superiors at the Foreign Office: 'Her orders, which are given imperiously, are obeyed as implicitly and with as much servility as those of the President himself.' In other words people were beginning to fear her.

When Brazil invaded Uruguay and became bogged down there, she urged López to invade Brazil. Still seething under the insult from Dom Pedro, who thought so little of him as a son-in-law, Francisco listened carefully. One day the largest steamer in the Brazilian merchant fleet was about to enter Paraguayan waters with a routine shipment of gold. It was seized and charged with a violation of national waters. Many of those on board, including the governor of Matto Grosso, were sent to a prison in the interior, never to be seen again. López now threw his soldiers into a war with Brazil that had never been declared. He took his troops up the Paraná river and the Brazilians, not prepared for invasion, fled leaving all their ammunition behind. Within 15 days all the territory claimed by Paraguay had been occupied. López sent news of his triumph back to Asunción. Eliza, glorying in his success, staged a four-hour military parade on the Campo

Grando, a huge plain outside the capital. She also gave a ball and other celebrations that went on and on and on.

But López, by his aggression and disregard for international law, had made everyone his enemy. As in some mad quadrille, everyone in South America changed partners. His three powerful neighbours, Brazil, Argentina and Uruguay, now joined against him in what was called the Treaty of the Triple Alliance. They were determined to crush him, though through bad leadership and ineptitude on all sides the war which ruined Paraguay was to drag on for five years.

Eliza had taken to collecting jewellery. She appealed to every woman to give up her treasured pieces to help López fight the war. That way she really got her claws into the aristocrats and the self-righteous ladies of Asunción who had snubbed her. She had memorized all the really fine pieces they owned. If they were not produced at the first asking, she asked again. She got her revenge. Most of the jewels were never seen again by their owners.

The war, bloody and terrible as it was, brought López to his knees. He lost half his army and most of his navy. It soon became obvious that only a miracle could save Paraguay from disaster. Eliza knew now she would never be Empress of anywhere. She had no intention of spending the rest of her life in a war-battered Paraguay and was determined not to leave as a pauper. Already a consignment of jewels had been sent to her agent in Paris. More followed as she continued her collection for the brave López. She also managed, through sheer bluff, to remove four cases of gold coins from the treasury, which she had loaded onto an Italian sailing ship heading for France.

Still, she did not abandon López. She moved up to the headquarters at Humaitá where the Brazilians were firing 4,000 shells a day, but so inaccurately that they caused little damage. She would order gourmet meals to be served to her with wine but López preferred plates of greasy food washed down with brandy. Sometimes, when he was drunk, the calamity of his position would strike him and he would order executions. Full of frustration he would cry out that he would pardon nobody. Before the war was over he had tortured and killed without mercy everyone from the common soldier to members of his own family. His brother-in-law, Treasurer General Bedoya, was accused of stealing four cases of gold coins and subjected to such terrible torture that he died. Eliza said not a word.

Humaitéa fell to the Brazilians on 25 July 1868 and soon most of the Paraguayan cities were in Allied hands. López gathered the remnants of his army together, along with his family and his mistress, and fled. In one final attempt at stopping the enemy reaching Asunción he threw everything he had into a pitched battle. In it, 5,000 Paraguayan troops died, most of them old men, young boys, cripples and women. López had lost or killed practically a whole generation.

The end came on 1 March 1870 when the Brazilians caught up with him and his wretched band of fugitives at his last 'capital' at Cerro Cora on the banks of the Rio Aquidaban. When he heard that the Brazilian cavalry, led by General Camarra, had broken through, he ordered his last few soldiers to make a human wall while he tried to make his escape on a horse. But the horse floundered in the mud and López was shot as he struggled to his knees. His final words were: 'I die with my country.'

His mother and two sisters, whom he had condemned to death only hours before as paranoia took him over, surrendered themselves. Eliza had made a dash to the carriage always kept waiting for her and attempted to escape with her youngest sons. But Camarra caught up with her and led her back to the place where López lay dead. She then buried him.

A Brazilian gunboat took the women back to Asunción. The López women returned to their homes but Eliza was kept on board for her own safety. Camarra was warned that if the women in Asunción had been able to get their hands on her they would have killed her. Refusing to hand her over to the provisional government, he put her on board ship for Europe. She had caused enough trouble.

Eliza Lynch was 35 when she got back to London. The most conservative estimate of the valuables she had managed to slip out of Paraguay was about a third of a million pounds, besides other investments she had been able to make. She lived in London for the rest of her life, presenting herself as the victim of a gross miscarriage of justice. She looked handsome and distinguished and was much admired.

Most of her time was spent over legal wrangles and trying to get what she considered belonged to her. For instance there was the matter of two small fortunes which she and López had given to a certain Dr William Stewart to send out of the country. They had gone astray. Some years later, she returned to Asunción, perhaps after Francisco's money which had been willed to her. Although she talked on her return of weeping women kissing her hand as she passed by, there was a move to have her brought to trial.

She died on 27 July 1886. Her death certificate gave her respectability. It described her as 'The widow of Francisco S. López'. Time, too, had its softening effect on her reputation. On the 144th anniversary of Francisco López's birth the urn bearing her remains was carried in procession to her last resting-place in Asunción. And the descendants of her liaison with the man who wanted to be Emperor had her proclaimed a national heroine.

Mae West

That high priestess of hussies, Mae West, once said that getting down to your last man was as bad as getting down to your last dollar. As the opulent forerunner of Hollywood's golden goddesses, Miss West, as she insisted on being called, also claimed she knew more about the opposite sex than would fit into an encyclopaedia. She proved it by issuing salty aphorisms about men nearly every time she opened her mouth.

She owned up to many lovers, the odd duke and a few oil tycoons among them, but when asked how many retorted: 'The score never interested me, only the game.' She avoided any scandals in her private life, which was conducted with surprising restraint. She neither smoked nor drank, refused to name her 'gentlemen friends' and seldom appeared in public with more than one at a time.

Her most famous line, 'Come up and see me some time', delivered with a lascivious wink and the lift of a white shoulder, did not have to be taken too literally. Mae West did not insist on being called Miss West for nothing. Her famous image – blonde curls, a voluptuous figure squeezed into a tube of sequins, lilting nasal voice and the arch smile of a temptress – had been carefully and cleverly built up over the years.

Mae West was born in Brooklyn in 1892. She got her blonde looks from her mother who was of Franco-German stock. Her father was a prize fighter. She must have been precocious, for her parents put her into stock drama at the Gotham Theatre, Brooklyn, when she was only five years old. Too young to read theatre scripts, she had them read over to her and learned them by ear, a habit she kept all her professional life. At 14, with a fast-ripening figure and a twinkle in her eye, she suddenly emerged as a juvenile vamp in skintight black velvet and paste diamonds.

About this time, too, she discovered that girls were a waste of time and boys much more interesting.

She married Vaudeville actor Frank Wallace in 1911 when she was 18 years old but domesticity and children did not fit in with the personality she was developing for herself. Their relationship did not last. Much later in life she said: 'I was sorry about Frank, but I was not in love with him. It was just one of those things. I should never have married him. But having made one mistake in marriage, I vowed I would never make another.' Instead she found safety in numbers. 'The recurring pattern of multiple men in my life was already showing itself. I start with one and usually five or six more put in an appearance.'

Miss West had developed her personality a little too far, according to the police. After years appearing in other people's shows she put on a play herself in 1927 at Daly's Theatre on Broadway. It was called simply *Sex*. It ran for a year before the powerful puritan element in New York managed to have Miss West hauled up on an indecency charge and jailed for ten days for 'corrupting the morals of youth' – largely because of a low-life scene, realistically depicted. She felt she had suffered a grievous wrong, and said so. The trouble was she could not now speak a line without people looking for a double meaning. She delivered every word with such superb insolence that everyone felt there must be more to what she said than appeared on the surface. Defiantly, she followed *Sex* with several more risqué plays, continuing to treat life with irreverence in such masterpieces as *The Wicked Age, Pleasure Men* and *The Drag*.

She reached the pinnacle of fame in the 1930s, invading Hollywood to play screen hussies with names like Peaches O'Day and Klondyke Annie. Her dresses were skintight, designed to show off her splendid bosom, and worn with enormous hats and diamond earrings like chandeliers. She batted eyelashes a yard long as she drawled her cynical wisecracks through insolently curved scarlet lips. 'A girl has to look out for herself,' she confided to her audience. 'A full moon and a wireless set, without a man, is just so much consolation.'

Surprisingly, many of her wisecracks were spontaneous, not studied. Asked in an interview if she had any formula for getting her man, she returned crisply: 'Girls don't like formulas.' Her most famous line, 'Come up and see me some time', occurred in a film called *She Done Him Wrong* made in 1933, but almost equally memorable was her quip 'When I act I don't make love and when I make love I don't act' – the last word spat out like a plum stone.

Off-screen and in private the hipswinging flamboyance was left behind. She looked smaller, prettier, with violet eyes, platinum blonde hair and an arched upper lip that gave her a girlish look. Her honesty made her popular among her fellow stars in Hollywood. She hated getting up early. Callers and telephone calls were barred before noon. Then she would dress herself with absolute care and put on her jewellery – a platinum and diamond bracelet with 17 gold charms, a 200-carat sapphire ring, diamond earrings that caught every light in the room. She dripped with diamonds, admitting that most of them had been given to her by admirers. At one time her jewels were estimated to be worth a quarter of a million pounds.

She loved the colour peach. She bought peach underwear, peach satin sheets, and decorated the dressing room and living room at her famous studio bungalow in peach and cream. Her best-known luxury was a huge, swan-shaped bed, smothered in silk and lace, with overhead mirrors reflecting 19th-century opulence.

Mae West said she had never knowingly allowed a married man to make love to her. One look at a wedding ring and she cooled off. 'But sometimes,' she admitted, 'it seems to me I've known so many men, the FBI ought to come to me for fingerprints.'

Men improved when they got to 40, she said. 'At 40 a man has come of age. He has more polish, poise, charm and more money. Money buys time, place, comfort and a private corner for the two of you to be alone. A man has more character at 40, too. He has suffered longer and the more suffering, the more character.'

Miss West wrote down a lot of this philosophizing about the opposite sex in a book she called *Goodness had nothing to do with it*, in which she gave advice to women on how to succeed in her line of business. 'I never set out to make men a career,' she drawled. 'It just happened that way. I had a certain something for them and the word got around . . .'

So she became rich, successful and popular. But the puritan community in America, consisting largely of church groups and women's committees, incensed by her attitude to sex, were waiting to catch her out. Their opportunity came in 1938 when she took part in a broadcast burlesque skit called 'Adam and Eve'. She played the part of Eve and Don Ameche was Adam. In the script Adam is made to appear cool towards Eve until the serpent gives her an apple from which she makes apple sauce. This raised a storm of protest and was described by Bible students as 'obscene, indecent and scurrilous'.

'I wouldn't do anything to hurt religion. I go to church myself,' pleaded Miss West. 'I know what's vulgar and what isn't,' she exclaimed. 'I make fun of vulgarity but people insist on getting me wrong.'

The protesters complained that it was not so much what she said but the way that she said it. 'I can't help my voice,' she retorted. Everyone enjoyed the scrap, and she went on from strength to strength.

During World War II her name entered the language. The lifejacket worn by airmen in combat was named after her. Her great creation was the character 'Diamond Lil', which she played on Broadway, on the screen and in theatres all over the world. She wrote, produced and appeared in it and, although the critics gave mixed reviews, no one denied her impact as a larger-than-life character.

She retired from films when she was 63 to live in her palatial beach house overlooking the Pacific at Santa Monica. At 70 she kept pretty much to herself, scorning drink, tobacco and Hollywood. When at last she gave an interview to the *Saturday Evening Post*, after people had been trying to talk to her for years, she received the reporter in her bedroom in full regalia – a pink satin négligée, blonde wig, false eyelashes and diamonds. 'Miss West still possesses overwhelming sexual force,' wrote the reporter. 'It comes and goes like distant music heard across a fairground on a summer night – but it is still there.'

Cleopatra

There is not a single portrait to show us what she really looked like. The nearest we can get to her is a profile on a coin. Yet, 2,000 years after her death, her name is still synonymous with temptation, seduction and love. She is one of the world's legendary women: Cleopatra.

She gave her love to only two men as far as we know. Both were giants. Both great heroes of Rome at the height of its power. One was Julius Caesar, the other Mark Antony. Both found her a bewitching woman, exotic, clever, dramatic in everything she did – and a superb lover.

Julius Caesar forgot his military and political strife in her arms and would probably have married her if he had not been assassinated. Mark Antony, a brave and fine soldier, laid his sword at her feet and in the end died with her.

She was 18 when, in 51 BC, she ascended the throne of Egypt as Cleopatra VII and formally married her brother, Ptolemy XIII, who was a boy of only ten at the time. The Greek-speaking dynasty of the Ptolemies, to which she belonged, had been ruling the country since the death of Alexander the Great in 323 BC. She was fiercely proud of her royal heritage and determined to preserve it, determined to keep Egypt free from the domination of Rome.

Cleopatra had not a drop of Egyptian blood in her veins. From ancient writings we know that she was fine-boned and well-proportioned and that she was exquisitely perfumed with all the rare concoctions of the East. A copper coin from Alexandria shows a young woman with a long, graceful neck, fine, large eyes, a distinctly semitic nose. The mouth appears to be large and beautifully formed. Being an eastern Mediterranean type, she no doubt had black hair and pale olive skin. Plutarch wrote: 'To know her was to be touched with an irresistible charm. Her form, coupled with the persuasiveness of her conversation and her delightful style of behaviour – all these produced a blend of magic . . . her voice was like a lyre.'

She had lived all her life in an atmosphere of intrigue, murder and corruption, so had learned to be cunning and ruthless herself. Before they had been married long, she and her brother, the King, were literally at war with each other, their armies confronting each other at Pelusium.

The historic meeting of Caesar and Cleopatra came about three years after she had ascended the throne at a crucial point in this family war. Caesar, returning to Rome after some bitter campaign which had wearied him, decided to stop at Alexandria, which loomed before him like a mirage with its cool fountains, gardens and flowers. Now, he thought, was as good a time as any to sort out these Egyptians. He knew Egypt could be brought fully under Roman control until the Ptolemies stopped fighting each other.

First, he summoned Ptolemy and told him to disband his army, then he sent a message to Cleopatra asking her to come back from Pelusium and meet him so that they could talk. She wanted to meet this Caesar, wanted to state Egypt's case in her own words. Her problem was how to get back. Her brother's troops were still fully mobilized, blocking her way to Alexandria by land and sea. However, by some skilful manoeuvre she managed to slip away by ship under cover of night. At the entrance to Alexandria harbour she transferred to a small boat in which Apollodorus, her faithful Sicilian servant, waited.

Apollodorus rowed the boat to a quay just below the walls of the palace. The following morning he was seen carrying a rolled-up carpet over his shoulder. Guards at the palace, who knew him, waved him on when he said he had a fine specimen to show Caesar. Admitted to the great man's presence, Apollodorus laid the rolled-up carpet on the floor and untied the cord that bound it. To Caesar's astonishment the Queen of Egypt rolled out, an exquisite little figure who smoothed her dark hair, sprang to her feet and hailed him.

He saw before him a 21-year-old enchantress. She saw a tall, fair man in his 50s with shapely limbs, a strong, attractive face, his thinning hair combed carefully forward over the crown of his head. His authority assured her that this was indeed Julius Caesar, conqueror of half the world, the greatest soldier, some said, since the famous Alexander.

This time it was Cleopatra who conquered. Caesar was a renowned womanizer in Rome but this Queen of the Nile, playful as a kitten one minute, wise as serpents the next, was unlike any woman he had known before. That night they became lovers. The whole ambience of this strange and ancient land seems to have had an effect on him, so that next day he wondered if he had been bewitched.

When the 13-year-old Ptolemy realized that Caesar and Cleopatra were lovers, he knew he had lost, that she would keep the throne and one day be Queen in her own right. Finding them together on obviously intimate terms, he rushed to tell his companions that he had been betrayed. For a time, however, Caesar brought sister and brother together and they consented to live in separate wings of the palace and keep the peace.

Caesar lingered in Alexandria for four months under the spell of Cleopatra. She enchanted him by showing different aspects of her character each day. Besides demonstrating the art of Egyptian love-making, which was renowned in ancient times for its subtlety, she would no doubt also have demonstrated her grasp of politics, surprising in one so young. When she entertained him it was with an exotic luxury different from anything he had known in the Roman world. On one occasion, wanting to show herself to the Egyptian people in company with the mighty Caesar, Cleopatra ordered a fleet of 400 ships to accompany them on a journey down the Nile. They themselves sailed in the state barge with its decks designed as arcaded courts and leafy grottoes.

Caesar's infatuation with the Egyptian Queen nearly cost him his life. As he was lulled into a delicious sense of ease and languor, his murder was being planned. The boy-King Ptolemy had secretly ordered his troops back from the East and they were surrounding the palace in Alexandria. Both Caesar and Cleopatra were trapped.

Only the arrival of Roman legions on the eastern frontier saved them. Fierce fighting broke out and Caesar had to extricate himself from what became known as the Alexandrian War. In the end, the Egyptians were routed and the boy-King drowned in the Nile, but Caesar, always the statesman, had his body recovered and buried in ceremonial gold armour.

By now Caesar knew that Cleopatra was expecting his child. Before he returned to Rome he confirmed her right to be Queen and arranged that her surviving 12-year-old brother should reign with her as Ptolemy XIV. The baby was born in late June or early July 47 BC and Cleopatra called him Ptolemy Caesar so that no one should forget his paternity, though he was generally known as Caesarion.

Great celebrations had been planned in Rome to celebrate the Alexandrian victory and to everyone's surprise Caesar sent for the Egyptian Queen to attend them. Her arrival caused a considerable stir. Those who had expected to see a half-savage were astonished at her exquisite appearance. She would be fully made-up for such an occasion with antimony and lamp black applied to eyelids and eyebrows, ochre to lips and nails, and henna, creating an orange-red colour, rubbed into the palms of her hands and soles of her feet. Besides her brother, the King, and her child, she boasted an imposing, elaborately dressed retinue.

Caesar installed her in a house on the right bank of the Tiber and made no attempt to conceal his passion for her. Though Cleopatra must have thought nothing stood in the way of her becoming his Queen Empress, there was one serious impediment. Caesar already had a wife, Calpurnia, and, though divorces were two a penny in Rome, marriage to a foreigner was not considered to be a marriage at all. But such problems were rendered theoretical by Caesar's murder on 15 March 44 BC.

When she heard the terrible news she must have realized the danger of her position. She had lost her lover, her ally, the man on whom the fulfilment of all her dreams for Egypt were based. She had been in Rome for one and a half years. Now she slipped quietly away amid rumours that she had miscarried Caesar's second child.

Consul Mark Antony was now the most powerful man in Rome though he had played no part in the murder plot. His rise to power had been almost entirely due to his association with Caesar, but now he emerged as a magnificent figure in his own right. He was a great soldier, tall, muscled like a gladiator, with a handsome, bearded face and curly hair. His good looks made him attractive to women and he was an insatiable lover. But he also had a reputation for being a man's man and his troops worshipped him. His talk was often bluff and ribald, and he had a taste for rowdy parties and drink. For all that, said Plutarch, there was a noble dignity about him.

The emergence of Antony did not worry Cleopatra. They had met before. When she was 14 he was the brilliant young soldier who helped to restore her father to the throne he had lost. He stayed in Alexandria for a short time, even then not unaware of the disturbing beauty of the young Princess. Now it was to him she had to turn to secure her own throne.

Violent crises convulsed the Roman Empire after Caesar's death. Antony found himself in direct conflict with Octavian, Caesar's adopted son, who was determined to claim his heritage. A clash between the two men was inevitable, but for the time being they divided the Roman world between them and gave the impression of being friends.

Antony assumed control of all provinces on the far side of the Adriatic. Since Egypt was already protected by legions under his command, and since he already knew the Queen, he decided to make Alexandria the capital of his eastern Empire. From there he would seek to defeat Octavian.

First, he felt it was his duty to carry on with Caesar's plans for a war against the troublesome Parthians. Egypt's position in such a war would be vital and he needed her money and material support. When he reached Tarsus he decided he could delay no longer and sent an intermediary to bring Cleopatra to him.

She was in no hurry to meet Antony. She knew about his voluptuous tastes, his vigorous sexual appetite, his military glory and his courage. She also knew he was married to the beautiful Fulvia, a woman of force and power in her own right. But Cleopatra was equally conscious of her own ancient royal dignity, conscious also of the fact that to her servants she was a goddess, Isis incarnate. She would meet him, but on her own terms, in her own time. So it was only after a suitable delay, designed to show that she was not at Antony's beck and call, that she set off for Tarsus.

Her arrival at the ancient port was never to be forgotten by those who saw it. Shakespeare, hundreds of years later, wrote: 'The barge she sat in, like a burnish'd throne, Burn'd on the water . . .' And Plutarch, the ancient writer from whom he gleaned his knowledge, recorded: 'She came sailing up the river Cydnus in a barge with a poop of gold, its purple sails billowing in the wind, while her rowers caressed the water with oars of silver which dipped in time to the music of the flute accompanied by pipes and lutes. Cleopatra herself reclined beneath a canopy of gold dressed in the character of Aphrodite, the goddess of love . . . all the while an indescribably rich perfume exhaled from numerous censers and was wafted from the vessel to the river banks . . .'

The whole population of Tarsus flocked to the water's edge to gasp at the sight of the Queen of Egypt reclining under her golden canopy. Antony, waiting for her in the marketplace, expected her to come ashore, but she had no intention of doing anything of the kind. He waited in vain. When eventually he sent a messenger asking her to dine with him she declined and invited him to dine with her instead. Unable to hold out any longer, he accepted.

That night, as the barge lay at anchor in the moonlit lagoon, Cleopatra proceeded to seduce Antony with all the skills she possessed. She was now 29 years old, at the peak of her physical and mental powers. Antony was fascinated from the start by her voice, her manner, her conversation. She led him to a banqueting hall below deck hung with purple tapestries, embroidered with gold. The whole room was brilliant with light reflected from 1,000 mirrors, the air delicately scented, the tables set with goblets and plates of gold studded with precious stones. He was overwhelmed. Again and again he returned, his senses dazzled by this amazing woman. At another banquet she had the floor covered with roses to a depth of several feet and dissolved a precious pearl in a goblet of vinegar to win a wager with him. Consummate lover that she was, she adapted her tastes to his. While his sexual experience was vastly greater than hers, she was versed in the exotic refinements of the East. By her intelligent assessment of his strengths and weaknesses she bound him to her.

He was a sensualist, like most Romans, and she knew that by enslaving him to his pleasures she could keep him by her side. He returned with her to Alexandria. Discovering Antony had a passion for gambling, she played dice with him; aware of his love of wine, she drank with him; and, aware of his love of practical jokes, she would join him in escapades in the streets of Alexandria after nightfall. They walked in her scented gardens and for a whole winter delighted in each other's company. Then Antony came to with a start. In Plutarch's words: 'At last, like a man roused from sleep after a long debauch, he realized he must leave his mistress and look to his laurels.'

Everywhere, it seemed, Octavian had triumphed while Antony's eastern Empire was tottering. From this moment on, his star began to wane. Fulvia, Antony's wife, had died while he had been dallying in Alexandria. He returned to Rome and, as an obviously political move, married Octavian's young and beautiful widowed sister, Octavia. The union was wildly popular in Rome for it seemed likely to avert civil war. But Cleopatra was filled with anger. Only a few weeks earlier she had given birth to Antony's twins. That Octavia was younger than she, and universally admired, only added to her fury.

Antony, however, could stand only so much of Octavia's virtue. She was a gentle paragon who lectured him about his drinking habits, his gambling and his health. He did not understand women like her. She suffocated him. Cleopatra was on his mind most of the time. She had understood his moods, joined him in his pleasures, laughed with him. Octavia had sailed with him on his return to the East, but when they reached Corfu he sent her home. He knew well enough that the act would be construed as an insult by Octavian, that he was, in fact, throwing down the gauntlet, but by this time he was in the hands of destiny.

He sent a trusted friend to bring Cleopatra to him at Antioch in Syria. His 'betrayal' was forgotten and forgiven and they spent the whole of that winter together. The following spring he set out with his legions to march against Parthia. If the campaign had been successful his military glory would have outshone anything Octavian had done. But it was a disaster ending with the proud legions in a desperate state. Antony's judgement and timing had been tragically wrong and even his soldiers began to murmur about his obsession with Cleopatra.

In the early months of 33 BC it became increasingly clear that the 'alliance' between Octavian and Anthony would not last much longer. The whole Mediterranean stirred uneasily. And as war loomed on the horizon the names of Antony and Cleopatra were besmirched in Rome. He was, if anything, even more enslaved to her. At some banquet or other in Alexandria he was said to have risen from his couch to rub her feet with sweet oils, usually the duty of a slave. On many occasions as he sat in the tribunal he would receive love letters from her on tablets of onyx or crystal and would stop everything while he read them. Once, while Furnius, the foremost Roman orator, was pleading a case, Cleopatra passed through the marketplace on her gold litter. Antony leapt to his feet, left the trial and accompanied her, hanging onto the side of the litter, laughing, completely forgetful of his duty.

The fate of these legendary lovers was coming to a

climax. In the year 31 BC Octavian declared war, using his strong fleet to seize Antony's eastern harbours and coastal fortresses one by one. Eventually he reached Actium, situated on the southern side of the Ambracian Gulf. Antony and his fleet arrived, anchored in the Gulf and Cleopatra joined him with her squadron of ships.

Octavian's plan was to stay offshore and lure Antony out to sea where his ships would be outflanked and outnumbered. For four months Antony refused to move. The sun poured down on the mosquito-ridden lagoon where he was trapped and conditions became intolerable. Disease was rampant and he was running out of supplies. On the second day of September, after advising Cleopatra to make for Alexandria, he decided to break out and the Battle of Actium began. Cleopatra's squadron, led by her flagship, the *Antonias*, moved swiftly through the two fleets locked in battle and made for the open sea.

Then Antony himself, in order to escape, transferred from his flagship to a lighter, faster vessel, caught up with Cleopatra and was taken on board her flagship. But, while the Queen went on to Alexandria, Antony and two companions dropped off at a small garrison town further up the coast. He had no intention of entering the Egyptian capital as a defeated man. News of Actium spread like wildfire and before long the eastern provinces went over to Octavian, leaving Antony with nothing but Cleopatra and Egypt.

Cleopatra knew that they were doomed. She begged Antony to join her in Alexandria and, while he sat desolate in a tower on the harbour wall, she began collecting all the Ptolemy treasures under one roof.

Octavian was closing in on Egypt. She took all the most precious items of the royal treasure and also great quantities of firewood and tinder and had them stored in the mausoleum she had built for herself in the royal cemetery of the Ptolemies. Then, with her two maids, Charmian and

Iras, she went inside and sealed the great doors.

Antony sent a message to his enemy offering to kill himself if he would spare Cleopatra, but he did not get an answer. Octavian's troops advanced steadily into Egypt until they reached the outskirts of Alexandria. There, Antony produced one last flourish of his military genius and forced them to retreat. But it was all over. His troops deserted him on land and his ships surrendered at sea.

At this moment of desperation a messenger arrived from Cleopatra. Her letter said either that she had killed herself or intended to do so. No one is certain which. At all events, believing Cleopatra dead, he took out his sword and asked his servant, Eros, to kill him. But Eros could not do it and turned the sword upon himself instead. Antony took another weapon and plunged it into his body, missing his heart.

When Cleopatra heard what had happened, and that he was still alive, she asked her servants to bring him to the mausoleum. As the great doors were sealed, Antony was bound to a stretcher and Cleopatra and her maids let down ropes from the window and gently drew him up. Cleopatra abandoned herself to grief, calling him her lord, her Emperor, her husband. He died in her arms, beseeching her to make terms with Octavian for her own sake. 'Be happy with me,' he begged, 'in remembrance of the good times we shared in the past.'

When the victorious legions arrived in Alexandria, she was tricked into opening the door of the mausoleum. Octavian allowed her to have full charge of Antony's burial at which she grieved loudly and bitterly. But she knew what she must do.

On 12 August, she asked her guard to take a sealed letter to Octavian. It contained a request that she should be buried beside Antony. Octavian knew this meant she intended to kill herself. Guards were sent immediately to the palace, but it was too late. Cleopatra was lying on a golden couch dressed in her full regalia as Queen of Egypt. Iras lay dying at her feet, Charmian, also on the point of dying, was trying to adjust Cleopatra's headdress. But the Queen was dead. One of the guards cried out: 'Charmian, was this right?' Charmian's reply was a fitting epitaph for her mistress. 'It is entirely right,' she managed to say, 'and fitting for a Queen descended from so many Kings.'

Earlier that day the guards remembered a peasant had been stopped at the palace gate with a great basket on his arm. He took off the leaves that covered it and showed them that it contained figs, choice figs for Cleopatra. Beneath, unseen by the guards, lay coiled a snake, probably the very poisonous blackish Egyptian cobra thought to be a special protector of the Egyptian royal house. Two faint, barely visible punctures were found on Cleopatra's arm. The snake was never recovered though marks which could have been its trail were noticed on the beach beneath Cleopatra's window. Octavian followed her last wishes and she was buried by Antony's side with full honours.

Sarah Bernhardt

Men would fight duels for her. She was a siren whose affairs were the gossip of half of Europe and who delighted in outrageous conduct as men like the Prince of Wales, Napoleon III and Victor Hugo fell on their knees before her. 'I have been one of the great lovers of my century,' Sarah Bernhardt told a close friend when she was old.

The legendary actress was not beautiful in a conventional way. Barely 5ft in height, she had a mass of unruly red hair, an aquiline nose and closely set, intense blue eyes. But her body was sinuously erotic, her voice was described as 'golden' and she exuded a femininity that was perfumed, exotic and magical.

Sarah loved to shock. In her bedroom she kept a coffin lined in rose-coloured silk. It travelled with her wherever she went. What did she do with it? Did she sleep in it, learn her lines in it, or, as scurrilous gossip hinted, lure her admirers into it for more intimate purposes? Stories about her affairs were so prolific that at one time the press distributed an astonishing pamphlet called 'The Loves of Sarah Bernhardt'.

For nearly 60 years her bizarre personal life and her magnetism as an actress held audiences captive all over the world. The 'divine Sarah', they called her. Yet as a child she was tossed aside, neglected, ignored, and told that she was ugly and that no man would ever love her.

Her mother, Judith van Hard, was a ravishingly beautiful Jewish courtesan who came from Holland. Her father, Edouard Bernhardt, was a law student. Sarah was born in Paris on 23 October 1844; shortly after her birth she was boarded with a peasant woman near Quimper in Brittany, and more or less forgotten. Appallingly neglected by her mother, she learned that the only way of getting attention was by creating a disturbance. Once she threw herself out of a window, breaking her arm, so that she would be noticed and listened to. After that, she was taken away from her nurse and sent to boarding school.

Only when she came into a legacy from her father was Sarah allowed to leave school and live with her mother in the elegant Paris apartment where Judith van Hard received her lovers and entertained the *demi-monde*. Sarah was well aware that her mother preferred her sister, Jeanne, who had inherited her looks and had been brought up in Paris with all the fuss and attention imaginable. Sarah, with her wild fits of temper and unruly hair, did not try to compete, instead producing disasters and crises at will in order to get her way.

When she reached 15 her mother suggested several suitors for Sarah's hand. The stubborn girl turned them all down. There was a family conference to decide what to do with her, to which her worldly Aunt Rosine brought her lover, the Duc de Morny. It was he who decided Sarah's destiny. 'Send her to the Conservatoire,' he suggested in an offhand manner, meaning the Conservatoire of the Comédie Française.

On the day she entered the Conservatoire her mother was too busy to go with her, as she should have done as Sarah was still a minor. Sarah decided she would have to make an impact on her own and arrived decked out in the height of fashion, in a carriage with footmen borrowed from Aunt Rosine. This did not go down at all well, either with her fellow students or with Thierry, the director. She hated the pompous, formal atmosphere of this theatre from the start. When she was eventually given a contract she felt no pleasure, only resentment that it was through the influence of the Duc.

To celebrate her entry to the Comédie Française Aunt Rosine gave a dinner party. The Duc de Morny brought with him an elegant young hussar, the Comte de Keratry. He did not take his eyes off Sarah, paid her many compliments and invited her to recite at his mother's house. He probably became the first of that long procession of lovers winding through her life. Now, even her mother could not deny that she had a certain magnetism.

Her first months at the Comédie were a sheer nightmare. She was badly affected by stage fright and received with faint praise by the critics. She struggled on but found herself frustrated by lack of parts and in the end, after a row with a powerful older actress, walked out. She obtained a new position at the 'Gymnase' theatre, but in 1864, at the age of 20, had to leave. She told everyone nonchalantly that she was off to Spain where she hoped to marry a matador. The fact was she was pregnant and did not want the whole of Paris to know.

Sarah had become the mistress of Henri, Prince de

Ligne, who came from one of the oldest and noblest families in Belgium. They met in 1862 and carried on a discreet but passionate affair. Just before Christmas 1864 she gave birth to his son, her only child, Maurice. The Prince gave her a choice: either to marry him or to return to the stage. There could be no compromise. The choice caused her great anguish but she already knew that she had a certain genius that must be fulfilled and she chose her profession.

After the birth of Maurice, life was not easy. She accepted any stage work offered to her and for the only time in her life took lovers for profit rather than for pleasure. Finally she succeeded in getting an engagement at the Théâtre de l'Odéon. She was charmed by the young and elegant director, Duquesnel, and settled down happily in what was to become her favourite theatre.

Now she radiated a vibrant energy and became the idol of the Bohemian world of Paris. Life sparkled at l'Odéon. It was so different from the stuffy, parochial atmosphere of the older theatre. Even rehearsals were fun. Prince Napoleon, the Emperor's cousin, better known as 'Plon Plon', came to rehearsals. He was gallant in his attitude to women, had impeccable manners and great appreciation of the arts. Most people were convinced that he became Sarah's lover, but she was discreet about it. She already had Pierre Berton waiting in the wings. He was one of the most handsome actors in France and madly in love with her. More than once she had refused his proposal of marriage, but their relationship lasted over two years and afterwards he said that their days together had been like 'pages from immortality'.

Her great talent began to unfold. She played the first unqualified success of her career in period male clothes when she took the part of a young minstrel in François Coppée's *Le Passant*. The critics said she spoke the poetry so exquisitely it was like listening to the song of the nightingale. From this time on she appeared in triumph after triumph.

The outbreak of war with Prussia, bringing about the end of the Second Empire, put an end to the applause but brought out unexpected patriotic fervour in Sarah. She persuaded the management to turn l'Odéon into a military hospital and volunteered to take on the task of getting food and supplies for wounded troops from the new Prefect of Police. To her amazement the Prefect turned out to be none other than her dashing first lover, the Comte de Keratry. He was soon under her spell again. He not only put his full resources at her disposal but also let her take his overcoat as a blanket, sent her ten barrels of wine, two of brandy, 30,000 eggs and hundreds of bags of tea and coffee. Sarah helped to nurse hundreds of soldiers during the siege of Paris and faced the greatest misery and suffering with compassion. The effect was to subdue the wilder side of her personality. Her fits of temper became quite rare.

After the war the role of Queen of Spain in Victor Hugo's *Ruy Blas* made her a star of the first magnitude. Sarcey, the great French critic, who could be so cruel, was in ecstacy. After the first-night performance the crowd of admirers around her backstage made way for Hugo himself. Before she could say anything he had gone down on his knees in front of her. Raising her hands to his lips, he murmured: 'Thank you, thank you.' Sarah wrote in her memoirs: 'He was so fine that evening with his noble forehead which caught the light, his stubble of silver hair like a crop out in the moonlight, his laughing, shining eyes.' Obviously delighted with each other, most people presumed they became lovers.

But Victor Hugo was not a young man and he had a rival. Playing 'Ruy Blas' to her Queen of Spain was an incredibly handsome young actor who seemed to have been born for romantic roles. Jean Mounet Sully was 31, dark, bearded with brooding eyes and a seductive voice. His performance was electric. Sarah had never looked more beautiful, wearing a white satin dress with silver embroidery, a train of figured silk and a little silver filigree crown on top of her blazing hair. Together they created magic. As she played opposite her lover Sarcey noticed 'She was all tender, languorous grace' and she spoke Hugo's most lyrical passages 'like a long caress'.

These were the great years. Sarah began to see herself as the new Renaissance woman and as a proper setting built herself a 'palazzo' at the intersection of the rue Fortuny and the avenue de Villiers in 1875. It was sumptuous, for she always loved luxury, and it was built without any consideration of how she would pay for it. The place was half-studio and half-mansion, for when she was not on stage she used her immense creative energy to produce works of art, all of which needed a home. Half-finished paintings and sculptures were stacked everywhere. The drawing-room window was like something out of a cathedral. There were dozens of dainty silk chairs, velvet couches, exotic hangings and towering tropical plants. Then there was her taste for the macabre: a skull autographed by Victor Hugo and that coffin, always ready for use. Her home also had a collection of dogs, cats, monkeys, fish, tortoises and other beasts – there was hardly space to put up a postage stamp.

Sarah made her debut in the English theatre in June 1869 and she was the sensation of the season at the Gaiety. English society loved her from the start and pardoned her eccentricity and her unreliability with regard to timekeeping. She did not disappoint those who expected something spectacular offstage. After a visit to a zoo she returned with a cheetah, six chameleons and a white wolfhound to add to her menagerie.

It was an agent called William Jarrett – she said he looked like King Agamemnon and had the most beautiful silver-white hair – who finally persuaded her to go to America and set the seal on a decade in which she became the most famous international actress ever known. She took America by storm with her performance as the dying consumptive Marguerite Gautier in *La Dame aux Camélias*, a role in which Garbo also triumphed. There were incredible scenes wherever she appeared. The role brought her dozens of offers of marriage and countless cures for TB.

It was at the peak of her radiant career that she fell in love as she had never done before. In September 1881, her sister Jeanne introduced her to Aristide Damala, the son of a wealthy Greek merchant. Damala had a colourful, if slightly dubious, background. One-time adventurer and officer in the Greek cavalry, he had also served his country for a time as a diplomat. He was forced to resign because of his habits, affairs and indiscretions. In Paris he had spent the last of his inheritance and involved himself in numerous intrigues. His oriental parties at which his guests took off their clothes and plunged naked into baths of champagne were notorious. Gambling and a taste for morphine were draining him of the last of the family fortune.

But Sarah put all this to the back of her mind when he called on her one morning. She found herself in the presence of a tall, dark, handsome man who had a strange effect on her. He told her of his ambition to be an actor and after hearing him read a part she agreed to take him into the company.

Sarah was intrigued not only by his looks and presence but by his apparent indifference to her charms, which she used on him with full force. She allowed him to play opposite her in a production of *Hernani*, a decision which made some of her friends wonder if infatuation had not warped her judgement. They took the play on tour to Vienna, St Petersburg, Warsaw, Genoa, Basle, Lausanne, Lyons, Trieste and, finally, Naples. By the time they reached Italy she was madly in love with him. The tables were turned this time. Usually Sarah called the tune and dictated the temperature of a relationship. She was both piqued and attracted by Damala's apparent aloofness. He alone of all the men she had known was not immediately conquered. But she made up her mind to marry him, and before the company left Italy they were engaged.

They dashed over to England where the formalities of two people of different nationalities getting married were kept to a minimum and at St Andrew's Church, Wells Street, London, on 31 March 1882, Sarah Bernhardt became Madame Damala.

Audiences that had been fascinated to see her on stage with her lovers were now even more intrigued to watch her play roles with her husband. Ellen Terry said of her: 'No one plays a love scene better, but it is a picture of love that she gives, a strange, orchidaceous picture rather than a suggestion of ordinary human passion.'

The marriage was a disaster. Damala continued to have affairs with other women and there were terrible scenes of jealousy. Professionally he was equally disastrous. Managements would not accept him as a leading actor and he became envious and bitter towards his famous wife, resenting her fame. Sarah did all she could to try to placate his injured pride, even to the extent of having a play written for him and leasing a theatre where he might be the undisputed star.

When they next appeared together Damala seemed to have improved and was given quite good reviews. For Sarah, however, it was another triumph. 'That electrical, chimerical woman had once again conquered Paris,' wrote critic Jules Lemaître. It was too much for Damala. After a terrible row in which he accused her of trying to wreck his stage career, he packed his bags and left the avenue de Villiers. By now he had become addicted to morphine.

She suffered greatly but carried on playing night after

night in Sardou's *Fedora*. In February 1883 he suddenly returned to her but his physical condition had deteriorated. In an attempt to end his dependence on drugs she threw away all the morphine and syringes she could find. Almost berserk with rage, Damala stormed out of the house again and this time she obtained a legal separation.

After his departure Sarah sought consolation in the arms of a burly, bearded poet, Jean Richepin, who produced several expensive theatrical failures for her, but, being handsome and adoring, he was forgiven. Richepin was involved in one of the most sensational scenes Sarah ever created offstage. A notorious book, *Mémoires de Sarah Barnum*, had been brought out by an actress called Marie Colombier who, Sarah realized, she must have slighted at some time. The book suggested that Sarah's rise to fame could be attributed to two things: publicity and sex. The young Maurice Bernhardt offered to defend his mother's honour by fighting a duel with anyone who would stand up in place of Marie Colombier. Fortunately, no one came forward. It was Sarah herself who settled the score. She headed for Colombier's apartment, taking Richepin with her. The actress, seeing La Bernhardt bearing down on her like a vengeful tornado, tried to hide behind a curtain. Sarah found her, hauled her out, and chased her through the house with a horsewhip, wrecking everything in sight as she went.

Philippe Garnier became her new leading man and, as she was always susceptible to handsome actors, he replaced Richepin in her arms. Actually, he had been there before. He was an old lover returned, a lover who had been displaced by Damala but who bore no grudge and was ready to worship her again. He played the Emperor Justinian to her Theodora in Sardou's play of that name. It was a production of Byzantine splendour. In one scene Sarah wore a dress of sky-blue satin with a train 4 yards long, covered in embroidered peacocks with ruby eyes and feathers of emeralds and sapphires.

Late in April 1886, with Garnier by her side, she set out on one of her mammoth tours. She travelled with her own company in special trains and steamers, always the centre of attention with her lover in attendance, her favourite animals and mountains of luggage. As many as 80 trunks would be needed to contain all her dresses, hats, shoes, personal linen and jewellery. Edmond de Goncourt, the French writer, gave a picture of Sarah in those years at the height of her fame: 'She arrived in a pearl grey tunic, braided with gold. No diamonds except the handle of her lorgnette. A mothlike wisp of black lace on the burning bush of her hair; beneath, the black shadow of lashes and the clear blue of her eyes . . . she must be nearly 50. She wears no powder and her complexion is that of a young girl.' Sarah wore no powder but she drenched herself with an expensive perfume so penetrating that a man's sleeve, if she took his arm, smelt of it for hours afterwards.

Offstage she was generally kind and good-natured with a great sense of loyalty to members of her family and old friends. What has been described as 'her greatest act of love' came in May and June of 1889 when Damala, dying of morphine addiction, turned up for the last time. He was penniless, a ghost of his former self, and pleaded to be allowed to act with her once more. Overcome with pity, she agreed. For several weeks she performed *La Dame aux Camélias* by his side. Half of Paris came to see them, but it was tragically obvious that he was dying. When he could no longer carry on, she traced him to a dark, sparsely furnished room in which the only decorations were a sabre he had once worn on stage, a gold crown and a Greek flag. She had him taken to hospital, assuring the authorities she would pay all the bills.

Aristide Damala was buried in Athens. Visitors to Sarah's house always noticed, in a place of honour, a marble figure she had sculpted of her husband in one of their few happy moments together, lying nonchalantly on his back, his hands under his handsome head.

She made her greatest world tour in the years from 1891 to 1893, and when she reached 55 had the ultimate satisfaction for an actress of seeing her name above her own theatre. Life had taught her aristocratic tastes and behaviour. Even in summer weather she usually appeared muffled to the ears in chinchilla or sables. But the house in which she now lived on the boulevard Pereire betrayed the real Sarah Bernhardt who had to be almost smothered in possessions before she felt secure. Most people, if they were honest, found it pretty awful. It was stuffed with bric-à-brac and animals both dead and alive. Dame Nellie Melba, the great Australian singer, never forgot her first visit. 'There were heavy stuffs hanging everywhere,' she recalled, 'drooping down and catching the dust; skins of animals on the floor, heads of animals on the walls, horns of animals on the mantelpiece, stuffed tigers, stuffed bears, even a stuffed snake.' Swarms of Buddhas inhabited dark corners and there were Chinese curios, bronze statues and ivories. The walls and ceiling were hung with red cotton material adorned with Mexican sombreros, feather parasols, lances and daggers. Amid all this tawdry splendour sat Sarah. Folding doors would be flung open to reveal an exquisitely dressed figure ready to receive her guests like a Queen giving audience.

It was in 1905 that the tragic accident occurred that was to affect the rest of her life. She was in Rio de Janeiro playing the name part in *Tosca*. The final scene required her to commit suicide by leaping to her death from a parapet. Mattresses were placed so that they would break her fall. One night someone forgot them. She fell heavily, taking the weight on her right knee, and fainted from the pain. The doctor called to attend to her had such dirty hands she refused to let him touch her. She insisted she would rather wait and see a specialist when they got to New

York. That meant a three-week delay and the delay was disastrous. Though she carried on with her career as though nothing had happened, she was never to be free from pain again, in spite of treatment with ether and morphine.

By 1914 she knew she had gangrene. She accepted the fate with typical courage and said to the doctors: 'Do what is necessary.'

They amputated her leg.

Even this did not mean the end of her career. She managed to invent dozens of clever little devices which enabled her to perform without revealing the extent of her disability. Still, in the final stages of her life, she gave a strange illusion of beauty. She invited the showman C.B. Cochrane to tea with her in Paris and he said he had never passed a more wonderful hour. 'After five minutes I felt this woman was not old and crippled but beautiful and strong.' The siren could still mesmerize. One of the last friends she saw, Mrs Patrick Campbell, arrived for dinner and found Sarah resplendent in a gown of pink Venetian velvet. She explained with great satisfaction that it was a gift from an admirer – Sacha Guitry.

Sarah continued working until nearly her last breath. In 1922 she announced she would appear as the clairvoyant in a film called *La Voyante*. But she was already suffering from uraemic poisoning and as the poison spread through her body her glorious powers began to wane. She died on the evening of 26 March 1923. Her last request had been for spring flowers so they covered her pillow with white and purple lilac, violets and roses. Then they laid her, dressed in a white satin robe, in the rosewood coffin lined with rose-coloured silk.

Pauline Borghese

Perhaps the hot, Corsican blood ran more strongly in her veins than in the rest of the family, but Napoleon's sister Pauline was a problem from the day she began to notice men. As one contemporary put it, she was a creature of 'bizarre moral habits'. Headstrong, wilful, beautiful and incredibly amorous, she became so exhausted by love-making during one affair that she had to be carried about on a litter!

All the same, she was Napoleon's favourite and he fondly called her 'Paulette'. Like him, she was intensely dramatic and the spoiled darling of the Bonaparte family. Born in Ajaccio, the capital of Corsica, just like her famous brother, she was only 15 when the family left and settled in Marseilles. Like most Corsican girls she matured early and was a great success in the social world at an age when most of her contemporaries were still at their books.

She had no education, no artistic talent, no dowry. Her sole asset at this stage was her beauty, and that was remarkable. Her small head was perfectly moulded, her face pure oval in shape with a clear, olive complexion. She had lovely hazel eyes and teeth like regular pearls. Her figure was superb and she knew it. The Duchesse d'Abrantes described her breasts as 'white as alabaster and seemingly ready to take flight from her corsage like birds out of a nest'. Canova, the famous sculptor, modelled the perfection of her form for the Villa Borghese. He was said to have adored her artistically, but most men adored her in quite another way.

She had scores of admirers among her brother's political supporters. One of the first to fall in love with her was Napoleon's aide de camp, dashing cavalry officer General Junot. He followed her everywhere, but as he had nothing but his army pay Napoleon refused to let him marry her.

Pauline's first serious affair happened when she was 16 with a man twice her age. Louis Stanislas Freron, with whom she fell hopelessly in love, was a violent revolutionary as well as a womanizer. He was said to wear rose-coloured breeches so tight that everyone wondered how, having got them on, he ever got them off. To such a worldly and practised seducer Pauline's freshness was enticing. She found it thrilling to be desired by a man of his distinction and notoriety. Besides, he was a godson of the King of Poland and the Bonapartes were always vulnerable when it came to titles.

Five months after their first meeting they were lovers. Madame Mère, her mother, forbade any further meetings when she heard what was going on. Pauline refused to give him up. She wrote him long, passionate letters and only the combined efforts of the family kept them apart. Napoleon, thinking it would give her time to cool down, offered her a comfortable apartment in the Serbolloni Palace, which he had taken for his own use. Here, Napoleon's wife, Josephine, showed her every kindness. Pauline hated her. 'This Creole woman', as she called her, had been the first to say she would disgrace herself by marrying Freron. For the rest of her life she treated Josephine with hostility for spoiling her love affair.

Pauline's daily life was a round of pleasure. Sometimes she behaved like a frivolous schoolgirl, playing tricks, mocking important people. Then Napoleon would give her one of his terrible glances which he used to cow the most formidable of men. But she would merely pout and carry on with her frivolity. She was an *enfant terrible* of the first order.

While in the social whirl of Paris at the age of 17, she ensnared the handsome General Leclerc – 'the only man I ever really loved', she said afterwards, though she said that about every man in her life. Napoleon was delighted. He had actually picked him out as a husband for her.

Leclerc was a curious man who copied Napoleon in every way, even trying to walk and talk like him, though he was as fair as Napoleon was dark. From the moment he saw Pauline, he adored her. Pauline shocked and hurt him, but they married and she gave him a son.

She was happy as long as they were in Paris, but to her horror Leclerc was posted to San Domingo in October 1801 and Napoleon gave specific orders that Pauline should accompany him. Wholly ignorant of geography, she imagined the island to be inhabited by cannibals and wild beasts. It was only when someone told her she would look charming in Creole costume that her temper cooled down. The truth was that Napoleon, growing disturbed by her amorous behaviour, wanted her out of Paris.

On 20 November she joined her husband at Brest to embark for San Domingo accompanied by a pyramid of trunks, boxes and suitcases. She was somewhat appeased on her arrival by a succession of balls and receptions in her honour. But the posting was ill-fated. Yellow fever swept the island, decimating the army Leclerc had taken out with him. Eventually the General himself was struck down. Pauline refused to leave him and nursed him with devotion. But he died and she became a widow. She had his body embalmed, Egyptian fashion, and laid a strand of her own hair across his forehead before the coffin was closed and shipped back with her to France.

Though she did not know it, she had also left behind in an unmarked grave another victim of the fever – her former lover, Freron. He had travelled out steerage on the same boat on which she was treated like a Queen.

On her return she was a pitiful little figure after all she had been through, but she soon began to recover and fret under all the restrictions demanded by her mourning. Her only consolation was knowing that she looked marvellous in black. But what was the use of looking marvellous if there were no men to admire her? In spite of Napoleon's watchful eye she managed to devastate the bluff and rather stout Admiral Decres, who became a shadow of his former self through unrequited love.

When the mourning came to an end she burst upon the world again with a devastating display of her charms. At a fancy-dress ball being given for Napoleon in Paris, she was met with gasps of astonishment as she triumphantly entered the ballroom dressed as a bacchante in a revealing, diaphanous white tunic embroidered in gold, her dark hair taken up with a band of tiger skin and grapes. In the splendour of her youth she was a vision. All the men applauded but the women called her dress 'une toilette effronte'.

Napoleon, secretly amused, decided he had better marry her off again to stop her scandalous behaviour. The man he suggested came from one of the greatest Italian families, so he felt that ought to please her. Prince Camillo Borghese was only 28, handsome and the richest man in Italy. But he was also utterly devoid of brains, a dandy who could not even write his own language properly. Pauline agreed to marry him. But he was to regret it.

They were married in 1803 and almost as soon as the wedding was over she started to plan how she could leave him. It was generally thought that Prince Camillo's fault lay in the fact that he was not a sexual athlete. Pauline already had a son by her first husband but Borghese did not seem able to oblige. She began to express herself volubly about the size of her husband's private parts and the insufficiency of his calves. In fact what actually happened was that for the next 12 years she waged what amounted to a terrorist war on the wretched man.

When Napoleon proclaimed himself Emperor on 18 May 1804, he made Pauline an Imperial Highness, which gave her precedence over her husband, a position she relished. Napoleon stopped her nonsense by making Borghese an Imperial Highness, too.

In Rome she assumed imperial airs and spent a fortune. Everyone was expected to wait for her as she could never be punctual. She would 'receive' guests at her morning toilette, chiefly, to display the beauty of her dark hair. Visitors would be admitted to her boudoir to find her reclining before a mirror in a floating white négligée. When she started to take it off, it was a signal to depart, though some lingered longer than others. Every day she bathed in milk, 20 litres being delivered early in the morning for this purpose alone.

After a time she told the Prince she no longer wanted to live with him in the Borghese Palace, though it was big enough for them to be able to avoid each other for weeks. She said she must have houses and villas of her own. For the sake of peace, he gave her one at Frascati and another in Rome. But Pauline hated the rigidity of the Roman social scene and continually rebelled against it. Napoleon wrote to her sternly, warning her that he would never receive her without her husband. Eventually, however, worn out by her pestering, he agreed she could return to Paris.

The Prince gave up any further efforts to gain her love and, with a sigh of relief, happily accepted the Order of the Golden Fleece from Napoleon and left Pauline to get on with her own life.

During the winter of 1805–6 she opened her salon at her fabulous house in the rue Saint Honoré. Her salon, with its yellow silk walls and crystal chandeliers, was the scene of the most glittering occasions in Paris. Of all the men jostling for her attention, she chose Jules de Canonville, a foppish man about town and one of Prince Wagram's aides de camp. They became lovers but Napoleon put a stop to the affair. For once he was really angry with her. He had, it so happened, just given her a present of a magnificent Russian cloak lined with sable. It had been presented to him by Tsar Alexander. The very next day, at a review, he was astonished to see the cloak thrown nonchalantly around the shoulders of Canonville. Within 24 hours the Colonel was ordered out of France to St Petersburg and when the Franco-Russian war broke out he was killed in action. Pauline threatened she would kill herself or go into a convent, but Napoleon eventually succeeded in calming her down. However Canonville had meant a great deal to her. She wore a miniature of him until the day she died.

Though devastated, she consoled herself with Auguste Duchard, a handsome young artillery officer, and with Talma, the actor, who was as romantic offstage as he was in performance.

Now she met the man who was destined to have a considerable effect on her as a lover – Nicolas Philippe Auguste de Forbin. At this time about 30 years of age, a successful society painter from an illustrious family, he was a polished, elegant, splendid figure and extremely well endowed sexually. Women raved over him and Pauline, intrigued, made him her chief chamberlain. He took control of her household in a most competent way and broadened her intellectual horizons. And, of course, he became her lover. She bought a charming little villa in Nice so that she could enjoy a summer idyll with him, but with the end of the summer came the end of the affair.

Pauline was in a state of utter exhaustion and had to be carried about on a litter. No one dared tell Napoleon the reason but they did tell Madame Mère, who delivered a stern moral lecture and told her she must never see Forbin again. Pauline was so angry and in such a nervous state that for a few weeks any dog that barked within her hearing was shot forthwith.

Forbin prospered. When the Bourbons were restored to the throne of France, after Napoleon, he became director of the Louvre.

Between lovers Pauline played the hypochondriac, forever calling for cashmere shawls and hot water bottles.

She spent much time lying languidly on her couch, complaining she was too weak to rise. But as soon as a possible lover came in sight her vanity forced her to her feet and to her interminable beauty routines.

She had begun to worry about her looks and took to wearing ten strands of pearls to conceal the slight wrinkling of her neck. She was as comically vain as ever. 'If you would like to see my feet,' she said to the Princess Ruspoli, 'come and visit me tomorrow morning.' The showing of the feet turned into an elaborate ceremony.

After Forbin's departure she appointed Felice Blangini as her director of music and took singing lessons from him, but it was soon obvious that she was more interested in finding out what he could teach her about love. Her last lover was Giovanni Pacini, a handsome young composer, chief rival to Rossini. She called him Nino, had his opera *The Slave of Baghdad* performed at her house, and hung on his every note. But for once in her life she had to face the fact that a man had lost interest in her before she was ready to declare the game over.

In spite of all her frivolity Pauline had one great loyalty and love throughout her life and that was for her brother Napoleon. She never let him down. When he was sent into exile she begged to be allowed to go with him. She offered to give him all her jewels if they would buy him comfort. When he was in the throes of his last illness she begged to be allowed to go and nurse him, but after he left the shores of France she never saw him again.

Pauline never got over the shock of his exile and death. In 1825, dangerously ill herself with cancer, desperately needing a friend, she asked her husband, Prince Borghese, to receive her at his palace in Florence. After some heart-searching, for he was perfectly happy as he was, he agreed. Though she had told him as long ago as 1812 that she wanted nothing more to do with him he treated her with great tenderness and she died in his arms.

La Belle Otéro

Her gypsy blood made her different from all the other courtesans in Paris during the Belle Epoque which followed the fall of the Second Empire in France. Dark, golden-skinned and fiery, La Belle Otéro, as she was called, had a temperament so sensational that even kings and emperors dealt with her warily.

Men committed suicide over her, several fought duels, others were ruined financially. She was one of the most acquisitive courtesans of all time and wildly jealous. Though she demanded the freedom to have as many lovers as she wanted, she would fly into jealous rages if those who were paying for her favours so much as looked at another woman.

Otéro has been called the last of the 'grandes horizontales'. She took her first lover in 1880 when she was 12 and she was still striking enough to make people turn and look at her in 1965, the year she died, aged 97.

Proud of her Spanish gypsy strain, she made the most of it. One of the most striking pictures taken of her shows her exquisite hourglass figure encased in a matador 'suit of lights'. She danced in flame-coloured Spanish skirts, slit to show a slender, black silk leg; in the days of her great wealth, like all the courtesans, she sparkled with diamonds under her silk Spanish shawls.

Before she was 20 she was a wild success both as a dancer and as a coquette. Passionate and impulsive, it was nothing for her to jump on a table at Maxim's and dance a fandango so sensual that every man in the room felt she was making love to him. When she added to that excitement the finesse of a practised courtesan she proved irresistible to half the crowned heads of the world.

Grand Duke Nicholas of Russia called her 'Ninotchka' – he was her favourite lover as well as being the most generous. Parisians gave her the name 'La Belle Otéro', by which she became famous. But she was born Augustina Carolina Otéro in the village of Puentavalga, near Cadiz, on 20 December 1868.

Her mother, Carmencita Otéro, was a gypsy dancer who lived in a caravan and performed in the steamy cantinas of Cadiz. One night a Greek ship put into port, its officers went seeking entertainment and one of them, Gregorios Karassou, saw Carmencita and became deeply infatuated. He pursued her, but she would have nothing to do with him. His ship sailed, but a few months later he returned with a Spanish-speaking friend to plead for him. Only when he satisfied her greed for possessions would she become his mistress. He bought a hacienda outside Cadiz and during the next seven years she bore him two sons and twin daughters, one of whom, Carolina, inherited her mother's beauty.

The gypsy grew restless and began to take other lovers, one of them a French winegrower from Cette. Their relationship became so flagrant that Karassou was forced to challenge the Frenchman to a duel. The Greek was killed and Carmencita married the winegrower. Carolina, who had loved her father, hated him and soon her mother, riddled with guilt, could stand her presence no longer and packed her off to boarding school. She would not contribute one peseta towards Carolina's education. The future favourite of Kings had to pay for it by scrubbing floors, washing dishes and waiting on fellow pupils.

After about a year, one of the teachers surprised her dancing stark naked on the desks before a crowd of cheering boys. Though only 12 she had the figure of an 18-year-old and was incredibly lovely. One of these boys, called Paco, persuaded her to elope to Lisbon with him where they became lovers. Carmencita found out where she was and had her brought home under police escort. The furious girl ran back to Lisbon, but Paco had disappeared.

Alone, her money running out, she became alarmed. But an amazing stroke of good fortune saved her and set her on the road to success. She used to sing Spanish songs to herself in the room of her hotel. In the room next door the artistic director of Lisbon's Avenida Theatre, staying there while his home was being decorated, heard her and was enchanted. He offered her a contract.

Otéro was a dazzling success, performing in whirling skirts to the click of castanets. Though still under age, she soon had her first lover, a banker, who bought her her first diamonds and established her in a luxurious suite of rooms. But he insisted she gave up the stage and before long she was bored. Hearing that Paco had left Lisbon for Barcelona, she wrote a note of thanks to her patron, packed her bags, gathered up her diamonds and went after him.

She discovered him at the Palais de Crystal, where all the fashionable men of the city hung about, watching performances of light opera on stage and playing the tables for high stakes. Otéro in her Lisbon diamonds and flame-coloured silk attracted their admiring curiosity as soon as she appeared. Paco, astonished but pleased to see his old love in such brilliant style, used his influence to get her a part in a frothy operetta called *Le Voyage en Suisse* at three times the salary she had earned before, and he introduced her to gambling. It became a lifelong passion.

Maturing swiftly, she soon jettisoned Paco for a handsome Italian opera singer, Count Luigi Guglielmo, to whom she was madly attracted. She married him, only to discover he was a philanderer and spendthrift. He took his child bride to the casino at Monte Carlo and there in 1881 lost the little money he possessed. Night after night he returned, gambling away her savings and even her jewels. Otéro decided she herself would try her luck at the roulette table. Idly, she risked two louis on the red. She lost, and the croupier raked in her money. She went in search of her husband, could not find him, and eventually returned to the original roulette table where she had placed her louis. The croupier, it seems, had made a mistake and unknown to her had replaced her money on the red. An old gentleman touched her arm. 'Mademoiselle would be wise to tempt fortune no longer,' he whispered. The red had come up no fewer than 28 times. She had won over 50,000 francs.

Though she forgave her Italian count, lived with him in Marseilles and took him with her to Paris, her eyes were on the higher stakes, that would give her the sort of life she craved. Luigi crept away one night and she never saw him again. She was too dazzled by Paris and its possibilities to care. It was 1889, she was 18 and she had experienced more already than most women do in a lifetime.

She was given a contract at the Cirque d'Eté and her debut in the spring of 1890 made her a star. The next day *Figaro* raved about La Señorita Otéro, supple as a panther in her Spanish finery. Admirers began to queue at her door. The great Duc d'Aumale, once the lover of Cora Pearl, took her to his bed. She knew well enough that the great courtesans, whose ranks she was planning to join, made sure they were rewarded by the finest jewels their lovers could afford. Otéro accepted diamonds from the Duc to replenish her collection.

From the start she caught the eye of the great connoisseurs of feminine beauty. The French writer Colette, who admired her, described her in her prime: 'She has the classic profile of a Greek statue: features without a fault, a low and pure forehead. Her nose and mouth are perfectly formed. Her hands and feet are small. Her bosom is white and beautiful. Her breasts are of an unusual shape – they resembled elongated lemons, firm and uplifted.' Barons, Princes and Dukes paid court to her. She moved around constantly living and performing first in one capital, then another, though always returning to Paris. While in Berlin, for instance, a millionaire banker, Baron Ollstreder, fell in love with her, set her up in a town house with servants, carriages, horses and every conceivable luxury, and in Paris she was never without a splendid villa paid for by some admirer.

Her lovers became more illustrious as the years went by. In turn she became mistress of two Grand Dukes of Russia, the Tsar, the Prince of Wales, Kaiser Wilhelm of Germany, King Leopold of the Belgians and King Alfonso of Spain.

Her first Russian lover was the Grand Duke Peter, son of Nicholas I, who showered her with jewels and pleaded: 'Ruin me if you like, but never, never leave me.' But she also became mistress of his elder brother, the Grand Duke Nicholas, Viceroy of the Caucasus. Even Nicholas II, the last Tsar, entertained her at clandestine suppers before his engagement to Princess Alix of Hesse.

Otéro first met the Prince of Wales at Marienbad, where he had gone to take the waters. She remembered him as an unfailingly kind and generous lover, who persisted in smoking large black cigars while they dined.

She always said she was afraid of the Kaiser. 'He had such strange, piercing eyes and I could not understand him.' He called her 'meine kleine Wildling', my little savage. He had to be flattered the whole time and his rage was notorious. One night she committed a *faux pas* that meant the end of her relationship with him. She made a careless but not unkind remark about his withered arm. His eyes blazed. 'Out you go,' he yelled. The valet came in to escort her and she curtsied her way out of his presence with all the dignity she could muster.

Her collection of jewels became notorious, and she was sometimes accused of greed because of her passion for them. But they were part of her stock in trade as a courtesan, to show how successful she had been, how grand

and wealthy her lovers. She had a waistcoat embroidered back and front with 240 diamonds of the finest quality. She only wore it on the greatest occasions and otherwise it remained safely in the bank vaults. But on one famous occasion she wore no jewels at all and scored heavily over her great rival Emilienne d'Alençon. While Emilienne sat weighed down with diamonds in her box at the opera, Otéro made her entrance in a black velvet gown, cut low, exposing her beautiful neck entirely bare of ornament. But behind came her maid carrying a small mountain of diamonds, emeralds, rubies and sapphires on a tray!

All her patrons were not royal. When she was 35 she met the American millionaire Vanderbilt. He wooed her with a lavish spending she had not experienced before. He gave her a yacht which she sailed to Monte Carlo. She gambled at the casino with reckless abandon and in one week lost £500,000. When Vanderbilt heard what had happened he offered to buy the yacht back from her for that sum with the promise that it was still hers to use as often as she liked.

She retired in her 50s so that she would be remembered in her full beauty. Her later years were spent in the south of France but she gambled away most of her wealth. When she died at the age of 97 she had only one treasure left: a golden spoon, the last of a set presented to her by the Tsar.

Blanche d'Antigny

She was one of the greatest courtesans in the world, but she brought about her own ruin by falling in love. Blanche d'Antigny, who blazed like a star in the *demi-monde* of 19th-century France, was, in fact, the inspiration for Zola's novel *Nana*.

Blanche was the convent-educated mistress of Kings and Khedives, Sultans and Shahs, but her love for a singer gave her the greatest happiness she had ever known. It lasted such a short time and brought an end to her life of bejewelled luxury, but through Emile Zola's pen made her immortal.

Her real name was Marie Ernestine Antigny. She was born in the country, the daughter of a carpenter in the little town of Martizay, near Bourges. She loved the fields and hedgerows and would probably never have left rural France but for a crisis in the family.

Her father suddenly left home to live with another woman and Madame Antigny went off in pursuit. She never found him, but decided to stay in Paris instead of returning to Martizay. She took a post as housekeeper with a gentlewoman called the Marquise de Gallifet who gave her permission to send for her daughter.

The Marquise helped Madame Antigny to send Marie Ernestine to a convent school, where most of the pupils came from rich and noble families. It would have been easy for her, as a simple country girl, to retreat into herself. She did at one time think of being a nun. But instead she set out to learn what she could of poise and good manners from these privileged m'amselles who christened her Blanche because of her milky-white skin.

The Marquise died when Marie was 14 and she had to leave the convent. Her mother found her a job in a draper's shop but this was not the sort of life she envisaged for herself. She wanted fine clothes, luxury, admiration. She was already fully aware of her power to attract men with her emerald-green eyes, pale gold hair and white skin. She yearned for a world in which she would be fully appreciated.

One evening a young admirer took her to the famous gaslit pleasure gardens of Closerie des Lilas where she caught a glimpse of the *beau monde*. She was enchanted by the atmosphere, and intoxicated by the wine, the scent of cigars and the music. She danced the can-can with abandon, surrounded by admirers. One of them bought her champagne – and seduced her. A few weeks later she went with him to Bucharest.

From now on she assumed the more aristocratic name of Blanche d'Antigny. After abandoning her lover, who proved tedious, she set out to discover what life could offer her in this new country. She knew there was only one profession open to her that would provide the luxury she craved . . . that of the courtesan. She had no difficulty in making conquests. An Armenian archbishop and a Prince were said to be among those who introduced her to high society. But life as a lady of pleasure exhausted her after a time and she became ill. Lying on her lace-trimmed pillows she began to think of Paris.

In 1856, when she was 18, she packed and left for home. Somehow or other she was determined to break into the glamorous world of the Paris *demi-monde*. She had no contacts. She would have to do it by her own efforts. First, she allowed herself to be admired riding in the Bois de Boulogne in the most elegant riding habit she could afford. After that she flirted with a journalist who, while he had no money, knew the right people. With his help she got herself taken on as a dancer at the Bal Mabille in the avenue Montaigne. Her final 'galop' in the can-can was as abandoned as when she first danced it in the Closerie des Lilas and people began to ask who she was. They were even more curious when she appeared next at the Théâtre de la Porte Martin as the living statue of La Belle Hélène. Every man in the audience gazed enraptured at the beauty of her figure and she was the talk of Paris.

Soon, instead of the artists and journalists who were her early lovers, she began to receive men whose very presence spoke of wealth and an assured place in society. Her income rose and she was able to move from her rather poor lodgings to an elegant, furnished suite of three rooms, the most elaborate being the bedroom with its four-poster hung with embroidered lace curtains, heavy with the scent of ambergris.

In her beautiful book *The Courtesans*, Joanna Richardson tells how Blanche arranged her day. At 11am she would install herself on the terrace of the Café de Madrid where perhaps her first lover would meet her and take her to lunch at Bignon's or Tortoni's. After lunch she would go home to dress for a regulation 5pm drive in the Bois de Boulogne. Since she needed to attract attention, she would hire a handsome coupé in winter, an elegant open carriage in summer. When it was time for absinthe she went to one of two cafés she regularly frequented where she met financiers, writers and actors.

While in her box at the theatre one night in the spring of 1863 she became aware of a dark, handsome man watching her. In the interval he asked to be introduced. He was Russian, and a Prince. That night over roses and champagne at the supper table he became so infatuated that he begged to be allowed to set her up in a palace in St Petersburg. But Blanche now had many admirers among the French nobility, including the Vicomte de Turenne, and she was not in a hurry to leave Paris.

The Prince was persistent, however, and when summer came and with it the grand exodus from Paris, she allowed him to take her to Wiesbaden, one of the most fashionable watering places of the era. There she created a sensation with her beautiful colouring, gorgeous clothes and magnificent jewels. She gambled wildly and attended every party in the calendar until the Prince was exhausted and glad to drag her off to Russia at last.

She had no idea what to expect. Her protector settled her into the Hôtel de France while he supervised the furnishing of a handsome house. Within a few weeks she moved into her residence with its fine carpets, magnificent tapestries and silver icons. Attended by her moujiks, her footmen and coachmen, her chef and her maître d'hotel, she received the Prince and his friends. The elite of St Petersburg would assemble for supper at her house after the theatre.

Perhaps all the adulation went to her head. After four years in Russia she committed a *faux pas* that even a Siberian peasant would have known was dangerous. Though she knew it was totally against the rules of society for a courtesan to attend the traditional gala performance which ended the winter season at the opera, she insisted on going. Even worse, she went in a dress which she had been warned had already been chosen by the Empress. She looked far more beautiful in it than its royal wearer. Next morning Mezentseff, chief of the secret police and one of her Russian lovers, was ordered to expel her.

She returned to Paris in the spring of 1868 with a suitcase full of diamonds and proceeded to wear most of them at once, so that people could see she had not been wasting her time in St Petersburg. She wanted to return to the stage and found a fabulously rich new protector, the banker Raphael Bischoffsheim, to support her. Some of the critics were more impressed by her jewellery than by her acting, for onstage and off, she glittered from head to foot with diamonds. She revelled in possessing them and seldom left them off.

Nevertheless, the composer Hervé asked her to play Frédegonde in the operetta *Chilperio*, a piece of froth now long forgotten. She did so, appearing on stage half-naked in nothing but her diamonds and a sheepskin! Following that she created the role of Marguerite in his light opera *Le Petit Faust*, looking, he thought, exactly like a golden-haired Rubens. These two parts established her as a star on the Paris stage.

As her fame increased so did the wealth and status of her lovers. They included royalty and heads of state as well as powerful industrialists and businessmen. In order to receive them properly she rented a charming house in the avenue de Friedland which she decorated and furnished richly. Her lovers were received by liveried footmen and led to a salon fragrant with hothouse flowers, hung with rich tapestries, royal-blue velvet and crystal chandeliers. She would lead them into an oriental smoking room, furnished with low red lacquered tables, encrusted with silver and mother of pearl, where they would be offered exotic cigarettes, cigars and tobaccos from gold boxes. The fortunate ones would progress to the lovers' boudoir, softly lit and furnished with deeply cushioned divans, or to her bedroom with its enormous four-poster hung with blue silk.

Blanche set the style with grand panache. Paris talked of her fabulous dinners at which Bischoffsheim presided, of her bath, made of finest Carrara marble which she filled with 200 bottles of mineral water, which she found reviving, and of the smart little Russian carriage which she had brought back from St Petersburg.

She was on tour with a play when the Franco-Prussian War broke out. She hurried back to Paris and was there for the siege, turning her beautiful house into a hospital where 40 Breton sailors were cared for at her expense. She looked after them herself, earning their adoration. After the war ended and they returned home, some of them sent her gifts of produce from Brittany, begging her to give their greetings 'to all your husbands'.

But the fall of the Second Empire also unleashed fear and violence among people and, quite irrationally, they turned on the courtesans, blaming them for sapping the nation's moral fibre. When the bombardment of Paris began, Blanche had to seek protection from the police. Her parties and gay receptions were condemned as wicked in the face of so much suffering.

When the siege ended she went back to the theatre with relief. But now, at the Folies Dramatiques, she fell deeply in love for the first and only time in her life. The man who won her heart, and who loved her in return, was a tenor known simply as 'Luce'. He had performed with her in *Le Petit Faust* and now their tender relationship gradually took over her life. Luce was not a handsome man; he was short and inclined to stoutness. But his love gave her the greatest happiness she had ever known. Early in 1873 he died of TB and she was heartbroken. She asked for an advance on her wages from the director of the Folies so that she could give him a decent funeral. With delicacy she explained she did not want to bury Luce with money she had earned in bed.

When she fell truly in love she could no longer bear the presence of her official lover, Bischoffsheim, and dismissed him. He never forgave her, and without his support her champagne-filled existence was doomed. Soon the creditors arrived at the house in the avenue de Friedland. They confiscated her carriages, her furniture and some of her jewels. She felt the only thing to do was to take flight.

With her maids, her companion Ambroisine, her daughter and her coachman Justin, she sailed for Egypt. The director of the Zizinia Theatre, Alexandria, had signed a contract with her for the winter season, paying her almost three times her salary in France. But at her first appearance she was booed off the stage. She left hastily and went to Cairo where the Khedive, who had no doubt at other times appreciated her other talents, received her splendidly. She was persuaded to return to Alexandria, but her reception was worse than before, and to her horror she found some of her creditors had discovered where she was. She was so afraid of arrest that she entrusted the rest of her jewels to her servants, keeping only a turquoise which Luce had given her. On 28 May 1874, her mother, whom she loved dearly, died. Hounded by creditors and with no home of her own, she booked into a room at the Grand Hôtel du Louvre. Soon after arriving she fell ill with a fever.

Blanche probably brought her death back with her from Egypt. It was either smallpox or typhoid; no one is quite sure which. The horrified manager turned her out of his hotel. Ironically, it was one of her own kind who took her in. The courtesan Caroline Letessier nursed her in her apartment in the Boulevard Haussmann until she died on 28 June 1874. She was not yet 35.

'Skittles'

Every man turned to look as she trotted down Rotten Row in London's Hyde Park. Her figure encased in a riding habit that fitted like a glove, her chestnut hair shining under a rakishly tilted hat, 'Skittles' was a match for every duchess in sight.

Her real name was Catherine Walters. She had come to conquer London from the dingy back streets of Liverpool. She had learned to ride like a duchess, and looked like a duchess, but she had a voice that 'shattered glass'.

Her amazing success on the London social scene in the 1860s was partly due to her superb seat on a horse, but mostly to the piquant contrast between how she looked and how she sounded. Skittles never lost her Liverpool accent, her native outspokenness or her bawdy sense of humour. That was why she became such a great courtesan. She was different from the rest.

She was born on 13 June 1839 in Henderson Street on the Mersey riverfront at Liverpool, close to Toxteth docks. Her father worked for HM Customs and had a regular job. Nevertheless, it was a hard world she was born into, tough and uncompromising. There seemed little chance of bettering herself unless she went into service, but while she was a child everyone could see that she was going to be a raving beauty.

When she was old enough she used to earn a few pennies stacking up skittles in the skittle alley at Black Jack's Tavern where her father used to drink. That was undoubtedly where she got her nickname. She matured early, as children did in those circumstances, and probably took her first lover when she was in her early teens.

Then something happened that changed her entire life. Her family moved to Tranmere in the Wirral, Cheshire. She was introduced for the first time to hunting country, the chase, beautiful thoroughbred horses and fine horsemen. She probably worked at a livery stables or those attached to an inn where the local hunt met. Somehow she was taught to ride, and to ride well.

Society people from London would come up to Cheshire for the hunt and she was fascinated by them. She began to look askance at local boys and told herself that one day she would have an elegant lover with fine manners. Sooner or later, as Henry Blyth says in his biography of Skittles, it was inevitable that she should find her way to London, following in the footsteps of the society people who, at the end of the hunting season, went back to their houses in Mayfair.

She was 20 when she headed south and she found the London of the 1860s an intoxicating place. She drifted into taking the odd lover to keep herself, and frequented the Argyll Rooms, beloved by army subalterns, where she thrived on the gay, noisy, permissive atmosphere.

After a few months she was introduced, by chance, to the owner of a prosperous livery stable in Bruton Mews, off Berkeley Square. She may well have spent the night with him. She was longing to go riding in the park and he could provide her with the sort of hack she could not otherwise afford. Skittles had watched the upper crust on display in Rotten Row and the Ladies' Mile, which separated Apsley House from Kensington Palace. Here could be seen the best riders in Britain, the finest horses, the cream of society. It was no place for novices. But she wanted to try.

By now she was earning a reasonable living and the owner of the stables was impressed by her style and elegance. He offered to mount her on the best horses in his stables, to allow her to drive the finest and most expensive little phaetons; then he took her to an exclusive tailor to have her fitted out in the most expensive habit, made all in one piece so that it fitted her like a glove.

They made a deal. She would be required to ride through the park each day to show off his horses. He would see she was fitted out.

No one riding in the park that spring of 1861 looked prettier. She even gained her first touch of fame. Sir Edwin Landseer, renowned for his animal paintings, used her as a model in his picture 'The Taming of the Shrew' in which a beautiful young woman is seen subduing a mettlesome mare.

One day, about a year later, Skittles, trotting happily through banks of spring daffodils, saw 'the greatest prize in London' coming on horseback towards her. Lord Hartington, 28, eldest son of the Duke of Devonshire and a bachelor, raised his hat, and what happened next no one is quite certain. Did she fall? Did she faint? Did he save her life as the horse bolted? Whatever happened, Skittles returned to the stables on the arm of 'Harty Tarty'. And the next thing London knew was that she was having a passionate affair with him.

Hartington installed her in a fine house in Mayfair with a retinue of servants and as many thoroughbred horses as she wanted. He was not very handsome for he had rather a long face, heavy beard and soulful expression, but they were very much in love. He was unconventional enough to take her to the Derby and be proud of showing her off. Most English aristocrats were more hypocritical about their mistresses and kept them away from society. She was riding on the crest of a wave, the lover of the next Duke of Devonshire. But, if she ever entertained ideas that she might be the next Duchess, they were soon dispelled.

After a time Hartington began to get restless, perhaps realizing that he was getting too involved. He went off to America to get a first-hand view of the Civil War, leaving Skittles with an annuity and a settlement from the Duke of Devonshire.

She had her next major affair in Paris. Out of love with London, she crossed the Channel to try her equestrian skill in the Bois de Boulogne. The displays there were just as elegant as in Rotten Row. When she first appeared in a royal-blue habit, so close-fitting it was said to have been stitched on to her while she stood naked, she created a sensation.

Watching closely as she played the field was a shrewd, intelligent man of the world, 63-year-old financier Achille Fould. Jewish, a man of taste, culture and wide interests, he had been French Minister of Finance five times. The more flamboyant courtesans did not interest him, but Skittles did. She amused and intrigued him. He enjoyed the possibility of turning her into a *grande dame*. He tried to stop her swearing, interested her in the arts, talked to her about pictures and encouraged her to read. She enjoyed his smooth sophistication and he bought her the most expensive thoroughbreds to ride.

Under his guidance she surrounded herself with a small but select group of wealthy and influential people. She did not try to copy the grand salons of the great courtesans in Paris. Her tastes were simpler and, quite naturally, more refined. She rode daily in the Bois, then gave select parties, laid out with the finest crystal and china, in the evening.

It was in France that she first met the poet Wilfred Scawen Blunt, a handsome, wild-eyed young man, then in the diplomatic service. She was his first mistress and he never forgot the few days of passion they shared. She glimpsed with him a hint of what true love would be like. The experience made her sparkle; it made him suffer. Temperamentally, they were light years apart. Realizing his brooding, romantic nature would eventually drive her mad, she left him to his tears. When he recovered, they became lifelong friends. For a long time after this she avoided younger men, determined never again to become emotionally involved.

Skittles loved hunting and first appeared on the hunting field in 1861 when she hunted in Leicestershire with the Quorn. Some of the women thought the presence of a 'London whore' an insult. But, in fact, she behaved very discreetly, putting up at the Haycock Hotel at Wansford, near Market Harborough, and troubling nobody to entertain her. She was the only woman to go over the jumps at the National Hunt Steeplechase and the men cheered her to the echo.

When in London, she held Sunday salons at her house in Chesterfield Street where one of her famous visitors was William Ewart Gladstone, then leader of the House of Commons. They had been introduced one afternoon in the park by Wilfred Blunt and found a common interest in horses. Gladstone asked Skittles 'about her childhood in Liverpool'. He was then in his 50s. His enemies called him a crank and his admirers a saint, as he went out on the streets of London trying to save 'fallen women'. He did not appear to have made any attempt to save Skittles. She was always shocked and angry at any suggestion they were lovers. They were very good friends.

Edward VII loved her tea parties with wafer-thin cucumber sandwiches, big creamy cakes and roaring fires in winter. He said he went there to hear the latest gossip. She probably became his mistress but he certainly enjoyed her company and her earthy good humour. Wisely, Skittles cultivated friendship, for she knew that, while lovers could vanish with her looks, friends she could keep.

Her nose was put out when the Empress Elizabeth of Austria came to England. The Empress was just as great a horsewoman as Catherine Walters, and a dashing figure. Her feats in the saddle became legendary. Skittles accepted that her heyday was over with the 1880s and settled comfortably at a house in South Street, Mayfair, where her old lover, Wilfred Blunt, now married to an heiress and turned Arabic, came to see her along with the Prince of Wales and others.

Quite suddenly she became Mrs Alexander Horatio Baillie and wore a gold ring on her wedding finger. Her husband, it emerged, was a friend of the Prince of Wales and his family had had close connections with Lord Nelson. He was a tall, handsome Edwardian gentleman, just the sort she had always admired. Perhaps she had really joined the upper crust at last. But when she died on 4 August 1920 the sad truth came out. She was named on the death certificate as 'spinster of the parish'.

Marilyn Monroe

On a sultry, hot day in August 1962 the world was stunned to hear that Marilyn Monroe had apparently taken her own life. That radiant, magical, vulnerable sex goddess, with her spun-gold hair and laughing eyes, lay dead in a bleak little bedroom, one hand on the telephone, as though even at the last moment she was calling for help. Was it suicide, or a terrible accident? Or even, as sinister voices began to murmur, murder by the CIA? Improbable theories were tossed to and fro. No one wanted to believe she had gone.

Marilyn Monroe had, in a sense, been calling for help throughout her life, but no one had been able to rescue her. By the time she died, from a massive overdose of drugs, her films had earned an estimated $100 million. But money meant nothing to her, and she remained what she had always been beneath the bright, shimmering exterior – a little girl lost.

Breaking out of a deprived childhood to win international stardom, Marilyn grew up to hate the spun-sugar image that made her famous, and longed to be taken seriously as an actress. Adjectives like 'gentle', 'vulnerable' and 'frail' were used to describe her, but she also had tantalizing physical beauty, and was packaged and sold by Hollywood as the greatest cinematic sex symbol of modern times.

There were three husbands and many lovers; her name was even linked with that of President Jack Kennedy, as well as his brother Robert, her deep feelings for the latter leading to humiliation and rejection. But at the end she was alone, with only a housekeeper to claim her body. She could never have suspected that, after her death, her fame would be even greater and she would be transformed into an icon, a legend, a tragic heroine.

Right from the beginning, life was an unstable affair for the girl who was christened Norma Jean Mortensen. Her mother, Gladys Pearl Baker Mortensen, worked as a film cutter and technician at various Hollywood studios. She had been abandoned by her second husband, Norwegian-born Edward Mortensen, only months after their wedding and had taken up with a salesman, C. Stanley Gifford. He was totally uninterested when she told him she was pregnant. Norma Jean never knew her father, and he never acknowledged her when she was born on 1 June 1926.

There was a frightening amount of insanity on her mother's side of the family, and Gladys Mortensen herself spend much of her adult life in a series of homes for the mentally sick. Norma Jean was fostered first in one home, then another. Her foster parents were mostly kind, but, nevertheless, failed to make her feel she 'belonged'. The great betrayal came when she was nine years old. Having run away from her foster parents, she was taken to the Los Angeles Orphanage, where she remained for 21 months. She remembered screaming: 'I'm not an orphan!'; but it made no difference. The experience scarred her for life.

Her mother's friend, Grace McKee, was named her guardian and eventually rescued her by taking her to live in her home with her new husband, 'Doc' Goddard. Norma Jean never felt close to Grace, but at least Grace gave her some sense of security.

The woman who really helped Norma Jean grow up was her Aunt Ana, a gentle Christian Scientist who, though a 62-year-old spinster, understood the turmoil she had gone through and tried to give her much-needed love. It was to her that Norma Jean recounted the trauma of having been raped at the age of eight by a lodger in one of her foster homes. No one else believed her, but in later years Monroe said that being sexually molested as a child made her feel of little value to anyone.

Next door to the house where Norma Jean lived with 'Aunt' Grace was the Dougherty family. While she was still at high school, one of the unmarried sons, James Edward, began to interest her. He was good-looking, extrovert and possessed a mischievous sense of humour. The attraction was mutual. Jim, six years older than Norma Jean, was fully aware of her early ripening attractions. When she was 16, he proposed. Marriage seemed to her like a safe haven and she accepted. They were married on 19 June 1942.

Norma Jean seemed perfectly content with being Jim's wife until 1944, when he enlisted as a PT instructor in the US Merchant Marine and took her to live with him in married quarters. Suddenly, she found herself surrounded by young men who stared and whistled when she walked by. Tight sweaters emphasized her curves, and she soon learned how to swing her hips in a provocative way. When she confessed to Jim her ambition to be a film star, he told her to forget it. He was old-fashioned, unimaginative, good, decent – and he didn't have the remotest idea how to cope with her.

When Jim was sent to Shanghai, Norma Jean stayed with his family and worked in an aeroplane factory at Burbank. One day, a photographer turned up from the army's pictorial centre in Hollywood. Seeing Norma Jean, he went to work with his camera. The pictures he took were printed in hundreds of army newspapers, including *Yank* and *Stars and Stripes*. She was on her way to a career in modelling.

Soon, Norma Jean was appearing in all the leading magazines, her soft brown colouring changed to platinum blonde for the sake of the cameras. At that time, Twentieth-Century Fox were on the lookout for new faces and casting director Ben Lyon, seeing potential in the young model, asked her to make a screen test.

It was Leon Shamroy, top cameraman at Twentieth-Century Fox, who first photographed her for the screen. He made her brush out her pale gold hair so that it caught the light, and put her into a clinging sequinned dress. All she had to do was light a cigarette and walk across the set. It was enough. When Shamroy first saw the 'frames', he felt a cold chill go over him. There was something about her that hadn't been seen on film since the days of Jean Harlow.

For the first six months with Twentieth-Century Fox, Norma Jean was groomed and processed through the studio publicity machine. Ben Lyon did not like her name. He suggested 'Marilyn' and left her to find the rest. Her guardian, Grace Goddard, called upon to countersign her contract, suggested her grandmother's name, Monroe. So, from August 1946, Marilyn Monroe it was. Two months later she accepted that her marriage to Jim Dougherty had crumbled away, and she got a divorce in Reno.

Monroe's agent in the early days was a man called Johnny Hyde, to whom she always gave credit for launching her career. Hyde fell deeply in love with her but, as he was 30 years older, she could only regard him as a father-figure and friend. Urged by fellow starlets to accept his proposal of marriage, they asked her: 'What have you got to lose?' She replied 'Myself,' and added 'I'm only going to marry for one reason – love.'

She despised the men who tried to buy her with money. Spending her own salary on drama, dancing and singing lessons, and buying as many books as she could afford, she struggled to improve herself and kill the 'dumb blonde' image that was threatening to engulf her.

Through Johnny Hyde she made the breakthrough from forgettable B films to major productions. He got her her first decent part in *The Asphalt Jungle*, a realistic crime film directed by John Huston. This was followed by a role in the famous Bette Davis saga, *All About Eve*. By 1952, playing Lorelei Lei in *Gentlemen Prefer Blondes,* she had graduated to stardom as the quintessential 'dumb blonde'. But she preferred her role in *How to Marry a Millionaire,* because it allowed her to wear glasses and display her talent as a delicious comedienne.

As a famous star, she had her own luxury bungalow on the film set, with a dressing room, bedroom, wardrobe and bathroom. When shooting had finished for the day, she usually went back to her suite at the luxurious and expensive Bel-Air Hotel to read and sip champagne.

One night, a girlfriend phoned to say she had fixed them both up with a date. Marilyn's escort was to be Joe DiMaggio, the great Yankee baseball player, who was a national hero. Marilyn tried to excuse herself: she was tired; she had an early start in the morning. But the friend was insistent. *Nobody,* she said, could offend the great DiMaggio in that way.

They were attracted to each other on sight. DiMaggio, already retired at 37, was in splendid shape, soft spoken with a touch of grey at the temples. Monroe had never been more vital and alive. She was ready for a serious affair. For two years they were almost inseparable, but whenever DiMaggio talked about marriage she steered away from the subject. Apart from making love, they had few interests in common. He did not like the 'phoneys' of the film world and was not very interested in her career. People noticed that he did not even accompany her to the spectacular première of *How to Marry a Millionaire.* They were very much in love, however, and eventually he swept aside her reservations. They were married in San Francisco on 14 January 1954.

Soon after the wedding, Marilyn went on an army morale-boosting visit to Korea, where American troops were bogged down in the aftermath of a bitter war. Throwing off the thick padded jacket she had been offered as a protection against the bitter cold, she sang to thousands of soldiers, wearing the sort of glamorous, low-cut dresses they had seen in her pin-ups. They adored her for it.

On her return she found DiMaggio was not impressed. There was a streak of prudery in him and he did not like his women to wear low-cut dresses. Some of her film costumes were so tight she had to be sewn into them; and they barely covered her breasts. He had thought, with marriage, things would change and she would settle down to a more domestic role, putting her career second. Disillusionment set in rapidly. DiMaggio sank back into his comfortable bachelor habits and began spending more time with his baseball cronies.

Marilyn started to film *The Seven Year Itch*, a delightful comedy directed by Billy Wilder. Although she had misgivings about the way she was always cast in dumb blonde parts, this role had style and class. DiMaggio, however, disapproved of what she was doing on screen. While the film was being made, a promotional photograph was taken of her standing over a subway grating. As the wind from a train passed beneath, it blew her white pleated dress above her sleek, bare thighs. DiMaggio watched from a distance. As her skirt flew higher and higher he turned away, his jaw set in anger. Later that night, guests at the New York hotel where they were staying heard sounds of quarrelling from their room.

They had been married for ten months and it was all over.

After the divorce, Marilyn fled Hollywood to study acting with Lee Strasberg at the famous Actors' Studio in New York, where Marlon Brando had also studied. Strasberg taught her to act 'from the inside out'; to *feel* a scene inside herself before she performed. For the first time, she found herself being accepted as a serious actress.

It was then that Marilyn astonished the film industry by forming her own production company, with the hope of being able to find more demanding roles. As 'Marilyn

Monroe Productions', she negotiated a new contract with Twentieth-Century Fox that vastly increased her profit and control. She then chose two films far above the usual level. The first was *Bus Stop*, directed by Joshua Logan, for which she gave a superb performance, and the second was *The Prince and the Showgirl*, with Laurence Olivier as her director and co-star.

If the industry was surprised by Marilyn's sudden business acumen, it was set back even more by the announcement of her next marriage. Quietly and persistently, Arthur Miller, America's foremost playwright and a considerable intellectual, had been wooing the sex goddess. They were deeply in love. She married him in White Plains, New York, on 29 June 1956, then again in a Jewish ceremony ten days later. When she left for England to work with Olivier on *The Prince and the Showgirl*, Miller went with her.

Monroe's reputation for being difficult to work with stems from this time. She had come very much under the influence of Lee Strasberg's wife, Paula, who was now her acting coach. Sometimes, everything on set would stop, while Marilyn rushed over to consult her. Never a good timekeeper, she now kept camera crews waiting for hours, while she soaked in a bath or compulsively washed and rewashed her hair.

Both Lee and Paula Strasberg had flown to London with the Millers, Lee to reassure Marilyn as she faced the challenge of appearing with the great Olivier, Paula to coach and hand out tranquillizers and sleeping pills. Miller could not stand the Strasbergs, and trouble was brewing even before they left the plane.

Marilyn was terrified of Olivier, and he did nothing to calm her. Although he claimed he treated her as 'an artist of merit', she found the whole experience of working with him a traumatic one. Filming in Hollywood had not prepared her for her encounter with the aristocracy of British acting. She flew to Paula Strasberg every time she wanted advice, forgot her lines and sometimes failed to appear for two or three days at a time, pleading illness. Olivier was beginning to think she was a troublesome shrew. Towards the end, he was a nervous wreck, and even the staunchly supportive Miller had begun to lose patience.

The first crack in the marriage came when Marilyn read an entry in Miller's black notebook, left open by accident. In it, he had written that he had once thought she was 'some sort of angel', but now he guessed he was wrong.

On the couple's return to America, they lived an idyllic rural life in Miller's beautiful colonial farmhouse. They had a deep love for each other and Miller hoped that, with the troubled weeks in England behind them, they could settle down to a happy married life. They were both ecstatic when Marilyn found she was pregnant but, tragically, she lost the baby and was soon back to pills and sessions with the analyst.

Miller, sad for her and sympathetic, said he would write a screenplay which would give her a fulfilling acting role. He started writing *The Misfits* – a tough, tormented story about two cowboys who round up wild horses to be killed for dogmeat. A tender-hearted blonde goes with them for the ride and ends up making her protest against what she sees as the destruction of all free, wild things. Clark Gable and Montgomery Clift were to be her co-stars.

Even as the screenplay was being written Monroe, in her everlasting search for love where she could get it, had started an affair with Yves Montand, who had been her co-star in *Let's Make Love*. Afterwards, the Frenchman ungallantly protested she had pursued him. Whatever the truth, it signalled the end of her four-year marriage to Arthur Miller.

In his complete and thoughtful biography of Marilyn, Fred Lawrence Guiles says at this time Paula Strasberg was telling columnists: 'She has the fragility of a female, but the constitution of an ox. She is a beautiful humming bird made of iron.' Friends of Marilyn were concerned to see this in print, says Guiles. 'She was barely pinned together emotionally at this time and would collapse altogether within a few weeks.'

The Millers both knew if they separated before the film was made *The Misfits* would be ruined. Marilyn was in limbo throughout the filming. All the stars, it turned out, were doomed. Clark Gable died of a heart attack not long after it was finished; Montgomery Clift ended his life with an overdose. Marilyn was heavily into narcotics and could probably not have got through without the help of Paula Strasberg and Gable, who treated her firmly but like a loving father.

As *The Misfits* came to an end, so did the Miller marriage. She did not realize how much she had depended on Miller for support until he had gone. Now, both physically and emotionally, she began to go to pieces. Her condition became so disturbed that her analyst persuaded her to enter the Payne Whitney Psychiatric Clinic at New York Hospital under the pseudonym Faye Miller. Once inside she began to panic, and turned to her old love Joe DiMaggio for help. When he became aware of the circumstances, he signed her out and took her to stay with friends. As she had no work in the offing, he invited her to join him at his home in Fort Lauderdale, where they went surf fishing. Though DiMaggio had failed her as a husband, he was a staunch friend.

It was now April 1961. Marilyn closed down her apartment in New York and returned to Hollywood to be greeted by old friends like Frank Sinatra and Peter Lawford. They drew her into the Rat Pack, a group of all-male friends, which also included Sammy Davies Jnr. and Dean Martin. Marilyn became their mascot.

Peter Lawford's wife, Pat, who was a Kennedy, became one of her closest friends. Through her, Marilyn came into contact with the President, Jack Kennedy, and his brother, Bobby, who was then Attorney-General. She began a discreet affair with the President, their trysts planned with the greatest secrecy. She knew that for him she was only one of many, for he was a notorious womanizer. It was Bobby, with his intense compassion for people, who interested her most. She felt deeply for him, and began to have daydreams that one day they would marry. When she faced reality, however, she knew he would never ruin himself politically for her. Only a few weeks before she died, he withdrew from the affair as delicately as he could, and carefully avoided a scandal.

In the spring of 1962, Marilyn started work on a new film for Twentieth-Century Fox. There was a dreadful irony in its title: *Something's Got to Give*. It was a light-hearted story, but from the first the production was bedevilled by her lateness on set, her inability to learn the script and her problems with the director and actors. When she slipped away to make an appearance at President Kennedy's birthday party, singing 'Happy Birthday' in a revealing cobwebby dress that sparkled and clung and made the audience gasp, it was the last straw. On 7 June 1962, the studios fired her for wilful violation of her contract.

She struggled on for two months. Other film offers came, but she couldn't make her mind up about any of them. She had bought herself a Spanish-style house, but it was only half-furnished and she wandered disconsolately through the unfinished rooms. Nothing in her life was working. Her career was in jeopardy. There was no man in her life and she had stopped caring how she looked.

Some time during the night of 5/6 August she went into the bathroom and took an overdose of barbiturates from the dozens of bottles in her medicine cabinet. She made a few blurred, indistinct phone calls. These could have been cries for help, but, by the time anyone came to realize, it was too late. The screen goddess was dead.

Divine Brown

The celebrity profile and film career of Divine Brown rocketed sky high after the very public revelation that she and the British film star Hugh Grant had been arrested for lewd and indecent behaviour in a public place in June 1995.

Grant, who was 34 at the time, was caught having oral sex with prostitute Divine Brown, 25, in a rented BMW off Sunset Boulevard on 27 June 1995. They were charged two days later, both facing jail sentences. Back in Britain, the tabloids went wild with headlines including 'Hugh Blows It With Hooker' and 'You've Blown It, Hugh!'

Divine Brown became instantly recognizable on both sides of the Atlantic, as the newspapers ran daily stories related to the incident. Both American and British Presses gleaned every detail they could from the case, and spared no taste in the pictures they used of Brown. However, it seemed she could only benefit from the media coverage; by July the British tabloid *News of the World* had paid £100,000 for her exclusive story.

The media hounding of Grant took its toll on his relationship with model girlfriend, Elizabeth Hurley. However, despite the alleged 'rocky patch' that they went through, Hurley stuck by him. It is thought that she forgave Grant since she herself had had an affair four years earlier.

Divine pleaded not guilty to the charge of lewd conduct, but the court had different ideas: she was sentenced to 180 days in jail, with two years' probation and a fine of $1,350. By this time, Divine had appeared on countless television and radio shows and she had capitalized on the lucrative cash deals her quick-found notoriety had given her. She also announced that her days as a prostitute were in the past, and that she wanted to be known by her real name, Stella Thompson.

In April 1996, Grant was back in the USA to film *Extreme Measures*. While Grant was filming in New York, Divine Brown was also there promoting her new film *Nine Minutes*, a pornographic movie based on her encounter with Grant.

Grant's film career also benefited from the incident. Despite the detailed Press coverage, the public were on the whole very forgiving. Grant's tearful and apologetic pleas that the incident was 'completely insane' were met with sympathy from the fickle cinemagoers, whose attendance at his films increased dramatically. (In the months after the incident, video orders for Grant's films went up by 30 per cent.)

The intensive media coverage for Divine Brown was, though, short-lived. Her act of notoriety had filled the pages of the tabloids for a good many months, yet it was the celebrity profile of Hugh Grant which reaped the long-term rewards of the publicity.

Scandalous Wives

Violet Trefusis

On 16 June 1919 a society wedding took place at St George's, Hanover Square, in London which caused many people to heave a sigh of relief. Looking exquisite in a gown of old *Valenciennes* lace, Violet Keppel became Mrs Denys Trefusis and that, they said, should settle the matter once and for all.

The handsome couple were waved off on their honeymoon, crossed the Channel and booked into the Ritz hotel in Paris. But, before the suitcases could be unpacked, Violet was scribbling tortured, passionate letters to her lover, letters crying: 'What am I now? A heartbroken nonentity, a lark with clipped wings. I feel so desperate . . .' Before the honeymoon was over, Violet Trefusis was in her lover's arms, leaving her husband to sob quietly in his room, and it was quite obvious that the matter had not been settled at all.

It was just one more stage in an affair that people felt they could only refer to in shocked whispers. For the lover Violet Trefusis refused to let go when the wedding ring was slipped on her finger was Vita Sackville-West, writer, poet, mother of two sons and wife of English diplomat Harold Nicolson.

The two of them first met at a tea party when they were only children and discovered both liked horses and read the same books. Both were the product of upper-class homes with nannies and governesses and both had forceful, glamorous mothers.

Violet was the elder daughter of Mrs Alice Keppel, the famous Edwardian society hostess whose good looks, charm and discretion made her a favourite companion of King Edward VII. Her father was third son of the Earl of Albemarle. As an exceptionally pretty little girl she was doted on, spoiled and usually managed to get her own way. She resented discipline of any kind.

When she grew into a young woman she was sent off abroad so that she could acquire polish and learn to speak French, Italian and Spanish fluently. She always wanted to be the centre of attention and usually managed it with her vivacity, her husky voice and great grey eyes. She became a terrible flirt, throwing over her first man, then another, perhaps in an effort to compete with her dauntingly fascinating mother.

Denys Trefusis was 28 when she was introduced to him, an officer in the Royal Horse Guards with reddish gold hair and startling blue eyes. Highly intelligent, there was something different about him that attracted her. Then she discovered that, though he had been brought up as an English public schoolboy and taught to love church, army and throne, he had run off to Russia where he had earned a living teaching the children of an aristocratic family. He had learned to speak Russian fluently and there was something of the Slav about him. He had come back to England to join up. Violet decided she was going to make him fall in love with her.

Trefusis spent a gallant war in the trenches and won the MC. Violet's warm, witty, clever letters had no doubt kept him going. She seduced him by post and when the poor, unsuspecting man proposed she said 'yes'. But there was, of course, the problem of Vita.

When they met again as grown women, the attraction was mutual: Violet, vibrantly feminine, reckless and free, and Vita tall, languid, and with the elegance of a handsome boy. But Vita was happily married and adored the husband she called 'Hadji'.

Their 'scandalous' affair started when Violet was a guest at the Nicolsons' beautiful country house in Kent in the April of 1918. She had asked if she might stay for a few days to get out of the London bombing. Vita was not too sure. She thought they might end up bored with each other. But Violet got her own way, as usual.

One night, Harold Nicolson did not return for dinner but stayed at his club in London for the night. That was when Violet with infinite subtlety and worldliness told Vita she loved her. Two kisses were exchanged. Vita did not sleep that night. Vita's son, Nigel Nicolson, told the story of what followed in his *Portrait of a Marriage* in which he is absolutely frank about both his parents' inclinations in the sexual sphere.

After that traumatic night they went off for holidays together staying at Hugh Walpole's cottage at Polperro in Cornwall. Vita's mother, Lady Sackville, told everybody 'they have gone to see the spring flowers', thinking they had. One of Violet's letters, recalling that time, says: 'Sometimes we loved each other so much that we became inarticulate, content only to probe each other's eyes for the secret that was a secret no longer.'

That autumn Vita began to write *Challenge*, the book in which she and Violet are depicted as the lovers Julian and Eve, and before long they began to act out their fantasy. Vita, dressed as a subaltern, would stroll through the streets of London with Violet on her arm and, as a laughing young couple they would join others enjoying a spot of leave at tea dances and restaurants. They took an enormous risk. Vita may have thought her disguise impenetrable, but Violet was such a well-known society girl they could easily have been caught out.

Denys Trefusis had appeared on the scene. He was desperately in love with Violet and did not look forward to having Harold Nicolson's wife as a rival. Violet made the almost impossible demand that if she married him she would not have to sleep with him and could continue her relationship with Vita. Thinking, no doubt, that things would work out in time, Trefusis agreed.

That same autumn the two women managed to get away to Monte Carlo for a short break. Amazingly Harold consented to get permits for them through his special influence at the Foreign Office as it was impossible to leave England without them at that time. As his son states, he could not have been ignorant of what was going on and even Lady Sackville was beginning to fear the worst.

Their little jaunt was supposed to last no more than a fortnight, but they stayed away for four months. When they reached Paris, Violet tried to get Vita to stay with her for always, saying she would kill herself if Vita did not agree. These scenes were repeated every time Vita tried to book a passage home.

Violet thought of herself as a true rebel. She wanted to shock society and thought that by openly flaunting convention she would show that love had more dimensions than people dreamed of. However, Harold Nicolson did not see it that way, as he first spent a Christmas without his wife, then found by New Year that she had even stopped writing to him. For the first time he became really angry. Lady Sackville relieved her feelings by calling Violet 'that viper' and 'that pervert' and by writing to all her friends that her daughter had been bewitched.

At last they came home. Violet, largely to please her mother whom she adored, got engaged to Denys Trefusis on 2 March 1919. This did not stop her writing to Vita, telling her how much she ached for her and demanding: 'Are you going to stand by and let me marry this man?'

She planned to elope with Vita the day before the wedding. They spent a lot of time together at Long Barn, the Nicolsons' home, and she nearly went mad with jealousy when Harold came home on leave.

'You and he, strolling about arm in arm (God I *shall* go mad!),' she wrote. 'I hate men. They fill me with revulsion. Even quite small boys.'

After the wedding and that travesty of a honeymoon Violet and Denys Trefusis came back to England to live at Possington Manor near Uckfield in Sussex. Violet was already talking of separation. She showed her husband all

Vita's letters and he angrily burned them. The passionate correspondence started up again and soon they were back to the old routine, pretending to be Julian and Eve, slipping across to Paris and making everybody thoroughly miserable.

The crisis came in January 1920, when the two women decided to go away together for good – and this time they meant it. By now Denys Trefusis was talking incoherently about shooting somebody, which was not really surprising considering the strain he was under.

Practically everybody turned up on the quayside at Dover. Violet had gone ahead to wait for Vita in Amiens. Denys confronted Vita while she was still hanging about waiting for a boat, and she confessed what was going on. He decided to travel across with her and perform the heavy husband act in Amiens. By this time, George Keppel, Violet's father, had also turned up. He insisted on joining them, and, on reaching Amiens, created a scene and refused to go back without his daughter.

The whole thing was too much, even for the ardent lovers. Violet felt they had been defeated by the forces of convention and finally agreed they had better go home. She continued to bombard Vita with letters and for a long time she and Denys hardly spoke to each other, but the great scandal was nearly over.

At the end of 1920 Violet was still passionately in love, but Vita was cooling off. By the end of 1922 Vita was looking back on the whole affair as a madness of which she would never again be capable, though she was on the brink of meeting Virginia Woolf . . .

The patience of Denys Trefusis was finally rewarded. Once the affair with Vita had died down they discovered they liked being married. They never had children but they had lots of things in common, loved literature and travel and had the same sense of humour. They lived in Paris together until his tragically early death from tuberculosis in 1929.

Violet still had another lifetime to live. She became a novelist, a great hostess and a focus of Paris intellectual society. Colette renamed her 'Geranium'. She did become a very close friend of the Princess de Polignac, who, as all the world knew, had tastes in a certain direction, but who preferred to keep her private life very private indeed. Violet, having had a taste of social ruin, decided in future to do the same. She died, considered by everybody a grand old lady, on 1 March 1972. She was 79.

Messalina

The Roman Empire, in its heyday, produced a bevy of women whose exploits chilled the blood. Livia, Agrippina and Poppaea were bad enough, but the monster of them all was Messalina, wife of the gentle Emperor, Claudius.

Her power over him was such that for years he went in ignorance of her cruelty, debauchery and avarice. When he began to suspect the truth, he was too timid to act. Beautiful to look at, she always knew how to soothe and flatter him, how to twist the truth and lull his fears.

Her education in the darker side of life began very early for her mother, Lepida, was a vicious woman who dabbled in magic as well as prostitution and carried on an incestuous relationship with her brother.

Messalina married Claudius before he became Emperor. She was his fifth wife. They had a daughter, Octavia, later to marry the Emperor Nero, and a son, Britannicus, born within the first few weeks of his reign. But she was a woman of such passionate desires that she could never remain faithful.

Claudius became Emperor in a coup that surprised him as much as the rest of Rome. He was bookish, some thought simple, with an easy, indolent nature, much addicted to the pleasures of eating and gaming. Every day he gave sumptuous feasts to which as many as 600 people were invited. He never troubled his head about what was going on in his household.

His wife, with her silky brown limbs and provocative eyes, had no difficulty attracting lovers. Only later, when her true nature was known, did those who were fascinated by her think twice. When she first became Empress she carried on her love affairs secretly and with discretion but, as she began to realize that no one dared oppose her, she flaunted her passions as she chose.

Ironically, her cruelty was first brought to light by a fit of jealousy. Her victim was Princess Julia, daughter of Germanicus and sister of the terrifying Caligula. This Princess and her sister had been banished by Caligula to the island of Pontia after he had abused and raped them both. Claudius, touched by their plight, recalled them from exile and restored them to their estates and former splendour.

Julia was a fascinating woman but unfortunately, as it turned out, being descended from the Caesars, had inherited a haughtiness and noble bearing which Messalina detested. It was also obvious that the Emperor seemed to have a great regard for her and they spent a lot of time together.

Mistaking her husband's regard for love, Messalina began to look upon the handsome Julia as a rival to be got rid of. She brought about her downfall by accusing her of crimes she could not possibly have committed. Claudius believed what he was told and Julia was banished. Soon after, through Messalina's agency, she was killed.

From now on anyone who stood in Messalina's way became the victim of her cruelty. She had only to accuse them of treason or an equal crime, and they were put to death without mercy. Her word became law. Appius Silanus was one of the first to die in this way. He had married her mother, Lepida, and become a close friend to

Claudius. He was universally well thought of and expected to achieve high office. But he had the misfortune to be found attractive by Messalina. She made advances to him which he repelled, reminding her of their family relationship. Humiliated, she swore to destroy him.

Claudius had a superstitious belief in dreams so when Messalina's servant, Narcissus, told him, on her instructions, of a dream in which he saw Silanus plunge a dagger into the Emperor's heart, he was disturbed. It only needed Messalina to add that she too had had the same dream several nights in succession, and Claudius fell into the trap set for him. Believing he was about to be assassinated, he gave orders for Silanus to be killed.

This served as a strong warning to the senate as to what they could expect from their Emperor under the spell of his evil wife. Several leading senators determined to get rid of Claudius and had plans for the Emperor of Dalmatia, with his vast army, to take over in Rome.

The plans came to nothing, but gave Messalina the opportunity for the violence she had been waiting for. Claiming to be acting for the good of the state she hunted down the guilty senators, in Claudius' name. Estates were confiscated, men tortured, anyone remotely connected with the plot put to death. Things came to such a pitch that many preferred to commit suicide rather than risk capture. She was intoxicated by her power and had reached a point at which she believed the least resistance to her should be punished.

She had a ravenous physical appetite, and heaped rewards on those who joined in her debauchery. Not being content with her own degradation, she forced women of rank to prostitute themselves. If they refused, she had them raped in front of their husbands. She ordered a room in the palace to be fitted up like a brothel, had the name of the most notorious whore in Rome inscribed over the top and amused herself by impersonating her, giving herself to every man that came.

Her infamy was common knowledge yet, incredibly, kept from Claudius. Messalina could make him believe what she wanted to and sometimes made a fool of him. This was so in the affair of Mnester, the most famous dancer in Rome. She was so madly in love with him that she had statues of him erected all over the city, but he did not give in to her, being afraid of what would happen to him if the Emperor found out. She pursued him until at last he said he would do whatever she pleased as long as the Emperor consented. Messalina went to Claudius and 'after a thousand deceitful caresses' complained that Mnester had refused to obey her over some petty business. She asked Claudius to give directions that her orders were to be treated with more respect. Claudius sent for the dancer and told him, in future, to obey Messalina implicitly. He obeyed and became her lover.

Greed was another of her vices. For years she had coveted the beautiful Gardens of Lucullus owned by Asiaticus, a senator of great distinction. As she could get them no other way she accused him of being responsible for Caligula's murder, saying he had boasted of the assassination. To everyone, it was obvious he was innocent, but by trickery she had him condemned and he was forced to choose his own death.

Messalina had fled to the Gardens of Lucullus. Her mother, Lepida, was with her. The centurions broke open the gates of the garden and the captain presented himself to her, without a word. He handed her a dagger, giving her the chance to kill herself but she couldn't do it. To make an end of it quickly, he ran her through with his sword.

Claudius was given the news of her death but did not seem to take it in. For some time after he would plaintively ask why the Empress Messalina did not come.

Jane Digby

English aristocrat, Jane Digby, shocked her upper-class world to the core by collecting and discarding husbands at an alarming rate before finally disappearing into the desert to marry a Bedouin sheik.

An exquisite woman with a streak of high-spirited wildness, she didn't give a fig for convention and as a result lived one of the most scandalous lives of the 19th century.

The Digbys knew, when their daughter blossomed from a tomboy into a raving beauty with pale gold hair, deep violet eyes, creamy complexion and a perfect figure, that she was going to be a handful. Not only was her beauty obvious by the time she was 13, but so was her power to attract men. At a family conference at Holkham Hall in Norfolk, it was decided she should be married off as soon as possible to keep her out of mischief.

Whoever became her husband had a daunting pedigree to live up to. She was a descendant of two extraordinary families; the Digbys, whose line could be traced back to Edward the Confessor, and the Cokes, whose roots went back to King John and the Magna Carta. Her father, Captain Henry Digby, was a hero of Trafalgar but it was the enormous wealth of her mother's family, the Cokes, that had built palatial Holkham Hall in north Norfolk where Jane spent her childhood.

When she was 16 she was taken to London for her coming-out season. At the great ball given in her honour in the spring of 1824 she met Edward Law, second Lord Ellenborough, who was regarded by everyone as a splendid 'catch'. Certainly he was a handsome man of distinguished bearing, wealthy, ambitious, respected. The fact that he was a widower more than twice her age, vain, lacking in warmth and, for all his brilliance, generally disliked by his peers, did not seem to worry anyone.

Jane was flattered by his proposal and agreed to marry him.

She had obviously imagined that being Lady Ellenborough would mean having a fine London house, taking her place as a leading hostess, constant dinner parties and balls. But once the honeymoon was over Lord Ellenborough went back to his politics and his sophisticated friends, leaving his beautiful child-wife – she was barely 17 – to pine with boredom at his country house in Roehampton.

He was generous enough and humoured her whims but otherwise condemned her to a life of paying calls and choosing dresses. Sometimes she attended grand receptions on his arm when she would bare her bosom as much as she dared. He seems to have married her for two reasons – to provide him with a decorative partner when necessary and to give him a son and heir. Once the latter was achieved he left her more or less alone and they moved into separate bedrooms.

But, if her distinguished husband was cold, Jane Digby was made of fire and passion and soon turned elsewhere for consolation. Since childhood she had been half in love with her first cousin, George Anson, and it was probably with him she first deceived Ellenborough. Then, before she had been married three years, she went to stay at Holkham Hall where she found a handsome young scholar, an official of the British Museum, in residence engaged in the tedious job of cataloguing the famous Long Library. She wooed him with her violet eyes, then seduced him and it was only when his journals were unsealed in 1920 that the story of their affair was told and the young librarian revealed as the future Sir Frederick Madden.

Back in London, with her husband's approval, she began to attend the fashionable Wednesday Night Balls, held under the patronage of great hostesses such as Lady Jersey and Princess Esterhazy. He would escort Jane to the door of the ballroom then leave to spend his evening elsewhere discussing politics. One night she was introduced to Prince Felix Schwarzenberg, the newly arrived Austrian attaché. She took one look at him and was hypnotized. He was her idea of a perfect Byronic hero, strikingly good-looking with a thick black moustache, dark eyes, magnificent shoulders and an air of mystery that was magnetic. Schwarzenberg had arrived in London with a reputation as a heart-breaker of international repute, but she ignored all warnings. Her intense passion for him was evident from the moment they danced together and he was captivated by her. Almost daily during the summer of 1828 they were seen together. Her elegant green phaeton, drawn by sleek, black ponies, would take her from Roehampton to the Prince's rooms in Harley Street and sometimes they even dared to slip away to Brighton for a weekend rendezvous.

Whether Lord Ellenborough had decided not to notice or whether he was too busy with his political ambitions to care, no one was quite sure, but soon gossip about the two lovers was so flagrant that the Austrian ambassador, Prince Esterhazy, began to concern himself. What if Ellenborough suddenly woke up to what was going on? The public scandal would do irreparable harm. Schwarzenberg, being warned, decided to safeguard himself by starting another flirtation. His reputation being what it was, nobody was in the least bit surprised, but, as it turned out, it was the worst thing he could have done. Jane complained loudly and tearfully to half of London that she had been abandoned by her lover until Prince Esterhazy, in desperation, had the amorous attaché recalled to Vienna.

Pandemonium followed. Jane, finding she was three months pregnant with his child, planned to leave Lord Ellenborough and accompany her lover to Vienna. This was not quite as he saw it. Begging her to make things up with her husband, he headed for the nearest Channel port. Ellenborough, having been told everything, and with one eye on the premiership, decided he would have to divorce Jane to save his honour.

The Digbys and Cokes, nearly prostrate with shock over the disgrace, descended on Roehampton *en masse* and tried to persuade their erring beauty to beg her husband's forgiveness. She would not, of course, do anything of the sort. Her parents were appalled.

Now in Vienna, a thoroughly embarrassed Prince Schwarzenberg was trying to persuade his ardent mistress to stay where she was. He could never marry her, he pointed out, because of the scandal! However, he could not ignore her passionate entreaties for ever and eventually promised that, if she left England and took up residence in Basle, he would look after her and the child. So, on the last day of August 1829 Jane Digby sailed from England. Ellenborough was unusually generous in the allowance he gave her saying that he did not want her to be without those comforts and conveniences to which her rank in life entitled her. The Ellenboroughs' divorce caused a sensation and, because of the distaste for such procedures in 19th-century England, it needed a private act of parliament before it was declared fully legal.

Jane gave birth to a daughter, Mathilde, in November that year. When the Prince was sent to serve with the Austrian Embassy in Paris he weakened and decided to take his beautiful mistress with him. She lived stylishly enough, first in the Faubourg St Germain, later in the Place du Palais, but because of her situation could not be received in the best circles. Jane became pregnant again and gave birth to a son, who died, but if there was ever a faint hope that the Prince might marry her then, it was soon crushed by the Schwarzenberg family who regarded her as a shameless English baggage.

Soon the Prince's name was being linked with other women in Paris and after a violent quarrel at the Place du Palais one night he left without a word of farewell, and arranged to be sent home to Bavaria. It was obviously the excuse he had been waiting for to extricate himself from the affair.

Desperate about what to do next, Jane arranged to meet her mother, Lady Andover, to discuss possibilities. The distraught parent suggested Munich where the family had connections. But on no account was she to return to England and embarrass everyone.

Jane made a splendid start in Germany by catching the eye of King Ludwig I of Bavaria who made a lifelong habit of collecting beautiful women and now fell madly in love with her. At the same time she accepted the passionate courtship of a great landowner, Baron Karl Venningen who escorted her to the opera, the balls, the outdoor cafés, all the public places where the King could not be seen with her. Between swooning over the memory of Schwarzenberg and dallying with the King, she drove poor Venningen half crazy. But, when she became pregnant again – the third time without a husband – and he proposed marriage, she agreed.

For a time she enjoyed the security and acceptance that came with being known as 'the beautiful Baroness von Venningen' but after only a year there were signs of friction. Jane continued to be on intimate terms with the King, and, though never quite sure whether she was his mistress or not, the Baron writhed with jealousy. He took her to live at Weinheim, a secluded, medieval watering spot 11 miles north of Heidelberg, but their relationship was not the sort that thrived on solitude. She became so bored and restless that he gave in to her pleas and took her back to Munich for the season.

Soon, however, both the middle-aged king and the gallant baron were to be obscured by the appearance of a dazzling figure rejoicing in the name of Count Spiridion Theotoky. He was only 24, fiery, magnificent to look at and a member of one of the most aristocratic families on the

Greek island of Corfu. From the moment Jane saw him at a carnival ball she knew she was on the threshold of another grand passion. As for the Greek, he was enchanted by the wild little Baroness with pale gold hair.

Not daring to breathe her love in daylight she would wait until the household was asleep, then saddle her thoroughbred mare and ride out in the moonlight to meet her 'Spiro'. They made one attempt to elope but the Baron gave chase, hauled Theotoky out of his carriage and challenged him to a duel in which the latter was slightly wounded.

After her dash for freedom, the marriage held together until the spring of 1839 when she fled to Paris with Spiro, leaving behind a heartbroken husband and two children. 'The misfortune of my nature is to consider love is all in all,' she wrote to King Ludwig, trying to explain her behaviour. As for the Baron, she had to admit he behaved nobly, even offering her his house as a haven should she ever need it. Jane Digby had that effect on people.

To her family this latest affair was the last straw. Her grandfather would not allow her name to be mentioned and, though she was reconciled with her mother who could never be cross with her for long, her father, Admiral Digby, never forgave her and never saw her again.

In Paris she posed first of all as Spiro's niece and later as his wife. In March 1840 she gave birth to his son, Leonidas. Though her other children were scattered around Europe in the care of various relatives, she seemed to cherish this child especially, little knowing how soon she would lose him.

The couple stayed in Paris until the spring of 1841 when with great excitement on Jane's part they set out for the Greek islands, staying first at Tinos where Spiro's father was governor then carrying on to Corfu to live on the family estates.

Before setting out for the Aegean they wanted to become

man and wife. As von Venningen had not even started divorce proceedings they decided to have that marriage dissolved through the Greek Orthodox Church. It is believed they were then married by a Greek Orthodox priest in Marseilles.

They arrived in Corfu as Count and Countess Theotoky. For three years they were blissfully happy there, living in an Italian style villa some 20 miles from the capital where they entertained lavishly and attended all the grand balls and receptions in town.

Their idyll was not to last long. King Otto called Spiro to Athens to become his aide de camp and the call was mandatory and included Jane. Once again her beauty proved her undoing for the King could not keep his eyes off her. Queen Amalia was furious and took an instant dislike to the Countess Theotoky while Spiro played the offended husband and in retaliation began a series of affairs. For a time it seemed as though their marriage was kept together by only one thing – their mutual love of their son.

Tragedy struck in the summer of 1846. The Theotokys went to their summer house, a tall Florentine villa in the Italian spa town of Bagni di Lucca. It was an imposing house with a reception hall three storeys high and inside balconies at all levels. One day, hearing his parents' voices in the hall the boy leaned over the balcony railing on the top floor, lost his balance and fell to the black and white marble floor below. He was killed outright at his mother's feet.

Jane never fully recovered. Shattered with grief she believed that his death was a punishment for the way she had neglected her other children. She and Spiro went their separate ways. She disappeared for a time and the rumour was that she took six husbands to console herself, a slander she fervently denied.

By 1849 she was back in Athens and her house became a meeting place for the liveliest and most interesting people of the day. Though she did not know it, the most colourful part of her life was about to begin.

King Otto, who frequently changed his aides de camp, had given Spiro's post to the most fantastic figure in Greece, the brigand chief, General Cristodoulos Hadji-Petros. This extraordinary man, leader of the fierce band of mountain freedom-fighters who initiated the Greek War of Independence and called themselves 'Pallikari' (the brave ones), was nearly 70 but with his sinewy body, shock of white hair and fine moustaches he carried his age lightly. Jane fell passionately in love with him.

When Cristos was made governor of the mountain province of Lamia, she did not hesitate to sell her house and follow her new lover to his rugged outpost. The life suited her as never before and she revelled in it, wearing coarse cotton smocks like the mountain women and sleeping between rough goats'-hair blankets as though she had never known the feel of silk. She galloped over mountains, slept in the open, ate and drank the roughest food. Nothing deterred her as long as she could be with Cristos. Her lover's small government salary was augmented by highway robbery, but he was careful to shield her from its more bloody aspects and she accepted it as part of mountain life. She was so happy she could think of nothing better than to be his wife.

Alas, her mountain venture was to last no more than a few months. Word got back to Athens that Countess Theotoky was living openly in the mountains with Hadji-Petros. Squeals of outrage went up from all sides and Queen Amalia, her old enemy, saw a way to avenge herself. She insisted that Cristos be dismissed from government for openly keeping a mistress. The old brigand wrote to the Queen explaining that he had only lived with the Countess for profit, not love – 'She is rich, I am poor. I have a rank to live up to, children to educate. I trust therefore . . .' The Queen had the note displayed publicly. Jane understood him enough to forgive this piece of ungallantry, but when he started to seduce young women she felt she had taken enough.

Without notice to anyone, she vanished from Athens, leaving Hadji-Petros and her dream of a mountain marriage behind.

She had been planning a trip to Syria to buy horses and decided to go through with the journey in order to distance herself from the persuasive Cristos. He usually had an explanation for everything and she might be tempted to listen. She sailed for Beirut on 6 April 1853, three days after her 46th birthday.

During the voyage she decided to give herself up to travel, to see as much as she could of the Middle East and perhaps even join a desert caravan. But, before she could set out for Palmyra or Petra, a young Bedouin sheik came into her life.

She was still as vulnerable to passion as she had been as a girl of 17. When she first saw Saleh against the background of low, black Bedouin tents she knew she would fall in love with him. She had been taken out to the encampment in the desert to buy a horse but dealing was soon forgotten. Saleh saw before him a beautiful, mature woman, and was fascinated.

Before the dealing was through he had invited her to his tent.

Jane became totally infatuated with Saleh, though he was 20 years younger than she was. She recognized something in the Arab of her own nature. She made up her mind she was going to marry him and embrace the Bedouin culture.

She had to return to Athens to settle her affairs and her friends threw up their hands in horror when they learned she was considering marriage to a Bedouin Arab. She could hardly wait to get back to him. She raced across the desert only to find, to her horror, that her place in his tent had been taken by a beautiful dark-eyed girl called Sabla, a brown nymph scarcely more than a child.

Jane realized that her passionately romantic nature had led her into one affair too many. As she turned towards Damascus she determined to eliminate men from her life altogether. But there was still one more to come, and that was worth more than all the rest.

Shortly after she had met and fallen in love with Saleh, she made plans to visit the ancient ruins of Palmyra. For this an escort was essential and the British Consul in Damascus told her to contact the Mesrab Arabs who for centuries had controlled the stretch of desert on the way to Palmyra. A younger son of their great sheik was sent to negotiate with her. His name was Medjuel el Mesrab. He was slight, graceful with a handsome olive face and dark beard; he could not only read and write but spoke several languages and was an authority on desert history.

In short he was a true aristocrat. By the end of their journey, which took them through dangerous territory and demanded cool nerves, Medjuel was full of admiration for the beautiful English woman. He admired her so much in fact that he asked her to marry him, but at the time she had thoughts for no one but Saleh.

Now on her way back to Damascus she thought about Medjuel again. He had never forgotten her, never taken another woman and never given up hope of marrying her. Hearing that Madame Digby, as he called her, was in the caravan approaching Damascus, he set out to meet her with a valuable Arab mare as a gift of welcome.

A few months later they were married.

Jane made one more journey home in the autumn of 1856 mostly for the purpose of being reconciled with her mother, but English society found her marriage to an Arab, when she still had three husbands living, too much to accept. She met members of her family but felt at a distance from them. Victorian England was no place for her and after six months she kissed her mother goodbye for the last time and set off back to her spiritual home, with a flock of Norfolk turkeys for her beloved Medjuel and ammunition for her Bedouin tribe.

She spent the rest of her life with him, sometimes in the desert as a Bedouin wife, but mostly in a charming house he bought for her in Damascus and where she received many English visitors. Most of all she loved riding by his side out into the desert and for her 73rd birthday in 1880 he bought her the most beautiful horse she had ever seen.

Only 12 months later, in August 1881, she fell ill with a virulent dysentery. Medjuel sat by her bed as she grew weaker day by day. When she died he obeyed her last wishes and she was buried in the Protestant cemetery in Damascus. Then, the grief-stricken Bedouin rode out to the desert and sacrificed one of his finest camels in her memory.

Caroline of Brunswick

On the morning of George IV's coronation, his wife, Caroline of Brunswick, rose from her bed at dawn, put on robes of white satin, pinned white ostrich plumes in her hair and then drove to Westminster Abbey, where the door was shut in her face.

'I am your Queen,' cried Caroline. 'Will you not admit me?' Lord Hood, who was among those who had accompanied her, on being asked for a pass replied huffily: 'I present you your Queen – surely there is no need for her to have a ticket.'

But, in spite of this farcical exchange, the party got no further. Orders had been given that on no account was Caroline to be allowed over the threshold. Inside, the coronation went on without her. The King had won his battle against the wife he detested. Now she would never be crowned.

The most extraordinary marriage in the history of

British royalty started to go wrong the moment the couple met. The Prince of Wales took one look at the short, bosomy German girl who had been chosen for him, walked sharply to the other end of the room and whispered to his friend the Earl of Malmesbury: 'Harris, I am not well, pray get me a glass of brandy.'

Caroline was astonished, but did not collapse in tears as many would have done. 'Mon Dieu!' she exclaimed in a loud voice. 'Is the Prince always like that? I find him very fat and nothing like as handsome as his portraits.'

That was the trouble with Caroline. She never knew when to keep her mouth shut. The Prince was fastidious, vain, sensitive. She was totally opposite. Her behaviour was like that of a hoydenish schoolgirl, lacking in feminine grace, with a freakish sense of humour and brashness which sealed her fate as far as the Prince was concerned. Little did he know the chaos she was to bring into his life, though most people felt they deserved each other.

Her parents, the Duke and Duchess of Brunswick, found her an odd, precocious child from the very beginning. There was a wildness about her which defied discipline and she told terrible lies.

When she was 16 she was quite a pretty girl with powdered curls, soft skin and bright eyes. But her behaviour was awful. Having been forbidden to attend a court ball by her mother, she retired to bed screaming that she was pregnant and about to give birth. All havoc was let loose and the midwife fetched. 'Now, Madam,' said the Princess to her swooning mother, 'will you forbid me to go to a ball again?'

At 26 she was still unmarried. Eligible Princes who had been considered for her were amused by her company but fled at the hint of a wedding. When, therefore, in 1794, the Duke was asked for Caroline's hand on behalf of the Prince of Wales, he was overjoyed. The Prince had never set eyes on her and had already contracted an unlawful marriage with a Catholic widow, Maria Fitzherbert, with whom he was very much in love. But his debts, due to over-rich living and gambling, were phenomenal and the King, anxious for his son to produce an heir, promised to wipe them out provided he would take a lawful wife. Caroline seemed eminently suitable as a Princess from a staunch Protestant family.

Lord Malmesbury was sent to fetch her. He tried hard to see her better points. She could be very kind and was good-natured on the whole. But, he had to admit, she was also far too easy in her manners, familiar and coarse. He tried to give her lessons in court dignity and to make her aware of the importance of being Princess of Wales. But the fact that worried him most was that Caroline was not very clean, for the dandified Prince was always immaculate. Caroline didn't wash very often and wore coarse underclothes and thick stockings which were seldom laundered. What's more, it seemed to be a subject on which she was singularly obtuse.

On arrival in England she was taken over by the bossy Lady Jersey, the Prince's favourite, who supervised her toilette and dressed her up like a Christmas chicken for that disastrous first meeting with the Prince. Caroline hated her and soon reverted to her old style.

The wedding took place in the Chapel Room at St James's Palace on 8 April 1795. The Prince was deathly pale and only got through the ceremony with regular prompting from the King. He apparently spent the greater part of his wedding night snoring in the fireplace 'where he fell, and I left him' as Caroline told everybody afterwards. There was no doubt he found her physically repellant and stayed in bed only long enough to consummate the marriage.

When it became obvious that Caroline was a 'wild child' as she put it, she roared 'I don't believe it' and suggested slyly that the Prince was not capable of fatherhood, a slur he never forgave her for.

She gave birth to a daughter, Princess Charlotte, on 7 January 1796 and her husband wrote in his diary: 'The Princess was brought to bed of an *immense* girl.' Of course he wanted a boy so that the whole thing was over and done with. The disappointment brought on one of his fits of hypochondria and he felt so miserable that he thought he must be dying. He made his will, leaving everything to Mrs Fitzherbert and stating that the care of his daughter should be in the hands of the King. 'The mother of this child,' he wrote, 'is to have no hand in her upbringing.' He went on: 'The convincing and repeated proofs I have received of her entire lack of judgement and of feeling make me deem it encumbent upon me to prevent, by all possible means, the child falling into such improper and bad hands as hers . . .'

After the birth of Charlotte they drew further and further apart. The Prince, who complained to his mother of her 'personal nastiness' – in other words she stank – would not even eat with her. He occupied one wing of Carlton House, his vast London home, the Princess another and the royal baby with its army of nannies a third.

The Prince was beginning to say openly that he despaired of the relationship ever settling down and in the end wrote to Caroline: 'Nature has not made us suitable to each other, but to be tranquil and comfortable is, however, within our power; let our intercourse therefore be restricted . . .' And they agreed to separate.

Princess Caroline set up her own household at Montague House, Blackheath, and rumours soon began to spread about the wild parties she held there. She invited naval officers from nearby Greenwich, including the famous Admiral Sir Sidney Smith and Captain Manby, a frigate commander. One servant claimed she had seen her mistress in such an indecent situation with Sir Sidney that she fainted! Caroline had taken a dislike to English women, so many of her parties were all male. She had a habit of disappearing with her favourite in tow, leaving her guests to fend for themselves. 'I have a bedfellow whenever I like,' she told a friend. She also exposed her bosom more than was thought decent and would dance about, exposing her garters when the mood took her.

Soon people began to refuse her invitations. When one of her ladies-in-waiting dared to suggest that she was going too far, Caroline turned on her in a fury and dismissed her for impudence.

At Blackheath Caroline struck up a friendship with her neighbour, Lady Charlotte Douglas, a fine-looking woman with a taste for scandal and indecency that equalled her own. The friendship was to cost Caroline dear and to lead to a humiliating investigation into her love life.

The trouble started when Lady Charlotte announced that she was expecting a child. Caroline, who was beginning to weary of her friend, decided to play a prank on her. She too would be pregnant. She stuffed her dresses with cushions and began to crave fried onion rings at breakfast. After a suitable time, when her Ladyship called one day, Caroline showed her a sleeping baby boy. Only when she had had her full quota of fun from Lady Charlotte's discomfort did she tell her the full story. Her Ladyship was not amused.

The boy's name, apparently, was William Austin, and he was the son of a Deptford dock labourer. One of Caroline's better habits had been to help poor and orphaned children and Mrs Austin, hearing of her good works in this direction and her husband having lost his job, pleaded for her help. Caroline offered to take her baby boy. He arrived just in time for her prank, but was to stay close to her for the rest of her life.

She called him 'Little Willum' and when someone referred to him as 'your son' she cried: 'Prove it and he shall be your King.' This, of course, was dangerous talk and got back to the Prince of Wales, who wanted to know what on earth was going on.

Lady Charlotte saw how to have her revenge. She was furious with Caroline for dropping her and also for her affair with Sir Sidney Smith. She had once been his mistress. She declared that Caroline had secretly given birth to 'Little Willum' in 1802. She also gave a list of her lovers.

It was obvious something had to be done. 'So much levity and profligacy . . .' moaned the old King George III, who was thought to be tottering on the brink of insanity. In 1806 a commission of inquiry was appointed to discuss Caroline's behaviour – it was called the Delicate Investigation. Only when Sophia Austin, the baby's real mother, was interviewed was the Princess cleared of adultery. The royal commissioners censured her over 'other particulars of her conduct' and she was rebuked by the King (but he had a soft spot for her and quite enjoyed a boisterous day at her house in Blackheath).

After the investigation, Caroline was determined to be reinstated at court and declared she would fight the whole royal family if need be. Her appearance at the King's birthday celebrations was not a success. She had grown fat, went without corsets, and dressed gaudily, showing too much bosom. The temperature was distinctly chilly and the Prince kept away from her.

But, whatever Caroline's faults, people throughout the country had sympathy for her over one thing: the enforced separation from her daughter, Charlotte. Ever since she moved to Blackheath they had only been allowed fortnightly meetings. But an incident occurred when Princess Charlotte was 16 that convinced many people that the Prince of Wales had acted wisely. The young girl fell in love with a Lieutenant Hesse of the 18th Light Dragoons. He was rumoured to be the Duke of

York's illegitimate son. Although her lady-in-waiting, Lady de Clifford, knew the affair should be stopped, Caroline thoroughly approved. She considered that at 16 a girl should take her first lessons in love and acted as their go-between. She arranged meetings for them and, when they paid her secret visits at her apartments in Kensington Palace, she would lead them to her bedroom, turn back the bedcovers and lock the door. What really pleased her was the thought of hoodwinking the Prince of Wales. Fortunately for her, Hesse turned out to be a gentleman and did not take advantage of the situation, and the Prince did not find out.

With the turn of history, things were to become much more difficult for her. On 6 February 1811, the King being desperately ill, the Prince of Wales was sworn in as Regent and in effect began his reign. A year later the King was pronounced incurable and the Prince took over full powers. Almost the first thing he did was to further restrict meetings between his wife and daughter.

Caroline, furious, published a highly indiscreet letter stating all her grievances in high-flown language. She gained unexpected support. The Whigs, who had been led to believe they would take office when the Prince succeeded, had been badly let down. He kept the Tories in power to please his new mistress, Lady Hertford. To show their disgust, the Whigs decided to champion Caroline. Suddenly she had a following. Loyal addresses began to arrive from all over the country and the Lord Mayor of London paid her a call.

The Regent, with new evidence up his sleeve, petulantly ordered another investigation into her morals. Twenty-three privy councillors were appointed to go through all the sordid details but the outcome was much as before. Caroline treated it as a triumph and was cheered in the streets.

But while the investigation was going on she was not

allowed to see Charlotte at all. From then on, mother and daughter were to meet only by accident. There was just one final scene between them in July 1813. Charlotte had broken off her engagement to the Prince of Orange, her excuse being that she must stay in England to be near her mother. The Prince suspected her of being in love with someone else and, in a temper, planned to close down her London household and send her to a lodge in the middle of Windsor Forest. Charlotte took refuge with the only person she knew who would defy her father – Caroline. But she had chosen a bad time. Her mother had plans of her own. Charlotte was persuaded to return to her father and obey his wishes. Mother and daughter never met again.

Caroline had decided to travel. She was now 46, had endured England for 19 years and decided she had suffered enough humiliation. She wanted to enjoy herself. The Prince, only too glad to see her go, arranged for a frigate to take her across the Channel with her entourage, which included a pale youth of 13 – William Austin. She left with untypical dignity wearing a sombre, military-style overcoat. As she watched the coast of England recede, she fainted with emotion.

Waiting on the other side was a bizarre collection of horse-drawn vehicles followed by an old London-to-Dover mail coach intended to carry servants and baggage. The party called first at Brunswick, where Caroline was well received by her elder brother, the Duke, then went on to Switzerland and Italy.

The behaviour of the Princess grew wilder and wilder. When she was warned that her indiscretions were being reported back in England she laughed. 'The Regent will hear it, as you say: I hope he will. I love to mortify him.' Most of the English aristocrats in her entourage went home. They couldn't stand the pace.

Caroline had taken to wearing a black wig which did not suit her. Lady Bessborough, who caught sight of her at a ball in Genoa wrote: 'I cannot tell you how sorry and asham'd I felt as an Englishwoman. The first thing I saw in the room was a short, very fat, elderly woman, with an extremely red face (owing I suppose to the heat) in a girl's white dress, but with shoulder, back and neck quite low (disgustingly so) down to the middle of her stomach; very black hair and eyebrows, which gave her a fierce look, and a wreath of light pink roses on her head . . .'

While she was in Milan Caroline engaged an Italian called Bartolomeo Pergami to be her courier. He was a splendid-looking man, who had fought for Napoleon, and he was rapidly promoted from being a servant to something far more intimate. Her long-suffering lady-in-waiting, Lady Charlotte Campbell, considered this the last straw and was regretfully 'obliged to resign'. Before long most of Pergami's relatives had joined the household, which was now almost entirely Italian. What Caroline did not realize was that her husband had spies everywhere, trying to catch her in the act which would give him his divorce.

She was having a marvellous time in Italy and was completely infatuated by Pergami. She bought the Villa d'Este on the shore of Lake Como for herself, and for him she purchased a small estate, south of Catania, carrying with it the title of Baron de la Francine. Full of high spirits, Caroline took her motley courtiers on to Sicily, where she had to be dissuaded from climbing a rumbling Mount Etna, then to Tunis, where she was received by the Bey, and then on to the Holy Land, where she created the Order of St Caroline and made Pergami the Grand Master.

Caroline and Pergami were obviously living as man and wife. At the Villa d'Este his sitting room was next to hers, his bedroom the only one near hers. His picture was in every room. There were rumours that the Pergami family were swindling her with impunity.

Caroline was on her way to Rome when the news came

through that George III was dead. With emotion she realized that she was now Queen of England. The Prince Regent, at the age of 47, was at last to ascend the throne.

She demanded a meeting with Lord Henry Brougham, who had always been sympathetic to her, and they met on neutral ground in France, at St Omer on the way to Calais. He had been told to offer Caroline an annual allowance of £50,000 to give up her crown. She refused it, with disdain. Brougham pleaded with her to return quietly and secretly, if she must. But Caroline had been waiting for this moment for years and was not going to be done out of it.

The Prince Regent was far from popular. His insane spending at a time when the poorer classes were at starvation level made many people despise him. But when Caroline arrived at Dover she was met by cheering crowds and accorded a 21-gun salute. She was treated as a heroine as she rode into London with William Austin by her side. 'Long live the Queen,' yelled the mob, 'and long live King Austin!' The King, appalled at this treachery, retired to Windsor with the rest of the royal family.

But before his departure he set in motion yet another investigation into his wife's morals – this time with the hope of gaining a divorce. He had been collecting scandalous information about her goings-on in Italy for above five years. Combined with what was known about her intimacy with Pergami, he felt sure he could prevent her from becoming Queen.

This time the hearing took place in the House of Lords.

On the day of the hearing, the court was in mourning for the Duchess of York so Caroline could not put on a show, as she would have liked. She appeared sombrely dressed in a largely black bonnet with ostrich plumes and a dress of black figured gauze with white bishop's sleeves and a frilled ruff at the neck. She was given a comfortable chair and a footstool, but could take no part in what was going on.

As it had been agreed that the King could not take direct divorce action against the Queen, the Prime Minister, digging in the archives, had produced an alternative – a Bill of Pains and Penalties. This was an obscure process which could, if the allegations against her were proved to be true, bring about an act of parliament with the forfeiture of her rights and the end of the royal marriage.

When the proceedings opened with a reading of this Bill, the grounds for the dissolution of her royal marriage were given as a most unbecoming and degrading intimacy between the Queen and one Bartolomeo Pergami, 'a foreigner of low station'.

The hearing went on for 40 days and wore everybody out but the public lapped up every scandalous detail and rolled in the aisles at the spectacle of the monarchy laundering its dirty linen.

One by one, Italian waitresses who had been paid good money to 'tell all' gave graphic accounts of Caroline receiving Pergami at her toilette in only her pantaloons; of Pergami visiting her in nothing more than a silk dressing gown; of Caroline being found asleep with her hand on his private parts; and of the pair of them playing silly games wearing nothing but fig leaves.

The intimacy was undeniable. The prosecution did a devastating job but then Lord Brougham took the stand in her defence and spoke for eight hours, by which time people were ready to agree to anything. His final point was astounding in the circumstances. The Queen, he thundered, could not have committed adultery with Pergami. The poor man was impotent. Smitten in his private parts while fighting for Napoleon!

On Friday 10 November, after a third reading, the vote was taken. Caroline had won – 108 in her favour, 99 against. Scenes of wild excitement broke out and congratulations poured in from all over the country. The King continued to sulk at Windsor but his supporters soon had all London singing this ditty:

> 'Most gracious Queen, we thee implore
> To go away and sin no more
> Or if that effort be too great
> To go away at any rate.'

Flushed with victory, Caroline informed the Dean of St Paul's that she intended to give thanks in his church for what had taken place. She arrived in procession, watched by a vast crowd, while the King hid himself and tried to puzzle out how he could get rid of her before the coronation. To his immense relief, the Privy Council met and decided that, as Caroline was living apart from His Majesty, she had no right to take part in the ceremony and the King could refuse her the crown.

By the beginning of 1821 the Queen was not as popular with the fickle crowds that had cheered her in the streets. Living at Brandenburg House she lay in bed complaining of the British climate and drinking too much brandy. She had been pestering the King with appeals to let her attend the coronation, but he refused point blank. He was terrified that she would make a scene.

So, on 19 July 1821, ignoring the pleas of her advisers, she put on her finery and drove to the Abbey . . .

Not many people noticed her depart. They were too interested in the magnificent show George IV was putting on for their benefit. His robes alone were known to have cost £24,000.

Soon after the coronation she went to Drury Lane Theatre with a group of friends. During the performance she was taken ill, though she refused to leave until the end. She looked haggard and was obviously in great pain. Her doctor diagnosed obstruction of the bowel and she went into a swift decline. Lord Brougham, who had spoken in her defence, was with her. She told him: 'I am going to die, Brougham, but it does not signify.' She had no regrets.

But it was her own daughter, Princess Charlotte, who probably summed up her life best: 'My mother was wicked,' she wrote, 'but she would not have turned so wicked had not my father been much more wicked still!'

Fall from Grace

Along with the marriage of Charles and Diana, there was another fairy-tale wedding in the 20th century. It was the marriage of the beautiful Hollywood movie star, Grace Kelly, to Prince Rainier of Monaco. In former times, the idea of a reigning monarch marrying an actress would have been a scandal. But, in this case, the Hollywood publicity machine had worked overtime to manufacture a virginal image for Grace. It was the antithesis of the truth.

True, Alfred Hitchcock had dubbed Grace Kelly 'The Snow Princess' during the filming of *Dial M for Murder*. But he did so ironically, because of her extraordinary promiscuity on the set. Screenwriter Bryan Mawr recalled a few years later: 'That Grace! She fucked everyone. Why she even fucked little Freddie [Frederick Knott] the writer.'

In the movie business, it was well known that Grace Kelly had slept her way to the top. The famous Hollywood columnist, Hedda Hopper, called her a 'nymphomaniac'. She was not quite the high-society gal that the studios made her out to be either. Her father, self-made millionaire Jack Kelly, was the son of an Irish immigrant and a former bricklayer, who qualified for the Social Register. But he took mistresses from among the wives of Philadelphia's socialites and groomed his daughter to marry a blue-blood. Eager to please Daddy, Grace cultivated a refined English accent and came on like a debutante.

She was barely 15 when men started proposing to her. Jack Kelly took it as a mark of esteem that herds of eligible young men would flock to the house. There were so many of them he could scarcely remember their names.

'You can take her out all you want,' he said. 'But don't think you are going to marry her.'

Only one of them meant anything to her. He was Harper Davis, the son of a brick salesman. Her father only discovered that the relationship was serious when Davis graduated from high school in 1944 and enlisted in the navy. He forced her to break it off,

Years later, when she got engaged to Prince Rainier of Monaco, he asked her if she had ever been in love before. She said: 'Yes, I was in love with Harper Davis. He died.'

When Davis returned from wartime service in 1946, he was struck down by multiple sclerosis. By 1951, he was totally paralysed. Grace would spend hours at his bedside, although he could not move or speak. He died in 1953. When she flew back from Hollywood for his funeral, the studio made great play of the 'Philadelphia socialite' returning for the funeral of her childhood sweetheart.

Grace enrolled in the American Academy of Drama Arts in New York in October 1947. But, before she left Philadelphia, she was determined to lose her virginity – but not to her own true love.

'It happened very quickly,' she explained later. 'I went round to a friend's house to pick her up, and I found that she wasn't there. It was raining outside, and her husband told me she would be gone for the rest of the day. I stayed talking to him and somehow we fell into bed together, without understanding why.'

She did not repeat the experience with the man in question, though she stayed on friendly terms with the couple.

Grace's first sexual encounter was not as accidental as she made it seem. She explained later that she had not wanted to move to New York without knowing what sex was all about, but none of the boys she knew could be trusted to keep a secret. When a friend commiserated saying that it was a pity that her first sexual encounter had not been suffused with love and romance, she replied: 'It wasn't that bad.'

At drama school, she dated the best-looking guy in the class, Mark Miller. But he had plenty of rivals.

'There were these guys who would call for her,' said Miller. 'I would be thinking that I'm the only love in her life, and some stud would arrive at school. So I'd ask her, "Who's that guy?" and she'd say, "Just some guy I know. He's crazy about me." She would laugh about it and brush it off, like she was just sort of doing the guy a favour. I never gave it too much thought. I was very naïve, I suppose.'

She also had a month-long fling with Hollywood leading man Alexandre D'Arcy, once hailed as the 'new Valentino'.

'She didn't dress as the sort of girl that would jump into bed with you,' D'Arcy said. But he tried it on anyway. In a taxi, he touched her on the knee. She just jumped into my arms. I could not believe it. She was the very opposite of the homely type of girl she seemed.'

She went back to his apartment on 53rd Street and made love to him without a second thought.

In her second year, one of the drama teachers at the Academy, Don Richardson, took her to his attic apartment on 33rd Street.

'I got the fire going and went out to make some coffee,' he recalled. When he came back, he found she had taken all her clothes off and was waiting for him in bed.

'We had no introduction to this,' he said. 'There was no flirtation. I could not believe it. Here was this fantastically beautiful creature lying next to me . . . That night was just sheer ecstasy.'

They had to be discreet at the Academy. But, somehow,

Mark Miller remained in blissful ignorance. Then he only broke it off when he found out she was seeing some stud from Philadelphia.

To make money, Grace would take on assignments modelling lingerie. At lunchtime, she would steal away to Richardson's apartment, and they would make love. Afterwards, she would put her clothes back on and run back to model. She said that these lunchtime sessions were important for her modelling career. They put lights in her eyes. Richardson also marvelled at how she would jump out of bed on Sunday mornings, run off to Mass, run back and jump back into bed with him, naked, with her little gold crucifix around her neck.

Sleeping with Richardson helped Grace at the Academy. He made sure she got good parts in the Academy's productions and coached her. He knew she would never make it on the stage. But when he took a photograph of her he realized that she had what it took to make a movie actress and he took her to the William Morris Agency.

Grace took Richardson home for the weekend to introduce him to her family. But they took against him. He was not a Catholic. He was married, although separated from his wife and currently in the throes of a messy divorce. And he was Jewish. Grace's mother went through his bags and found a packet of condoms. Richardson was thrown out of the house and Grace was lectured on immorality.

She was only allowed to return to the Academy for her graduation. But she seized the opportunity to move in with Richardson. Grace's father tried to buy Richardson off with a Jaguar. Her brother phoned, threatening to break every bone in his body. Richardson refused to be intimidated, but the affair cooled when he discovered Grace was seeing other men.

One of them was the Shah of Iran, who spent a week with her when he was visiting New York. He plied her with gold and jewels. When her mother read about this in the newspapers, she insisted Grace return the jewellery. Grace also received jewellery from Aly Khan.

Richardson recalled her putting on a fashion show for him. She appeared in gown after gown. He could not imagine where she had got them from. Then she appeared, naked, wearing nothing but a gold and emerald bracelet. Richardson had known several girls who had been out with Aly Khan.

'When he first had a date, he would give them a cigarette case with one emerald on it,' he said. 'When he fucked them, he'd give them the bracelet. I was broken-hearted. I put my clothes on, and said that I was leaving.'

On his way out, he dropped the bracelet in the fish tank. He left her, naked, fishing around the tank for her bracelet.

She had an affair with Claudius Philippe, banqueting manager of the Waldorf-Astoria, who was on first-name terms with everyone from Gypsy Rose Lee to the Duke and Duchess of Windsor. She also set her cap at Manie Sachs, the head of Columbia Records, who was a close friend of her father.

While touring with the Elitch Gardens stock company in the summer of 1951, she began an affair with actor Gene Lyons. Lyons was another divorcee and 10 years older than her. Then, on 28 August 1951, she was asked to report to Hollywood to appear in the film that would make her name, *High Noon*.

Her co-star was Gary Cooper. He was a well-known womanizer and, although he was nearly 50, he still lived up to the nickname Clara Bow had given him in the 1920s – 'Studs'.

The movie began with Gary and Grace in a wedding scene. All Cooper had to do was say 'I do', take Grace in his arms and kiss her. The scene was shot over and over again. Cooper kissed her at least 50 times. Grace made no secret of the fact that she preferred older men and seduced him.

Grace's affair with her co-star in *High Noon* was the first of many. Gore Vidal, then a scriptwriter in Hollywood, said: 'Grace almost always laid her leading man. She was famous for that in town.'

She also slept with screenwriter Bob Slatzer.

Cooper made a point of not being seen out with Grace. Nevertheless the affair made the gossip columns and Mrs Kelly was soon on her way to Hollywood to chaperone her wayward daughter.

Grace flew back to New York and Gene Lyons, but they were soon parted. She signed a seven-year contract with MGM and headed to Africa to film *Mogambo* with Ava Gardner and Clark Gable. From the moment she landed at Nairobi airport, she began flirting with Gable. He was unimpressed, but once they were out on the set and he found that Grace was the only available white woman for hundreds of miles he succumbed. He was 28 years her senior.

When they arrived in London to shoot the interiors in Boreham Wood, the Press asked him about the affair. He denied any involvement.

'I hear you two made Africa hotter than it is,' said Hedda Hopper.

When Mrs Kelly turned up in London, Gable had had enough. He had a guard mounted at the top of the stairs at the Connaught to keep Grace out and he did not return her phone calls. A few weeks later, he was seen doing the town in Paris with model Suzanne Dadolle, with whom he had started an affair before he went to Africa.

Back in New York, Grace consoled herself with Gene Lyons, while seeing Don Richardson on the side. Her affair with Lyons ended when she started an intense affair with leading French heart-throb, Jean-Pierre Aumont, during the shooting of *The Way of the Eagle* for TV. Afterwards, he returned to France and she went back to Hollywood, where she and Gable talked of marriage. Gable considered the age difference insurmountable. In the end, she had to agree.

'His false teeth turn me off,' she told a reporter.

During the filming of *Dial M for Murder*, both Tony Dawson, who played the murderer in the movie, and Frederick Knott, who wrote the original play, fell for her. So did her 49-year-old leading man, Ray Milland.

Milland had been happily married for 30 years. Although he had had the odd peccadillo, he had steered clear of actresses, which had kept him out of the gossip columns.

His long-suffering wife, Mal, kept her eyes judiciously shut. But she could not turn a blind eye to his affair with Grace, especially when the scandal sheet *Hollywood Confidential* got hold of the story.

When Milland was spotted getting on a plane with Grace, Milland and his wife separated and Grace moved in with him. However, when Milland's wife agreed to a divorce – their property was in her name – he thought better of it.

Hitchcock was also in love with Grace in his way, and she was happy to gratify his voyeuristic yearnings. She lived a mile down Laurel Canyon from him. He had a powerful telescope and she would purposely leave the curtains open when she got undressed, slowly, at night.

Throughout this period, Grace had also been seeing Bing Crosby. He was married, but his wife of 22 years, Dixie, was an alcoholic and was incapacitated with cancer. Crosby pretty much came and went as he pleased. He lived next door to Alan Ladd, and would use the Ladds' pool house for his trysts with Grace. This upset Ladd as he and his wife were close friends of Dixie. Ladd suggested they go to a motel, but Crosby was a well-known skinflint. Besides, going to a motel risked a scandal.

Grace was cast in *The Bridges at Toko-Ri* with William Holden, who was just 11 years her senior and her youngest co-star yet. Although he was married with children, Holden was on the rebound from Audrey

Hepburn at the time and he and Grace had a fling.

In New York, she met up with Jean-Pierre Aumont again, who introduced her to fashion designer Oleg Cassini. An accomplished seducer, Cassini set to work. Aumont and Cassini had long been rivals in love, first over Cassini's wife, then over actress Gene Tierney. Cassini bombarded her with flowers, but Grace was heading back to California where she renewed her romantic attachment with Crosby.

Crosby's wife had died and the newspapers were soon proclaiming the affair between the 25-year-old actress and the 50-year-old crooner 'Hollywood's newest romance'. He proposed. She turned him down. But he carried a torch for her for the rest of her life.

Grace invited Cassini out to the coast. But when he arrived in LA she had little time for him, as she had resumed her affair with Holden. *Confidential* magazine got wind of the affair when reporters spotted his white Cadillac convertible parked outside her apartment one morning. The studio claimed that he was just picking her up for an early call. Holden claimed that the convertible was Mrs Holden's.

'Does anyone think I'm so dumb as to park my wife's car outside another woman's apartment all night?' he told Hedda Hopper.

While Holden's lawyers were demanding a retraction from *Confidential*, Grace's father and brother went to *Confidential*'s office and threatened to beat up the editor. The scandal sheet changed its tack. In the next issue it said: 'Hollywood wives stop biting your nails . . . this new Hollywood heat wave wasn't grabbing for a guy who already had a ball and chain.' It went on to say that Grace had forsworn married men and implied that she was only bedding single men from now on.

Even though Grace was occupied elsewhere, Cassini did not waste his time in LA. He was seen at Ciro's with Anita Ekberg, Pier Angeli and other beauties. He made sure his adventures made the gossip columns so that, even when Grace was out on location, he could pique her jealousy.

It worked. When she went to France to film *To Catch a Thief* with Cary Grant, she sent him a postcard saying: 'Those who love me shall follow me.'

He did and they became lovers. But again her family thought he was a poor choice as a husband. Her mother thought there were too many women in his background. Her father dismissed him as a 'wop', although he was actually a Russian Jew by descent. Hollywood looked down on him, too. Hedda Hopper wrote: 'With all the attractive men around town, I do not understand what Grace Kelly sees in Oleg Cassini. It must be his moustache.'

Cassini did not improve the situation by cabling Hopper saying: 'I'll shave off mine if you shave off yours.'

In the face of this opposition, Grace was determined to marry Cassini. But during the filming of *Tribute to a Bad Man* there were rumours of an affair with her co-star, Spencer Tracy. She was seen out with Bing Crosby and Frank Sinatra, who was a well-known stud and freshly divorced from Ava Gardner. This was all grist to Hedda Hopper's mill. Grace also began a discreet affair with David Niven.

Years later, Prince Rainier asked Niven which of his Hollywood conquests had been best in bed. Niven replied without thinking 'Grace'. Then, seeing the shocked expression on the Prince's face, he tried to recover the situation by saying unconvincingly: 'Er, Gracie . . . Gracie Fields.'

Sensing the affair was coming to a close, Cassini poured out his heart to Joe Kennedy, the future President's father. Kennedy offered to intercede with Grace for Cassini, then used the opportunity to pursue Grace himself.

At the 1955 Cannes Film Festival, Grace bumped into Jean-Pierre Aumont again and they rekindled their affair. Then she received an invitation to visit Prince Rainier in Monaco. She accepted, but then tried to wheedle out of it when she found she had a hairdresser's appointment that day.

Aumont stepped in, explaining that she could not turn down an invitation from the reigning monarch because she had an appointment at the hairdresser's. At the very least it would be a diplomatic embarrassment for America.

So Grace drove the 50 miles to Monaco. She found that Prince Rainier was a good deal more attractive than she had expected. He showed her around his palace and gardens. It was not love at first sight, but Rainier was very taken with Grace. He was in the market for a Princess. As things stood, if he died without producing an heir, the principality of Monaco would be swallowed up by France.

Although charming, the Prince plainly did not make much of an impression on Grace. Two days later, she was photographed kissing and cuddling Aumont in Cannes. One picture showed Grace nibbling Aumont's fingers. *Time* magazine's caption read: 'Grace Kelly, commonly billed as the icy goddess, melted perceptibly in the company of French actor Jean-Pierre Aumont . . . had Aumont, who came and thawed, actually conquered Grace?'

Cassini's brother Igor, who was a syndicated columnist, claimed that it was all a put-up job, an attempt by Aumont to revive his flagging career. But Aumont told the Press 'I am deeply in love with Grace Kelly' – although he admitted that he did not think that she felt that way about him.

The Kellys were horrified. Grace immediately cabled her family, denying any romance. Her mother, who knew better, cabled back: 'Shall I invite Mr Aumont to visit us in Philadelphia?'

Prince Rainier was upset. Two years before, at the Cannes Film Festival, his mistress Gisele Pascal had had a fling with Gary Cooper.

Grace received a curt note from the Prince's spiritual adviser, Father Francis Tucker, thanking her for showing the Prince 'what an American Catholic girl can be and for the very deep impression this has left on him'. And that seemed to be the end of that.

Grace and Aumont left for Paris, pursued by the Press. The papers printed rumours that they were going to get married. When the reporters caught up with Aumont, they asked him whether he wanted to marry Grace. He replied: 'Who wouldn't? I adore her.'

To the same question, Grace replied: 'A girl has to be asked first.'

Then she launched into a diatribe against the Press.

'We live in a terrible world,' she complained. 'A man kisses your hand and it's screamed out from all the headlines. He can't even tell you he loves you without the whole world knowing about it.'

The couple managed to give the Press the slip and it was reported that they had eloped. When they were found at Aumont's weekend home in Rueil-Malmaison with his family, the newspapers took this to mean they were already married.

It was not so, but she was keen. When Grace flew back to America alone, she told reporters: 'Differences in our age or nationality present no obstacles in marriage between two people who love each other.'

Once more her family were against her choice of marriage partner. A few days later, she issued a formal statement saying that she and Aumont were 'just good friends.' And she began seeing Cassini again.

Aumont conceded that, with her in Hollywood and him in France, things would not have worked out. Nevertheless, Aumont was one of the few people who got a telegram from Grace, informing him that she was going to get engaged to Prince Rainier, before the formal announcement. He married actress Pier Angeli's twin sister, Marisa Pavan, three weeks before Grace's wedding.

By 1956, Prince Rainier had another reason to get

married. Three years before, Aristotle Onassis had bought the casino in Monte Carlo, but the economy of the principality was flagging and he was losing money. Gardner Cowles, publisher of *Look* magazine, suggested that if Prince Rainier married a movie star it would help lure rich Americans there. Top of Onassis's wish list was Marilyn Monroe.

'Do you think that the Prince will want to marry you?' Cowles asked her.

'Give me two days alone with him and of course he'll want to marry me,' Marilyn replied.

But the Prince had plans of his own. By chance, friends of the Kellys had been in Monaco. Unable to get tickets for the Red Cross Gala at the Sporting Club, they had called the palace. Once they mentioned the two magic words 'Grace Kelly', they were invited to the palace. Rainier told them that he was going to America and wanted to see Grace again. Delicate negotiations between Monaco and Philadelphia began. Rainier wanted to see Grace on the set of *The Swan*, which she was filming in North Carolina, but Aumont was with her there.

Instead, the Prince made arrangements to meet her in Philadelphia on Christmas Day. Father Tucker told Grace's father that the Prince wanted to marry his daughter. As always, Jack Kelly was against it.

'I don't want any broken-down Prince who's head of a country that nobody ever heard of marrying my daughter.' He scowled. Jack Kelly suspected that Prince Rainier was only after Grace for her money. But when Rainier proposed Grace accepted. There were some advantages to the arrangement.

'I don't want to be married to someone who feels inferior to my success or because I make more money than he does,' she explained. 'The Prince is not going to be "Mr Kelly".'

Oleg Cassini protested: 'You hardly know the man. Are

you going to marry someone because he has a title and a few acres of real estate?'

'I will learn to love him,' replied Grace.

Before Grace could marry her Prince, there was a formal marriage contract to be drawn up. Monaco was going through a political and financial crisis at the time and the Prince demanded a dowry. A figure of £2 million was mentioned. Jack Kelly went through the roof, then paid up. At last, he had one over the Philadelphia blue-bloods.

Grace then had to submit to a fertility test. Rainier had taken the precaution of taking his own doctor to America with him. Rainier had had to reject his previous love, the model Gisele Pascal, because she had failed the fertility test. When he had finally given her up, he told Father Tucker: 'Father, if you ever hear that my subjects think I do not love them, tell them what I have done today.'

Later, when Gisele married and gave birth to a child, Rainier was devastated. The fertility tests had been falsified as part of a plot by Father Tucker who did not consider Gisele a suitable candidate for the role of Princess.

Grace was terrified that the examination would reveal she was not a virgin. Far away from Hollywood gossip, Prince Rainier had apparently been taken in by Grace's chaste screen image and actually believed she was a virgin! Grace took the simple precaution of explaining to the Prince's doctors that her hymen had been broken when she was playing hockey in high school.

Scandal dogged the match from the beginning. At their first public appearance together at a charity gala at the Waldorf-Astoria in New York, a woman rushed up to Rainier and kissed him on the cheek. Grace caused a stir by ordering the Prince to wipe the woman's lipstick off his cheek. Who was that woman? Grace demanded to know. The Prince said he had no idea. The next day, the woman identified herself to the papers as Ecuadorian socialite Graciela Levi-Castillo.

'He knows who I am,' she said.

Grace had one more movie to make. It was *High Society*, co-starring Bing Crosby and Frank Sinatra. Fearing the worst, Rainier rented a villa in Los Angeles and appeared on the set every day. He appeared puzzled by the private jokes that passed between his fiancée and her two male co-stars.

Although Jack Kelly was pleased that his daughter was marrying into royalty, it was generally considered that Grace was marrying beneath her station. The *Chicago Tribune* wrote: 'She is too well bred to marry the silent partner in a gambling parlour.'

Much of Hollywood confused Monaco with Morocco and wondered how Grace would fare among camels and sand dunes. When he discovered that Monaco was actually a tiny Mediterranean principality, the head of MGM complained that it was no bigger than the studio's back lot.

The myth of Grace's virginity was shattered by her mother, of all people. Overjoyed at the prospect of her daughter's royal marriage, Mrs Kelly talked to reporters and spilled the beans on her daughter's former love affairs. Her revelations ran as a ten-part series in newspapers across America, headlined: 'My Daughter Grace Kelly – Her Life and Romances.'

To escape the scandal, Prince Rainier headed for home. But all was not lost. Although it was too late to do anything about the stories running in the American papers, the studios managed to get their hands on the articles and edit them before they went out in Europe. So as far as the citizens of Monaco were concerned, Grace Kelly was still *virgo intacta*.

Grace still had four years to run on her contract. She wanted to make *Designing Woman* with Jimmy Stewart, but the Prince put his foot down. Realizing that they could hardly sue a Princess for breach of contract, MGM swapped her appearance in *Designing Woman* for exclusive rights to film the royal wedding.

Grace made the rounds of Hollywood farewell parties, 'chaperoned' by Frank Sinatra. Then, with a party of 65 guests, she sailed for Monaco on board the *Constitution*. They were met in the Bay of Hercules by the royal yacht. Artistotle Onassis arranged for a plane to drop red and white carnations in the harbour when they docked in Monte Carlo.

Then the problems started. The Kellys and Rainier's family, the Grimaldis, did not get on. Jack Kelly could not find the bathroom in the palace. Since the servants spoke no English, he could not ask them where it was. So he took a limousine to a nearby hotel to take a leak.

At the civil wedding, Grace married her Prince in a religious ceremony at St Nicholas's Cathedral in Monte Carlo.

'Bride is film star, groom is non-pro,' *Variety* reported.

Of her myriad former lovers, only one – David Niven – turned up. Frank Sinatra had been invited, but turned down the invitation when he discovered that Ava Gardner would be there. Press speculation about a possible reconciliation between them would have overshadowed the wedding, he said. Cary Grant also cried off. He was filming *The Pride and the Passion* in Spain.

After the reception, the couple sailed off together on the royal yacht. Grace was not a good sailor and started throwing up as soon as they got out of port. A few days later she fell pregnant.

She spent her confinement alone in the palace. Five months after she gave birth to a girl, she was pregnant again. Despite this, the marriage was soon on the rocks and she would spend long hours on transatlantic calls, pouring out her heart to her friends.

When Grace was away visiting her dying father, Rainier was seen out and about with one of her ladies-in-waiting.

On her return, Grace confronted the Prince. He denied everything, but the lady-in-waiting was fired anyway.

To get her own back, Grace invited Cary Grant to stay. Pictures of them kissing at the airport appeared in the papers. Rainier promptly banned screenings of *To Catch a Thief,* which shows them in steamy love scenes together. In fact, they had not had an affair at the time. Grant was one of her co-stars whom Grace had overlooked. That was because Cassini was fresh on the scene at the time. But in the 1970s, after grant had separated from his third wife Dyan Cannon, they began an affair. It lasted, on and off, for seven years.

By the early 1970s, like many royal couples, Prince Rainier and Princess Grace had stopped sharing the same bedroom. Soon they went one step further. They stopped sharing the same country. Prince Rainier made a life for himself in Monaco. Princess Grace lived, largely, in Paris. In 1979, there were rumours that she was having an affair with Hungarian documentary film-maker Robert Dornhelm, whom she saw a great deal of in France. He denied any romantic involvement, but he told the Press that he thought having affairs would do her good.

Dornhelm knew that Grace was seeing a number of younger men, whom her friends called her 'toy boys'. One of them was Per Mattson, a 33-year-old Swedish actor who was considered for a part in a film about Raoul Wallenberg that Grace was planning with Dornhelm. They had met at a formal dinner in New York in 1982. He had been whisked up to her hotel room and had stayed there until 5am.

'Grace was used by some of these men,' said her old friend, actress Rita Gamm. 'For them it was not so serious, but for her it was. They did not suffer as desperately and silently as she did.'

New York restaurateur and former model Jim McMullen spent a week in Monaco with her. They were also seen together at a New York disco, Studio 54. She picked up executive head-hunter Jeffrey Fitzgerald on Concorde.

'I thought he would hate my lumps and bumps,' she told a friend, 'but he doesn't mind one bit.'

As the years drew on, Grace drank too much, ate too much and put on weight. Meanwhile, the torch of sexual misadventure was passed to a new generation. Both her daughters, Caroline and Stephanie, became notorious. Stephanie threatened to run off with her boyfriend, racing driver Paul Belmondo, son of the French movie star Jean-Paul Belmondo. In a moment of turmoil, Princess Grace confessed to biographer Gwen Robyns: 'How can I bring up my daughters not to have affairs when I am having affairs with married men all the time?'

On 13 September 1982, Princess Grace crashed on a hairpin bend on the Moyenne Corniche and was killed. Although the crash had taken place on French soil, Prince Rainier invoked diplomatic protocols and hampered the police investigation. This promoted all kinds of theories into why she had crashed. A lorry driver said that he had seen the car being driven erratically and that the brake lights had never shown once as the car plunged over the mountainside.

The Mafia was active in the area at the time and it is said that they cut the brake lines. Others claimed that Stephanie, who escaped unscathed from the wreckage, was actually driving. But the most likely theory was that Princess Grace had had a minor stroke while at the wheel and had lost control of the car.

At the time of Princess Grace's death, her eldest daughter Princess Caroline, a ravishing young divorcee, was the toast of the European tabloids. In 1983, she was married for a second time to Stephano Casiraghi, the son of an Italian industrialist. He died tragically in a speedboat accident in 1990 leaving her with three small children. As her brother Prince Albert shows no sign of getting married and settling down, Caroline has changed her children's names from Casiraghi to Casiraghi-Grimaldi, with the aim of putting her son on the throne.

Princess Stephanie maintained the role of Monaco's enfant terrible as a wannabe movie star, rock star and fashion designer. She is noted for being the first Princess of the house of Grimaldi to give birth out of wedlock.

Fifteen years after the death of Princess Grace she hit the headlines again with an even more bizarre scandal. In December 1997, *The Sunday Times* revealed that, before her death, Princess Grace had become a member of the Solar Temple. According to the newspaper article, her initiation into the cult involved nude massage and ritual sex.

In October 1994, 23 of the Solar Temple's followers were found dead in a farmhouse in the village of Cheiry in Switzerland. Another four were found dead in the cult's headquarters in Canada. Now, if Princess Grace had survived to participate in this ritual murder and mass suicide, that really would have been the biggest royal scandal of all time.

Crooks and Outlaws

Myra Hindley – the Moors Murderer

Ian Brady and Myra Hindley still rank as perhaps the world's most infamous killers. Their bizarre and deviant sexual relationship drove them to torture and murder defenceless children for pleasure in a case of serial killing that appalled the world. The idea that Hindley may one day be released from prison elicits howls of protest from the public. Nobody – least of all himself – however, has ever contemplated freeing Brady.

When Hindley met Brady he was already deeply warped: a 21-year-old stock clerk at Millwards (a chemical company in Manchester), his mind was full of sadistic fantasies. He had a collection of Nazi memorabilia and listened to recordings of Nazi rallies, while in his lunch hour he read Adolf Hitler's autobiography *Mein Kampf* ('My Struggle') and studied German grammar. He believed in the Nazi cause and regretted that he had not been part of its terrible excesses.

For her part, Hindley was known as a loner. Her first boyfriend had died when she was 15; she had not been able to sleep for days afterwards and had turned to the Roman Catholic Church for consolation. At school it was noted that she was tough, aggressive and rather masculine, and that she enjoyed contact sports and judo, none of which suited her to the genteel life of 1950s Britain. At the age of 19 she became a typist at Millwards, where she met Brady. He impressed her immediately: she considered most of the men whom she knew to be immature, but Brady dressed well and rode a motorbike. 'Ian wore a black shirt today and looked smashing . . . I love him', she confided to her diary.

For nearly a year Brady took no notice of her, however.

'The pig. He didn't even look at me today,' she wrote more than once. Finally, in December 1961, he asked her out. 'Eureka!' her diary says. 'Today we have our first date. We are going to the cinema.' (The film that they saw was *Judgement at Nuremberg*, which was about the trial of Germany's leading Nazis following World War II.) Hindley rapidly surrendered her virginity to Brady, later writing: 'I hope Ian and I love each other all our lives and get married and are happy ever after.' Yet their relationship would not be as innocent as her hopeful words suggest, for Hindley soon became Brady's sex slave. He introduced her to sexual perversion and urged her to read his books on Nazi atrocities. They took pornographic photographs of each other and kept them in a scrapbook; some showed weals across Hindley's buttocks that had been left by a whip.

Hindley subsequently gave up babysitting and going to church. Within six months she and Brady were living together at her grandmother's house; because her grandmother was a frail woman who spent most of her time in bed they had the run of the place. Brady persuaded Hindley to bleach her brown hair a Teutonic blonde and dressed her in leather skirts and high-heeled boots. He often called her Myra Hess – or 'Hessie' – after a sadistic, Nazi, concentration-camp guard.

Life with Brady made Hindley hard and cruel. She did anything that Brady asked of her and did not balk at procuring children for him to abuse, torture and kill. Their first victim was the 16-year-old Pauline Reade, who disappeared on 12 July 1963 on her way to a dance. They persuaded Pauline to go for a walk on the nearby Saddleworth Moor, where they killed and buried her. Four months later Hindley hired a car and abducted the 12-year-old John Kilbride; when she returned the car it was covered with mud from the moors. Brady and Hindley laughed when they read about the massive police hunt that was undertaken to find the missing boy.

In May 1964 Hindley bought a car of her own, a white Mini van. During the following month the 12-year-old Keith Bennett went missing; like the other victims, Hindley and Brady had buried him on Saddleworth Moor. At Brady's behest Hindley then joined a local gun club and bought pistols for them both, which they practised firing on the moors. While they were there they visited the graves of their victims, photographing each other kneeling on them.

On 27 December 1964 they abducted the ten-year-old Lesley Ann Downey. This time they were determined to derive the utmost perverted pleasure from their defenceless victim. They accordingly forced her to pose nude for pornographic photographs and then tortured her, recording her screams, before strangling her and burying her with the others on Saddleworth Moor.

Brady now wanted to extend his sphere of evil influence, aiming to recruit Myra's 16-year-old brother-in-law, David Smith, to their perverted circle. Brady showed Smith his gun and talked to him about robbing a bank. He also lent him books about the Marquis de Sade (from whose name the word 'sadism' is derived) and persuaded him to write down quotations dictated by Brady. 'Murder is a hobby and a supreme pleasure' or 'People are like maggots, small, blind, worthless fish-bait' Smith obediently wrote in an exercise book under Brady's guidance.

Brady believed that he could lure anyone into his world of brutality and murder and bragged to Smith about the murders that he had committed. They were drinking at the time and Smith thought that Brady was joking, so Brady decided to prove his capacity for murder and simultaneously ensnare Smith by making him party to a killing.

On 6 October 1965 Brady and Hindley picked up Edward Evans, a 17-year-old homosexual, in a Manchester pub. They then called Smith and asked him to come to their house at midnight. When he arrived he heard a cry coming from the sitting room. 'Help him, Dave,' said Hindley, and Smith rushed into the room to find a youth in a chair with Brady sitting astride him. Brady held an axe in his hands which he brought down onto the boy's head, hitting him at least 14 times. 'It's the messiest,' Brady said with some satisfaction. 'Usually it takes only one blow.' Brady then handed the axe to the dumbstruck Smith. (This was an attempt to incriminate Smith by putting his fingerprints on the murder weapon.)

Although Smith was terrified by what he had seen he helped to clean up the blood while Brady and Hindley wrapped the boy's body in a plastic sheet; the couple made jokes about the murder as they carried the corpse downstairs. After that Hindley made a pot of tea and they all sat down. 'You should have seen the look on his face,' said Hindley, who was flushed with excitement; she then started reminiscing about the murders that she and Brady had previously committed. Although Smith could not believe what was happening he realized that he would be their next victim if he showed any signs of disgust or outrage. After a decent interval he made his excuses and left; when he got back to his flat he was violently ill.

Smith told his wife what had happened, who urged him to go to the police. At dawn, armed with a knife and screwdriver, the couple went out to a phone box and reported the murder. A police car picked them up and took them to the police station, where Smith told his lurid tale to incredulous policemen. When the police visited Hindley's house at 8.40am to check out Smith's story, however, they found Edward Evans' body in the back bedroom.

Brady admitted killing Evans during an argument and then tried to implicate Smith in the murder. Hindley merely said: 'My story is the same as Ian's . . . Whatever he did, I did.' The only emotion that she showed was when she was told that her dog had died. 'You fucking murderer,' she screamed at the police.

The police found a detailed plan that Brady had drawn up for the removal from the house of all clues to Evans' murder. Curiously, one of the items listed was Hindley's prayer book; when the police examined it they discovered a left-luggage ticket from Manchester Station. The police reclaimed two suitcases containing books on sexual perversion, as well as coshes and photographs of a naked and gagged Lesley Ann Downey. The tape that had recorded her screams – which was later played to the stunned courtroom at Chester Assizes – was also discovered. Other photographs showed Hindley posing beside graves on Saddleworth Moor, and it was these that subsequently helped the police to locate the bodies of Lesley Ann Downey and John Kilbride.

At Brady's and Hindley's trial the truly horrific nature of the murders was revealed. The pathologist disclosed that Edward Evans' fly had been undone and that dog hairs had been found around his anus; John Kilbride's body was discovered with his trousers and underpants around his knees. Hindley, it seemed, had been turned on by watching Brady perform homosexual acts on his victims. Later Brady let it slip that both he and Hindley had been naked when they had photographed Lesley Ann Downey in the nude, but otherwise the pair refused to talk about their crimes.

They were sentenced to life imprisonment. Brady did not bother to appeal against the sentence; Hindley did, but her appeal was rejected. They were refused permission to see each other in jail, although they were allowed to exchange letters.

Brady showed no contrition in prison and refused to allow his spirit to be broken, regarding himself as a martyr to his own perverted cause. He gradually became insane.

Hindley, however, broke down and petitioned to be released. When her appeal was refused a warder (who was Hindley's lesbian lover) organized an abortive escape attempt, for which Hindley was sentenced to an additional year in jail.

She took an Open University degree and gave additional information about the whereabouts of her victims' graves to the police in a bid for mercy. Brady, however, countered her every move by revealing more of her involvement in the crimes, considering any attempt on her part to go free as an act of disloyalty to him. 'The weight of our crimes justifies permanent imprisonment,' Brady told the Parole Board in 1982. 'I will not wish to be free in 1985 or 2005.'

Hindley still hoped for parole, but public opinion was resolutely against it: after all, the families of their victims were still suffering.

Mary Frith

When Mary Frith strode through the streets of 17th-century London with her great mastiff 'Wildbrat' panting at her heels, people would step into the gutter to let her pass. A huge woman with a glittering eye and the air of a pirate, dressed like a man and smoking like a chimney, she was obviously someone to be reckoned with. The London underworld knew her well enough, but by another name. This was the notorious Moll Cutpurse, queen of the pick-pockets, fearless highway robber and receiver of stolen goods.

No one expected Mary to turn out as she did. The only daughter of an honest shoemaker, she was born in 1584, near the Barbican at the upper end of Aldersgate Street. Her parents doted on her and prepared to give her a good education and find her a well-to-do husband. But from the earliest days she proved hard to handle. She hated sewing and stitching, found the company of girls boring and would tear off her white linen cap and apron so that she could fight and sport with boys in the street. Her temper was unruly and she swore like a trooper. Her poor parents must have wondered what they had produced but, as someone at the time remarked, they were spared the worst as they died in her youth.

Mary grew into a fine, lusty, plain young woman fit to put out to service, everyone hoped, as she had no money to maintain her without working. But as a domestic she was a disaster. She had no time for children, in fact she hated looking after them. She would lose her temper at the slightest thing, then go off to the ale house where she would spend every penny she had, then join in the bawdiest and wildest escapades with a laugh that echoed round half of London.

At last, her embarrassed relatives seemed to have reached the decision that as nothing would change her they had better be rid of her. She was tricked into going aboard a merchant ship lying off Gravesend but discovered in the nick of time that when it sailed for New England she would be one of the passengers. The night before it was due to leave she jumped overboard and swam ashore determined never to go near her treacherous relations again.

The underworld was waiting with open arms. She fell in first with a group of fortune-tellers who travelled about the country reading palms and gazing into crystal balls. But her income from this proved totally inadequate for her tastes. She was far more interested in the gangs of pick-pockets and thieves who swooped down on the great fairs and markets like vultures and obviously took home rich pickings.

Once admitted to their ranks she threw off her petticoats for good and took to masculine attire. She realized by now that she was not attractive to the opposite sex, that she had no feminine charm and no hope of a husband. Far better, she reasoned, to wear the trousers that suited her and prove herself the equal of any man. Rumours that she was a hermaphrodite were quite untrue.

Mary Frith soon showed herself superior to most of the petty criminals she associated with for she had a brain and a smattering of education as well as the longest, niftiest fingers in the business. It was the fashion during the early days of the 17th century for men and women to wear a pocket or purse attached to a belt round the waist and it was her extraordinary dexterity in separating these purses from their owners by cutting them off that earned her the name 'Moll Cutpurse'.

Fame came to her quickly, for in 1610 there was entered in the register of the stationers' company a book called *The madde prankes of merry Moll*, written by John Day, and she was presented on stage as a 'bold virago straight and tall' in Middleton's *Roaring Girl*. She lapped this up along with the rich pickings but after a few years, having been in prison several times and burned on the hands as punishment, she decided to leave petty crime and take to the highways.

Moll, as she was known from now on, already had a wide circle of friends among the aristocrats of the road, including the legendary highwayman Captain Hind. She was a staunch, declared Royalist and insisted she would only rob Roundheads or any other enemies of the King. Together she and Captain Hind made a daring attack on a wagon containing pay for Commonwealth soldiers in the neighbourhood of Shotover. At other times she went out alone. Her nerve never failed and she became as feared as any man.

Over the years she relieved her victims of thousands of pounds without turning a hair. Though of huge proportions she was a fine horsewoman and nimble on her feet.

Escape was never a problem. Then one day she took part in the famous hold-up of General Fairfax on Hounslow Heath. In the fracas he turned on her. She shot him through the arm, then, to stop pursuit, fired on and killed two of his horses. After he had been relieved of his money, Fairfax managed to struggle to the town of Hounslow where some of his officers were quartered and he gave orders that she was to be found at all costs. This time she was out of luck. Her own horse had failed her and she was captured at Turnham Green, carried off to Newgate Prison, tried and condemned. But so rampant was the corruption at the time that she was able to buy her freedom from a prison official with a bribe of £2,000!

Moll bought a house in Fleet Street, only two doors away from the Globe Tavern. She preferred to live in the hustle and bustle and never shunned the limelight. An official attempt to shame her failed miserably. One day she was summoned to appear before the Court of Arches to answer a charge of wearing 'indecent and manly apparel'. Her defence was considered inadequate and she was ordered to do penance in a white sheet at St Paul's Cross during a Sunday morning sermon. She turned up in her sheet, wept bitterly and seemed truly contrite until someone discovered she was maudlin drunk having consumed three quarts of sack (white wine) before making her appearance. Those who knew her said they might as well have shamed a black dog as Moll for she would have travelled all through the market towns of England in her penitential habit if she had been offered a fair sum.

As though to thumb her nose at the Court of Arches she made a bet of £20 with a vintner in Cheapside that she would ride astride in breeches and doublet from Charing Cross to Shoreditch. She hired two men to walk in front of her, one with a trumpet, the other with a banner. It was too much for the crowds that watched her brazen progress. They called her 'thou shame of women' and threatened to pull her off her horse. But she won her bet.

The Fairfax disaster had actually scared Moll and she decided to try yet another branch of criminal activity. She became a fence, a receiver of stolen property, and her transactions were on a huge scale. By now she was known to all the greatest rogues in the Kingdom and most of them at one time or another called at her house in Fleet Street. Highwaymen like Hind, Hannam and Crowder even left their booty with her while they went off looking for fresh game along the country roads.

She lived comfortably surrounded by dogs, parrots and ornate gilt mirrors and was 'mightily taken with the pastime of smoking'. She was well dressed and her house was said to be pleasantly, if curiously, decorated and furnished. But perhaps she missed the excitement of the road. She took to displaying stolen goods in her front window. One day a gentleman passing by saw his own watch, of which he had recently been relieved, fetched a constable and took Moll and his watch to court. She was duly committed for trial but when the constable entered the witness box he found the watch in question was missing from his pocket. The jury had no alternative but to let her go free. Her friends were waiting for her. They had, of course, accompanied the constable to the court and simply taken it back again!

In her later years she turned her house into a brothel even though she herself had a reputation for chastity. She procured for either sex and became part of a sordid world which included characters like Aniseed-water Robin who wore skirts and petticoats. Her reason was probably lack of money. Though she had stolen a fortune in her time and was known to have put by £5,000 in gold, she had barely £100 left. She willed £30 to three maids and the rest of her estate to a kinsman called Frith, master of a ship at Rotherhithe, whom she advised to stay at home and get drunk rather than go to sea and be drowned in salt water.

Moll Cutpurse died on 26 July 1659 and was buried in St Bride's churchyard with a marble headstone. It disappeared in the Great Fire of London. Near the time of her death she had given instructions that she was to be buried face down so that she might be as preposterous in her death as she had been in her life.

Belle Starr

In legends of the Wild West, Belle Starr is always depicted as a fascinating hussy who combined sex appeal with bravado – a sort of Cleopatra of the range.

Reality was very different. Although she had herself photographed in a velvet gown there was usually a six-shooter dangling from her hand. Belle was, in fact, an ugly woman, a horse thief with a venomous disposition, and she takes her place in Western history with the worst of the outlaws.

Born Myra Belle Shirley on 5 February 1848 in a log cabin near Carthage, Missouri, her background was surprisingly proper. Her father, John Shirley, was an ex-judge, a Virginia aristocrat who survived the Civil War and bought a 800-acre homestead to make a new life for himself in Missouri. Nothing is known of her mother, Elizabeth.

When she was eight Belle was sent with lots of other nice little girls in clean white pinafores to the Carthage Female Academy where she had a chance to learn from a prospectus offering reading, writing, spelling, grammar, deportment, Greek, Latin and Hebrew. But her studies were violently interrupted when war broke out on the Kansas-Missouri border and marauding gangs set fire to John Shirley's cabin. His son, who had joined a Missouri regiment, was killed. The ex-judge decided to move the rest of his family, including Belle, out of trouble and into the state of Texas. The move certainly did not keep Belle out of trouble!

Belle grew up in Scyene, 10 miles east of Dallas. By the time she was 18 it became obvious that she was no beauty. It also became obvious that she had a taste for rough company and no respect at all for law and order. Her heroes were all thieves and outlaws who didn't give a damn and got away with murder. It was when she was 18 she met Cole Younger, one of the gang of handsome, laughing brothers who rode the outlaw trail with Jesse James. Cole was on the run after robbing a bank with James in Liberty, Missouri, and was planning to hide out in Texas. Belle swore to the end of her life that she gave him shelter and he fathered her first child, a daughter she named Pearl. Younger denied this and utterly rejected Pearl, who was born exactly nine months after they met. She was certainly in love with him then and she never forgot him.

Three years later, in 1869, she had a new lover, a prospector called Jim Reed from Vernon County, Missouri, who had taken to bank and train robbery to boost his income. With Reed and two other outlaws she rode to the North Canadian river country in search of gold. They were unsuccessful until one day a fellow prospector, an old Creek Indian, revealed when he was drunk that he had 30,000 dollars worth hidden away. They tortured him until he revealed where it was.

When the loot was shared out Belle decided to buy herself some finery and return to Texas in style. She paraded around in a flowing velvet gown and wide-brimmed, plumed hat with matching six-guns and fine leather boots. She also bought a black mare which she called Venus. In their marvellous *Pictorial History of the Wild West* James D. Horan and Paul Sann say that at the turn of the century there were still residents of Scyene who remembered Belle in her velvet gown, shiny boots and six-shooters, riding

Venus into town with a riding crop dangling from her wrist.

She presented Jim Reed with a baby boy, Edward, in 1871 but he didn't live long to appreciate his son and heir. He was killed by one of his own murderous gang in a gunfight.

Belle rode out of town, leaving her children with her mother, and joined up with a gang of cattle and horse thieves operating in an area known as the Oklahoma Strip. She hated being without a man for long and a flat-faced Indian outlaw with the curious name Blue Duck became her next lover. She soon became undisputed leader of the gang and masterminded all their criminal forays for the next five years.

Blue Duck did not last long. His place was taken by another Indian, a tall, slim Cherokee called Sam Starr. Sam was different from the rest and seemed to have some influence over Belle who was now a leather-faced woman of 28 and notoriously hard to handle. She married him and when they weren't out on the rampage, rustling and stealing cattle and horses, they lived in a log cabin with a sloping roof near Fort Smith, Arkansas. Belle, in memory of the man she couldn't forget, called it Younger's Bend. She acquired some pretty awful relations by her marriage to Sam Starr. One was a terrible old man called Uncle Tom who boasted that he had burned a whole family to death in his heyday.

Younger's Bend became a hideout for some of the most wanted bandits of the day. Once Belle had a special visitor. He was a cold, silent man with incredible, flickering blue eyes and a straggly dark beard. She told Sam he was a friend from Missouri and he needed a bed for a few days. Sam was suspicious. She seemed to treat the stranger with respect, an odd thing for Belle. He never took off his guns, even when he slept. He left as silently as he had come and many people said that Sam never knew that his house guest had been Jesse James.

Belle was charged four times with horse-stealing but was only imprisoned once. That was in 1883 when she became the first female ever to appear for a major crime in front of Hanging Judge Parker. He managed to make the charge stick and sentenced her to six months in the Federal Prison in Detroit. Sam was given one year.

They served their time and returned together to Younger's Bend. After about a year Sam disappeared and Belle was seen hanging on the arm of a criminal type called John Middleton, wanted for murder in Texas. Rumour began to spread that Middleton had also done away with Sam Starr so that he could have the pleasure of Belle's company all to himself. Things appeared in a different light, however, when one day Middleton was found full of bullet holes and Sam reappeared to take up where he had left off.

The pair were soon being featured on US Government posters promising 10,000 dollars in gold coins for information that led to their arrest. They were wanted, the poster stated, for 'robbery, murder, treason and other acts against the peace and dignity of the United States'. In 1886 they were arrested by US Marshals, taken to Fort Worth and brought before the dreaded Judge Parker. But Belle knew a legal trick or two and the Judge had to dismiss them for lack of evidence.

Belle rode out of town laughing. She was totally unrepentant, thoroughly enjoyed the limelight and gave long, indiscreet interviews to local editors. But she wasn't laughing for long.

That Christmas Sam went into town to drink at a local bar, had too much alcohol, got into an argument with a deputy sheriff and in the ensuing gunfight was shot dead.

Belle mourned him but didn't waste much time before finding herself a new lover. His name was Jim July, a Creek Indian with long black hair falling to his shoulders. He was wanted for robbery and hid out at Younger's Bend until Belle persuaded him to turn himself in at Fort Smith. From experience she felt certain there was not enough evidence to convict him. She advised July to plead 'not guilty' and she said she would support him.

On 3 February 1889 the pair set out towards Fort Smith. They stayed the night at a halfway house but the following morning July was seen to go on alone while Belle turned back. Riding Venus alone on the trail she was shot out of the saddle by an unseen gunman. She was found dying in the dust.

The identity of her killer was never established. Someone called Watson who had been seen arguing with her shortly before her death was charged, then cleared. Some said July himself had offered a gunman 200 dollars to kill her because she had decided not to help him. There was even a theory that her own son, Ed Starr, with whom she was said to have had a stormy, incestuous relationship, had done it. She had recently given him a savage thrashing for riding Venus without her permission.

Whoever killed Belle Starr remains a mystery. But, when she was buried in the front yard of the cabin at Younger's Bend, her daughter, Pearl, had a splendid stone monument erected at the grave in her mother's memory.

The memorial verse read:

> 'Shed not for her the bitter tear
> Nor give the heart to vain regret
> 'Tis but the casket that lies here
> The gem that fills it sparkles yet.'

A more fitting epitaph might have been Belle's own words: 'I regard myself as a woman who has seen much of life!'

The Ugliest Gals in the West

Beauty, grace, fresh-faced femininity . . . the famous gals of the old West had none of these. Despite their portrayal on cinema screens as glamorous, gun-totin' ladies, these women were often worse than their violent menfolk. And, from the photographs that have been passed down to us, we know that the one thing they lacked was good looks. In fact, most of them were downright ugly!

They had names like Calamity Jane, Belle Starr, Dutch Annie, Blonde Marie, Madame Moustache, China Mary and Big Nose Kate.

Often they would just as soon shoot you as take you to bed. And for 30 roistering years in the mid-1800s they drank, fought, shot and loved their way into Western legend.

Calamity Jane (born Martha Jane Caaery) earned her nickname because so many of her lovers wound up on Boot Hill. She was a drunkard, chewed tobacco, swore like a cavalry trooper and packed an equally hefty punch.

She became a mule-skinner, an army scout, served under General Custer and fell in love with Wild Bill Hickok, near whose grave she was buried in 1903. Calamity was also the biggest liar in the West.

Poker Alice was really Alice Ivers, daughter of an English schoolteacher, who married a card-sharp mining engineer. She won her nickname by spending more time at the gaming tables than at home.

She smoked large cigars, wore outlandish, expensive clothes and, after the death of her husband, opened a brothel. She was as fast with a gun as she was with the cards, and in her long career she shot dead at least two men. She died virtually penniless in 1930 at the age of 79.

Dutch Annie, Blonde Marie, Madame Moustache and China Mary were all brothel queens, vying with each other for the favours of the hard-drinking, hard-loving frontiersman. They had their counterparts in every cattle town from the Dakotas to New Mexico.

Big Nose Kate, born Kate Fisher, was a dance-hall girl who attached herself to the Earp gang and became girlfriend to 'Doc' Holliday somewhere between Dodge City and Tombstone.

Holliday must have been shortsighted as well as an alcoholic for Kate was the ugliest of the lot. But she did establish Tombstone's first dance-hall in a specially built marquee.

Pauline Cushman was one of the sexiest, wildest, man-destroying predators in the West. A one-time actress turned bar-fly, she would goad men into gunfights and then sleep with the winner. In San Francisco music-halls, men would go wild as she came on stage, firing six-guns into the ceiling.

Bonnie Parker

She was barely 5ft tall with a tiny waist and well-manicured hands. She liked good clothes, fast cars and guns. Apart from those closest to her she didn't give a damn for other human beings and when they got in her way she mowed them down. Her name was Bonnie Parker.

With her partner in crime, Clyde Barrow, she has become as much a part of American folklore as the gunfighters of the Wild West and, like them, over the years has gained an aura of spurious glamour.

Laughing and killing she tore through the southern states at the time of the great American Depression, when robber barons, gangsters and strikebreakers were all part of the scene. Her partnership with Clyde Barrow was short, but bloody, and she paid the final price in a hail of bullets.

The legends began before she was buried but those who knew her saw her for what she was: a small-time crook with a taste for murderous men and no mercy for those who stood between her and money.

There was nothing about her childhood that made her different. She was born in 1911 into a family of devout Texan Baptists. He father, a hard-working bricklayer, died when she was only four. Her mother took her to live in Cement City, near Dallas. At 16 she married her childhood sweetheart, Roy Thornton. He soon left her – to serve a 99-year sentence for murder.

She was working as a waitress in a downtown café when she ran into Clyde Barrow in January 1930. She was just 19 and he was 21. He fell immediately for the petite, fair-haired girl with provocative red lips and she, sizing up his somewhat effeminate looks and narrow, snake eyes, came to the conclusion that he could be interesting. Bored, restless, missing her husband, Bonnie Parker decided that Clyde Barrow was her new man.

She found out very soon after meeting him that he had been in and out of trouble since the cradle and was, in fact, an incurable criminal. The son of a poor Texan farmer, who just scraped a living to keep his eight children, Clyde was in a boys' reformatory before he was ten and fell into a life of petty thieving. His habits had not improved. Before their relationship could settle down, he was carted off to spend another two years in jail, leaving Bonnie in a fit of rage and frustration.

When he was 'inside' she managed to smuggle a gun to him. He broke out with two other prisoners, only to be recaptured a few days later after an armed robbery at a railway station. This time he was given 14 years but only served a few months. When Texas elected a woman governor, he was one of those released on parole. Nobody had an idea of what mayhem they had just let loose.

When Bonnie saw him again in March 1932 he was on

crutches. He had bribed a fellow prisoner to chop off two of his toes with an axe so that he would not be suitable for hard labour. Bitter and hard, he vowed he would never let himself be caught again. Bonnie agreed to join up with him.

Lying to her mother, who was the one person she really loved, she said she had taken a job demonstrating cosmetics in a Houston department store. In fact she and Clyde had formed the 'Barrow Gang' and were planning to launch their violence on an unsuspecting community.

By April, Bonnie had been picked up for questioning about a stolen car and when she was released three months later, without being charged, the killing had already started. A jeweller in Hillsborough, Texas, had been gunned down for a measly 40 dollars and the Sheriff and deputy Sheriff of the little town of Atoka in Oklahoma had also been shot dead. Bonnie climbed onto the bandwagon and they set off on a hell-raising tour of Michigan, Kansas and Missouri.

Clyde Barrow had a passion for guns. They accumulated a formidable array of firearms with which Bonnie liked to pose for photographs. She never hesitated to use any of them. Small-town banks, cafés and filling stations were their main target. He had a quick temper and a streak of sadism. Killing people made him laugh.

At first when they had a run of good luck they stayed in decent hotels, ate at fancy restaurants and bought themselves smart clothes. Both were fussy and immaculate in their dress. Bonnie regularly took her clothes and his to a laundry in the country and went to beauty parlours to have her nails painted. She liked the soft life and wished she could have more of it. But the biggest snatch they ever made was 1,400 dollars and, in spite of all the blood they shed, their grand total one month was 76 dollars.

Their exploits made headlines everywhere and they revelled in the publicity. She had been named 'Suicide Sal' and he was 'The Texas Rattlesnake'. But fame meant no more hotels. They travelled constantly sleeping in the cars they had stolen or in empty houses or tourist camps, living off a diet of peanut-butter sandwiches and ice creams.

They had been joined by William Daniel Jones, a gas station attendant who had grown up with Clyde and hero-worshipped him. He is said to have become Bonnie's lover for she had a voracious appetite for sex which Clyde, with his latent homosexual tendencies, could not satisfy. Jones proved himself a worthy acolyte. While the three of them were trying to steal a car in Temple, Texas, he shot dead the owner's son. Later, when Bonnie and Clyde walked into a trap at Dallas, set for another bank robber, he shot and killed the deputy sheriff.

The robbing and killing went on non-stop. If anyone stood in their way or pursued them, they were shot. By now there were two more additions to the gang: Clyde's brother, Buck, and his wife, Blanche. From the time they joined, things began to go wrong.

In March 1933 they all rented an apartment in Joplin, Missouri. It was a mistake. The neighbourhood was respectable and anything unusual did not go unnoticed. One resident reported to the police that he had seen a great deal of coming and going from there and that the occupants scurried in and out like frightened animals. The police sent two squad cars on a routine investigation which ended in a desperate shoot-up. They all escaped, leaving two policemen dead on the pavement and another badly wounded.

Unable to rent any more apartments, they had to sleep in their stolen cars. One day Bonnie, always a realist, said: 'It can't be long before they get us now. I want to see my mother before I die.' A secret rendezvous was arranged.

Strangely enough, Clyde himself nearly killed Bonnie shortly after. One day, driving in his usual mad fashion, he failed to notice a sign warning that the bridge over a gorge near Wellington, Texas, had collapsed. He approached at

70 mph and plunged over a precipice, turning over twice in mid-air. He was thrown clear but Bonnie had been pinned underneath the wreckage. It caught fire. She pleaded with him to shoot her if he couldn't pull her clear. But a farmer and one of his hands had seen the accident and ran to help release her. She was badly burned and the farmer offered to let her stay and rest while he phoned a doctor. At the mention of a doctor they began to behave very strangely, arousing the farmer's suspicions. He phoned the police. Clyde threatened him with a gun, took his car and escaped with only seconds to spare.

Bonnie was delirious and unless she had medical attention was sure to die. For once in his life, Clyde was frightened. He contacted Buck and his wife and told them to book a double cabin on a tourist site near Fort Smith, Arkansas. Clyde told everybody she had been injured in an oil-stove explosion while they were camping. She refused to go anywhere near a hospital and a doctor and nurse had to be brought in to look after her. The gang robbed another bank to pay the bills, shooting dead a newly elected marshall and, as usual, making their escape in a stolen car.

Again, they were on the run. To give Bonnie a decent night's rest the four of them booked two cabins at a tourist camp near Platte City, Missouri. They kept their curtains drawn all the time, which aroused suspicion among the other campers. They had to shoot their way out when police arrived in droves and this time they didn't get away scot-free. Buck was shot three times in the head and Blanche was temporarily blinded by shattered glass. With Bonnie still in agony from her burns, Buck half-dead and Blanche needing a doctor for her eyes, they were in a sorry mess. They hid out in some thick woods near the river at Dexter, Iowa, and Bonnie sent Jones to fetch five chicken dinners from a nearby take-away. The police followed him back. In the bedlam that followed Bonnie managed to get away across the river with Clyde and Jones following but Buck was shot again and was taken to hospital to die. Blanche, who had stayed by his side, was clapped in jail to await trial.

After that, because of Bonnie's presentiment that time was running out, they went back to Texas, sleeping in stolen cars and meeting their families in secret. It was Bonnie's idea that Clyde should dress up as a woman in a blonde wig. The police, she reasoned, were looking for a man and a woman, not for two blondes. The ruse worked.

Recovered from her burns, Bonnie drove the getaway car when they organized a prison break at the beginning of 1934. They got out a man called Ray Hamilton, shot dead a warder and allowed four other prisoners to escape. A few weeks later they machine-gunned two highway patrolmen in Grapevine, near Dallas.

They were as nervous as cats and knew they had reached the point of no return. They had killed at least 18 people in their merciless capers. Now the police of Texas, Oklahoma, Louisiana, Arkansas and Kansas were determined to put an end to it.

On the morning of 23 May 1934 Texas Ranger, Frank Hamer, received a tip-off from one of Clyde Barrow's so-called friends. Six police officers in plain dress waited in bushes by the side of the road just outside Gibsland, Louisiana. Shortly after 9am a Ford V-8 Sedan appeared on the dusty, white road. As it drew nearer they could see Bonnie Parker laughing and munching a sandwich. Suddenly guns were rattling out death and the two of them lay sprawled in a river of blood.

They were taken home to Dallas for burial and the crowds were so great that members of their families could hardly get to the graveside. People snatched flowers to take home as souvenirs. Bonnie had written her own epitaph:

'Some day they will go down together
And they will bury them side by side.
To a few it means grief
To the law it's relief
But it's death to Bonnie and Clyde.'

Madame Rachel

Like a black satin spider Madame Rachel sat in her exotic Bond Street beauty parlour waiting for vain little society flies to become her victims. She lured them in with the promise of everlasting youth and the opportunity of purchasing her fabulous preparations. Miracles, she assured them, could be performed with her royal Arabian soaps, her luxurious Circassian baths, her peach-blossom lotions and alabaster creams. Wrinkles and other tiny signs of age could be banished for ever with her greatest discovery of all – magnetic rock water dew from the sands in the Sahara.

Unfortunately many gullible women in the 1860s found Madame Rachel's advertisements for her famous beauty salon quite irresistible. What they did not know until they were trapped in her web was that the lotions and creams were a cover for a far more lucrative profession. Once Madame had chosen her victims she proceeded to strip them of their money and their reputations and to blackmail them with great cunning.

Many dared not tell their husbands how foolish they had been until it was too late. Fear of scandal, even when there was no truth in the allegations, was like a disease in Victorian England. It was a brave man who eventually exposed the truth and brought Madame to her deserved end. Not, though, until she had wrought havoc in some quarters of London society.

Typical of her method was that used on a woman of wealth and position who had been wheedled into taking a course of baths under Madame's personal supervision. One day this lady removed some diamond earrings and valuable rings she was wearing and slipped them into a drawer in the dressing room before stepping into the Circassian waters. On her return she found her jewels had gone. She rang the bell and told Madame Rachel of her loss. The old virago fell into a towering rage and declared she did not believe the lady had any jewellery with her. When she persisted Madame raged: 'It's no use giving yourself airs here. I have had you watched. I know where you live. How would you like your husband to know the real reason for your coming here? What if I tell him about the man who has visited you . . .' The wretched woman crept home in despair. Though there was not a word of truth in the allegations she did not dare tell her husband the story until after Madame had been arrested.

Sarah Rachel Russell was born into a Jewish theatrical family about the year 1806. Though in her later years she was said to resemble a somewhat dissipated Queen Victoria, in her youth she was good-looking with a magnificent head of hair. She was first married to an assistant chemist in Manchester, then to a Mr Jacob Moses who went down with the wreck of the *Royal Charter* off Anglesey in 1859 leaving her a young family to provide for, and finally to a Mr Philip Leverson who gave her more children but removed himself from the scene by the time she was operating in Bond Street.

In her early days she was a clothes dealer and used to be allowed to take her goods backstage at the London theatres. But she added procuring to her business activities and was thrown out of Drury Lane for making an insulting proposition to one of the dancers, who threw a pot of ale in her face.

Soon after marrying Leverson she fell desperately ill with an unspecified fever. She was taken to King's College Hospital where her head was shaved and she lost every bit of her beautiful and abundant hair. Her distress was so acute that the doctor treating her gave her some lotion to rub on her scalp which, he promised, would produce an even finer crop of hair than she had before. To her amazement his promise came true and she begged him to give her a copy of the prescription. He did so gladly. The prescription was probably the scientific basis of all the lotions and creams which she later described as 'the purest and most fragrant productions of the East!'

By 1860 she was ready to launch out with her new skills. She opened a shop in Bond Street for the sale of cosmetics and other toilet requisites, but the venture was a flop and she found herself in the Insolvency Court and later the debtors' prison. Nevertheless she knew she was on to something good and determined to try again, this time using her genius for self-publicity and her florid imagination.

Her new premises under the name Madame Rachel were in New Bond Street where she was assisted by her clever young daughters Rachel and Leontie. Madame herself could not even write her name but, if she provided the ideas, her daughters could present them.

The new business was launched with a pamphlet entitled *Beautiful for Ever*. It was snapped up by every woman in London who cared about her looks and had money to spend. Its language was wildly romantic and idiotically far-fetched but it worked. Madame claimed to be the sole possessor of the delicate and costly arts whereby the appearance of youth could be produced in the face and figure of an older woman. The secret? Her magnetic rock dew water of the Sahara at two guineas a bottle. She gave her customers an insight into how this magic liquid was obtained: collected in the early morning it was carried from the Sahara to Morocco on swift dromedaries, there to be used exclusively by the ladies of the court. She had gained the sole right of importation from the Sultan of Morocco himself 'at an enormous outlay'. As it was guaranteed to 'increase the vital energies, restore the colour to grey hair and remove wrinkles, defects and blemishes' it sold like a bomb.

She offered her customers about 60 preparations including her own special brand of face powder. One shade was called 'Rachel' and brunettes still buy powder of that name in the shops today to suit their darker skins. Her most expensive treatment was the *Complete Royal Arabian Toilet of Beauty* which, she claimed, she had planned for the Sultana of Turkey with marvellous results. She did not say how much the Sultana paid but she charged ordinary mortals around 200 guineas.

However, word had begun to spread that beauty treatment was not all that Madame had to offer at her Bond Street establishment. Business flourished and soon she had enough money to take and furnish an elegant house in Maddox Street and to reserve a box at the Opera, which cost £400 for the season. Creams and lotions did not pay for such luxuries. Procuring, fraud and blackmail did.

Sometimes she played for the highest stakes. At other times she would risk everything for a relatively small sum. One day the wife of an Admiral called at her salon to buy perfume. Madame, singularly plausible, persuaded her to call again, then again. Each time the Admiral's wife bought a few small items. Eventually she received an exorbitant bill. She managed to pay but stopped calling in at Bond Street. Madame did not intend to let her escape so easily. She sent a bill for £1,000 to the Admiral, claiming she had cured his wife of an unpleasant skin affliction. Protests only brought further demands and a threat that unless the bill was settled promptly details of a scandal concerning his wife would be spread throughout London. Fortunately the Admiral went straight to his lawyers and refused to pay a penny. Madame dropped the claim.

The victim who eventually turned on Madame Rachel was a weak, vain little woman of almost unbelievable gullibility, called Mary Tucker Borradaile. The widow of an Indian army colonel, she lived alone in London on her military pension and the modest interest on her investments. She was thought to be about 50 though she refused to reveal her age even in court. She had an almost morbid desire to cling to the pretence of youth and by the autumn of 1864 it seemed she had found the answer to all her problems. She read an advertisement for Madame Rachel's fabulous oriental treatments for enhancing youth, beauty and grace and decided to consult her at all costs.

Madame looked at her new customer with satisfaction. She was 'a skeleton apparently encased in plaster of Paris, painted pink and white and surmounted by a juvenile wig'. Her voice was childish and affected, her lack of brains sadly evident. Madame smiled sweetly and assured her of complete and lasting rejuvenation.

On her first visit Mrs Borradaile spent a modest £10 though in the following 12 months her treatment added up to £170 and she paid out other sums of money for cosmetics. By the spring of 1866 it was obvious that despite all the baths, creams and lotions Mrs Borradaile looked pretty much the same. Disappointed and peeved she told Madame she had expected to see a better result for her money.

Madame decided she had better move on to the second part of her plan. She informed Mrs Borradaile that a nobleman, Lord Ranelagh, had seen and fallen in love with her. A few days after this extraordinary announcement when they were both sitting in Madame's parlour a tall, elegant man came into the shop. Madame addressed him as Lord Ranelagh. 'Are you *really* Lord Ranelagh?' asked the bemused widow. He bowed, presented her with his card and left. On several occasions after that she saw his Lordship in the shop and once he bowed to her.

His Lordship, it appeared, had first seen her in the days

of her beauty when her husband was still alive, and her impression had been imprinted on his heart, only to be revived when he saw her again in Madame's parlour. He begged her to allow Madame to proceed with her 'Beautiful for Ever' programme. This meant an immediate outlay of £1,000 to which the widow at first objected but, seeing that she could not be brought to the pinnacle of perfection required by her suitor for less, the silly woman agreed to foot the bill.

Madame now began to bring her letters from Lord Ranelagh, which she explained, would be signed 'William' for the sake of discretion. All their courting would be done by letter and they were eventually to be married by proxy. If Mrs Borradaile began to have her doubts they were no doubt calmed when she received a tender note decorated with Lord Ranelagh's crest and monogram accompanied by a little perfume box and pencil case which had apparently belonged to his 'sainted mother'.

His Lordship had requested his beloved to deliver up to Madame all her jewels as they were not worthy of her future rank. More costly pieces would of course be provided by him in the future. Meanwhile he advised her to buy a few diamonds for their wedding. A coronet and a necklace were ordered from a New Bond Street jeweller for £1,260 and as the widow hadn't got that much in cash she sold some property in Streatham to pay for them. The money was handed to Madame Rachel, never to be seen again. Nor did she see the diamonds. Lord Ranelagh, it seems, had needed the cash for some project he had in mind and had suggested that a coronet which had belonged to his mother might be altered for her.

The letters which Lord Ranelagh continued to send to his future wife were extremely coy but included phrases like: 'My own sweet love I am worried to death about money matters . . .' He claimed he had tried to see her, referring to Madame in a conspiratorial way as 'Granny'. It was obvious, from the letters, that his Lordship was most anxious to preserve an amiable relationship between his fiancée and 'Granny'. If she once jibbed at the demands made on her purse he was quick to reply: 'My own darling Mary, why don't you do as Granny tells you . . .'

Even the bride-to-be could not help but notice that sometimes the letters appeared to be written in a different hand. Often there were spelling mistakes and grammatical errors she did not expect from such an aristocratic fiancé. Once the writer inexplicably signed himself 'Edward'. Madame hastily assured her that Lord Ranelagh had not lost his memory but had injured his arm and had had to ask a friend to write the letter for him.

As the wedding day approached it was suggested that she should visit a coach builders in New Bond Street to select a carriage for herself and also a quantity of silver and plate. All her own things, even rings, brooches and trinkets, had been packed away by Madame Rachel – they were not considered suitable for her future station in life.

Finally, having stripped the poor creature of everything she owned apart from the clothes she stood up in, Madame dealt the final blow. She had her arrested for debt and taken to Whitecross Street Prison where she could only obtain her release by making over to her 'creditor' her pension of £350 per annum.

That, according to Madame's calculations, should have been the end of the affair. But the worm turned. Poor, brainless Mary Borradaile wanted revenge. She made contact with her brother-in-law, a Mr Cope, and he came to her rescue. Having obtained her release he instituted proceedings against the woman who had ruined her.

On 20 August 1868 the case of the Queen v. Leverson came before the Central Criminal Court in London and provided entertainment for days as the whole ludicrous story spilled out. There were in fact two trials, the jury at the first having failed to agree. Mary Borradaile, it had to be admitted, was hardly a credible witness, tottering into the box with her yellow wig awry and giving her evidence in a childish, lisping voice while Madame, resplendent in black satin and ostrich plumes, watched her through narrowed eyes. Even *The Times* called her a 'self-confessed idiot'. But, by the time the second trial started on 22 September, Mrs Borradaile had got her spirits up and at one point, when she was being cross-examined by Mr Digby Seymour, cried out: 'She's a vile and wicked woman and you are bad too!'

Madame Rachel, accused of obtaining money by false pretences, claimed in her defence that her client was in fact having an affair with a man called William, that she had concocted the story of her engagement to Lord Ranelagh herself and that all her money had been squandered on her real lover. She had merely been a go-between and had helped Mrs Borradaile to deceive her relations out of the kindness of her heart.

There was a great stir when Lord Ranelagh entered the box. He said he recalled meeting the lady in question on two occasions. He had been introduced to her by Madame but had never had the slightest intention of marrying her and had never corresponded with her in any way. He was extremely embarrassed.

Mr Digby Seymour, summing up for the accused, failed to convince the jury that the pathetic widow was the loose conniving woman he would have them believe. The appearance in the witness box of Madame Rachel's two daughters did nothing to help her. In spite of their charm and good looks it soon became obvious that they were lying for all they were worth and the court came to the conclusion that the younger of the two had in fact written the 'William' letters.

The jury was only out for 15 minutes before returning a unanimous verdict of 'guilty' sending Sarah Rachel Leverson to prison for five years. She was, said one counsel, 'a most filthy and dangerous moral pest'.

Madame served her time in jail then emerged, apparently undaunted, to start up business again as 'Arabian perfumer to the Queen'! No longer welcome in exclusive Bond Street she established herself in a shop at 153 Great Portland Street where she was soon up to her old game. Her sign caught the eye of a young woman called Cecilia Maria Pearce, wife of a Pimlico stockbroker, who though she was only 23 was dissatisfied with her complexion. Before long the old rogue had her deeply involved. This time, however, she had not taken on a fool but a bright young woman who soon realized she was in trouble and consulted her eminent solicitor, Sir George Lewis. For the third time a warrant was issued for Madame Rachel's arrest. She was tried at the Old Bailey in April 1878 and sentenced to five years' imprisonment, the judge regretting he could not give her more. But Madame did not serve out her term. She died in Woking Jail on 12 October 1880.

Perhaps the evidence given by Sabina Pilley, one of her assistants, finished her off. For Sabina had torn aside the veil of mystery and divulged her exotic secrets. The fabulous Arabian complexion treatment, for instance, consisted of starch, fuller's earth, pearl ash and water with a dash of hydrochloric acid. As for the Royal Arabian and Circassian baths, so much enjoyed by the Sultana of Turkey, alas, they were just hot water and bran.

Evita: the Glamour and the Greed

Eva Perón was the champion of the poor. They adored her. They lavished their humble devotion upon her with an almost religious fervour. They called her Santa Evita – 'Little Saint Eva'.

In the years following World War II she was a heroine to Argentina's descamisados – the 'shirtless ones' – whose idolatry made her, for a while, the most powerful woman in the world.

As wife of Argentinian military leader Juan Perón, Eva moved regally among the masses, distributing gifts to the poor. Without warning, she and her retinue would dramatically appear in a peasant village and hand out sweets to the children and food packages to their parents.

The grateful recipients of her largesse wore rags. Eva boasted furs, finery and glittering jewellery. To outside observers, the contrast seemed incongruous. Yet that, Eva always insisted, was how her people wanted it. She was the only glamour in their impoverished existence, she argued, and they needed her.

But that glamour was not just for show. It was many years before the full truth was known, but beautiful Eva and her handsome husband – those two champions of Argentina's poor and oppressed – had spent all their years in power busily lining their own pockets.

Eva Duarte was the illegitimate child of a poor provincial woman. She was born in 1919 – though she always claimed, with ruthless feminism, that it was 1922. By the time she was 15, she had moved to Buenos Aires with her first lover and was trying to get jobs as an actress.

She was 24 when she met Colonel Juan Perón, who was twice her age. She was then a small-time radio starlet earning £4 a week as a disc-jockey and heroine of the station's soap operas. Perón and the other leaders of Argentina's right-wing military junta arrived at the radio station to appeal for funds for the victims of an earthquake. Colonel Perón, still straight-backed and athletic, was captivated by her deep, seductive voice.

From that moment on, it was Eva who regularly appealed for funds for Perón's Social Services Ministry. In doing so, she built his political charisma. She became his spokeswoman.

'He doesn't care a button for the glittering uniforms and the frock coats,' she purred. 'His only friends are you, the descamisados.'

When the too-powerful Perón was ousted by the junta in 1945, it was Eva who single-handedly regimented the support of the young officers and the workers to reinstate him.

Two years later she married him. And the following year, with Eva at his side, Juan Perón was swept into the Presidential palace on the shoulders of the descamisados and with the backing of the powerful unions.

As wife of the President, Eva Perón's ambitions and her past became even more starkly conflicting. She dripped with diamonds, and wrapped herself in mink.

When she was snubbed by the genteel, aristocratic ladies who ran the nation's charities, Eva sacked them all and launched the Eva Perón Social Aid Fund. She ordered dresses from France and directed second-hand clothes to the farms and shanty towns. Children were showered with toys. The people were mesmerized. They worshipped her.

Juan Perón's power was based on the trade unions, Eva's on the descamisados. Their regime seemed unassailable. But when Eva sickened with incurable cancer Juan Perón faced the loss of his popular 'voice'.

Eva grew thin and shrunken. At those few political functions she attended, she had to be physically supported by her husband. She complained: 'I am too little for so much pain.'

On 26 July 1952, at 8.25pm, Eva Perón died. She was 33. Almost on her last breath, her body was rushed away to be embalmed by an eminent pathologist who had been standing by for weeks. He operated on her emaciated body, replacing her blood with alcohol and then with glycerine, which kept the organs intact and made the skin almost translucent.

The nation went into an orgy of mourning. Two million people filed past her coffin. Seven were killed in the crush. There were plans to build memorials to her throughout Argentina. Most of them got no further than the drawing board. For in 1955 a period of roaring inflation led to Perón's overthrow.

The deposed President fled to Spain, where he remained in exile for 20 years. Meanwhile, his successor, General Lonardi, made every effort utterly to discredit the Peróns.

He opened the Peróns' homes to the public. On display were 15 custom-built sports cars, 250 motor scooters, and the safes where Peron kept his $10 million in 'ready cash'. Much, much more had been salted away abroad. Also revealed were Juan Perón's secret Buenos Aires love nests – apartments lined with furs and mirrors where 50-year-old Perón had satisfied his predilection for teenage girls.

The new military rulers also put on display Eva's vast wardrobe of clothes and jewels. But strangely, in her case, the effect was only to gild her glittering reputation. Eva had never hidden her beautiful clothes and gems from her worshipping descamisados. It seemed not to matter to them that almost all of her wealth had been milked from the charities she had so ostentatiously championed.

Satan in Satin

When his Great Army of the Potomac was crushed at Bull Run, Abraham Lincoln knew there had been treason in his government – and that behind the treachery was a beautiful but deadly woman.

He called on General George B. McClellan to take command of the shattered Union Army. And together they turned to Allan Pinkerton, founder of Pinkerton's Detective Agency and internationally known man-hunter. Now he was to become a hunter of women. Specifically, his prey would be Mrs Rose O'Neal Greenhow – 'Rebel Rose' –

whose Washington spy ring was like a noose around the Union throat.

Rich, brilliant and seductive, the 44-year-old widow lived in an elegant mansion that had become the favourite gathering place of Washington's elite. She made no secret of her Southern sympathies or her flaming love affairs. She claimed to have been James Buchanan's mistress and the power behind his Presidency. She also boasted that her current affair with Senator Harold Wilson had led to the trapping of Union forces at Manassas and the Bull Run catastrophe. There would later be documentary proof of her claim when Rebel archives were taken after the fall of the Confederate capital of Richmond, Virginia.

As chairman of the Senate's Military Affairs Committee, Wilson knew Lincoln's secret war plans. He had confided those secrets to Rose Greenhow, who routed them to another of her lovers in the Confederate high command, using as courier a female operative who crossed Union lines disguised as a farm girl.

The contest between Rose and Pinkerton became a classic duel of wits. Rose made the first move, inviting him to a lavish house party where she tried every blandishment on the no-nonsense Scot. But, when Pinkerton failed to take the bait, she became his deadliest enemy.

In the weeks that followed, Pinkerton and his men kept a constant watch on her home. Rose knew of the surveillance and openly laughed at it. Her own female operatives, all stunningly beautiful, continued to pass in and out of the house, and the great of Washington still vied for her favours.

The treacherous Wilson was a constant caller, and General McClellan angrily told Pinkerton that military secrets were reaching the enemy daily. Without further delay, Pinkerton arrested Mrs Greenhow in her home. Under the lady's furious eyes, he ordered a search of the premises and turned up damning evidence.

There was the cipher by which she had communicated with the enemy. There were Senator Wilson's passionate love letters. There was a list of Rose's couriers and fellow conspirators, most of them wealthy and powerful. Worse, there were copies of official information on the movement of troops, the sizes and quantities of ordnance, and blueprints of the forts defending the city.

The grim-faced Pinkerton wanted Rose and her co-conspirators hanged, but Lincoln and McClellan vetoed the idea. Some of the traitors were so highly placed that the already shaky administration could have toppled.

For five months Lincoln wrestled with the problem, while Pinkerton kept Rose under house arrest in her home. But, on 18 January 1862, she was transferred to Washington's Old Capitol Prison.

No spy in history has enjoyed kinder prison treatment. With the Greenhow fortune still at her disposal, she was given a suite of rooms on the second floor where guards brought her catered meals and champagne from her own cellars.

In Rose's case, prison discipline was suspended entirely. Her powerful friends came and went at will, and the guards retired politely when Senator Wilson was a guest. Another frequent caller was Gustavus V. Fox, Assistant Secretary of the navy, who was reckless enough to divulge the government's naval plans.

To everyone's surprise, Rose had taken up knitting, and balls of coloured wool were delivered to her through the Provost Marshal's office. She turned out an endless supply of socks, sweaters and tapestries and presented them as gifts to some of her callers.

Suspicious, Pinkerton intercepted one of the female visitors and took a close look at her tapestry. It held a cunningly concealed message for the Confederates – a coded outline of the information Rose had gleaned from Fox.

Even Lincoln agreed now that a woman who could spy from behind bars was too dangerous a prisoner to keep.

In June 1862, Pinkerton escorted her to Fortress Munroe, where she signed a pledge 'not to return north of the Potomac' until the war was over. 'But then I shall return,' she assured him. 'And after we have burned your White House to the ground, I think we shall hang Old Abe in my yard to frighten away the crows.'

In fact, she was never to return.

Jefferson Davis, President of the Confederate States, sent her from his capital of Richmond to London in order to recruit money and sympathy for the Rebel cause. There she published a book of memoirs reviling Allan Pinkerton and detailing her affairs with Lincoln's traitorous friends. Suppressed in the United States, her book was an overnight sensation in England.

But, on Rose's return voyage, the blockade runner carrying her was grounded on a shoal off the coast of Wilmington, North Carolina.

Too impatient to wait for rescue craft, Rose set out for shore in a small boat. The boat capsized in heavy seas, and her body was never found.

She left many questions behind her.

Never exposed during his lifetime, Harold Wilson went on to become a Vice-President of the United States. Gustavus V. Fox escaped without a rebuke. And, though he knew their identities well, Lincoln took no action against any of the traitors who had worked so intimately with Rebel Rose.

It may have been a fatal mistake. Historians agree that these same conspirators could have been in league with John Wilkes Booth, the demented actor who brought Lincoln's life to a violent end.

Thérèse and her Priceless Brick

Thérèse Humbert was the daughter of a French peasant, and she made a fortune out of a most audacious confidence trick. She drew inspiration from her father, who had lived his life in Toulouse on borrowed money raised against a vast inheritance – 'proof' of which he kept in an old sealed chest. When he died, his creditors called to claim the contents. They opened the chest and found a solitary house brick.

Like father like daughter, Thérèse fashioned a master plan. She moved to Paris where she found a job as a washerwoman in the household of a government official. Here she deceived the boss's son into believing she was coming into money and he married her.

In due course, Thérèse had what appeared to be a fantastic windfall – a legacy of $20 million. She explained that it had been left her by Robert Henry Crawford, an American from Chicago. She had met him on a train two years previously and nursed him when he later suffered a heart attack.

The amazing story soon got around and, when the young ex-washerwoman arrived at the bank, she received a warm welcome. She explained to the manager that Mr Crawford had actually left half of his fortune to be split between his two nephews in America and Thérèse's younger sister Marie. Out of the latter, Thérèse was to get an annual annuity but the full amount would not be realized until Marie reached the age of 21.

In addition, Thérèse explained, under the terms of the will and by agreement with the Crawford nephews, all the documents and deeds relating to the settlement were to be kept locked in her safe.

Thérèse told the manager: 'I am not allowed to open it until Marie comes of age, under penalty of forfeiting all claim upon the Crawford millions.' Then, predictably, she asked for a loan. It was readily granted.

The conniving trickster used the same ploy on several other banks. One Lille banker alone advanced her, over the years, several million francs. And nobody ever questioned the contents of her safe – a massive contraption she kept hidden and locked in her splendid mansion bought with borrowed money.

Thérèse's position was now practically unchallenged . . . until the Lille banker, M. Delatte, happened to visit America. While there he tried to contact the Crawford family in Boston, where they were supposed to be living. Nobody in Boston or Chicago had ever heard of them or of the deceased millionaire, Robert Henry Crawford.

The investigation proved disastrous not for Thérèse but for Delatte. His body was found floating in the East River in New York. The murderer was never caught.

With Marie's 21st birthday looming up, Thérèse now concocted a plan to make more crooked money, financing her brothers in a life-insurance scheme that offered tempting returns. Instead of investing the incoming money, she spent it or paid off her more pressing creditors. Now she was 'La Grand Thérèse' and bankers and financiers pleaded with her to allow them to invest money in her schemes.

Then one high-ranking banker, Jules Bizat, decided to investigate. What he discovered shocked him – particularly as his own family had given the Humberts a small fortune – and he alerted the Prime Minister, Pierre Marie Waldeck-Rousseau.

The Premier decided against exposure but investors had to be warned. A series of scathing articles appeared in the influential newspaper *Le Matin*. Yet Thérèse's own lawyer believed so fervently in the truth of the Crawford inheritance that he threatened to sue the newspaper for libel and offered to open the safe to prove her virtue.

Thérèse, understandably, was horrified at this suggestion and covered up by protesting that such a procedure would dash all hopes of her getting her money. But the lawyer insisted that the safe should be opened to clear her name. Thérèse was trapped in the web of her own lies.

Two days before the safe was due to be opened, a mysterious fire broke out in Madame Humbert's apartment, totally gutting everything inside the room – except the safe. It was fireproof.

Some of France's leading financiers gathered around the safe on 10 May 1902. Thérèse was not present when the door was swung back to reveal . . . a brick!

Thérèse was later caught and sentenced to five years in prison. The safe, complete with brick, went on show in a Paris shop window, where it became one of the great tourist attractions of the year.

Ruthless Rulers

Livia

Livia was one of the most cruelly ambitious women the world has ever known. Her portrait was painted with fine precision by Robert Graves in his book *I, Claudius* as the she-wolf of all the Roman Empresses.

Her family was one of the most illustrious in Rome and her ancestral stock more ancient than Rome itself. She had a high-bred kind of beauty and a disdainful air that came naturally to her. Her mind ranked as one of the finest but when she chose to she could ensnare men with her seductive manner.

When she was at the height of her beauty and married to Tiberius Nero, Augustus became intrigued by her. Caesar was then in his prime, a splendid-looking man with fair, tightly curled hair, a typical Roman nose and sparkling eyes. He was also blessed with an affable temperament, except when at war when he was as cruel as any. He found Livia, with her satin smooth charm, vastly different from his wife, the odd and gloomy Scribonia.

Livia could not have left Augustus in doubt for long about her own feelings for she was soon pregnant and general gossip assumed the child to be his. Unfortunately Tiberius Nero was an old enemy and could not be bought. So, taking the bull by the horns, Augustus asked Tiberius to give him his wife and left him in no doubt as to what would happen if he refused. It did not take the lady long to assess who would further her ambitions better.

Augustus consulted the oracles pretending to be anxious about whether he might marry a woman already with child. The oracles were favourable, so the wedding took place. Tiberius was asked to give her away and, perhaps to soothe his ruffled ego, was guest of honour at the great feast that followed.

Three months later Livia had a son who was named

Drusus. Augustus sent the baby to be brought up by Tiberius in case it should be thought his own, but ribald jokes about who was really the father caused a great deal of laughter among the ordinary people.

Two historic battles soon separated the Emperor of Rome and his new Empress. In the first he defeated the great Roman general, Pompey, in one of the bloodiest battles known at that time. He went on to bring an end to Mark Antony at the famous battle of Actium, after which Cleopatra took the asp and killed herself rather than be taken back to Rome in triumph.

Augustus returned home to be loaded with honour and glory and Livia basked luxuriously in its reflection. A town called Liviada was built in her honour. She was given the most pompous titles, poets celebrated her in verse and temples were erected in her name.

Victory meant a time of peace. In Rome Augustus anticipated all her wishes so that in time her authority was as absolute as his own. She always showed great tenderness towards him, but there was also a great deal of art and cunning in her behaviour, which he did not find out until it was too late. She took care at that stage that nobody should have anything to reproach her with. One day, some young men, sporting about, had appeared before her stark naked. They were condemned to death but she had them pardoned saying that a naked man made no more impression on the imagination of a virtuous woman than a statue.

Her two sons, Tiberius by her former husband, and Drusus, grew to be men. She saw to it that they were given important status in the Roman army and that their victories, however trivial, were treated as triumphs. Tiberius was cruel and arrogant and addicted to debauchery of the worst kind. Augustus gave his opinion that if he ever came to power he would cause the greatest misery and suffering. Drusus, on the other hand, was such a fine man that the Emperor would have liked to have named him as his successor but felt it would confirm people's suspicions that he was his own son.

As it was he chose his nephew and son-in-law, Prince Marcellus, as heir presumptive, a soldier he considered to have noble qualities. This was not what Livia had in mind. Her one aim now was to pave the way to the throne for her son, Tiberius. Soon after Augustus had made his announcement, Prince Marcellus died in great agony. Livia had struck her first blow.

As if in answer, fate threw a tragedy across her path. Her son Drusus was killed on his way back to Rome after a battle. Her grief was so great that philosophers were sent for to give her what comfort they could. From then on she became more deadly and doubled her efforts for Tiberius. With Prince Marcellus out of the way she thought matters could be arranged quite easily for she had advised Augustus so skilfully in other matters that he began to think her always right. But then he took the step of marrying his daughter, Julia, widow of Prince Marcellus, to Agrippa. She gave birth to two sons, Gaius and Lucius, both in direct line to the throne. For a time there was nothing Livia could do.

But as the years passed and Augustus grew older she determined afresh to get rid of any obstacle that stood between her son and the throne. She made her plans without any outward show of treachery or violence, like a snake creeping up in the night. By now the Emperor was completely under her domination and her word had become, if anything, more respected in Rome than his. People did not dare disobey her.

The day came when the two young Princes Gaius and Lucius met sudden and tragic ends, the first in Lycia as he was returning from war, the second in Marseilles. People were aghast at the awfulness of the tragedy and Augustus could not be comforted. Feeling that soon he would have no kin of his own left in the world, he adopted his daughter's youngest son, Agrippa, together with Tiberius. This step divided the Empire between his own grandson and Livia's son. He thought she would be pleased, but she was furious that all her well-laid plans had ended in this. Agrippa had to be got rid of but another death, so soon, would not be satisfactory. She set to work to poison the Emperor's mind with malicious talk and rumours about his grandson, none of which were true. But Augustus, believing her implicitly, wept and had him banished to the island of Planasia. To all Rome the punishment seemed unjust and cruel. Agrippa had not the polished style of the other Princes, but, as far as anyone knew, this was his only crime.

Augustus often complained of his cruel destiny in losing one by one so many members of his family. He began to think back on all that had happened and suddenly longed to see Agrippa, the grandson he had exiled. He made up his mind to go to his island prison. He kept his visit a secret from anyone, even Livia, for perhaps at last he was beginning to have suspicions. Only his friend Fabius Maximus knew. But this man told his wife and his wife told Livia. This produced such venom, such anger, that Caesar should have acted without her knowledge, that she made the most terrible decision of all – to kill Augustus and his grandson.

Even with her smooth tongue she could not conceal her true feelings on his return, when she told him there was 'no occasion for all this secrecy'. One day at his palace in Nola, lying in the very room where his father, Octavius, had died, she brought him a dish of figs. He ate them with pleasure, but they were full of poison. As he died, Augustus spoke to Livia with words of tenderness, but those close enough thought they saw a light of dawning horror in his eyes.

His death was kept secret for some time because Tiberius

was absent. Livia fretted and paced her palace floors willing her son to come home. As soon as he arrived, the death of Augustus and the succession of Tiberius were announced simultaneously. Poor Agrippa was murdered. Livia said that Augustus had ordered it in his will but everyone knew this was just another of her crimes.

The Romans, by now afraid of this she-wolf, lavished fresh honours and titles upon her. This was just what she had schemed for. Now, the glory of being mother of the Emperor would give her even greater stature. But she had not reckoned with Tiberius. She had bred a son worthy of her.

He was jealous of her honours, looking upon them as diminishing his own stature. He gave orders that her household was not to be increased by a single officer. He was in fact indifferent to her. She irritated him by constantly reminding him that he owed his throne to her.

This ingratitude did not stop her. She took every step necessary to ensure that he should reign without trouble or threat. She persecuted all those of Augustus's family she had still left alive. However, there was still Prince Germanicus, her own grandson, who, like his father, Drusus, was brave and honest. Tiberius himself was jealous of his fame, hated hearing of his triumphs and resented his victories. Orders were sent to Syria where he was in charge of the army and he was killed by poison.

Mother and son grew further apart. Tiberius hated Livia's boundless ambition. The pomp and magnificence with which she surrounded herself were anathema to him. He was just in time to stop her putting her name before that of Augustus on a memorial dedicated to the great Caesar.

Finally, to escape her, he left Rome and went to Capri where he spent the rest of his life indulging his taste for nameless debauchery. Livia reigned absolute in his place. She enjoyed herself and lived until she was 80. When news of her end was carried to Tiberius in Capri he said he could not go to Rome. He excused himself with weak stories of ill health and other difficulties, but it was thought he dared not let it be seen how terribly his appalling life had aged him.

Livia was placed in a mausoleum with Augustus, and her grandson, Caligula, pronounced her funeral oration. The Senate wanted to make her a goddess, but Tiberius, in a fit of retaliation, would not allow it. He said he did not think she would want such a thing. At that, she must have stirred in her grave.

Catherine the Great

'She is romantic, ardent and passionate. She has a bright glassy hypnotic look like that of a wild animal. She has a big forehead and, unless I am mistaken, a long and terrifying future marked upon it. She is thoughtful and friendly and yet when she approaches me I automatically back away. She frightens me.'

So wrote the Chevalier D'Eon, secret agent and wily observer at the Russian Court in 1756. The woman he was writing about became Catherine the Great, Empress of Russia, and, to this day, one of the most remarkable women ever to sit on a throne.

D'Eon summed up her complexity. She was no tyrant, yet she demanded blind obedience. She thought only of making Russia great, yet treated the wretched serfs as scarcely human. She could never be directly accused of murder, yet the assassinations of Tsar Ivan VI and her husband, Peter III, undoubtedly left blood on her hands. She remained a virgin until she was 23, then for the rest of her life she hardly ever went to bed without a lover.

Strangely enough, Catherine had not a drop of Russian blood in her veins. She was German.

Her given name was Sophie Augusta Frederica of Anhalt-Zerbst and she was born at Stettin, Pomerania, in April 1729. Her father was Prince Christian Augustus, an impoverished royal who had been given the post of Commandant at Stettin. Her mother, related to the great ducal house of Holstein, was a discontented woman who considered she was living a dull, provincial life, unworthy of her status and talents. She had no real affection for her daughter. But, in spite of her father's lack of money and her mother Princess Johanna's coldness, the young Sophie had a normal childhood.

Life changed dramatically when she reached the age of 15. Mysterious comings and goings, letters with Imperial seals and her mother's excitement were all for one reason. She had been chosen as a possible bride for the Grand Duke Peter of Russia. Frederick of Prussia had probably suggested her because her humble place in the list of German Princesses was thought more likely to make her grateful for the honour and, therefore, easy to manipulate.

Summoned to the Russian Imperial Court by the Empress Elizabeth, mother and daughter set off with a scarcely adequate wardrobe, the Prince refusing to spend money on fancy clothes. They were received with great splendour. Princess Sophie nearly fainted when the Empress approached her, looking like a goddess in silver watered silk and diamonds. This beautiful, imposing woman, known only too well for her vanity and cruelty, examined her coolly and liked what she saw. Princess Sophie, with her beautiful pale skin, long dark hair, blue eyes and natural grace, could be the right choice. After days of further scrutiny, during which she felt like a piece of merchandise, she was accepted as the Grand Duke's bride.

When she first saw him, she was appalled. Twisted and deformed with an ugly, thick-lipped face, he behaved like a whimpering child one minute and a drunken sadist the next. But what mattered was her destiny. She took the name Catherine on 28 June 1744, the day of her conversion to the Orthodox faith, and the following day became engaged. The Grand Duke was not much older than her. They sometimes found enough in common to keep each other company and play games in the palace corridors. But as the days went by a growing mutual dislike became obvious. It was decided to bring forward the day of the wedding.

They were married in Byzantine splendour, both dressed in cloth of silver and smothered in jewels. That night, after a great dinner and ball, he fell into bed brutishly drunk. Catherine did not know whether to be angry or relieved. On following nights he often took his toy soldiers to bed and played with them on the counterpane. It was obvious to everyone that the marriage was a failure.

The Grand Duke, pitifully aware of his own ugliness, took a perverse pleasure in rousing Catherine's disgust. He was impotent by night and repulsive by day; terrified of the Empress and irritated by his wife's devotion to her duties. She had almost made herself ill by spending long hours learning the Russian language and Orthodox rites.

After several years of marriage, Catherine was still a virgin. She was desperate for love. One day she decided to flirt with one of the chamberlains at her court whose name she discovered was Sergei Saltykov. He was attractive to women and he knew it. Although married to one of the Empress's ladies-in-waiting he had travelled and learned sophisticated manners and habits. Catherine, whose appetite for beautiful young men became a mania, was bowled over. Before long they were lovers. Nobody seemed to mind. The Grand Duke had his whores and the Empress turned a blind eye for state reasons. There was still no heir.

In 1754 Catherine became pregnant and when she gave birth to a baby son he was called the Grand Duke Paul.

Saltykov was advised to travel for the sake of his health and the Empress whisked the child away to bring him up herself. Catherine was heartbroken, but made up her mind never to be hurt by a man again. When she returned to court, the steel in her nature had begun to show.

'My misfortune is that my heart cannot be happy even for an hour without love,' she was to write later. Fortunately for her there now appeared a romantic young Pole, Count Stanislas Poniatowsky. He was not as handsome as Saltykov but had a cultivated mind and great sensitivity. Catherine yearned for him. Once she fixed her eyes on a man, he was as good as lost. Though nervous at first, Poniatowsky agreed to disguise himself as a tailor or musician to gain access to the Grand Duchess's apartment. He was caught slipping out one morning and dragged before the Grand Duke. 'Confide in me,' said Peter smoothly, 'and it can all be arranged.' He was indifferent to his wife's amours, but liked to know what was going on. It was a dangerous moment. The Grand Duke was terrifyingly unpredictable and could have run him through with a sword. As it turned out, Peter fetched his mistress and the four of them played a game of cards.

Poniatowsky became a pawn in an intricate game of diplomacy that was being played in St Petersburg and in the end he was driven from Russia. Years later Catherine broke his spirit by a callous political manoeuvre, making him King of Poland one day and forcing him to abdicate the next. The humiliation killed him.

Swift on the heels of the Pole came one of the most important and useful men in her life.

Grigori Orlov was a magnificent Tatar, one of five brothers, all noted for their looks and their strength. He was only moderately intelligent and had no deep conversation to offer her, but he had marvellous sensuality and made her feel alive. Politically he was a brilliant choice. The whole Orlov clan was proud of having one of themselves chosen to be the Grand Duchess's lover and they vowed undying life-long loyalty, raising support among their fellow officers. Having the army behind her was to be vitally important.

On Christmas Day 1761 the Empress Elizabeth died and suddenly the ugly, debauched nephew she had terrorized was Peter III, Tsar of all the Russians. He went wild with his newly attained power. He mocked Elizabeth's coffin, refused to wear mourning and played the fool in her funeral procession. Catherine, to give a good impression, wore black from head to foot and kept vigil by the embalmed body of the woman she had hated.

Once again she was pregnant, this time by Orlov. When her baby son was born, he was sent out to foster parents. Peter, who had made threats to crush the wife who was ice cold to him, shouted across the table at a banquet: 'God knows where she gets her children from, but at least I know they are not mine!'

That sealed his fate. From that time on Catherine began to scheme against him and to await his downfall. He dug his own grave. Mad with power he made enemies on every side, mocking the Orthodox religion and courting his great Hero, Frederick the Great, who had beaten Russia to her knees.

The coup d'état which made Catherine the ruling Empress came so swiftly that people scarcely had time to realize what had happened. It took place dramatically, by night, with the Orlov brothers predominant and the army solidly behind her. Next day, Sunday 30 June 1762, she made a triumphal entry into St Petersburg, with all the bells ringing.

It had been bloodless and swift. She took power at the head of 20,000 soldiers, dressed in officer's uniform, and all the important factions submitted to her.

Peter, green with fear and whimpering like a child, had been bundled off his throne and into a carriage to be imprisoned in the fortress of Schlusselburg, a place long associated with torture and misery and which he dreaded. He pleaded with Catherine to let him keep his mistress, his dog, his negro and his violin. She wrote sardonically: 'Fearing scandal, I only granted him the last three.' There was nothing but hatred left in their feelings for each other.

A short time after he had been deposed, Peter was dead. Catherine always maintained he had died from apoplexy, but this was not true. It was known that he did not die of natural causes but from violence. The full story of his death has never been told but at the time it was universally believed that he had been poisoned by a glass of burgundy; then, when that did not work fast enough, strangled with a table napkin by one of the Orlov brothers. Catherine swore she had nothing to do with it, but she was not believed. Feeble though he was, as long as he remained alive he had been a threat.

Another threat, infinitely more pathetic, was removed very soon after. Catherine had been to visit a prisoner in his cell. He was a young man of 22 with a thin white face and wild eyes whose mind had slowly atrophied in isolation. He was called Prisoner Number 1 but he was in fact the rightful ruler of Russia, Tsar Ivan VI. Shut away since he was six years old by the Empress Elizabeth, he knew nothing of the world but damp prison walls and iron bars. As Catherine stood before him he mumbled his claims over and over again. The fact that he should have been Emperor was the only thing he could remember. She stared at him with cold eyes, then left.

Her orders were that the guard on him was to be doubled and he was to be killed outright if any attempt was made to rescue him. She knew she had enemies and sure enough certain groups began to talk of restoring the martyr to his rightful place and getting rid of the German woman. One night, Ivan was stabbed to death by a hot-headed lieutenant called Basil Morovitch. But Morovitch had not acted alone and again the rumours started. Was he merely an agent for Catherine?

Only one rival remained – her own son. She loved the Grand Duke Paul in her way but had him brought up to be submissive. After he asked why his 'father' had been killed she made sure he remained a nonentity.

Her whole aim was to raise the power and might of Russia over all other empires and to expand her frontiers as far as possible. She had a rock-like will when it came to achieving her ends. She claimed to hold liberal views but did nothing to change the barbaric, cruel and miserable life endured by the millions of human beings called serfs. She handed them out by the thousand to reward the architects of her coup d'état. Serfs had no more rights than defenceless animals and were often valued at less. In Catherine's Russia a pedigree dog was worth 2,000 roubles but you could get a male serf for 300 roubles and a young peasant girl cost less than 100.

Catherine never forgot what the Orlovs had done for her. Grigori and his brothers, over a period of ten years, received seven million roubles as tokens of her gratitude. This did not include gifts of palaces and jewels. On their estates they were absolute lords of 45,000 serfs.

Grigori Orlov remained her great love and she allowed him to behave with such familiarity that people began to resent his influence on her. He wore a miniature of her, studded with diamonds, as a mark of her special favour and soon became so aware of his power that he was no longer satisfied with his role as lover. He tried to persuade Catherine to marry him so that he could be consort. When he received her refusal with a show of haughty bad temper she began to see that it was time for him to go. She conferred on him the title of Prince then sent him off on his travels. He dazzled Europe with a succession of magnificent uniforms but caused one wit to remark: 'He is like an ever-boiling pan of water which never cooks anything.'

On his return the Empress gave him a marble palace and he presented her with an enormous blue Persian diamond, the 'Nadir-Shah', which became known as the Orlov diamond.

She was glad to see him and put up with his behaviour because he had such a special place in her life. But there was already another lover in her bed, a dark, good-looking young man called Vasilchikov. The shock brought him to his senses but it was too late.

Waiting in the wings was the most famous of all Catherine's lovers, the great Prince Potemkin. She was 45 when he stormed her emotions, causing her to write him scorching letters confessing her greed for him. 'Every cell in my body reaches towards you, oh, barbarian! . . . Thank you for yesterday's feast.' Yet it was power not love that Potemkin was seeking and it was her mind that he valued. Between kisses they would discuss affairs of state and gradually Catherine began to see that he was more than a lover to her. He was indispensable and worked with her to further her ambition and all the great schemes she had for Russia. When she heard he had died, she fainted.

At a time of life when her ardour should have been on the wane Catherine started on a string of young lovers whose only qualifications were beauty of face and form. She adored young men, even the most humble. The money Catherine lavished on her favourites is almost without parallel. In cash alone, forgetting all the lavish presents and houses she dispensed, she cost Russia 100 million roubles. Potemkin had 50 million of this sum but at least he gave Russia the Crimea, the Caucasus and the Black Sea!

Potemkin's death was such a terrible blow to Catherine that she never wholly recovered. Her last favourite was a brilliant, handsome courtier called Platon Zubov, who soon began to show a taste for insolence and intrigue. He was 40 years her junior, and, though she was never to know it, he was to strike the first blow in the murder of her son after he ascended the throne.

Her end came suddenly, as the snow fell on St Petersburg. She suffered a stroke, from which she never recovered, and died in her bed on 7 November 1796.

Queen Christina of Sweden

Through the Monaldesco affair the whole world came to know that Christina of Sweden meant what she said when she cried: 'I never forgive.' This strange Queen, who dressed as a man, despised women and after abandoning her throne spent a lifetime storming about Europe, shocked even the most worldly by her part in a cold-blooded murder.

It took place while she was staying at Fontainebleau in France, an unwelcome and uninvited guest as far as the French Government was concerned. With her were two of her Italian courtiers, Count Santinelli, her captain of the guard, and the Marquis Monaldesco, her chief equerry. The two men loathed each other. They were constantly plotting and scheming to see which of them could find greater favour with the Queen. Santinelli had cheated and swindled her over her property in Rome and the Marquis, seeking to incriminate her, forged a series of letters in his hand including, for good measure, insinuations about her relationship with a Cardinal in Rome and her ambition to take the throne of Naples.

The whole thing went desperately wrong for Monaldesco. Christina, always in the habit of opening other people's letters, recognized his hand through the forgery and came to the conclusion that it was he who was betraying her. She summoned him to her room and asked him what he would consider a fitting punishment for a traitor. 'Death,' said Monaldesco, thinking she was convinced of Santinelli's guilt. 'Good,' said the Queen. 'Remember what you have said. For my part, let me tell you, I never forgive.'

The climax to the terrible affair came on 10 November 1657 when the Queen summoned him to the Galerie de Cerfs at Fontainebleau. She had also summoned Father Lebel, prior of the nearby Mathurin Monastery, and told him to read the letters. Monaldesco had a sudden premonition of what was to happen, but it was too late. The doors were guarded by soldiers and the Queen, dressed in black and toying with an ebony cane, talked of trivial matters for a while as though playing for time. Suddenly Santinelli and two guards strode into the room, drawn daggers in their hands.

Trembling, Monaldesco threw himself on his knees and begged for her pardon, confessing the forgery was in his hand. He pleaded with her to listen, to let him tell the whole story. She turned to the prior and said: 'Prepare his soul for death.' Then she left the gallery.

Lebel followed her asking her to have mercy. Serene and unmoved she replied that after the treachery this man had shown towards her he could not have mercy. Even the rogue Santinelli went down on his knees and begged her to change her mind, to let the case come before the Royal Courts. Christina merely urged him to make haste.

Monaldesco died a terrible death. He had put on armour underneath his ordinary clothing and his executioners found it hard to kill him. He took 15 minutes to die and his screams must have reached her ears. She salved her conscience by sending money to the local convent to have prayers said for the repose of his soul.

To her enemies the affair offered proof of what they considered her arrogance and lack of humanity. They thought that far from being executed for political treachery Monaldesco had probably come into possession of some delicate personal secrets which Christina preferred to remain unknown.

Queen Christina was an extraordinary woman whose whole life was an enigma. She amazed everybody by her learning, the brilliance of her mind and the vivacity of her conversation. She also worried them by her odd sexuality, her meddling in politics and her lack of feeling for people generally. She always preferred the company of men and was awkward in feminine pursuits. When young she thought nothing of hunting reindeer in snow and biting cold for ten hours at a time, galloping at such a crazy speed that no one could keep up with her. Whenever she could she dressed in men's clothing. Her sexual leanings were not straightforward. Although she fell deeply in love with one of her ladies-in-waiting as a young woman, the other great loves of her life were all men.

Christina gave up the throne of Sweden because she had become bored with the plain, Protestant life and bored with being Queen. She also refused to marry. For the rest of her life she went flinging and swaggering about Europe, creating such problems that men went pale when they saw her coming.

When she was born on 8 December 1626 she was so hairy and cried with such a deep voice that everyone told her father, the great King Gustavus Adolphus, that he had a son. The mistake caused great embarrassment but Gustavus was typically good-natured about it and said: 'The little thing will grow up to be clever. She has already fooled us all.'

He was killed in battle in 1632 when she was six and five regents took over until she reached her majority. They kept her away from her mother's melancholy influence as much as possible. After Gustavus's death, Queen Marie lived in a room hung with black in which candles burned night and day. She kept a shroud by her side and Gustavus's heart, encased in gold, above her bed. As a result Christina received a somewhat masculine education, directed almost exclusively by men.

On her 18th birthday she took the oath as King of Sweden as it was not considered suitable to have the first woman to sit upon the throne called merely Queen. For ten years Christina handled politics vigorously and well. Europe was agog at this extraordinary girl whose statesmanship was remarkably mature, whose thirst for knowledge had become a mania and who was so unorthodox. It seemed she only required four hours' sleep a night, spent the minimum of time on her appearance, preferring Hungarian riding clothes of masculine cut, and had declared her love for a woman.

The great passion was for the beautiful Ebba Sparre, a lady-in-waiting. The girl was already betrothed to the Count Jacob de la Gardie and Christina tried in every way to take her away from him. The Queen's intensity must have frightened her and she had no intention of turning down a splendid offer of marriage to become an old maid. She married the Count while Christina suffered agonies of jealousy. Typically, she never forgave him.

But Christina was never predictable. Just as everyone had made up their minds she was lesbian she took as her favourite the brilliant, French-oriented brother of this same Count, and it was obvious she fell deeply in love with him. In the eyes of the world he was her lover but eventually she loaded him with honours and sent him away, perhaps because she was aware of the ambiguity of her sexual nature.

Christina had become bored with Protestant Sweden. She began to regard the teachings of Luther and Calvin as 'moth-eaten' and called her Prime Minister an 'Old Goth'. She wanted to strengthen Sweden's alliance with France, a move which her ministers regarded as a sin against the Protestant cause. She admired French culture and the French way of living and had already enlivened the court with considerable style. She came under the influence of four foreign *bon viveurs* who were only too ready to help her change and life became all festivals and ceremonials, ballets and masquerades. She began to neglect the affairs of state to such an extent that sometimes she would let a month go by without seeing her ministers. What they did not know was that one of her friends, the elegant Spanish ambassador, don Antonio Pimentel, had already brought numerous Jesuit priests to Stockholm in disguise and that she was on the verge of conversion.

Christina had two shocks ready for her government. First, she refused to marry. She told them: 'Marriage would entail many things to which I cannot become accustomed and I really cannot say when I shall overcome this inhibition . . .' Then she told them she intended to abdicate and suggested the throne should be offered to her cousin, Prince Charles Gustavus, who would be better able to secure the succession. Their reaction, and that of her people, was as though she had committed high treason. Who would have believed this of the daughter of the great King Gustavus!

She greeted the day of her abdication with relief. There was a rather ludicrous little ceremony in which she had to put on her crown, her blue velvet coronation robe and her insignia, then have them stripped from her. No one dared touch the crown and she had to take it off herself. The coronation of Charles X took place the same day.

Seeming to care little for the chaos, anxiety and disappointment she left behind she dressed in male clothes, took the name Count Dohna and set off for Denmark, promising she would return, though she had no intention of doing so. The new King found his palace in Stockholm so emptied of furniture and carpets that he had difficulty finding somewhere to sleep. Christina had shipped them off to Rome, where she intended to bask in the approval of the Pope.

On 23 December 1654 Christina made a triumphal entry into Brussels where she declared herself a Catholic. Those who knew her doubted her motives and thought she made the change because she liked the colour and pageantry. People crowded round to catch a glimpse of her. They saw a woman of medium height dressed in a strange mixture of clothes with a ribbon tied carelessly round her unruly hair. Her face was rather sallow and her features strong, her nose being somewhat aquiline. She rode like a man.

She enjoyed herself in Brussels with one long round of festivities, but her reputation for unconventional behaviour became so widespread that the government in Sweden threatened to stop her income. The scandal sheets accused her of every kind of sexual irregularity. She was called the 'Queen of Sodom'.

The Pope, Alexander VII, sent word that he would receive her in Rome just before Christmas in 1655. It was the moment she had been waiting for. Dressed magnificently for once, but riding her horse astride like a man, she made her way towards the Vatican through streets festooned with flowers, triumphal arches and flags. Fanfares and salvos greeted her all the way along the route. Then she walked in a brilliant procession to where the Pope waited to give her the sacrament of confirmation. She was the sensation of Rome.

But if the Pope thought he had gained a model convert he was soon to be disillusioned. She had had her fill of piety and had other things to do. Humility was never one of her virtues and it did not suit her to be openly humble as His Holiness wished. She made fun of the relics and jabbered away to her companions during mass. Being informed of this the Pope sent her a rosary and begged her to tell her beads while in church. She answered bluntly that she had no intention of being a mumbling Catholic.

Worse was to come. She won over two of his cardinals by her brilliant talk. One of them, Cardinal Colonna, became so involved that he fell in love with her and the exasperated Pope had to send him away from Rome to avoid a public scandal. The other was Cardinal Azzolino, whom she undoubtedly loved and who became a devoted friend to her, though no one is sure of the relationship.

Though she made fun of Italian tastes and manners, the intellectuals gathered around her and she pleased them by inaugurating an Academy of Moral Science and Literature. She began to concern herself with politics with the most unfortunate results and Alexander began to wish his guest would go. She too had become tired of being under the eye of Rome.

She decided to leave for a time but was obliged to sell horses, carriages and jewellery to get herself to Paris. It was worth it. The French gave her a state reception watched by 200,000 people. She rode into the city astride her charger wearing a hat trimmed with sable plumes and a tunic heavily trimmed with gold and silver lace. She was escorted by 16,000 men of the Paris militia and 10,000 horses.

People were rather surprised at the coolness with which she accepted this display in her honour. 'Providence arranged that I should be born surrounded on every hand with laurels and palms . . .' she explained sanctimoniously. 'All Sweden went on its knees and worshipped me in my cradle.' She was not liked by the ladies of the court but impressed the men by her intellectual brilliance and mastery of languages.

She stayed at Fontainebleau and it was then that the Monaldesco execution took place. The French were appalled at what they described as a medieval barbarity. She had to wait several months for the affair to blow over before she could return to Paris. Cardinal Mazarin, her host, gave her to understand that the sooner she went the better, and she set out once more for Rome.

Her reception in Rome was very unfriendly. Only the devoted Cardinal Azzolino, who had written to her regularly while she was away, seemed delighted to see her. The Pope wanted nothing to do with her and complained to the Venetian ambassador that she was a barbarian. He neither replied to her letter informing him of her arrival nor received her at his summer palace. He was furious with her and suggested she took residence outside Papal See. But he did grant her an annuity and appointed Azzolino to look after her financial affairs.

As the years passed Christina began to be plagued with regrets. She no longer seemed to have any place in the world. Her position was too humble for her liking. It was at about this time she heard that a woman called Gyldener who was the same age as herself and strongly resembled her had been passing herself off as Queen Christina in Sweden. Several months elapsed before her real identity was discovered. Full of rage the exiled Queen sent word to King Charles to have the wretched woman put to death. The King decided to be more merciful and put her in prison for a month on a diet of bread and water.

Christina now began to meddle in European politics and at one point even suggested a new crusade to unite all Christian countries against the Turks, saying that modern Turkey must be completely destroyed. Nobody took much notice of her.

She seized upon another ambition: to rule another European country so that her name would mean something again in the councils of the world. The throne of Naples was vacant and she wanted to be Queen. First, however, she wanted to drive the Spaniards out of Sicily and asked France to help her. But France would not commit herself to Christina in any way.

Then, in February 1660, another throne became empty, the one she had once abdicated so joyfully. Charles X had died suddenly leaving as his heir a five-year-old child. Christina made up her mind to go to Sweden. When she got as far as Hamburg the Swedes sent her a letter more or less asking her to go away, but she ignored it. For one thing she wanted to find out what would happen to the already desperate state of her finances. She also wanted to revive her image as a great Queen and possibly spy out the land for the future. In Stockholm she was received with due respect and even given her apartments in the royal palace. But her hosts were wary. They were afraid that she was beginning to regret her abdication and would take this opportunity to make a claim to the throne. They allowed her to retire to one of her estates for a time where she ordered Mass to be said regularly, then, after a decent interval the government hinted that it was high time she left.

The remaining years were spent wandering about the world, often dishevelled, and as she grew older any charm she once had disappeared under a layer of fat. Her eyes, too, took on a steely, hard look and she was inclined to make extraordinary statements like 'to attack me is to attack the sun'.

She returned to Rome at last and lived for a while in a villa where the Garibaldi Monument now stands. Her relationship with Cardinal Azzolino had become more and more remote. She swore she would love him to the end but he was in line for the Papal crown and had to watch his reputation.

There was one more throne she had her eye on: that of Poland. But the Poles, thinking over her reputation, her life as a man-woman and her material dependence on the Pope, declined her offer. They chose the Duke of Lithuania instead and sternly reminded her of Monaldesco's assassination.

Her last years in Rome were full of cultural activity and she gathered a loyal circle around her. In February 1689 her health began to waver. She contracted a lung disease. The Pope gave her his absolution and promised to visit her in person but before he could do so she died, on 19 April, with Azzolino at her side.

Tzu-hsi – the Dragon Empress

The hatred and cruelty of one woman, Tzu-hsi, Dragon Empress of China, came to a terrifying climax in the celestial city of Peking one hot summer's day in 1900.

At the height of the Boxer rebellion – that great upsurgence of Chinese against foreigners and Christians – the French cathedral was burned to the ground killing hundreds of men, women and children. She watched the blaze from a nearby hill. Her order for a ceasefire in the bombardment came, not from mercy, but because her head ached.

While the red-turbaned hooligans she championed rampaged around the city yelling 'Burn, burn, burn. Kill, kill, kill', she was engaged in painting delicate designs of bamboo on silk or arranging exquisite water picnics on the palace lake. While Christians were massacred, thousands of Chinese converts among them, she tended her 4in-long fingernails, shielded with jade, and tottered round her gardens in jewel-encrusted shoes.

'Let no one escape,' she had ordered, 'so that my Empire may be purged . . .' Her soldiers were offered money for the heads of Europeans. Yet many of those who barricaded themselves in the British Legation, and staunchly held out until rescue, remembered taking tea with her and being charmed, especially when she confided that she had a great admiration for Queen Victoria and kept a photograph of her beside her bed.

This extraordinary, complex woman, who controlled the destiny of 400 million people for nearly 50 years, believed herself to be the cleverest woman in the world. But eventually her feudal outlook, her conviction that China was the centre of the world and that all foreigners were barbarians, brought about the end of the great Ch'ing dynasty. Her death in 1908 opened the floodgates to change.

Though she stood only 5ft tall her appearance was often dramatized, especially in her youth, by mask-like make-up and magnificent garments jewelled and fantastically embroidered in brilliant colours. Her raven black hair was never cut. She took great care of her appearance and her health, eating vast amounts of milk curdled with rennet but only small amounts of other foods, always of the finest quality.

She was the daughter of a minor Manchu mandarin. Born in November 1835 her destiny, according to the structure of the society she lived in, was to become a concubine. She was sent to the Imperial court at the age of 16 and a contemporary description of her, given in Marina Warner's biography of the Dragon Empress, is enchanting. Like all Manchu girls she whitened her face and rouged two spots of high colour on her cheeks. Her bottom lip was painted in a scarlet cherry drop. Sometimes she added blue to her eyelids and outlined her eyes with khol. Above this mask-like visage her hair was gathered up from the nape of the neck into an enormous, weighty decoration of jewels, shaped like flowers and insects, which fanned out on either side and hung down with tassels of pearls. She wore the Manchu costume of tunic and trousers in vivid silk and her shoes had a central high wedge hung with pearls and encrusted with jewels.

But she was only one of 3,000 concubines and 3,000 eunuchs whose lives were dedicated to the dissolute 20-year-old Emperor, Hsien-Feng. She was of the fifth and lowest rank and it was quite likely that she would never even meet him, but would spend her days as an exalted servant. Given the name Imperial Concubine Yi she set out to make what she could of her position. The palace had a fine library and as, unlike most girls, she had learned to read and write, she took every advantage of the books and scholarly tutors now available to her. She also befriended and flattered the 15-year-old concubine of higher ancestry who had been chosen to be Hsien-Feng's wife.

After three years her cunning was rewarded. The Empress proved barren and one night she was sent for to share the Emperor's bed. Nine months later, in April 1856, she gave birth to a son, his Imperial Majesty's only male child.

Her status was immediately enhanced. The powerful eunuchs, who infiltrated and dominated court life with their intrigue and malicious gossip, sensed a new star rising and gathered round her. Tzu-hsi never underestimated their influence and enjoyed their silken subservience. Hsien-Feng was amazed at his new concubine's grasp of affairs and her dynamic energy and in the end found it easier to let her take part in politics and run things for him. Effeminate, weak and ill he seemed unable to cope with the terrible wars launched by the Taiping rebels in the north. When these troubles were added to by an invasion of north China by joint forces of England and France, it was the last straw.

To escape the advancing 'foreign devils' the royal court fled from Peking to Jehol, away in the mountains. Signs of a shift in power came with a special decree from the royal palace ordering the decapitation of all prisoners as a warning to the 'bandits' who had dared to invade the Forbidden City. The voice that gave that order was not the Emperor's but that of the Concubine Yi.

Blood flowed in Peking but Hsien-Feng's brother, the statesman-like Prince Kung, was wise enough to realize that the killing of Europeans could not go on. China's only hope lay in submission. He ignored further Imperial decrees and made a peace treaty with the French and English.

The Emperor was to return to his capital in the spring of 1861 but, before the winter storms had ceased, he was dead. His Empress and Tzu-hsi became regents. At the first sign of good weather they set out on the long, stony road from Jehol to Peking, taking the child Emperor with them. They had been warned of a plot of conspirators who wanted to seize power and who planned to kill the two regents and leave their bodies for the vultures. The royal route over the wild mountain passes was changed at the last minute.

All eyes were on Tzu-hsi as she made a triumphal entry into Peking with her son, borne shoulder-high on a yellow throne through streets hung with yellow banners and strewn with yellow sand.

This was the point at which she had to decide who were her friends and who were her enemies. The Empress Niuhuru had no interest in political power, so could be discounted. But Tzu-hsi gave orders immediately that Su Shun, the wealthy man behind the assassination plot, was to be decapitated and his supporters ordered to commit suicide. She grabbed his estates and laid the foundations of an immense fortune.

Civil war at its most terrible raged through five provinces and 20 million people died in the first years of her reign, as the Taiping rebellion continued to run its terrible course in the mountains of the north. During these years she relied heavily on the wisdom of Prince Kung. He saw her every day, taught her state craft and did his best to curb her warlike tendencies.

At first their meetings were conducted with the strictest formality and etiquette. As time went by, however, Prince Kung became a little too familiar for Tzu-hsi's liking. She had had enough of the pupil-teacher relationship and decided to get rid of him.

Her moment came in the fourth year of her regency. One day Prince Kung absentmindedly started to rise from his knees during a long and tedious audience. (A judicial rule of etiquette forbade anyone to stand in the sovereign's presence to safeguard against attack.) Tzu-hsi shrieked for help, worked herself into a terrible rage and claimed that he had moved towards the throne to attack her. He was seized by eunuchs, dragged from her presence and stripped of all honours and duties.

Later, probably because she could not do without him, she extended her forgiveness and he was re-admitted to the Grand Council. But she had made her point. She had brought down the most powerful man in the country and subjugated him to her will.

Her private life became more and more extravagant and she encouraged her officials to increase taxes on an already impoverished Chinese people in order to keep the Dragon Court in feudal magnificence. Still not satisfied she began selling all positions of authority for large donations to her coffers.

Meanwhile, the young Emperor, Tung Cheh, was being brought up in a hot-house environment dominated by painted concubines and eunuchs. It was as though Tzu-hsi was plotting his downfall from the very beginning, looking ahead to the day when he assumed power and she would no longer be needed. She indulged the eunuchs and took no notice of the terrible influence they had on him from the earliest age. By the time he was 15 it was obvious that he had all his father's ambi-sexual tastes and was steeped in debauchery. The eunuchs planned orgies and she encouraged them to introduce him to the whores in the back streets of Peking.

By 1872, when he was 16, he was considered old enough to marry and daughters of Manchu officials were ordered to appear at the Palace. He chose as his bride a beautiful 18-year-old girl called Alute who proved to have brains as well as looks. Tzu-hsi became fiercely jealous of her and extremely angry when she realized that Alute was encouraging the wretched Tung Cheh to think for himself and resist the influence of the eunuchs. But it was too late.

When the time came for the young Emperor to assume the throne officially and for Tzu-hsi to retire and do her embroidery, her chagrin was felt in every corner of the

Forbidden City. She gave orders that the old Imperial Summer Palace, destroyed by the British and French, should be rebuilt for her in all its glory. Vast sums were raised for the purpose but many, Prince Kung among them, complained of such extravagance while China was still suffering from the terrible results of the Taiping rebellion. The rebuilding was abandoned and Tzu-hsi shut herself away in fury.

She did not have long to wait. The Emperor's exploits with the whores and transvestites of Peking were beginning to take their toll. He was found to be suffering from venereal disease; then his weakened frame succumbed to smallpox. Little was done to help him. In the flowery language of the court, he 'Ascended the Dragon' on 13 January 1875. He was only 19.

His loving Empress, Alute, had never left his bedside. Tzu-hsi, hearing her complain to him of her overbearing ways, flew into one of her terrible rages and ordered the eunuchs to take her away and beat her. Alute was pregnant and there was no doubt among court officials that Tzu-hsi had made up her mind to get rid of the girl before the birth of her child.

On the day of her son's death, sitting on the Dragon throne with the compliant Niuhuru by her side, she called a Grand Council. Tung had left no heir. An Emperor had to be chosen. Sweeping aside all tradition she insisted it should be her nephew, the son of her only sister. She was flagrantly manipulating the ancient dynastic law and only ten men dared to defy her. She made a note of their names. She could not stand opposition and had unscrupulous methods of getting rid of those who stood in her path.

She immediately adopted her nephew, Kuang-hsu. The thin, delicate three-year-old was fetched in the middle of the night, hastily dressed in Imperial robes and taken to pay homage at the bier of his dead cousin. On 25 February 1875 he became Emperor. Tzu-hsi knew she could remain in power as regent for another decade at least. The neglected, humiliated Empress Alute, denied the succession for her expected child and made ill by her mother-in-law's treatment, killed herself with an overdose of opium. It was even said in some quarters that Tzu-hsi had ordered her to commit suicide because her presence was repugnant to her.

With the arrival of Kuang-hsu unexpected rivalry grew up between the two regents. The child was obviously terrified of Tzu-hsi and much preferred the gentle Niuhuru. Stories vary as to the actual nature of the dispute which finally brought about the latter's death, but it is known that one afternoon Tzu-hsi sent her some rice cakes, and by the evening she was dead.

After that the Dragon Empress ruled alone as regent for six years, her constant companion being the chief eunuch, Li Lien Ying, a corrupt, avaricious, cruel man who was, nevertheless, utterly devoted to her. She totally dominated the young Emperor, a languid, listless youth with 'a voice like a mosquito'. He was said to have been frightened of her and one can understand why. A court official, describing her rage, said: 'Her eyes poured out straight rays, her cheekbones were sharp and the veins on her forehead projected. She showed her teeth . . .'

In 1887 Kuang-hsu attained his majority and the regent, now 55, went into retirement. She chose a luxurious retreat just outside Peking, where she could keep a close watch on him. What she saw amazed her. The Emperor was not the puppet she supposed. He had, in fact, a thirst for Western knowledge and ideas and visions of ending the repressive regime he had inherited and creating something nearer to European democracies. Tzu-hsi came to hate him for his outward-looking politics. There was only one sort of China for her and that was the China of her ancestors. She set her chief eunuch to spy on him and blamed him for China's humiliating war with Japan whereas the blame in fact lay at her doorstep for she had ruined the navy by taking funds.

Great bitterness developed between Tzu-hsi and her nephew. At last he decided the only solution was to kill her favourite, Jung Lu, and imprison her. But he was betrayed by officials who feared what changes the coup might bring and instead found himself a prisoner.

The enraged Dowager Empress, as she was now called, dared not kill him but had all his attendants put to death or banished and replaced them with her own. Pearl, Kuang-hsu's concubine, knelt before her imploring her to spare the Emperor further humiliation. She even dared to suggest that as Kuang-hsu was the lawful sovereign anyway she had no right to set aside the mandate of heaven. Tzu-hsi dismissed her and had her imprisoned.

As for the pitiful young Emperor with his dreams of a better world, his reign was virtually ended. But the rest of the world was becoming interested in China, which had been a closed book for centuries, and there was great sympathy for Kuang-hsu. The British Prime Minister went so far as to say that foreign countries would view with displeasure and alarm his sudden demise. She was incensed by this sympathy for him and her old hatred of 'foreign devils' began to fester.

The Boxer movement started among gangs of reactionary youths in the Kuan district of Shantung. They were violently anti-foreign and derived their name from the gymnastic exercises and shadow-boxing they performed to work themselves into a frenzy. Their blood-chilling rites and ceremonies were accompanied by cries of 'Exterminate the barbarians'. But, as they were fiercely loyal to the Ch'ing dynasty and fanatically nationalistic, Tzu-hsi chose to regard them as a 'people's army' and gave them support.

Soon the killing and the burning began. No missionary or Chinese convert was safe. Some of her ministers dared to warn all Europeans to get out while they could; they were beheaded. When a dispatch came from the foreign ministers demanding her immediate abdication and the restoration of the Kuang Emperor she roared: 'How dare they question my authority – let us exterminate them.'

Appalled by what was going on, foreign governments made plans to invade China and rescue those who were holding out, mostly in the only important European building left standing – the British Legation. An international force landed and captured Tientsin, then started moving up the railway line to Peking. The Dowager Empress watched with dismay as turmoil grew in the city and people began fleeing to the hills. As foreign troops drew nearer she made no attempt to control what was happening but made plans to leave with the Emperor.

All the concubines were ordered to appear before her, the Emperor's favourite, Pearl, among them. The unfortunate girl, who had still not learned her lesson, suggested that the Emperor's place was in Peking. Tzu-hsi was in no mood for argument. 'Throw this wretched minion down the well,' she ordered. Pushing aside Kuang-hsu, who fell on his knees pleading with her to spare the concubine's life, she ordered: 'Let her die at once.' There was certainly no time to waste. The enemy was at the gates. Dressed as peasants and riding on an old cart, Tzu-hsi and her nephew fled Peking.

For the first time in her life the Dowager Empress began to experience what it was like to live as an ordinary Chinese. During the first days in exile she had to sleep like the poorest traveller in wretched, flea-ridden inns and eat the coarse common porridge made from millet. She saw the suffering of peasant families and professed pity for them, handing out gifts of money, and saying she had not appreciated their plight in the seclusion of her palace.

But she did not have to share their life for long. Even in exile she was soon surrounded by luxury. With great relief she heard on 1 June 1901 that peace terms had been agreed and she could fix a date for the court's return. Fully convinced that she would be exempt from blame, she left for Peking in a blaze of pageantry with silk banners, painted lanterns and flowers. Before she entered the city she made offerings to the river god.

She gradually managed to convince herself that she had nothing to do with the atrocities and greeted every foreigner she met with the utmost charm and civility. She demanded that history be rewritten and all decrees favouring the Boxers wiped from the records. At last she realized the full power of the Western world and in the last few years of her life issued edicts that brought about major reforms that even Kuang-hsu would have approved.

The Emperor had been badly treated ever since their return from exile. He was given insolent eunuchs to serve him, provided with stale and unpalatable food and, when the rest of the palace was converted to electricity, his apartments were left out.

But the end was very near for both of them, an extraordinary end that could have been a twist of fate but was more likely due to human venom.

In the summer of 1907 the Dowager Empress suffered a slight stroke and the following year became weak and ill with dysentery. Her usually robust health seemed to be failing. As she took to her bed, the Emperor became desperately ill and took to his. He was suffering from a disease of the kidneys and his health was ruined, but the doctor who was fetched to see him found him writhing in agony and suffering from symptoms he had never seen before. Kuang-hsu lay back on his satin cushions and died early in the morning on 14 November 1908. Before he died he scribbled a curse on the woman who had put him on the throne.

Twenty-four hours later Tzu-hsi asked for the traditional robe of longevity, turned her face to the south, and died.

Those present said when told of the Emperor's death she had seemed relieved. Had she, in a last act of hatred, had him poisoned? No one could be quite sure.

She was buried with great splendour. Twenty years after her funeral, bandits broke into her tomb and stole the treasure that had been buried with her. Her body was carelessly flung to one side.

Female Fanatics and Cults

Ulrike Meinhof

Early in the evening of 16 June 1972 a tense German policeman, acting on a tip-off, knocked at the door of a flat in the suburban village of Langenhagen, near Hanover airport.

The door was opened by a sullen-looking woman with straggling hair, who immediately realized her mistake. Suddenly police were swarming everywhere. She struggled hysterically, fought and shouted obscenities. But it was all over for Ulrike Meinhof.

After the biggest and most sustained search in German police history, the middle-class anarchist, who had come to be regarded as the most dangerous woman in Europe, was in their grasp. As she was led away they opened one of her suitcases, packed for a flight from Hanover airport. They were not really surprised to find it contained three 9mm pistols, two hand grenades, one submachine-gun and a 10lb bomb.

With university drop-out Andreas Baader as her partner, Ulrike had been waging war on the established order for nearly three years. The terrorist group they formed committed so many crimes, ranging from murder to forgery, that it needed 354 pages to list them when they came to trial. Baader and two other gang leaders were already in prison. But, until that June evening when Ulrike Meinhof was captured, the authorities could not rest for she was undoubtedly the intellect, the driving force behind everything.

The story of how she changed from an idealistic student into a fanatical anarchist ready to tear down everybody and everything is full of violence and hatred. Yet in the middle of it she remains a sad figure.

Ulrike Meinhof was born into an intellectual, upper middle-class family at Oldenburg, Lower Saxony, on 7 October 1934. Both her parents were art historians but her father died when she was only five, her mother when she was 14. During her formative years she was fostered by her mother's friend, Professor Renate Riemeck, an intellectual woman of strong radical views. It was said that Ulrike learned from her many of her socialist ideas and the importance of never accepting the edicts of authority without first questioning them.

The attractive, red-haired girl soon showed signs of academic brilliance. In 1957, when she was 23, she went to Munster University to study sociology and philosophy. She campaigned against the atom bomb, the Americans in Vietnam and most of the burning issues that radical-minded students were interested in.

One day she was introduced to a thin-faced, handsome man called Klaus Roehl. He ran a lively, left-wing magazine called *Konkret* and when he asked her to join its staff she agreed.

Before long Ulrike had acquired a reputation as a first-class radical journalist, writing columns of such brilliance that she began to be talked about in circles outside the university. She probed into the economy of Germany, dealt with social questions many people felt were being brushed under the carpet and wrote about the misery that existed among those who had no part in Germany's so-called Economic Miracle.

Klaus Roehl made her his editor and his wife.

The magazine was successful enough in its own way, but not a best-seller. When Roehl hit on the idea of adding sex to the political content, it took off. They made a lot of money, lived in a fashionable house and drove round in a large white Mercedes.

Ulrike, now the mother of twin daughters, found herself the darling of radical chic society and became a familiar face on television. But the success and the gloss were superficial and inwardly Ulrike was burning with resentment. Her husband, she had discovered, was a womanizer. His affairs became too much for her and after seven years together they were divorced.

She gave up her job with her marriage, moved to Berlin and put her daughters, Regine and Bettina, into an old-fashioned, strict-discipline boarding school. This left her free to mix with a group of well-off young people with extreme radical views, who believed the only way to change society was through violence. The idea took root. She was soon publicly defending arson, violent protest and the crimes of urban guerrillas. But before she acted politically she had to get rid of some personal bitterness. She started a campaign against her husband and his magazine which culminated in a night of fury in which she and her friends vandalized the home in which she had once taken such a pride.

Through the grapevine she heard a lot about a young agitator and arsonist called Andreas Baader who was serving a prison sentence for his part in burning down a Frankfurt department store. One day she met Baader's 'revolutionary bride', a tall, blonde girl called Gudrun Ensslin, a pastor's daughter, who had studied philosophy. Gudrun told her his friends were determined to get him out and they wanted her to help. On certain days he was allowed to work outside the prison in a Berlin library, and it was decided to 'spring him' from there. On 14 May 1970 Ulrike led the raid with a gang of armed terrorists, leaving the librarian severely wounded and several prison guards with bullet holes. The violence had started.

After Andreas and Ulrike had had time to sum each other up, they agreed to form the Baader-Meinhof gang with a hard core of about 24 fellow anarchists. Apart from themselves the leading members would be Baader's girlfriend, Gudrun, and Jan Carl Raspe, who became Ulrike's lover.

Andreas Baader was officially the leader of the group. He was a dark, brooding, handsome man, attractive to women, who based his image on the young Marlon Brando. He was also indolent, spoiled and aggressive. Ulrike Meinhof supplied the drive and the brains in their partnership.

The four of them managed to flee the country after the raid and turned up in the Middle East to train with the Palestine National Liberation Front. But the Germans and Arabs did not get on too well, each accusing the other of being cold and arrogant. The two women were considered domineering and a damned nuisance and before long the PLO decided that their trainees were rebels without a true cause and asked them to leave.

Ulrike remained passionately pro-Palestinian. On her return to Germany she made the shocking decision to send her two small daughters to a refugee camp in Jordan to be trained along with the Palestinian children to become kamikaze fighters against Israel. Fortunately for them, her plans went wrong. Karl Roehl had been scouring Germany for his children and had even engaged private detectives. He was tipped off just in time and they were snatched from a hideout in Palermo. They hated him at first because their mother's indoctrination had been very thorough. But for all his faults he was a good and devoted father and won back their affection.

The gang grew to be about 150 strong. Most of its members were from quite prosperous backgrounds, the only two working-class recruits being garage hands, useful for dealing with stolen cars.

They were armed to the teeth with small firearms, sub-machine-guns, hand grenades and bombs and set out on a series of bank raids and robberies to raise funds to buy more. There was one particularly terrible assault on a branch of the Bavarian Mortgage and Exchange Bank in the small provincial town of Kaiserslautern, 35 miles west of Heidelberg, in which a police officer was murdered with callous deliberation.

Taking part in the raid was a new recruit, a long-haired blonde called Ingeborg Barz. The girl was so horrified by the bloodshed that she made up her mind to go home. She telephoned her parents in Berlin. It was the last they ever heard of her. According to Gerhart Muller, who turned state witness, she was summoned to a meeting with Ulrike Meinhof then driven to a remote spot near some gravel pits where she was executed.

Violence piled upon violence while the ordinary man in the street watched with horror. During two years of urban terror five people were shot or blown to bits, and there were 54 attempted murders, countless vicious assaults and a series of bombings directed against the US army in general. Ulrike had developed a complete disregard for human life and categorized some people, including policemen, as 'pigs'. Her aspirations were supposed to be humane: to do something about the injustices she saw in human society. In fact she seemed to be using terrorism to work out of her system a load of hatred and bitterness.

The police put all their manpower into an attempt to crack the terrorist hold on West Germany and their chance came one day early in 1972 in a quiet Frankfurt Street. They had received an anonymous tip that a garage there was stuffed with ammunition. They drove up in two lorries, loaded with sandbags, and began to build a wall – but because they were dressed in overalls they looked more like corporation gardeners delivering bags of peat. After a time a smart lilac-coloured Porsche drew up. Three young men in leather jackets climbed out. Two of them went into the garage, the third, waiting outside on the pavement, was grabbed by the police. They found they had got Jan Carl Raspe, the arch terrorist who was also Ulrike's lover. After a long, tense siege, first a gang member called Holger Meins was brought out. Then, after a brief exchange of fire the police dragged out a dark young man writhing with pain from a bullet in the thigh. It was Andreas Baader.

Not long after, Gudrun Ensslin was captured in a Hamburg dress shop when a shop assistant discovered a gun in her jacket and phoned the police. Ulrike began to feel very much alone. As the months went by she found that even her friends from the trendy left felt she was too dangerous to be associated with.

Then came the night in June when she decided to head for Hanover airport. She knew a left-wing teacher who had a flat nearby and turned up on his doorstep with several suitcases. He was in a terrible dilemma. He now held a respected position as Federal President of the Teachers' Union. The last thing he wanted was Ulrike Meinhof as house guest. He went to seek the advice of some friends and they urged him to phone the police at once. He made the phone call and stayed clear of the flat . . .

The rest of Ulrike's life was spent in prison or in the courtroom where she yelled and shouted abuse at her judges. The trial of the Baader-Meinhof gang was considered so potentially explosive that a fortified courtroom and special cells were built at the top-security prison at Stammheim in Stuttgart. There was great fear that reprisals and countermeasures would be launched by terrorists still outside.

Though members of the gang were kept apart she became aware as the trial went on of the enmity of the others, especially in the case of Gudrun Ensslin. Solitary, apart from her typewriter and her books, she began to brood. Eventually the pressure must have become too great. On the morning of 9 May 1976 she was found hanging in her cell.

Her followers refused to believe that she had committed suicide and for a time insisted she had been murdered by the authorities. Four thousand people marched in the cortège at her funeral in Berlin, many of them masked to avoid identification. The police felt they were watching over a time bomb and later they had to deal with revenge terrorist attacks.

But, of Ulrike Meinhof, a priest who knew her said afterwards: 'I think she finally decided she had come to the end of the wrong road . . .'

Mary Tudor

Henry VIII's elder daughter has been condemned to be known for all time as 'Bloody Mary'. Her face, with its tight, narrow lips and short-sighted eyes, peers out at us from Tudor portraits with frightening intensity. Even so, it is hard to imagine how in the short years of her reign this pious woman left England reeling as she sought to gain her religious ends by acts of appalling cruelty and fanaticism.

By the time she came to the throne in 1553, Mary Tudor was an embittered woman of 37. She suffered from a disorder of the womb, complained of violent headaches and had a deep-rooted aversion to sex. She had survived some traumatic experiences but instead of making her aware of the sufferings of others she had become hardened. It soon became clear that she would let nothing stand in the way of her one great passion – the restoration of the Roman Catholic Church and the supremacy of the Pope in England.

Gathering her forces round her she began her reign of terror against the Protestants with an order that the neglected statutes against heretics were to be brought back into full use. She gave her commissioners power to investigate all rumours of heresy and to arrest offenders on the spot. Protestant homes were broken into, premises searched for heretical books, and torture used on men and women alike.

But the real horror began one February morning in 1555 when the first Protestant martyr was tied to the stake at Smithfield and perished in full view of his wife and children. Before her own death four years later, Mary was to be responsible for committing 283 martyrs to the terrible death by fire. At the worst period there was an average of one burning every five days. She seemed to be a woman without mercy.

So obsessed was she with rooting out heretics that she allowed the country's economy to get into an appalling state. Prices were so high that people were driven through hunger to grind acorns for bread meal and to make do with water instead of the universal drink – ale. Mary thought it far more important to concern herself with the spiritual needs of her subjects rather than their general welfare. As the flames rose higher and higher, so did people's anger. She had to abandon any plan for showing herself on royal 'progresses' as other Tudor monarchs had done. She became so hated that her safety could not be guaranteed.

Yet when Mary Tudor first ascended the throne the bells of London rang out joyously and people stood for hours in the streets to cheer as she passed on her way to Westminster. She was a heroine in many eyes for the way she had borne so many injustices and for the way in which she had stood firm against her royal father's tyranny.

Born at Greenwich on 18 February 1516, the daughter of Henry VIII and his first wife, Catherine of Aragon, Mary was out of favour from the start. She should have been a boy. Though Henry showed his disappointment he seems to have been fond of her as a child and saw to it that she had a good, classical education. Her misery began with the appearance at court of the beautiful, bewitching Anne Boleyn. Henry, passionately in love with her, was determined somehow to obtain a divorce and make her his wife. How many people he hurt and destroyed in the process was of no importance.

Cranmer was appointed Archbishop of Canterbury and the King ordered him to sit as a judge and try his divorce case. Catherine refused to recognize the court or to appear before it, but Cranmer still gave judgement that her marriage to Henry had been unlawful. This meant that Mary was considered a bastard and had no right to the throne. She never forgave Cranmer and, in spite of the fact that his intervention probably saved her from the Tower, she later had her revenge and sent him to the stake.

When Henry married Anne Boleyn in January 1533 and she gave birth to the future Queen Elizabeth the following autumn, Mary was told she must no longer call herself Princess and she was to give precedence to Anne Boleyn's daughter at all times. She was forcibly parted from the mother she loved and had every pressure put on her to make her renounce her Catholic faith.

Both Queen Catherine, isolated with her Spanish ladies-in-waiting at a cold and cheerless manor at Kimbolton in Northamptonshire, and Mary, placed in charge of Anne Boleyn's sister at Hatfield in Hertfordshire, went in fear of their lives. Each morning when they woke they dreaded being forced to take the Oath of Succession declaring that Anne's children were heirs to the throne or the Oath of Supremacy declaring Henry supreme head of the Church in England. There was a great deal of sympathy for them throughout the country especially when it became known that Queen Catherine had died on 7 January 1536, still declaring her love for the King but without Mary being allowed to visit her, write to her or receive any memento.

Mary still stubbornly refused to bend to her father's will. Throughout this period her only ally was her mother's nephew, the powerful Emperor Charles V of Spain. His ambassador to England, Eustace Chapuys, frequently tried to intervene on her behalf when he thought her in danger and at the same time warned her that, unless she tempered her fierce Tudor pride with a little humility, she might lose her head. Many believed that it was only the fact that the powerful Emperor of Spain knew of her danger and had sympathy for her that kept her head on her shoulders. Mary did at one time consider escape to Spain but her heart was not in it. What she really wanted was for Charles V to invade England.

Things began to improve for her when Anne Boleyn was sent to the block for adultery and Henry married the gentle Jane Seymour, daughter of a Wiltshire knight. The new Queen felt pity for Mary and advised her for her own sake to show humility and beg Henry's forgiveness. Eventually after being urged by Chapuys, who told her she was 'the most obstinate and obdurate woman, all things considered that ever was', she agreed to sign the papers acknowledging her parents' divorce. Six months later she returned to Greenwich.

On the day before Anne Boleyn was beheaded Cranmer obligingly annulled her marriage to Henry in a farcical trial. This made both Mary and Elizabeth bastards. So when, on 12 October 1537, Jane Seymour gave birth to a son who would become King Edward VI, Mary, in good temper, recognized that her new brother took precedence over her and she did in fact become very fond of him.

For the next decade she lived at court when she was in her father's favour and in confinement in some isolated castle whenever there was an upsurge of Catholic feeling in the country. There was an attempt to marry her to the Duke of Orleans but it came to nothing.

One bitterly cold night at the end of January 1547, the tyrant Henry died and the throne passed to his frail but staunchly Protestant son.

It was clear from the beginning that Edward would not live for very long. He had a mind of his own and an affectionate nature, but power lay in the hands of his uncle, Edward Seymour, Jane Seymour's brother, who became Lord Protector and with Cranmer set out to firmly establish England as a Protestant country. This made it extremely difficult for Mary to remain at court in spite of her fond relationship with her brother, so she retired again to the country and was allowed to say Mass in private.

By the summer of 1553 the whole country knew that Edward was dying. He had survived serious attacks of measles and smallpox but his constitution was weakened and he succumbed to tuberculosis. Mary diligently prepared herself to take up her duties for, by act of parliament and under Henry's will, she was next in line to the throne. First, however, she had to contend with one of the most shameful power struggles in English history.

It was led by the corrupt and unscrupulous Duke of Northumberland, who was determined to keep Mary from the throne in order to preserve his own power and the power of the Protestant nobles. His pawn was the poor little innocent Lady Jane Grey. She was cousin to the young King and third in succession after Mary and Elizabeth. Northumberland married her to his son, Lord Guildford Dudley, then persuaded Edward to make a will bequeathing her the crown and excluding both Mary and Elizabeth on the grounds that they were illegitimate. The dying King, anxious to support Northumberland and his Protestant cause, signed away his sister's birthright.

When Lady Jane Grey was told that she was to be Queen of England she fainted from shock. She protested she had no desire for the crown. But even her own father, the cowardly Duke of Suffolk who changed sides as often as he changed coats, pushed her on to her tragic destiny. She was only to reign for nine days.

Meanwhile Mary's supporters were rallying to her at Framlingham Castle in Suffolk. Added to them were thousands who hated Northumberland. Soon it became obvious that a movement to put Mary on the throne was gathering momentum and when they saw which way the tide was flowing all the leading nobles and officials, including those who had fervently supported Lady Jane Grey, scurried to Framlingham to acknowledge Mary as their rightful Queen and to beg for her pardon.

On 19 July 1553 she was proclaimed in London. She made a slow and dignified progress towards the capital, receiving Elizabeth on the way, then entering the city in triumph. People cheered, sang and danced in the streets, but little did they know that the fountains which were filled with wine would soon run with blood. On 1 October Mary was crowned at Westminster by the Catholic Bishop Stephen Gardiner, Cranmer having been already sent to the Tower.

Mary set about disposing of those who had acted against her. It soon became clear that she was prepared to be ruthless and, though her accession had seemed popular with the masses in spite of the religious problem, those close to her began to urge her to marry to reinforce her position. Her old friend and protector Charles V put forward his own son, Prince Philip of Spain, as a suitable husband. Mary's dislike of sex made her very reluctant to take this step, especially as Philip was only 26, 11 years younger than herself, and reported to be virile. Charles sent Renard, his ambassador and one of the most skilful and cunning diplomats in Europe to persuade her. When finally she agreed it was only to find her choice so unpopular from a political point of view that riots broke out all over the country. The most serious of these revolts was led by a 23-year-old Catholic, Sir Thomas Wyatt, supported by an army of 15,000. They actually reached the city before being crushed.

Shaken and angry, Mary's attitude hardened towards those she considered her enemies. Although she had accepted Lady Jane Grey as a pawn of ambitious men she now saw her as a dangerous focal point for rebellion. Dressed in black from head to foot, the pathetic 16-year-old girl was executed as a traitor.

Unrest in England had only made Mary more determined to proceed with her plans. Philip landed at Southampton in July 1554 'in a wild wind and down-pouring rain'. They were married at Winchester Cathedral having only set eyes on each other once before. Philip, a dazzling, handsome figure in white, was kept waiting for half an hour before Mary arrived, resplendent in cloth of gold. She fell deeply in love with him but he found her so unattractive that one of his friends remarked sympathetically: 'It would take God himself to drink this cup.' Philip was gallant and attentive to her in public but privately admitted the marriage was a failure and that she lacked 'all sensibility of the flesh'. Soon rumours of his amorous intrigues were all over London. During their marriage she twice declared herself pregnant and had a *Te Deum* of thanks sung in churches all over London. But it proved to be only a disease of the womb that made her swell like a pregnant woman. At this point of her life she was truly to be pitied.

But the stage was being set for the last dreadful years of her life. Ambassador Renard had been instructed by Charles V to urge Mary to be ruthless in punishing traitors and ridding herself of political enemies but he also begged her to try to restrain her religious fervour and to proceed cautiously in restoring the Catholic religion and persecuting Protestants. She turned a deaf ear to his wishes.

The victimization of Protestants began only a few months after her wedding when the statutes against heretics came into force. The Bishop of London, Edmund Bonner, who with Bishop Gardiner was the Queen's chief prosecutor, led a procession through the streets of London to celebrate the restoration of Rome's power. A tribunal was set up at Southwark to examine suspected heretics.

The first martyr of her reign, the married priest John Rogers, burned at Smithfield in February 1555, was soon followed by others. That same week Lawrence Saunders, Rector of All Hallows, Coventry, Dr Rowland Taylor of Hadleigh and Bishop Hooper of Gloucester also went to the stake. No one could understand why Mary allowed

Hooper to be burned. He had always been loyal to her in spite of their religious differences. In the course of the year most of the Protestant bishops and leading theologians who had not escaped abroad were sent to the fire. By the end of it, the toll had reached 90. They included men like Hugh Latimer, Bishop of Worcester, who with Cranmer had taken part in establishing the Protestant church, and Ridley, Bishop of London, who had supported Lady Jane Grey. The two of them were taken to Oxford, chained back to back and tied to the stake. As the flames rose Latimer cried out the immortal words: 'Play the man, Master Ridley. We shall this day light such a candle in England as by the Grace of God shall never be put out!' Latimer died quickly but poor Ridley suffered a terrible death as the fire on his side was slow-burning. After Latimer and Ridley came Archbishop Cranmer who signed six recantations on the promise of a pardon but in the end found the courage to stand by what he truly believed. He was said to have met his end with fortitude.

Most of the Protestant martyrs, however, were simple folk, more than half of them coming from London, Kent and Essex. There was a great outcry as the burnings went on for, though this method of dealing with heresy had been accepted in earlier reigns, it had never been on this scale. Mary could have stopped the terrible deaths at any time but it seemed as though mercy and pity had died in her. Her supporters claimed that she was encouraged by her Spanish husband but in fact he argued moderation because he knew these Inquisition-like executions would not be accepted by the English temperament.

Philip, though considerate and courteous, had become increasingly disenchanted with his wife and secretly appalled at what was happening in England. Mary looked old for her age. Though not yet 40 her complexion was heavily wrinkled, her mouth thin and tight. She was very short-sighted and would sometimes stare at people for a long time in a way that frightened them. Her court had become increasingly sombre as though in perpetual mourning and though her own clothes were rich and her jewels rare she took no pleasure in them. She never slept for more than three or four hours a night, went to Mass nine times a day and worked hard on her state papers. But she was still in love with her husband and, when Philip announced he had to leave England for a time to deal with his territories abroad, Mary wept bitterly.

With Philip gone, her barren condition known to everyone, Mary turned with wrath on her heretics. She introduced a new and terrible element into the persecutions. Heretics would no longer be given an opportunity to recant before they died. Many people, though not prepared to be martyrs themselves, began to regard those who went to the stake as saints. They would touch them as they went to their deaths and ask for a blessing. This made Mary so angry she declared that anyone showing compassion for a heretic at the stake was to be arrested. A man in Norwich who protested against the agony he saw was flogged through the streets.

To Mary's great joy Philip returned to England in March 1557, but it was not for love of her. His reason was political. During the three months of his stay he persuaded her, against the advice of her ministers, to join him in declaring war on France. Mary never forgave herself for allowing herself to be drawn into this war. Through it she lost Calais, which had been part of England for more than 200 years.

In the spring of 1558 Mary became seriously ill. She seems to have suffered from dropsy and, some say, a malignant growth of the womb. Certainly she was in a desperate way and also suffering from melancholia. Most of the time she spent weeping for Philip, for Calais and for her cause. It was becoming increasingly obvious that her policy of suppressing heresy had not been successful.

Secret prayer meetings were being held everywhere, forbidden books circulated and more and more vocal demonstrations held in support of the martyrs. When seven people were burned at Smithfield in the summer of that year a large crowd cheered and sang hymns.

Mary raved about all that was reported to her but, as the year turned to winter and its darkest days, she began to sink rapidly. On 10 November she signed the order for five heretics to be burned at Canterbury. They were to be the last victims of her reign. Three days later, though she knew herself to be near to death, she found the strength to sign the death warrant of two more London Protestants. They were the luckiest men in England. There was no time to carry out the order. Mary died at 4am on 17 November. At daybreak the two men were set free and sent home to their wives.

Elizabeth began her glorious reign by giving Mary a Catholic funeral of great splendour, but the Catholic cause in England did not recover from her fanatical cruelty for centuries to come.

Elizabeth Bathory

The Countess Elizabeth Bathory who lived in the Carpathian mountains in the 16th century was one of the original vampires who inspired Bram Stoker's legend of Dracula.

She was Hungarian by birth. Records give her entry into the world as 1561. As a girl she was beautiful with long fair hair and an exquisite complexion. She was married off to an aristocratic soldier when she was 15 and became mistress of the Castle of Csejthe in the Carpathians.

Life in the dark, gloomy Csejthe Castle, while her husband was away on his various military campaigns, became very boring indeed. She was determined to liven things up.

First she gathered round her a sinister band of witches, sorcerers and alchemists who taught her the black arts. Then, armed with her special flesh-tearing silver pincers, a manual of tortures her husband had used when fighting the Turks and a taste for flagellation learned from her aunt, she set out to indulge herself and while away the lonely hours.

When her husband died in 1604 she had reached the difficult age of 43. She longed for a new lover to replace him but her reflection in the mirror showed her that time and indulgence had not improved her looks. One day she slapped the face of a servant girl and drew blood with her nails. She was convinced that that part of her body where the girl's blood had dripped was much fresher and younger than before. It only needed the alchemists to add their opinion and she was convinced that drinking and bathing in the blood of young virgins would preserve her beauty for ever.

So, at the dead of night, the Countess and her cronies would tear about the countryside hunting for girls. They would be taken back to the castle, hung in chains and their blood used for the Countess's bath, the finest saved for her to drink.

The terrible woman carried on like this for five years until she began to realize the blood of peasant girls had not been terribly effective. In 1609 she turned to the daughters of her own class. Offering to take in 25 girls at a time to teach them social graces, she soon had a flourishing academy.

Helped as usual by her peasant procuress, Dorotta Szentes, known as Dorka, she treated the 'pupils' with the same inhuman cruelty as she had treated the others. But this time she became too careless. The bodies of four girls were thrown over the castle walls. Before she realized her mistake villagers collected them and took them away to be identified. Her secret was out.

News of her reign of terror finally reached the ears of the Hungarian Emperor, Matthias II. He ordered that the Countess be brought to trial. But as an aristocrat she could not be arrested, so parliament passed a new act so that she would not be able to slip through their hands. At her hearing in 1610 it was said she had murdered 600 girls.

Dorka and her witches were burned at the stake. The Countess escaped execution because of her noble birth. But she was condemned to a living death – walled up in a tiny room of her castle and kept alive by scraps of food pushed through the bars. She died four years later without a word of remorse.

Lady Caroline Lamb

After Lady Caroline Lamb met Lord Byron for the first time she summed him up in her diary as 'mad, bad and dangerous to know'. Looking into the poet's handsome face she felt faint and had to turn away.

Nine months later it was he who was tempted to say the same thing about her for she had driven him frantic with her obsession for him. 'Let me be quiet. Leave me alone,' he wailed in most uncharacteristic tones for such an infamous womanizer.

A dainty, delicate sprite with fair curls clinging to her head she was in many ways an altogether delightful creature when she wasn't tearing everyone's nerves to shreds – including her own.

She was the daughter of Lord and Lady Bessborough and at a very early age showed a vivid, volatile nature, high-spirited and fearless. But she also had a tendency to become nervous and over-excited, which perhaps should have warned of things to come. She was a Ponsonby and one caustic observer at the time wrote: 'The Ponsonbys are always making sensations.'

In 1805, looking prettier than anybody had ever seen her, she married William Lamb, Lord Melbourne's second son, who was extremely rich, and settled down to be a worthy wife. She tried very hard to please her husband, though it as soon obvious that they were basically incompatible. He was anchored to the earth while she was up in the clouds. The birth of a son, named Augustus, delighted her but he was a poor sick child from the start and, though she proved to be a devoted mother, he had to be taken away to be nursed.

Living out in the country, at Brocket Hall, the Hertfordshire house she dearly loved, time hung heavy on her hands. She really had nothing to do. Reading and writing letters did not get rid of her extraordinary nervous energy. Her husband, William, was a splendid man but somewhat lethargic. She tried to cure her own boredom and rouse him by flirting with other men. When her mother-in-law, Lady Melbourne, heard she had been seen with Sir Godfrey Webster, an experienced rake, and that he had given her presents, she wrote to tell her that her behaviour was 'disgusting'. After a while Caroline's riotous carrying-on did become a source of some concern to the rest of her family. She admitted on one occasion: 'I behaved a little wild, riding over the downs with all the officers at my heels.'

But it was not until she was nearly 30, in 1814, that she read Byron's great poem *Childe Harold* and declared she had to meet him. She was told he had a club foot and bit his nails. She answered: 'If he is as ugly as Aesop, I must see him.'

She first set eyes on him in an admiring circle of women at Lady Jersey's ball. The impact of his physical beauty was so unexpected she had to turn away. She refused to be introduced to him at that point, but went home to write the famous words in her diary. She also wrote: 'That beautiful, pale face will be my fate.'

One day, out riding, she paid an impromptu call on Lord and Lady Holland at Holland House. She was told that Lord Byron was expected. Hot, dusty and dishevelled she protested she could not be presented to him in that state. She ran upstairs to wash and as she came down again Byron watched with mounting interest the entrancing little figure in riding habit, eyes sparkling and gold curls tumbled from the exercise.

'I must present Lord Byron to you,' said Lady Holland.

Bending towards Caroline he whispered: 'The offer was made to you before. Why did you resist it?'

She could certainly resist him no longer. He begged permission to call next day, then again after that. Once he brought her a rose and a carnation with the sardonic comment: 'Your Ladyship, I am told, likes all that is new and rare – for a moment.' Perhaps it would have been better for him if the attraction had been fleeting.

For the next few months she was at his side all the time, everywhere. She was obviously in the throes of a passion she could not and did not care to hide. People began to ask them to parties together as if they were man and wife, but that was a result of her behaviour. Byron was always a little aloof. The Duchess of Devonshire commented tartly: 'She is, as usual, doing all sorts of imprudent things for him and with him . . .'

She kept her wildness in check because she knew he preferred tranquil women. But she poured out her admiration in letters: 'How very pale you are . . . a statue of white marble. I never see you without wishing to cry.' Her cousin reported wryly: 'Lord Byron is still on his pedestal and Caroline doing homage.'

By September of that year Byron was longing to be rid of her. He felt suffocated, worn out by her clinging, obsessive attention. He was tired of being made conspicuous, weary of restless vivacity and endless chatter. She refused to let him go.

First she bombarded him with letters, in one of them assuring him that if he was in need of money all her jewels were at his service. If she met him at a party, purely by accident, she would always make sure she returned from it in his carriage and accompanied by him. This made him irritated. But even worse was her habit of waiting in the street for him if he was attending a party to which she had not been invited. One night as he left Devonshire House after a particularly grand reception she was seen to run after his carriage and stop it from leaving, her body half in and half out.

Byron still wrote to her, trying to assure her of his affection, for he was not an unkind man. But she knew now that he was trying to get away from her and all the wildness that had been kept in control for his sake broke loose.

She began to watch him endlessly, to find out where he was going, who he was going to see. She arranged for someone to spy on him at his lodgings and report back to her in detail. One day she disguised herself as a tradesman – she always looked convincingly like a young man in masculine dress – and called round at his house at 9pm. Byron's valet, who did not see through this disguise, let her in to speak with him. She let her cloak fall, then threw herself at his feet. He had a very difficult time persuading her to go home.

The climax of the whole affair came when Caroline ran away. She left a house in chaos behind her and her mother, Lady Bessborough, so ill with worry she nearly had a stroke. Lord Byron found her and brought her back. She threatened that if he ever as much as stirred from London she would do it again. It seems she had heard rumours that he was planning to return to Greece.

Lady Bessborough's pitiful condition, brought on by

her daughter's behaviour, was the main topic of talk among her servants. Caroline received a letter from Mrs Peterson, the housekeeper, in which she called her 'cruel and unnatural' to upset her mother so. 'Shame on you,' wrote the old servant. 'You have exposed yourself to all London.' And indeed she had. People did nothing but talk about Caro Lamb and Lord Byron.

Caroline's husband was persuaded to take her for a holiday to Ireland for the sake of her health and to give everybody a bit of peace. She was pale, thin, nervous and her eyes strangely dilated. She had driven herself to the edge of madness. Even from Ireland she wrote telling him of her 'lonely, lovelorn condition'. He answered: 'Amuse yourself. But leave me quiet.'

Lord Byron now made it clear to everyone that if she persisted he would leave England. 'I shall enter into no explanations, write no epistles, nor will I meet her if it can be avoided and certainly *never* but in society.' He went to stay with Lady Oxford, but kept his whereabouts secret from Caroline. She began to suspect the truth and wrote to everyone in an attempt to find out. She did not hear from him for weeks and one day threatened to cut her throat. Lady Bessborough, the best of mothers, grasped the blade as she flourished it in the air and defied her to pull it through her hand.

There was another flurry of scandal when Caroline forged Byron's signature perfectly in order to get hold of a picture of him she desperately wanted. But worse was to come. The two of them met at Lady Heathcote's ball. They exchanged a few barbed pleasantries about Caroline dancing the waltz, then moved in to supper. Precisely what happened next goes according to whether you read Caroline's version or Byron's, but there was suddenly a knife in Caroline's hand and blood on her dress. There was some excuse about scratching herself with a piece of glass, but nobody believed it. Whether she intended just to maim herself or use it on Byron will never be known. People crowded round, took it away from her, then went on with the dancing.

Despite all that had been said Byron agreed to see Caroline once more before he left England for good. She went to his rooms in the Albany. 'Poor Caro,' he said, 'if everyone hates me, you, I see, will never change – not even with ill usage.' She answered him calmly. 'Yes, I am changed and will come near you no more.'

William Lamb, having decided to stay with Caroline, against the advice of his family, began to think how he could repair her reputation and re-establish her in society.

Unfortunately Caroline felt the urge to write. She began a novel which she called 'Glenarvan', and, as though in an attempt to purge herself, finished it at breakneck speed in a fortnight and delivered it to the publishers. Its central character was obviously Byron, but in her indictment of a false society she also clearly outlined the figures of her husband, mother-in-law and dozens of famous people she knew. The book was a best-seller. People read it avidly, identifying themselves and their friends sometimes with shock and horror at what she had revealed.

This, coming after the Byron affair, nearly ruined her.

There was never anything in her life to compare with Byron. She never really recovered from her love for him. The night before he died she dreamed of him for the first time since they parted and jumped out of bed screaming.

By some stroke of fate they were to meet once more. She had been ill. On the day of her first outing her carriage was held up by a funeral cortège. It was Lord Byron's.

Unity Mitford

She would sit at Hitler's feet while he gently stroked her hair. At night before she went to sleep in a bedroom hung with swastikas, she would pray before his photograph. She thought he was the saviour of mankind, the Messiah.

For a time not even Eva Braun came as close to the Führer as Unity Mitford, the blonde English aristocrat who looked so like the embodiment of splendid Aryan womanhood that he admired, and who was one of his most devoted and fanatical admirers.

As far as she was concerned Adolf Hitler could do no wrong. Even his solution to the Jewish problem was perfectly acceptable. 'They're Jews,' she would say contemptuously, 'just Jews, and they must be got rid of.' For him there was fascination in the very fact that an upper-crust English girl could so embrace the Nazi creed. He treated her with the utmost courtesy and at times, in company, referred to her as Lady Mitford.

Lord and Lady Redesdale, her parents, both eccentric and nostalgically Edwardian, had produced an astonishing crop of daughters. The Mitford girls were to become famous everywhere. But Unity was the one who took some swallowing and in the end spoiled her parents' lives.

Fate gave some strong signs of her future, right from the beginning. Her grandfather was a friend of the German composer Wagner. When she was born on 8 August 1914 she was given the names Unity Valkyrie, the second being that of Wotan's maiden and Wagner's great opera. She always preferred to spell it 'Walküre' in the original German form. Then Lord Redesdale bought a gold mine near Culver Park in Canada, where the family went prospecting for fun but found no fortune. It was called the Swastika Mine.

Compared with their past wealth, the Redesdales were

beginning to feel the pinch. Lord Redesdale, a roaring bull of a man who could not understand anyone not like himself, such as Jews, Catholics or foreigners, made some unwise investments which dipped the family fortunes still lower. However, by the time Unity reached an impressionable age in 1926 they still had a town house at 26 Rutland Gate in London, a vast place with a ballroom and five floors of bedrooms, and a house on the family estate at Swinbrook in the Cotswolds, which Lord Redesdale had designed with a cottage atmosphere in mind, but which turned out to be more like a barracks.

As Rutland Gate was usually 'let out' they led a country life at Swinbrook, each of the Mitford girls having the freedom to develop her own strikingly different character. Unity, a big, ungainly girl with fair hair chopped off in a hard fringe above baleful blue eyes, intimidated all the governesses. She could unnerve her father too. She would sit at the dinner table staring at him while he chewed mouthfuls of mashed potato, until he flew into a rage. Her mother, called Muv, sailed through it all, quietly getting on with her embroidery and good works.

By the time she was 15, Unity became bored with Swinbrook and was sent off to St Margaret's boarding school at Bushey in Hertfordshire. She was expelled a year later. When she was old enough she did the round of debutante balls and dances, dressed in the required chiffon or satin, but very soon the only garment she was to be interested in was the black shirt of the Fascists.

She had become very close to her sister, Diana, in spite of the four-year age gap between them. Diana, the older of the two, was deeply influenced by Oswald Mosley, leader of the British Fascist movement, a dramatic-looking man with black hair and an intense white face. After Mosley had been to Rome in 1932 for an audience with Mussolini, he came back determined to copy the European Fascists and soon his supporters were wearing black shirts on the streets of London. Diana decided to throw in her lot with him. Unity, impressed and excited, swallowed the Fascist bait whole.

When Mosley visited Swinbrook to see Diana on 14 June 1933, he gave Unity the emblem from his own lapel together with a Fascist salute, which she returned. She could hardly wait to sign the pledge. Proudly wearing Mosley's emblem on her coat, she strode into party headquarters in Lower Grosvenor Place, London, five days later to tell them she wanted to join. She was given a frosty reception. They had had enough of frivolous society girls, attracted by the uniform. She had made a mistake. Next time her approach was more respectful. She drove from Swinbrook into Oxford to the local branch of the British Union of Fascists where she was eyed sceptically by a roomful of black shirts. She told them she knew Mosley personally and had read his book. Vincent Keens, a 30-year-old Canadian, who was the Oxford leader, listened to her for a while and was amazed. This was the genuine upper-crust article all right. And she was serious. He handed her the membership card and she was sworn in.

People began to duck out of the way when they saw her coming. She wore the swastika, signed herself with the swastika and talked continually about Hitler. Worst of all was her increasing fanaticism about the Jews. One day, out shopping with a friend, she suggested popping into Selfridge's to make a record of their own voices, just for fun. The friend made her contribution to the disc then was appalled to hear Unity chanting 'The Yids, the Yids, we've got to get rid of the Yids' – the standard cry of the black shirts as they marched through the streets of London.

She enrolled at London County Council's School of Art in the spring of 1933 but only stayed long enough to be able to call herself an art student. Far more momentous things were happening.

In August that year the Nazis staged their first Nuremberg Rally, a colossal, frightening expression of power in which 400,000 party members, including members of the dreaded SS and Hitler Youth saluted their leader. Unity was chosen as one of the BUF representatives to go to Nuremberg. She gloried in every minute of it. For the first time she saw Hitler, and heard his voice. 'From that moment I knew there was no one else in the world I would rather meet,' she said. The official Nazi brochure published after the rally has a photograph of Unity in a tweed suit with a black shirt, her black-gloved hand held up in salute – the only woman in the British delegation.

Some time in the spring of 1934 she told her parents that she would like to live most of the time in Germany. They sent her to a finishing school run by a Baroness Laroche, a haunt for upper-class English girls in Munich before the war, where they were taught the German language, printing, painting, piano, singing and how to look the other way to avoid endangering their own lives. In other words if they saw a scuffle and suspected it was a Jew being beaten or harassed, they should avert their eyes and hurry by. Unity was heard to say: 'Jolly good. Serves them right. We should go and cheer.'

Baroness Laroche began to feel that Miss Mitford was an alarming pupil. The school was not very big and she seemed to fill it with her overpowering fervour for the Nazis and their leader. She was constantly singing the *Horst Wessel Lied* and other Nazi songs, had portraits of Hitler on her bedroom wall and would sometimes bring SS men back to the house, much to the Baroness's horror. Wearing her black shirt and black-leather gauntlet gloves, Unity took part in torchlight processions and attended every ceremony and reception where she knew Hitler would make his appearance.

She was determined to meet him, but had no intention of joining the thousands of women who threw themselves at Hitler's feet, who moaned and fainted and sometimes even swallowed the gravel upon which he had walked. She had a better way.

Hitler's favourite restaurant was the Osteria Bavaria in Munich. He went there often, with two or three others, quite informally dressed in a raincoat holding his favourite Alsatian dog with one hand and a whip with the other. Unity took the same table every day and waited to see him arrive. At last he became curious about the attractive blonde who seemed to turn up everywhere and one day sent an aide to her table asking if she would join him for lunch.

It was the beginning of their remarkable relationship.

David Pryce Jones, who went to see Albert Speer, Hitler's Minister of Armaments, when he was writing his biography of Unity Mitford quotes him as saying: 'She was highly in love with him, we could see it easily. Her face brightened up, her eyes gleaming, staring at Hitler . . . and possibly Hitler liked to be admired by this young woman, she was quite attractive – even if nothing happened he was excited by the possibility of a love affair with her.'

But Unity Mitford herself described Hitler as a celibate man and it is not considered likely that she ever became his mistress. Her attraction, for him, was something quite different. To start with, she was an aristocrat and educated to be a lady. She addressed him adoringly as Mein Führer and talked to him about art, literature, music, dogs, travel, in a lively and interesting way. He enjoyed her company.

Before long she was seen in his entourage on every big occasion and she was invited to join him on many informal outings at which he was always an exemplary host. He seemed to be very fond of asking people for tea. She would receive a call instructing her to be at the Chancellory by 4pm and would find he had bought mountains of cream buns which she was expected to eat, though he only nibbled a dry cracker. She was never alone with him, however. There would always be others present.

Lord and Lady Redesdale, bewildered by what was happening, went out to Munich in the winter of 1934–5 to find their daughter had turned into a fully fledged Nazi maiden. She introduced them to Hitler. Later she tried to draw them even more into her German life and succeeded to a certain extent, though they never got over the tragedy which her life was leading up to.

Some of those close to Hitler felt that her constant presence was a nuisance. Obviously convinced she was not an agent, he would talk about party politics and far-reaching policy while she was there. Goebbels, the womanizer, liked her but thought that her intensity did more harm than good to the cause. Unity became close friends with Goebbels's wife, Magda, and would sometimes stay with the family for weekends. If there was a big party at the Chancellory in Berlin, Hitler would ask Frau Goebbels to invite Unity to stay the night.

Her own favourite among the Nazis was Julius Streicher, the Jew Baiter and torturer. It was to hear him that she attended one of those Nazi get-togethers that turned out to be so sinister. They were all gathered in the pretty, rolling countryside at Hesselberg for a weekend of bread and circuses. Plump party members in Lederhosen and swastika armbands swilled down gallons of beer and fair-haired Nazi maidens twined flowers in their hair. Streicher spoke to them at 10pm, his voice ringing out in the darkness, telling them to be revenged on the Jews 'who after the last war had tried to make an end to the German race'.

'The English are ready for peace,' he yelled, 'it is the Jew who does not want peace.' Unity, blue eyes shining, fair hair drawn back from her face, was called by him to the microphone and she affirmed her solidarity with the German people and with the struggle of Julius Streicher.

After that people began to be very wary of her. It was not safe, they realized, to criticize anyone in her hearing.

People had been known to be arrested 48 hours after being in her company. Once she boasted that it was such fun to have supper with Streicher as he'd have the Jews in after a meal and make them eat grass to amuse his guests. She was obviously setting out to shock people, especially the English women still left in Berlin and Munich, for they loathed her.

Hitler invited both Unity and her sister, Diana, who had just married Mosley secretly in Germany, to attend the 1936 Olympic games. These games, planned on a Roman scale, were intended to show the world that the Nazi party had reached its zenith. Hitler, a solitary figure in an aura of blue white light projected by 180 searchlights, had never seemed as hypnotic to the awestruck Unity. But Hitler had played a trick on her that took the glory out of the proceedings. He had given her a ticket in the reserved stand next to Eva Braun. The two women, deeply jealous of each other, did not bother to hide their mutual dislike. Eva Braun had been known to say of Unity: 'She is known as the Walküre and looks the part, including her legs. I know these are the dimensions he prefers but . . . !'

She was home for Christmas 1936 and for the final spasm of the abdication crisis. She went to the House of Lords to hear the abdication speech read and commented: 'Hitler will be terribly unhappy about it. He wanted Edward to stay as King.'

Back in Germany she was happy to be able to sit at Hitler's feet while he talked. They used to flip through the pages of *The Tatler* together and mark the names of those people who might come over to them when he occupied England. He showed an unusually light side of his nature by imitating Mussolini and Göring and other top Nazis. Sometimes he even imitated himself – and Neville Chamberlain, then British Prime Minister.

Some of the German hierarchy began to question just what Unity Mitford wanted. Did she have an assignment from the Secret Service? Was she an agent? In the end they used a word for her which implied she was a fellow traveller. Ribbentrop disliked her, as did Rudolf Hess, who was jealous as well as suspicious.

Wild stories began to circulate about Hitler asking her to marry him. Unity was angry because she knew it was out of the question and she was afraid that he might think the rumours had been inspired by her. Lord Redesdale did what he could to put an end to it. A statement by him appeared in the *Sunday Pictorial*: 'There is not, nor has there ever been, any question of an engagement between my daughter and Herr Hitler. The Führer lives only for his country and has no time for marriage.'

Home for another visit she was given a roasting by the Press and had a taste of British feeling which shook her more than she liked to admit. With a small group of BUF members she attended a Labour Party rally in Hyde Park protesting at non-intervention in the Spanish Civil War. They stationed themselves beside Sir Stafford Cripps, hoisted the swastika banner and gave the Fascist salute. She had not said anything but someone recognized her. Her badge was ripped off and thrown away and she was surrounded by a crowd of men and women who threatened to chuck her in the Serpentine. Three police officers arrived to escort her away but she kicked and some people tried to follow her onto a bus.

She felt it was time for her to go back to Germany and stay there. But the sands were running out and things would never be the same again. Hitler's march into Austria in the spring of 1938 and the signing of the Anschluss thrilled Unity. He had given her an invitation to join him in the victory celebrations at the Imperial Hotel in Vienna. But to her great disappointment she only saw him for a few minutes.

By the end of May Hitler was in a rage with Czechoslovakia and threatening to crush the state that had dared to partially mobilize its army because of his sinister troop movements. Unity set off for Prague and stayed at the Esplanade Hotel. She wore the swastika provocatively and was asked by the Czech Government to leave as these were sensitive times. But she set off instead for Carlsbad and was arrested en route. When a representative of the British Legation arrived to help he was told bluntly that she was a Nazi and had been warned at several road blocks not to drive through. She was asking for trouble, and had got it. In her luggage they found a Nazi dagger and a portrait of Hitler. She promised to leave immediately. On her return she told how she had been 'revoltingly molested' in Prague.

By the summer of 1938 Unity found it was not possible to see Hitler in the old informal way. She had to wait for an invitation and would then be conducted to his table by an aide. He was always pleased to see her and greeted her, even when surrounded by his top men, with great affability. When she attended the Nuremberg rally in September, taking her parents who had been converted by her, she found Hitler grave and preoccupied.

For the next 12 months, while Europe slid from peace to war, she divided her time between Germany and England. The Führer had offered her a flat from a number that were to become empty in the Agnesstrasse. She went along to find they were owned by Jews who had been warned to remove their belongings and whose tragic fate was only too obvious. Behaving as though they were faceless, without identity, not even there, she went about brightly making her selection. She had been thoroughly indoctrinated by the Nazi creed.

When her flat was finished it was very colourful, very chic, with deep-pile carpets. The whole thing was a present from Hitler. Behind her bed hung two great swastika flags, their ends draped over the pillows, and by her bedside the inevitable photograph of the Führer. In her sitting room was a writing table, one drawer of which contained a revolver. 'When I'm obliged to quit Germany,' she told a friend, 'I'll kill myself.'

She never thought England would stand firm. She began listening to all the news bulletins and heard Lord Halifax, the Foreign Secretary, pledging support for Poland should Hitler invade, in accordance with the repeated pledge to do so.

Distraught, she went to the British Consul for news. He told her that all British nationals were leaving and he advised her to go home too. 'I don't contemplate it,' she answered. 'Then,' answered the Consul, 'you no longer have the protection of Great Britain.' Always determined to have the last word Unity flung back: 'I have the much better protection of the Führer.'

By 29 August she was listening to every news bulletin on her radio. She could not believe what was happening. The thought of a war between Germany and Great Britain was more than she could stand.

On the morning of 3 September when war was declared she locked her flat, got into her car and drove to the Ministry of the Interior. She handed in a heavy envelope which was found to contain all her badges and emblems and a farewell letter to Hitler.

A few hours later the police discovered a young fair-haired woman slumped on a seat in the English Garden. She had shot herself in the temple, but was still alive.

It was some hours before she was recognized as Unity Mitford by doctors in the Munich clinic to which she had been taken. Hitler was informed immediately. He instructed the clinic to do all they could to save her. He would pay for everything.

At first her case seemed hopeless. The bullet had lodged in her head and any operation to remove it would probably cause brain damage. After long consultations it was decided to leave the bullet where it was. At first she could not speak properly, then refused to admit she had shot herself. 'I had such a terrible fall,' she would say.

Hitler went to visit her at the clinic on 8 November, taking sheaves of flowers. It was the last time she was to see him. He was deeply shaken by the change in her and when she told him she would like to go back to England he made no objection. He not only set the wheels in motion for her return but also gave instructions that her parents were to be allowed into the country to fetch her.

Her arrival home was a nine-day wonder. Too many other things were happening. There was some talk about why wasn't she interned as a traitor but Herbert Morrison, the Home Secretary, said that in her present condition she was no threat to security.

The old Valkyrie was no more. Unity Mitford was now a quiet, slightly odd young woman with a bit of an obsession for kind clergymen. She went to church regularly but became increasingly lonely in spite of the efforts of her family. Her parents had parted, so after the war Lady Redesdale decided to take her daughter to live on the tranquil island of Inchkenneth off the coast of Mull. She had a good life there until the old wound began to make itself felt. Though outwardly fit she began to need special nursing. On 28 May 1948 she became very ill and was taken by boat to the little West Highland Cottage Hospital in Oban. She was past help and died from meningitis caused by a cerebral abscess brought on by the festering bullet. Such a quiet end for one of Wotan's maidens.

The Theosophists

In 1859 Charles Darwin published *On the Origin of Species* and thus drove an apparently immovable wedge between science and religion. The Theosophical Society sought to breach that rift, and by the end of the 19th century it had become enormously influential.

The word 'theosophy' comes from the Greek words *theos* – 'God' – and *sophia* – 'knowledge'. The Theosophical Society, which was founded in New York in 1875, aimed to create a universal brotherhood of humankind – regardless of race, religion or class – in order to study ancient religions, philosophies and science and thereby liberate the psychic powers that it maintained were latent in humans. It reclaimed the concept of evolution from what it saw as the brutal materialism of Darwinism, by insisting that humankind was evolving towards a more spiritual existence and individuals towards a higher state through reincarnation. There were already masters, Theosophists said, who held the secret knowledge, but who held themselves back from the bliss of merging into the universal oneness in order to show others the way.

The driving force behind the Theosophical Society was Helena Petrovna Blavatsky, known the world over as Madame Blavatsky, but to her friends and intimates as HPB. She undoubtedly led a remarkable life, but exactly how remarkable we shall never know. Like many of her circle who claimed to possess the universal truth, she seemed incapable of telling the truth in the ordinary sense, so her life story probably represents a heady cocktail of fact and fiction.

It seems that she was born in the Ukraine in 1831. Her father was an army officer, her mother a romantic novelist. From an early age she claimed that she could make furniture move and objects fly about by touching them only with her invisible 'astral arms'. At 17 she was married off to the 40-year-old Nikifor Blavatsky, a Tsarist general and provincial governor. She said that the marriage was never consummated, and after three months she left her husband and made her way to Constantinople (Istanbul). The couple never divorced and she kept his name for the rest of her life.

From Turkey, she set off on her travels. It is not quite clear where she went. She simply referred to this period, from 1848 to 1858, as her 'veiled time'. On various occasions she claimed to have visited the Orient, most of Asia, India, Africa, Europe, the United States and Canada, as well as Central and South America. During these trips she allegedly whirled with the dervishes, learnt magic in Japan's mountain-worshipping Yamabushi sector, traversed the Rockies in a covered wagon, discovered the mysteries of the Mayan ruins on the Yucatán, was initiated into Voodoo, became a Druze, slept in the Great Pyramid of Cheops and became an independently wealthy woman by trading in Sudanese ostrich feathers. Or so she said.

Apart from all of that she also found the time to spend seven years in Tibet, living in a remote valley in the Himalayas with a group of mahatmas, or masters, who revealed to her the secrets that later became the basis of Theosophy. Yet Tibet had been closed to foreigners since 1792 and there is absolutely no evidence that she went there. She certainly went to Egypt, however, where she began smoking hashish. She took a course in snake-charming and consulted a Coptic magician, whom she later dismissed as a charlatan. After that she travelled around Europe with a Hungarian opera singer, who claimed to have married her. There were several other putative husbands, although she claimed to her dying day that she was a virgin. Yet a child lived with her for a time: Yuri, a hunchback who died in late childhood. The child was adopted, she said.

She briefly managed a factory producing artificial flowers in Tiflis, but the main thrust of her career was in spiritualism, which she practised in Russia. In England, she was the assistant to the celebrated medium Daniel Dunglas Home.

Back in Cairo, in 1871, she formed the Société Spirité. Its occult teachings, she said, came from an Egyptian order called the Brotherhood of Luxor, which was so ancient and exclusive that no one had ever heard of it. The Société was a failure, so she made her living as a medium until she was exposed as a fraud and fled back to Europe.

In Paris in 1873, she received a message from the spirit world telling her to go to the United States and complied. At a séance in Vermont she met the Civil War veteran, lawyer and newspaperman Henry Steel Olcott, who was covering the event. He was impressed by her large size and her massive, Mongoloid face. She was wearing the scarlet shirt that had been popularized by the followers of Garibaldi and had short, crinkly, blonde hair, which, he said, put him in mind of the fleece of a Cotswold ewe.

They hit it off immediately. Though not as widely travelled as HPB, Olcott fancied himself as a cosmopolitan and a free-thinker. Olcott dropped what remained of his journalistic scepticism when, back in New York, he received a letter written in gold ink on green paper. It said: 'Sister Helen will lead thee to the Golden Gate of truth.' It was signed by the grand master of the Brotherhood of Luxor.

Within a year Olcott and Blavatsky were living together in an apartment in Manhattan. He did the cooking and the housekeeping while she ran a salon for those who were interested in the occult and the esoteric arts. He was much impressed by her ability to conjure things out of thin air – though the lights had to be dimmed while she did so – and by the way in which she summoned him by ringing an invisible bell. Olcott suggested that they form an organization to investigate all things mystical. They toyed with a number of names, eventually coming up with the 'Theosophical Society'.

They appear to have picked their moment well. For two centuries rationalism had seemed to have been on the advance and now Darwin had dealt God, the creator, a possibly fatal blow. But scientific materialism offered people nothing beyond the grave and it was this vacuum that the Theosophical Society and its spin-offs intended to fill.

Using spirit writing, Madame Blavatsky dashed off the occult masterpiece *Isis Unveiled*. The Egyptian goddess Isis had appeared to her several times, she said, but the majority of the book was nevertheless about the masters whom she claimed to have met in Tibet. They had written it and then projected it around the world into her room in New York by using 'astral light', she explained. If this was true then the masters were plagiarists: much of the book is lifted verbatim from other texts. Despite damning reviews, the massive, two-volume, 1,300-page *Isis Unveiled* was an instant best-seller. It maintains that all human religions and philosophies originally sprang from a single, hidden source. That source was 'universal science'. Knowledge of it was held by the masters, who were using her, Madame Blavatsky, to convey the truth to humankind, she added.

The success of *Isis Unveiled* gave the Theosophical Society a great fillip. Thomas Edison and Adner Doubleday, the latter the celebrated Civil War general and supposed inventor of baseball, both joined. Lodges were opened in London and Bombay. However, Blavatsky's occult credentials soon came under attack from her former spiritual mentor, the medium Daniel Dunglas Home. Blavatsky's private life also came under scrutiny and it was rumoured that she was about to be charged with bigamy. Olcott and Blavatsky set off for India.

Although the two Theosophists had formerly poured scorn on the idea of reincarnation, once in India, where the concept was widely accepted, they took it on board, too. After all, it explained how the masters had amassed their secret knowledge: they had built it up over the course of their successive lives. Two of the masters became particularly important to Blavatsky. One was Master Morya, whom she claimed that she had met in England during the 1850s when he was already 125 years old. The other was Master Koot Hoomi, who had also spent time in Europe, where he frequented the beer halls of Munich.

Under the guidance of the mahatmas, Blavatsky began to recruit future Theosophists. One, an impressionable youth named Ramaswamier, set out after her when he thought that she was going to visit the masters. Although it was Madame Blavatsky, he believed that he saw a master on horseback. He knew that the figure was a master, he explained, because he had already seen him in an astral projection back at the Theosophical headquarters. Ramaswamier's claims were given wide circulation through Theosophical journals.

Olcott and Blavatsky then had a parting of the ways. Although he dressed like a Hindu and was bearded like a Sikh, Olcott became a Buddhist. He travelled widely, setting up numerous new lodges and recruiting thousands. But he had lost interest in the mystical side of Theosophy and instead concentrated increasingly on social reform and the idea of a universal brotherhood.

Madame Blavatsky, however, plunged deeper into the occult. She used her enormous charms to woo Alfred Percy Sinnett, the editor of the British daily newspaper in India, *The Pioneer*. Already interested in the occult, Sinnett found that letters from the masters fell from the skies whenever he visited the headquarters of the Theosophical Society. And when Madame Blavatsky went to stay at his house in Allahabad more letters mysteriously appeared on his pillow in the morning. In 1881 Sinnett wrote a book extolling both Theosophy and Madame Blavatsky, which aroused interest in England. This did not impress the paper's owners, however, who were conservative Christians, and Sinnett was sacked.

Sinnett, Blavatsky and Olcott then headed for London, leaving Blavatsky's handyman and housekeeper, Alexis and Emma Coulomb, in charge of the Theosophical Society's headquarters, which had recently moved from Bombay to Adyar, near Madras. The Coulombs soon fell out with other members of the Theosophical Society and talked freely to the staff of *Christian College Magazine*, which was run by Protestant missionaries who thought little of Blavatsky. The astral projections of the masters were nothing but turbaned dummies that were paraded on moonlit nights, the Coulombs said. And the letters from the masters that fell from the sky were, in fact, pushed through a crack in the ceiling.

Blavatsky threatened to sue her detractors, but Olcott counselled caution: a court case would put all the claims of the Theosophical Society on trial. Blavatsky never set foot in India again. Worse was to come. The recently founded Society for Psychic Research was eager to prove Madame Blavatsky's outlandish claims for Theosophy and she agreed to co-operate. But then the society sent an investigator out to India. Despite openly admitting being pro-Theosophy, the investigator found that the Coulombs' claims were true, and in a 200-page report added numerous other examples of Blavatsky's fakery – including revealing that the 'master' whom Ramaswamier had seen on horseback was, in fact, a man hired by Blavatsky to play the part. This news distressed one Indian devotee so much that he set out to Tibet to make his own investigation. Sometime later his frozen corpse was found. The resulting scandal would have sunk anyone else, but Madame Blavatsky's greatest triumph was still to come.

After a quick tour of the Continent she sat down and wrote the 1,500-page *The Secret Doctrine*. In this, the tenets of Theosophy were, at last, fully unveiled. Published in 1888, *The Secret Doctrine* purports to have been based on the world's first book, *The Stanzas of Dzyan*, which, unfortunately, scholars through the ages have failed to unearth. The heavens, it says, are full of numerous universes, each containing countless solar systems. Every solar system has its own god; beneath him are seven planetary spirits, each in charge of a phalanx of angels. Evolution takes place in steps, from mineral to vegetable to animal to human to the superhuman, or spiritual being, to come. The first inhabitants of the Earth, the book stated, were descended from the residents of the moon and lived on a continent called the Imperishable Sacred Land. Then came the Hyperborean race, also known as the Boneless or the Sweatborn. They lived at the North Pole (but since they did not have bodies they presumably did not feel the cold). Next came the Lemurians, who were the first to have bodies and reproduce by means of sexual intercourse. Their homeland, Blavatsky said, is now at the bottom of the Indian Ocean.

The fifth of these so-called 'root races' was the Aryans, who spread south and west from northern Asia. Apparently, we are still in the Aryan phase. Madame Blavatsky revealed that there will be two more root races. Then the cycle will be complete and humans will move to another planet to start all over again. Meanwhile, individual humans progress from having physical bodies, through the astral, mental and ethereal states in incarnations. Progress is regulated by karma. Obviously, those with the best karma have arrived at the highest ethereal state. These are the masters.

Even though she had been exposed as a fraud, *The Secret Doctrine* brought Madame Blavatsky many plaudits. New members flocked to the Theosophical Society and Madame Blavatsky formed an inner circle, called the Esoteric

Section, as a rival to the recently established Hermetic Order of the Golden Dawn. She established the magazine *Lucifer* and published two more books, *The Key to Theosophy* and *The Voice of Silence*, before she died in 1891. Even sceptical newspapers conceded in their obituaries that she was one of the most remarkable women of the 19th century.

Her final work, *The Theosophical Glossary*, was published posthumously. However, during her lifetime she had promised two more volumes of *The Secret Doctrine*, which would finally explain all the secrets of the occult. Some Theosophists are still waiting for them.

Madame Blavatsky had left instructions that after her death the British Annie Wood Besant, the head of the Esoteric Section, should take over as the leader of the Theosophical Society. As a teenager Besant had been obsessed with Anglo-Catholicism and at 20 had married an elderly clergyman. But she was not cut out to be the wife of a country vicar and left him after six years of marriage. She became a socialist, a free-thinker and an atheist. A friend of George Bernard Shaw, she rose rapidly through the ranks of the British Fabian Society and thc national Secular Society. As a feminist campaigner she was unsuccessfully prosecuted for selling obscene literature – in the form of a booklet on contraception – through the post.

When *The Secret Doctrine* was published she had reviewed it favourably. Madame Blavatsky had quickly recruited her and had made her head of the Esoteric Society, the occult wing of Theosophy. As the successor of Blavatsky Besant was an inspired choice: she could not be accused of fakery because she professed neither psychic nor spiritual powers. However, she had a rival for the post: William Q. Judge, one of the founder members of the Theosophical Society in New York. He headed the American Section and thought that he, rather than the parvenue Besant, should be in charge of the society. He suggested that they share power and then set sail for England to meet Besant.

When Judge turned up in London to discuss the matter Besant received a mysterious letter from the mahatmas telling her that Judge was right: he should be in charge. This was very puzzling, as Madame Blavatsky had said that the letters would stop when she died, but they nevertheless kept on coming. They looked just like the ones that had arrived during Madame Blavatsky's lifetime and were in exactly the same handwriting. Besant was so convinced by the letters that she went public and told a meeting that she had received them from an 'unseen world'. If Madame Blavatsky was a fraud who had written the letters to her then she, too, was a fraud, Besant said. This statement caused a sensation. Besant had a towering reputation and not even her worst enemy would have called her a liar. People began to believe that the Society of Psychical Research had judged Blavatsky too harshly.

Membership of the Theosophical Society accordingly rose again. A novel called *The Mahatma,* about a master, was serialized in a magazine. Mahatma hats went on sale and fashionable Londoners greeted each other by asking 'How's your karma?' Even William Gladstone, the once and future Prime Minister, was asked questions about Theosophy at a working men's club, according to *The Times*.

By 1894 Judge was trying to force Besant out of the society. Letters from the mahatmas now claimed that Besant was controlled by 'dark powers'. Besant retaliated by revealing that the letters were a fraud. Presumably Judge had got hold of the crayons and rice paper that Blavatsky had used, along with the great seal of the mahatmas, and after a little practice he had managed to forge Blavatsky's handwriting.

Judge sailed back to the United States and formed the 85 US chapters of the Theosophical Society into the Theosophical Society of America. Besant struck back with a speaking tour of the USA and managed to found 37 new lodges that were loyal to her.

The game was up in England, however. The Theosophical Society had been exposed for the second time as a fraud, so Besant headed to Adyar, where the Indian wing of the organization was still expanding. Besant became a passionate advocate of Indian independence, establishing the Indian Home Rule League and becoming the president of the Indian National Congress. The Theosophical Society in India turned itself over to humanitarian work and social reform. It established a number of schools, including the Central Hindu college, where Mahatma Gandhi and Pandit Nehru learnt much of the background of Hinduism. Although critical of Theosophy, Gandhi acknowledged that it was Besant who had brought the idea of Indian home rule to every household in the Subcontinent. She bought a newspaper with which to propound the idea of Indian independence, renaming it *New India* and making it one of the biggest-selling dailies in the country. During World War I she was even interned for her anti-British views, but was released after three months as a result of the public outcry.

Having been estranged from one Anglican priest, she then became involved with another: the Reverend Charles W. Leadbeater, who had earlier been expelled from the Theosophical Society for telling the boys in his charge that it was all right to masturbate. (Besant miraculously came up with a letter from the masters saying that Leadbeater was right.) Together they wrote a number of books which turned the Theosophical Society more towards Esoteric Christianity than the Esoteric Buddhism that was Olcott's legacy. (However, Besant did write *An Introduction to Yoga* and translated the Indian scripture the *Bhagavad-Gita* into English.)

In 1908 Leadbeater became entranced by the 14-year-old Jiddu Krishnamurti, apparently because of his remarkable aura. Leadbeater announced that Krishnamurti would become the long-awaited fifth Buddha, the living incarnation of a master and a new world teacher. The wisdom that he would deliver, Leadbeater believed, would begin a new root race as described in *The Secret Doctrine*. Besant adopted Krishnamurti and established the Order of the Star in the East as a vehicle for his mission. This caused dissent among many Theosophists, who accused Besant and Leadbeater of trying to start a new church, the antithesis of everything that Theosophy was supposed to stand for.

The head of the German chapter, Rudolf Steiner, quit Theosophy in order to start Anthroposophy. Rather than evolving towards becoming god-like beings, such as the masters, Steiner taught that human beings had once, in the dim and distant past, possessed those divine qualities and should now struggle to find them within themselves again. Through Christ, Steiner said, people could ascend to higher spiritual levels, but the two evil powers of Lucifer – through human pride – and Ahriman – through the material world – held them back. Steiner introduced a spiritual theory for what is now known as organic farming – with natural times for sowing and harvesting being prescribed and chemical fertilizers being prohibited. He also pioneered 'child-centred' education, with his Anthroposophical theories emphasizing the importance of awakening the talents that lay within the child rather than imposing learning on it.

Leadbeater was indeed trying to start a new church and in 1916 he founded the Liberal Catholic Church. For her part, Besant persisted with Krishnamurti. But as the boy grew up he began to have doubts about the destiny that Leadbeater and Besant had thrust upon him. In 1929, at a Theosophist summer camp in front of Besant and 3,000 others, he denied that he was a new incarnation of the Messiah and disbanded the Order of the Star in the East.

He became an independent teacher and lectured until his death in 1986. The Krishnamurti Foundation, based in Ojai, California, promotes his work, and his followers call themselves Liberal Theosophists.

Besant never really recovered from this setback. She withdrew to the Theosophist headquarters at Adyar, where she died in 1933. Her body was cremated Hindu-style; it was Leadbeater who lit the funeral pyre.

As well as Anthroposophy, Theosophy had further spin-offs. New Revelation Theosophy, for example, claims that it possesses new teachings from the masters. Another, the Arcane School, was established in California by Alice Bailey. An English Theosophist, Bailey moved to California in 1917, opening a vegetarian café and marrying the national secretary of the Theosophical Society, Forst Bailey. In 1919, while walking in the Hollywood Hills, she said that she had bumped into one of the Tibetan masters, Djwhal Khul, who asked her to be his secretary and began dictating books to her at a prodigious rate. The central tenet of these volumes, which otherwise resembled existing works of Theosophy, is that Christ will reappear as a new world leader and that devotees should meditate in order to prepare themselves for the event.

In 1949 another cult developed from the Arcane School; the new cult ran Full Moon Meditation groups, which meditated at every full moon. And the Astara Foundation, which was established in California in 1951 by Robert and Earlyne Chaney, has attempted to return to the early teachings of the Theosophical Society.

It is interesting to note that the influence of Theosophy can furthermore be seen in the works of a number of modern artists, including Piet Mondrian and Wassily Kandinsky.

Mary Baker Eddy

Christian Science was founded by the redoubtable Mary Baker Eddy. Born in 1821, she was a sickly child and remained ill until well into her 20s. Her first husband died of yellow fever soon after they married; her second husband introduced her to the hypnotist and faith-healer Phineas P. Quimby, who cured her of what she believed was a crippling spinal disease.

She began lecturing on his methods. Then, a month after Quimby died in 1866, she slipped on some ice and hurt herself. While she was convalescing she read the Bible and came across a passage in the Gospel of St Matthew in which Christ healed a man who was sick with the palsy. After reading this she said: 'The healing Truth dawned on my sense and the result was that I rose, dressed myself and ever after was in better health than I had before enjoyed.' She then sat down to study the Bible for more hints on health. By 1870 she had started lecturing on the subject and in 1875 published the book *Science and Health with a Key to the Scriptures*. Critics say that it borrows heavily from Quimby's work.

With the encouragement of her third husband, she established the Church of Christ, Scientist, in Boston, Massachusetts, in 1879. She also opened the Massachusetts Metaphysical College in Boston, where she ran courses for which she charged hefty fees. The church nevertheless grew quickly.

Eddy accepted no deviation from the truth as she saw it. She allowed no churches in which an individual pastor might give an independent view. Instead, she instituted Christian Science reading rooms in which her works would be read, along with the Bible, which she considered to be apocryphal. There was no Holy Communion in Christian Science because Mrs Eddy did not believe that

God had been made flesh. Members were denied the comfort of tobacco and alcohol; strict adherents even forswore tea and coffee. But Christian Scientists are more famous today for rejecting all forms of medical treatment, including blood transfusions, on the grounds that God alone will provide salvation from sickness. Disease is regarded as a mere 'error', since God intended humankind to be healthy and happy.

Christian Scientists are also required to buy the *Christian Science Monitor* every day, along with the weekly *Christian Science Sentinel*, the monthly *Christian Science Journal* and the *Christian Science Quarterly*. Not surprisingly, when she died in 1910 Mary Baker Eddy left $3 million.

Witchery

Alice Kyteler

In the dusty, mouldering pages of some 14th-century archives lies the story of a beautiful woman, rich, influential, probably of Anglo-Norman stock. She lived in the town of Kilkenny in Ireland where, it was recorded, she had been married to three wealthy husbands in succession and in the year 1324 was about to lose her fourth. Her name was Lady Alice Kyteler and she was one of the most sinister figures of her time.

Lady Alice was not popular with her neighbours partly because of her inordinate wealth, partly because of her arrogance and haughty, overbearing manner.

There were also rumours that her Ladyship was involved in the practice of witchcraft and sorcery, though no one could prove it.

Her first husband had been one William Outlawe, a banker and money-lender who died before 1302. Then she married Adam le Blund of Callan who expired by 1311 to be followed by Richard de Valle who also went to his maker rather quickly.

Two of these husbands had been widowers with children who lost their inheritance when the besotted fellows left everything to Lady Alice. If they suspected foul play, they said nothing at the time.

However, when Lady Alice's fourth and latest husband, Sir John le Poer, fell dangerously ill in 1324 with a wasting disease which made his nails fall from his fingers and toes and caused his hair to come out in handfuls, the children began to hint that their fathers had died from equally strange illnesses with similar symptoms.

Sir John, in love with his wife, did not want to hear what they were implying. But ,when one of his maidservants began to give such broad hints that it would have been foolish to ignore her, Sir John decided it was time for him to act.

He demanded his wife's key to her room. When she refused he seized her and, after a struggle, wrenched it from her belt. A search soon brought to light a number of boxes and chests, all heavily padlocked. Forcing them open the wretched man found inside all the evidence he needed to prove that his wife was a poisoner and deeply involved in witchcraft.

Sir John gathered together all the strange powders, phials and potions, the wicked-looking instruments and wafers of sacramental bread inscribed with the name of Satan, and sent them, in the safekeeping of two monks, to the Bishop of Ossory, whose diocese it was. The Bishop was to prove a formidable prosecutor.

He was an English Franciscan named Richard De Ledrede, known to be a fanatic in hunting out those who dabbled in sorcery and a man greedy for funds. Should Lady Alice be found guilty her wealth would be confiscated by the Church.

After an investigation the Bishop accused her of being involved in 'diverse kinds of witchcraft' and ordered her arrest along with 11 accomplices including her own son William Outlawe and her personal maid, Petronilla de Meath.

This Bishop's indictment contained no fewer than seven formidable charges to which the inhabitants of Kilkenny listed with fascinated horror. Lady Alice, it emerged, had crept from her home in the dead of night to hold meetings with her accomplices in local churches where religious ceremonies were mocked and appalling rites performed. Living animals were sacrificed to the devil then, torn limb from limb, scattered at the crossroads. She had been expert in making charms and ointments from such hideous ingredients as the hair of criminals who had been hanged, nails from dead men's fingers, the intestines of animals, worms, poisonous herbs and flesh of babies who had died unbaptized.

All these things she was said to have boiled together in the skull of a robber who had been beheaded.

The indictment also included 'an unholy and obscure association' between Lady Alice and a demon called Robert Artisson who was described as her familiar and who would appear sometimes in the shape of a huge cat, at other times like a shaggy beast or yet again in the disguise of a black prince with two tall companions, each carrying a rod in his hand. Lady Alice was said by her maid to have had sexual intercourse with this 'apparition'. Who was this creature?

Under the influence of witchcraft he was believed to be supernatural but in fact he was probably a fellow practitioner from another town or village. The Bishop cast his net wide to try to trap him, but he never succeeded. It was rumoured he must have been an educated man or a noble for no peasant would have had the wit or resource to have escaped Ossory's Inquisition for long.

That she had used her potions to kill her former husbands and to bring Sir John to the point of death was soon obvious. She had an insatiable greed for money. Her only true allegiance was to her favourite son, William Outlawe, who had proved a willing disciple in her diabolical craft. She used to perform a rite which was meant to make him rich. She would take a broom out into the streets of Kilkenny at sunset and raking all the dirt and dust towards the door of her son's house chant:

'To the house of William my son
Hie all the wealth of Kilkenny town!'

It was one thing for the Bishop to order Lady Alice's arrest, quite another to take her into custody. He found himself obstructed on every side. Up to this time sorcery had been a secular crime, not under the jurisdiction of the Church, so the Bishop had to ask the Lord Chancellor of

Ireland to issue a writ for the arrest of the accused.

Unfortunately, the Chancellor was one Roger Outlawe, a kinsman by her first marriage who supported her.

Taking the law into his own hands, the Bishop sent two representatives to call her in person before the court of the Bishopric. She refused to accept his jurisdiction. The ecclesiastical court, she said, was not empowered to judge her or anyone else on a matter of this kind. Nevertheless, the court sat and the Bishop excommunicated her.

Her supporters took revenge by making him a prisoner in Kilkenny Castle for 18 days and while he fretted and fumed the accused coolly indicted *him* in a secular court for defamation of character.

All this only served to stiffen the Bishop's resolve to get 'the Kyteler' in the end. Time after time he was asked to leave secular courts where he demanded her arrest. When at last, after being obstructed at every turn, permission came to bring the accused sorceress to trial in an ecclesiastical court, it was too late. The bird had flown. Helped by fellow aristocrats, the Lady Alice had gathered up her jewels and escaped to England where she lived for the rest of her days.

Her fellow witches were left to face the fire. Bishop Ossory found an ally in Lady Alice's husband, Sir John, who helped him to arrest William Outlawe. This gentleman begged to be reconciled with the Church and pardon was granted him as long as he fulfilled certain penances and paid for the re-roofing of St Mary's Cathedral in Kilkenny.

Lady Alice's maid, Petronilla de Meath, eventually brought to trial with the other accomplices, paid the greatest price. She was the first witch to be burned in Ireland. Yet, she declared, compared with Lady Alice she was a mere novice. Her mistress had taught her everything. She believed there was no more powerful witch in the world than her Ladyship, Alice Kyteler. The abandoned and unrepentant Petronilla went to the stake and was burned on 3 November 1324.

Lady Alice was tried and found guilty 'in absentia', but she remained safe as long as she stayed away from Ireland. The Kyteler case nevertheless became something of a landmark, not only because it was the first trial of its kind in Ireland.

The dusty, 14th-century records also showed that by her instruction and teaching Lady Alice Kyteler had set out the complete witch creed for centuries to come.

La Voisin

Queen of all the witches in France during the reign of the Sun King, Louis XIV, was a woman called Catherine Deshayes, better known simply as La Voisin.

Some of the most famous and dazzling women of the day, Madame de Montespan, the King's mistress, among them, were known to have sought her help through the black arts. She thought herself invincible as she dabbled in wickedness. 'Nothing is impossible to me,' she told one of the clients. 'Only another god can understand my power.'

Only when the miasma of her dark deeds threatened to touch the King himself was she brought to justice in a great purge which swept up half the witches in Paris and aired a great many scandals at high level.

La Voisin was a short, plump woman, not unattractive apart from her eyes which were piercing, like those of a bird of prey. She was said to have inherited her powers from her mother who practised as a sorceress and was so famous that even the Emperor of Austria and the King of England had asked her advice.

She lived in a neat, secluded villa in the Paris suburb of St Denis and claimed that her occupation was most innocent. 'I am a practitioner of chiromancy, a student of physiognomy,' she would boast. She was indeed an uncanny fortune-teller, skilled at crystal gazing, reading the Tarot cards, reading palms and reading faces. 'The lines on a face are far easier to read than the lines of the hand,' she would say. 'Passion and anxiety are difficult to conceal.'

She made up love potions and happiness powders and sold them in silk and taffeta pouches, prescribed herbs for unwanted pregnancies and supplied aphrodisiacs for lagging lovers or husbands. When challenged with far worse things she had the gall to say: 'I rendered an account of my arts to the Vicars General of Paris and to several doctors at the Sorbonne, to whom I had been sent for questioning, and they found nothing to criticize.' She had indeed been to the Sorbonne to discuss astrology with some of the professors and had paid a social call on the rector of the University of Paris. She even attended early Mass at her parish church.

How she must have laughed, for she was queen of the most powerful coven of witches in Paris and dedicated to evil. Only her enemy, Marie Bosse, could be compared with her. At first she had sought her clients among the common people but as her fame as a sorceress spread so did her ambition. She was brought into contact with high society and the court. Moral restraints, she found, did not matter greatly to the very rich. Men and women of great eminence would pay anything to get rid of an unwanted partner, to eliminate a rival or ensure the continuance of their power.

Poison was her speciality. She had secured the services of two women who were capable of genius when it came to making up prescriptions. They provided La Voisin with 57 different poisons from which she could improvise in hundreds of ways. By varying the fatal doses she gave to clients she was sure that the symptoms would be different. This meant that no one could establish a pattern of death and trace the poison back to her.

Curiously enough, she had made several attempts to

finish off her own husband, a bankrupt jewel merchant, as she had taken as her lover an infamous criminal character calling himself Le Sage, but each time she failed. He had an ally and protector in La Voisin's maid, Margot. The poisoned dishes were usually served up to him at the family table. Once Margot saved him by jogging his elbow just as he raised a lethal bowl of soup to his lips. Another time she gave him a counter-poison which worked well enough but left him with incurable hiccups and a bleeding nose. It was a great joke in La Voisin's circle of intimates. 'Bonjour Madame,' they would greet her. 'How is your husband? Not dead yet?'

The most shocking and repulsive aspect of what went on in the demure villa at St Denis was in the saying of Black Mass for which she provided priest, altar, vestments and sacrifice. For these ceremonies and séances she wore a dramatic vestment specially designed and woven for her which included a vast cloak of crimson velvet elaborately embroidered with the double head and wing spread of golden eagles. The same motif was stitched in pure gold thread on her slippers. She admitted at her trial that she had a furnace in the garden where she had disposed of the tiny corpses of hundreds of infants or embryos, aborted, premature, still-born and newborn, that had been used in the Black Mass. She scattered their ashes on her garden.

It was in 1679 that Louvois, the King's Minister of War, sent him a secret message saying that the woman called La Voisin had started to talk too much. She had said openly that Madame de Vivonne and Madame de la Mothe had come to her for something to do away with their husbands. Who would be talked of next? The whole court was in a stew while the King insisted that someone must get to the bottom of this poisons affair, regardless of rank, sex or position.

The name that had shocked him was that of Madame de Vivonne, sister-in-law to Madame de Montespan, who was in the intimate circle around him at court.

La Voisin, with her accomplices, was arrested with scores of others in the great purge of his capital which the King demanded. Le Sage, who had been supplanted in La Voisin's bed by a man named Latour, betrayed all her secrets. Many names were mentioned of the aristocrats involved, but La Voisin kept silent about Madame de Montespan and any services she had rendered her. It was Le Sage who blurted out her name under brutal interrogation, telling how the King's mistress had come to La Voisin for help when she thought she was losing his love. Apart from the potions given her to stimulate the King's interest, she had also taken part in the Black Mass.

The police chief, Nicolas de la Reynie, alarmed by what was emerging, reported to the King. Louis ordered that any documents mentioning Madame de Montespan should be delivered to him personally. He burned the incriminating evidence with his own hand and hardly spoke to the lady again. But the police had copies and the evidence survived.

In a last-minute attempt to save herself La Voisin protested that the only drugs to be found in her house were purgatives for the personal use of her family. As for the small furnace or oven in the garden, concealed by a tapestry, she said it was for baking her pâtés.

But when the police broke in they found what amounted to a small factory for making poisons, copies of the Luciferian Credo, a store of black candles and incense and a collection of wax figurines bristling with needles and pins.

La Voisin protested in vain. She was burned alive for her sins. Unrepentant to the last, she repelled the crucifix held in front of her as the flames climbed higher.

Scandals

Amelia Dyer

Her name was used, like that of the bogeyman, to scare young children into being good. If you don't behave, Victorian parents would say, you'll go and stay with Amelia Dyer. And everyone knew what that meant. It meant you didn't come back.

Amelia Dyer was a 'baby-farmer' who, when finally charged with her appalling crimes, was discovered to be a monster who had been quietly killing off unwanted infants for a period of about 20 years.

She was originally a Bristol woman who had been born, brought up and married in that city. Short and squat, with a well-scrubbed look, her hair dragged into a bun at the back of her head, she belonged to the Salvation Army and went out at weekends to sing hymns on draughty street corners. Her husband worked in a vinegar factory.

When the Dyers split up, in about the year 1875, she found it necessary to earn money to keep herself and her daughter, Polly. Rather than take in washing, she became the local midwife, occasionally fostering those she brought into the world. But, she discovered, far more lucrative than midwifery or casually looking after children for whom she might, or might not, get paid was the business of baby-farming. This was a practice that sprang up towards the end of the 19th century. It was considered illegal, but thrived nevertheless. Mothers with unwanted or inconvenient infants farmed them out to working-class women sometimes for a few months, sometimes for years. The women were suitably paid at the start, then left alone to get on with the job. Sometimes, the real mother never came back.

Amelia Dyer realized she could earn a reasonable living if she was clever about it. The more babies she 'farmed' the more money she would earn. Her problem would be how to accommodate them all, how to make room . . .

She started a baby farm at her cottage in the village of Long Ashton, southwest of Bristol, but eventually she was discovered and jailed for six weeks. After that she fell on bad times, was taken into the workhouse at Barton Regis and did not leave again until June 1895.

She left the workhouse with an old crone called Granny Smith and the pair of them went to live in Cardiff with Amelia's daughter, Polly, now married. It must have been a wretched household. Polly's husband, Arthur, was unemployed; they had a baby that died of convulsions, and there was no money.

Soon it became necessary to get out of the way of creditors and the police, so the entire household packed up its belongings on an old cart and took to the road. They came eventually to the village of Caversham, outside Reading, and took a cottage there in Piggott's Road.

Amelia Dyer decided to go back to her old business, using a false name. She inserted an advertisement in the local paper: 'Couple having no child would like the care of one or would adopt one. Terms £10.' She made it known by word of mouth that the house was open for boarders.

First to arrive was the ten-month-old baby daughter of a barmaid, then came a nine-year-old boy, Willie Thornton, followed by another baby and a girl of four. Amelia was also paid £10 by a woman called Eleanor Marmon, who asked her to take care of her illegitimate daughter, Doris. A baby boy, Harry Simmons, was received from a lady whose maid had given birth to him, then disappeared.

Amelia took them all into her loving care. But on 30 March 1896 bargemen working on the river Thames near Reading fished a brown paper parcel out of the water. To their horror they found it contained the body of a baby girl, strangled with tape, and a brick used to weigh her down. Then on 2 April two more parcels, this time in a carpet bag, were dragged out of the water. They contained the tiny bodies of Doris Marmon and Harry Simmons, who had also been strangled with tape.

The police made a discovery that led them straight to the murderer. On one of the pieces of brown paper they could just decipher the address 'Mrs Thomas, Piggott's Road, Lower Caversham'. Two days later, having identified Mrs Thomas as Amelia Dyer, they arrested her.

There was pandemonium when she was taken to the police station. First she tried to kill herself with a pair of scissors; then, that having failed, she tried to throttle herself with a bootlace. Both her daughter, Polly, and her son-in-law, Arthur, were also taken in.

Police continued dragging the river and found four more of Amelia Dyer's tiny victims, bringing the number to seven. She never revealed how many she had killed altogether but it was known that at the time of her arrest she was still taking payment for infants long dead. She said, without emotion: 'You'll recognize mine by the tape.'

While in prison she did try to save her daughter and son-in-law and clear them from suspicion by writing a letter to the Superintendent of Police. 'I do most solemnly swear that neither of them had anything to do with it,' she wrote. 'They never knew I contemplated doing such a wicked thing until too late.' As it happened, Polly, the daughter she loved, became chief witness for the prosecution, giving evidence against her mother both at the magistrates' hearing and later at the Old Bailey.

Amelia Dyer was charged with the murder of Doris Marmon and tried before Mr Justice Hawkins on 21 and 22 May 1896. Polly described how her mother had turned up at her home in Willesden carrying a ham and a carpet bag and holding the baby girl, Doris Marmon, whom she said she was looking after temporarily for a neighbour. It was cold and Polly sat her mother down by the fire in the kitchen while she went out to fetch more coal. When she came back, the baby had disappeared, and her mother was pushing the battered old carpet bag under the sofa. That night she insisted on sleeping on the sofa. By next morning Harold Simmons, a baby Polly was minding for her mother, had also disappeared. She was puzzled, but didn't know what to do. Later that day, the Palmers took her to Paddington station to catch the Reading train. While she went to buy some cakes to eat on the journey, her son-in-law held the carpet bag, remarking on how heavy it was. It was of course the same carpet bag she later dumped in the Thames with the two tiny strangled corpses huddled inside.

Her defence lawyer, a Mr Kapadia, accepted that she was guilty – she had in fact never denied her actions – but that she was insane. There was much argument and contention over this point, but the jury took just five minutes to find her 'guilty' but 'not insane'. For she had kept a careful list of those she fostered and an even more careful list of the money paid to her, often long after the babies were dead.

She was hanged at Newgate Prison on 10 June 1896 leaving a letter stating 'What was done I did do myself' and regretting the trouble she had brought on her daughter.

But Amelia Dyer's trial achieved something. It brought about a sharp decline in the practice of baby-farming. For who knew whether there might be another Mrs Dyer, waiting to earn an honest £10?

Frances Howard

As a family the Howards were a violent crowd, full of valour in wartime, full of passion in peace. But few of them had as little respect for human life as the bewitching Frances, one of the great beauties at the court of James I.

Their lineage was ancient and powerful, dating back to

William the Conqueror and Lord Howard of Effingham who improved their image by defeating the Armada in 1588. But throughout history they had also been famous for a record of intrigue and plotting, violent temper and greed that made all men wary of them. They had managed to stay in power and royal favour by sheer skill.

Frances was the daughter of Lord Thomas Howard, created Earl of Suffolk when James I came to the throne in 1603. He was an unscrupulous man whose career ended in disgrace when he was accused of gross embezzlement of public funds. Her mother was no less greedy. She was born and brought up at the family's country seat at Audley End, near Saffron Walden, and for a time her charm and sweet face hid her true character. It was her father's uncle, the Earl of Northampton, who detected the embryo of something evil and, with devilish cunning, began to wield a sinister influence over her.

She was married at 15 to Robert Devereux, Earl of Essex, but the young couple were separated almost at once as the King, who had taken the handsome boy under his wing, insisted that Robert return to Oxford to finish his degree, then join the army abroad.

This left Frances free to practise her powers of seduction at court as Countess of Essex, and she used them to great advantage. Her first affair was with the Prince of Wales but his attractions paled to nothing once she set eyes on the King's favourite, the darkly handsome Robert Carr, Viscount Rochester, a Scot who had come to England on the accession of James I.

Lord Northampton, aware of her passion and thinking to further his own interests, brought them together. Though Rochester was at first wary of becoming involved because of the King's affection for the absent Devereux, he soon succumbed to the advances of this most seductive woman.

He insisted their intrigue must be carried on away from the eyes of the court. But he had one disadvantage. He was not an educated man and had no skill in writing love letters. He realized he needed an accomplice, a go-between who would also write the letters for him. The man he chose was Thomas Overbury, son of Sir Nicholas Overbury of Bourton-on-the-Hill in Gloucestershire. Rochester had first met him in Edinburgh when he himself was page to the Earl of Dunbar. They became inseparable friends and travelled south together to join James's court. The arrangement was successful and for a time the lovers had no cause for alarm.

The first cloud came on their horizon with the return of Essex, who was eager to sample the joys of married life with his beautiful 18-year-old wife. At first she pretended to be timid. When he became more pressing she was frigid. Though they occupied the same bed and the same room she would not yield. She cared only for Rochester and any other man repulsed her. Desperately, the Earl asked her father 'to remind his daughter of her obedience as a wife'. But a father can do little in such circumstances. The stalemate lasted until Essex was struck down with smallpox and was too ill to bother about his wife.

This gave Frances time to scheme. She had two objects: to kill her husband's natural desire for her and to inflame Rochester's passion still further. She decided the only effective course would be through witchcraft. She was given, in utter secrecy, the address of a Mrs Anne Turner, widow of a doctor of physics in London who apparently worked hand in glove with the sinister and infamous Dr Simon Forman. At night she paid a visit to their 'surgery' and was prescribed evil-looking potions and powders which were guaranteed to be effective.

When Essex recovered his health and strength and began to act like a normal husband she started to administer her poison. After a few doses he should have been utterly debilitated, but there was no effect. However strong she made the potion, he remained lusty, hale and hearty. Sending a note to Mrs Turner, with instructions to burn it after she had read it (the instructions were never carried out) she begged frantically for a more effective remedy. She wrote the damning words 'I cannot be happy as long as this man liveth'. She had also, it emerged later, consulted a Norfolk witch called Mary Woods who swore she had received a diamond ring and a promise of £1,000 if she could produce a poison that would dispatch Essex within three or four days.

At court Rochester was now at the height of his power, and Frances watched jealously as he moved freely among the beautiful women who sought his favour. She was even more incensed as she realized that her lover was anxious not to jeopardize his favourable position by associating too openly with her. She resorted again to spells and potions and even took part in black-magic ceremonies. The repulsive Dr Forman made wax figures of Frances and Rochester in the act of love.

Whatever the reason, Rochester seemed to be drawn more and more towards her, eventually declaring he could not live without her. The lovers met whenever they could either at Mrs Turner's lodgings in Hammersmith or at a house in Hounslow which Frances had bought specially for the purpose. Their meetings were known to only one other person and that was Thomas Overbury, who had now been knighted for his loyalty, Rochester having told the King what a staunch friend he was.

Overbury did not like what was happening. He did not like Frances. He saw her as a vicious woman whose evil practices would bring down his friend. When he heard that she was determined to seek a divorce from her husband in order to marry Rochester he could hold his tongue no longer. 'If you do marry that filthy, base woman you will utterly ruin your honour and yourself; you shall never do it by my advice or consent,' he blurted out to the man he loved and admired more than any other. But

Rochester was blinded by his infatuation and the relationship between the two men was never the same.

Frances heard what had happened, heard that Overbury was talking about her openly at court, and with hatred vowed she would destroy him. The King had already shown some sympathy for her divorce. If he discovered she was not the virtuous woman he thought, he might change his mind. From that moment Overbury's death was certain.

She turned to her old mentor, Lord Northampton, for help. He was jealous of Rochester's influence as the King's favourite and was only too anxious to work against him, whatever the reason. Together they set out to poison Rochester's mind against his friend, making great capital out of their insinuation that Overbury was plotting to step into his shoes and was already being shown great favour by the King.

Poison was also poured into the royal ear so that when Overbury refused James's offer to send him as ambassador to the Low Countries, the King suspected him of ulterior motives and sent him to the Tower for 'a matter of high contempt'.

Frances was going to make sure he never came out alive. She paid an agent called Weston to work for her, and managed to get him a position in the Tower, eventually arranging for him to become personal assistant to the wretched Overbury. It would be his task to administer the poison to the prisoner's food, making sure that nothing was left on the plate as evidence.

The first attempt to poison Sir Thomas failed because Weston was caught red-handed by Sir Gervase Elwes, Lieutenant of the Tower. After some thought Elwes decided to keep silent. For all he knew Weston might be acting on instructions from the highest level and he did not want to make life difficult for himself. But he was a humane man and did not intend to let Overbury be poisoned if he could help it. He must have intercepted most of the jellies and tarts, cold meats and sauces that Frances sent in for him. They contained so much poison that had he eaten them he would have had enough in his system to kill 20 men. Frances had paid Mrs Turner and an apothecary, James Franklin, to supply her with seven different poisons. That none of them had worked seemed inexplicable, unless she was being cheated. When a rumour began to circulate that Overbury was due to be released from the Tower, she got rid of the useless Weston. She took an immense risk. With Northumberland, she contacted a young man called William Reeve, assistant to Dr Paul de Lobell, the French physician who was attending prisoners in the Tower. For £20 reward Reeve stole from his master a solution of mercury sublimate. It was given to Sir Thomas Overbury as a medicine. He swallowed it without any suspicion and died in agony.

Frances had already petitioned for divorce from the Earl of Essex and on 16 May 1613 a commission was at last appointed to examine her claim that her marriage was null and void, because her husband was impotent. Essex denied this emphatically and people were inclined to believe his side of the story. However, after some interference on the part of the King, who found the whole thing distasteful, nullity was declared. The pair of them were free to start again. Essex had no idea at the time how lucky he had been to escape with his life.

The marriage between Rochester, now created Earl of Somerset, and Frances Essex took place towards the end of that year, the bride radiant in white with her long fair hair flowing loosely down her back as a symbol of purity and innocence. The whole court attended with the King and Queen and a great deal of money was spent on the occasion.

Rochester still had no idea that he had married a murderess.

But if Frances thought she could now settle down

happily with the man who had obsessed her and dominated her passions and emotions, she was mistaken. For very soon after the wedding her health seemed poor. She was nervous and curiously ill-tempered for a new bride. No wonder. All her accomplices were starting to blackmail her. She now lived in dread that she would be found out.

Somerset himself seemed to be out of favour with the King, who had grown rather tired of his favourite's overbearing manner and was tending to prefer George Villiers, who was to become Duke of Buckingham. There was nothing he could do to stop Villiers's rapid advancement and his enemies scented blood.

In the autumn of 1615 when Frances had been married for two years, William Reeve, who had given Sir Thomas Overbury the fatal dose of poison, fell dangerously ill and began worrying about the fate of his immortal soul. He unburdened himself of his guilty secret and recovered.

The facts were eventually laid before the King who gave orders that justice must be done. Somerset and his Countess were told not to leave their apartments until a preliminary hearing had been held. Gradually the whole story came out, and both of them were arrested on a charge of murder.

From the beginning Somerset protested that he knew nothing of the murder of his friend and stood firm in his denial right to the end. He was sentenced to death but there was a general wish that the King should spare his life and at the 12th hour he was granted a pardon. On the other hand, feelings ran high against the Countess and at one stage it was thought likely that she would have to submit to the death penalty pronounced in court. The King granted her a pardon, on the grounds that her family had done the country so much good service and that she had sworn to be truly penitent. But there were demonstrations against her in the streets and one day a mob attacked a coach in which the Queen was travelling with a young friend. They had made the mistake of thinking it was 'that vile woman' and her mother.

Both Frances and Somerset were imprisoned in the Tower. She pleaded with the lieutenant not to put her in the room where Overbury had died. They stayed there until January 1621 when the King allowed them to go to Grey's Court in Oxfordshire where Lord Wallingford, brother-in-law of Frances, had offered them accommodation. The only condition was they were never to leave. They were under house arrest for the rest of their lives.

The punishment was worse than anybody could have dreamed. Somerset loathed the woman who had brought about his downfall and disgrace, turned him against his friend and then had that friend cruelly murdered. He hardly ever spoke to her again. Day in, day out, they were forced together in an intimacy that was sheer torture. And when Frances died from a terrible wasting disease in August 1632 the last thing she saw was the contempt in his eyes.

Belle Gunness

There was only one name they could give to Mrs Belle Gunness and that was 'the female Bluebeard'. How else could you describe a woman who had coldly and systematically murdered at least 100 people?

To her neighbours she had seemed pleasant enough. She was a widow and ran a small but successful farm in the green hills of La Porte County, Indiana, USA. There was something a bit foreign about her and perhaps she was a bit flighty but that did not mean to say she was not hard-working and respectable.

They were terribly shocked when they heard one morning in April 1908 that there had been a terrible fire at the Gunness farm during the night and the comely widow and her three young children had been burned to death in the flames.

But they were even more shocked when the police arrived and started digging up the farmstead and excavating fields, finding graves and corpses everywhere they looked.

The truth might not have come out for years but someone remembered that a farm hand named Lamphere, who had worked for Mrs Gunness for years, had left the farm suddenly a day or so before the fire. He was thought to have had some grievance against her and would mutter threats when he had had too many beers in the local bar.

Following up this clue the police managed to track down Lamphere and subjected him to continual and intense questioning. He broke down under it and confessed that he had killed his employer and her children with an axe while they slept and had set fire to the farmhouse to destroy the evidence of what he had done.

Why did he do it? 'I had to,' he exclaimed. 'If I hadn't killed her, she would have killed me. I knew too much.'

'Knew too much? How do you mean?' asked the policeman in charge of the case.

'The woman was a murderess. She killed people the way you and me would kill rabbits.'

Hardly able to believe what he was hearing, the policeman asked softly: 'How did she kill them?'

'With an axe, after she'd chloroformed them,' groaned Lamphere. 'She buried them on the farm.'

For weeks following his confession, the Gunness farm was full of grim-faced men, digging. Bodies of men, women and children were found neatly interred, mostly in separate graves, but sometimes two buried together. Beneath the cement floor of the farmhouse they found a deep pit full of human bones. Belle Gunness must have been at work for years, filling her own private cemetery.

Eventually the whole story was pieced together and it chilled the blood of even those used to dealing with murder. The scale of her wickedness was beyond anything they had come across.

She was Norwegian by birth and had emigrated to America as a girl. While still in her teens she had met and married a Swede called Albert Sorenson. She poisoned him in 1900 after having insured him for a tidy sum.

With this money she bought the farm in Indiana, and, thinking she needed a man about the place to do the heavy work, married Joe Gunness. There was some evidence that she was already deeply involved with a murderer named Hoch whose speciality was advertising for wives then killing them off for their money. Some of these unfortunate women were sent to stay with Mrs Gunness and never heard of again. Her husband must have tumbled onto her secret and was killed with an axe one night to make sure he didn't talk. The man Hoch was arrested and executed and she decided from that time she would operate on her own.

The only difference was that she advertised for husbands. She inserted the same notice in small provincial papers all over the United States. It read as follows:

> 'PERSONAL – Comely widow, who owns large farm in one of the finest districts of La Porte County, Indiana, desires to make the acquaintance of a gentleman unusually well provided, with a view to joining fortunes. No replies by letter will be considered unless the sender is willing to follow an answer with a personal visit.'

Whether they were attracted by the thought of the comely widow or by her fortune makes no difference. Gentlemen replied to her advertisements with alacrity – scores of them. She could pick and choose her victims, telling them to bring substantial sums of ready cash with them when they came to inspect the farm, just so that she could be sure of their good faith.

One by one they fell into her trap. The prospective husband would be received with open arms, shown round the farm, then, when he had eaten a huge farmhouse supper he would be shown into her guest room. It was really a death cell. The bed was comfortable enough but the thick oak door was fastened with a spring lock, the windows had iron bars and the walls were of double thickness, the cavity packed with sawdust, making the room completely soundproof. First there would be the chloroform, then she would kill with an axe. She had got the routine down to a fine art.

She had the skill of a siren when it came to those who did not respond quickly enough to her initial overture. This is a letter which was sent to a man called Andrew Helgelein in December 1907:

> 'To the dearest friend in the world – I know you have now only to come to me and be my own. The king will be no happier than you when you get here. As for the queen, her joy will be small when compared with mine. You will love my farm, sweetheart. In all La Porte County, there's none will compare with it. It is on a nice green slope near two lakes. When I hear your name mentioned, my heart beats in wild rapture for you. My Andrew, I love you!'

At the bottom of the page she had scrawled: 'Be sure and bring the three thousand dollars you are going to invest in the farm with you and, for safety's sake, sew them up in your clothes, dearest.'

Andrew Helgelein visited Mrs Gunness. He was seen by some neighbours as she drove him in her pony and trap towards the farm. But he never came out again.

As her lust for money and possessions grew, she killed more frequently. Sometimes whole families were wiped out. It had always been presumed they had left the district hurriedly until they were discovered in their graves. Something of the sort happened on Christmas Day 1906. Mrs Gunness invited two married women she knew who wore particularly fine jewels. She told them to bring their husbands along to the farm and help a lonely widow celebrate the festive season. As she had anticipated, they came wearing all their best trinkets. By Boxing Day not one of them was left alive and all four were identified when they were found by the police.

Exactly how many people she murdered was never known. The authorities could only make estimates with the help of the imprisoned Lamphere, who had made a long confession. He said she had carried on her foul trade for roughly five years and that she averaged three victims a month. His estimate was thought to be exaggerated. Still, even allowing for that, the police found that, by adding on the victims of other murders she was known to have committed outside the farm, the total must be well over 100.

Why did no one suspect her before? It appears there had been inquiries about some of the men who disappeared after visiting her at the farm and Andrew Helgelein's brother was about to start an investigation at the time of the fire.

But, after all, she seemed such a nice woman and the farm was so well run. No one accused her and, if a farm hand called Lamphere had not set fire to the place, she might have gone on for years.

Chicago May

Her real name was Mary Vivienne Churchill. She wafted through the foyers of the world's great hotels in crepe de Chine and pearls, a vision of loveliness with her spun-gold hair, green eyes and white satin skin. Men were captivated by her, and willingly became entangled with her, only to find that one morning when they awoke she had turned on them with the venom of a rattlesnake, demanding more money than they dared to think of.

She was known to the police as Chicago May, a leading member of the underworld and one of the most vicious blackmailers of modern times. Her one object in life was to make as much money as possible and, using the bedroom as her centre of operations, she bled her victims white.

Born in Ireland, the daughter of respectable, well-off parents, she was thought to have 'a bit of a devil' in her as a child, but nothing to worry about. By the age of 16 she had turned into a beauty and began to show her true colours. With cool calculation, she threw herself at the son of a leading Irish family, seduced him, then threatened to tell his parents if he didn't pay her handsomely to keep her mouth shut. The young man paid up, but she told them nevertheless. To get rid of her they gave in to her demands: £1,000 and a passage to America.

It was 1912, still a decade before Al Capone, but the underworld was bristling with gangsters, hoodlums and big-time grafters. May dressed herself in the height of fashion and headed straight for Chicago. Before she was 20 she had been accepted into the fraternity as a high-class operator.

Her victims were mostly very rich men in their 50s or 60s, tycoons, heads of industry, public figures and bored husbands all on the lookout for a beautiful woman to flatter them and on whom they could spend their hard earned money. Her technique was simple. She would use her considerable charm to enslave some hapless male, modestly accept his homage of jewellery then cash, then allow herself to be seduced. Before he knew what was happening incriminating photographs had been produced, threats made and his reputation put up for sale.

As a result of these tactics Chicago May could soon afford a splendid house with servants, her own personal bodyguard and a film-star wardrobe. Then, at the height of her success, she met the criminal Eddie Guerin, a tough, unscrupulous bank robber with flinty blue eyes and a chilling presence. They seemed made for each other. They became lovers and he dominated the rest of her life. Eddie had no squeamish feelings about May sleeping with rich old men. That was business. But, if she showed any sign of being attracted to someone nearer her own age, he turned very nasty indeed.

Her reign in Chicago lasted for about four years during which time she was estimated to have gained over half a million dollars by blackmail. Her victims' lives were never the same again, even after they had paid their dues. The head of one huge steel combine went straight to the police, only to find that the high-ranking officer to whom he complained was already in her pay. Another threatened to shoot her but was frightened off by her henchmen. One younger man she had seduced, then bled to the point of ruin, killed himself.

Just when she was at the height of her career in Chicago, the Press decided to run a series of exposure articles that would involve not only some very distinguished citizens but also her part in their corrupt goings-on. She was told to quit before something unpleasant happened to her.

May felt that what she had done in Chicago she could do anywhere else. She packed up her sables and headed for New York. Eddie followed in a very short time. But, as she drifted round the luxury hotels, planning her campaign, she began to have an unpleasant feeling that things were not going to work out. The social scene in New York was entirely different. She had no contacts. And the top criminals, sensing that she spelled trouble, didn't want to know her. The police, having been warned by their colleagues in Chicago, hinted that they had enough evidence to put her away for a long stretch. It was all going wrong. May decided there was only one thing to do. She had to return to Europe.

She started her tour of the major European cities in high style. Booking herself into the most expensive and fashionable hotels she performed her old routine and, for a year or two, tasted something of her old success. In Berlin she managed to separate a great industrialist from a quarter of a million marks. In Vienna she compromised a Prince of a royal house and the family paid a huge sum to get her out of their lives. It was the sort of thing she thrived on.

Eventually she crossed the Channel to London, booked into a luxury hotel and prepared to start work. London was not as easy as she had expected. The British male, she found, was far more reticent, more suspicious than his counterpart in America or on the Continent. She made a few minor conquests but had to admit to herself that she had failed. Was it anything to do with the fact that too many late nights and too much brandy had coarsened her skin, left pouches under her eyes and added an inch or two to her exquisite figure?

With great relief she heard that her old lover Eddie Guerin had arrived in Paris and wanted her to join him. She found him staying in seedy lodgings in Montmartre, planning the biggest job of his criminal life. He was going to break into the strongroom of the American Express Company. After that, he promised her, they could retire.

The night that Eddie and his gang blew the safes and brought out nearly half a million dollars in American currency, May was standing on a street corner, playing the uncharacteristic role of lookout. She wouldn't have done it for any other man. The money had to be moved out of the country without delay. Every minute counted. The gang split up and began swiftly to put their plan into operation. But they were not quick enough. An informer gave the French police two names: Eddie and Chicago May. They were picked up as they were packing their suitcases with dollars.

Eddie knew he was finished but when May denied she had taken any part in the raid he backed her up. The French police were pretty sure she had been an accomplice but they let her go, content that they had managed to capture one of the most dangerous bank robbers in the world. But May loved Eddie. Though she had managed to escape to London she couldn't bear to think she might not see him for years. She returned to Paris to see him in prison before his trial and this time the French authorities pounced. She was sentenced to five years' imprisonment for her part in the robbery. She nearly collapsed when she heard that Eddie had been sent to the dreaded French penal colony on Devil's Island for life.

When she came out of prison she had to face the fact that her beauty was fading fast. The sort of life she had led was etched on her face. Back in London she set up her own organization: the Northumberland Avenue Gang. She was deep in blackmail again but this time using prostitutes. It was a lucrative but dangerous racket and, to her cost, May found that the police in London were not, on the whole, open to corruption. When the law caught up with the Northumberland Avenue Gang many of its members were arrested but May managed to slip through a back door and lie low.

Next time she surfaced it was in another trade. With her looks no longer what they were and her gang dispersed she decided to give up blackmail. With the money she had saved she opened a plush opium den only a stone's throw from Piccadilly Circus. It became a 'must' for young male tourists who wanted to see the *real* London and soon she added a brothel as an extra attraction. As Gerald Sparrow writes in his account of her life: 'The whole thing was filthy, unsavoury and weird and attracted the dregs of humanity.'

One morning May heard a sharp knock on her front door and opened it to find Eddie Guerin standing there. The shock was almost too much for her. He had escaped from Devil's Island – in one of the greatest prison breaks ever made – and had come to find her. She still loved him but she knew how much she had changed and wondered if she could hold him.

For the first six months they were happy enough together then May started to notice any attention Eddie gave to younger women. Soon she was jealous of every female he looked at. There were violent scenes and Eddie's eyes became colder and colder. One day he vanished as suddenly as he had appeared. He had taken with him an 18-year-old girl who was working for her.

When May realized what had happened she went berserk. In her fury and jealousy she only knew she had to destroy him. She hired a young professional gunman and became obsessed with hunting him down. The terrible confrontation came one afternoon in a street in Bloomsbury. As soon as May saw Eddie with his girlfriend she rushed at him with a knife, but the gunman shot him before she could use it. They left him sprawled on the pavement in a pool of blood with the girl sobbing over his body.

By some miracle Eddie Guerin did not die. He lost several pints of blood but the doctors pulled him through and he went on living. Chicago May was arrested in 1926 and charged with attempted murder, along with her hired gunman. There was no trace left of her golden-haired beauty. She sat huddled in the dock like an old woman and when they sentenced her to 15 years she turned and left the court without saying a word.

The Raving Romanovs

It is not only British royals who misbehave. Indeed, the most famous of all scandalous royals was Catherine the Great, who ruled Russia from 1762 to 1796.

From an early age, the German-born Catherine was a very sensual woman. She would lie in bed at night and masturbate with her pillow between her legs. At 16 she was married to her 17-year-old cousin, Peter, the German-born grandson of Peter the Great and heir to the throne of Russia. However, the marriage bed did not hold all the delights Catherine longed for. Peter was an alcoholic, impotent and feeble-minded. For him, bed was where you played with your toys.

For several years, Catherine contented herself with horseriding and voracious reading. But the Empress Elizabeth, Peter's aunt, who was Russia's reigning monarch, wanted her to have children to continue the Romanov line. So, on an out-of-the-way island in the Baltic, Elizabeth arranged for Catherine, who was still a virgin, to be left alone with Sergei Saltykov, a Russian nobleman and accomplished womanizer.

After one night with Saltykov, Catherine could not get enough sex. Two miscarriages occurred in rapid succession. Then she went to term with Paul, who was whisked away by Elizabeth and presented to the Russian people as heir to the throne.

Soon after, Catherine's husband Peter underwent an operation, which corrected a malformation of his penis and left him potent. He began taking a string of mistresses. However, he does not seem to have had sex with his wife, who by this time had had a second child by a young Polish nobleman named Count Stanislas Poniatowski.

'I do not know how it is my wife becomes pregnant,' Peter said.

He soon found out when he caught Count Poniatowski leaving their country home in disguise. He accused the Count of sleeping with his wife. Naturally, Poniatowski denied it. Peter then had Catherine dragged out of bed. She and Poniatowski were then forced to have supper with Peter and his latest mistress. Afterwards, Poniatowski was sent back to Poland in disgrace.

Catherine replaced him with an officer in the Horse Guards, Count Grigori Orlov, who soon got her pregnant. She managed to conceal her belly under the huge hooped dresses then in fashion. When she felt the child coming, one of her servants set his own house on fire to distract Peter, who never could resist a good fire. She had three children with Orlov. But they were always farmed out to servants as soon as they were born and only introduced to the royal nursery once no one could really be sure to whom they belonged.

Catherine's infidelity drove Peter crazy and, when he came to the throne in 1761, he was determined to divorce her. But Peter was deeply unpopular. He made no effort to conceal his hatred of Russia and his love of all things German. Worse still, he worshipped Frederick II of Prussia with whom Russia was then at war. After just six months on the throne, Peter concluded a peace treaty with Frederick and was planning a disastrous war against Denmark.

Although Catherine had been born in Germany, too, she was much more popular than her husband. Dressed in a lieutenant's uniform, she rode to St Petersburg where Count Orlov was stationed. With the army behind her, she proclaimed herself Empress in Kazan Cathedral. Peter was arrested. He abdicated, but was murdered anyway a short time later by Orlov's brother, Aleksei.

Once on the throne, Catherine refused to marry Orlov, preferring to preserve the Romanov dynasty. He got his own back by seducing every attractive woman who came to court. He became a political liability when he bungled peace negotiations with the Turks. He capped that by seducing Catherine's 13-year-old cousin. Catherine kicked him out of court and he died mad, haunted by the ghost of the murdered Emperor Peter.

Catherine had already met the cavalry officer, Prince Grigori Potemkin. They had fallen instantly in love. This had so infuriated Orlov's brother that he beat Potemkin so hard that he lost an eye. When Catherine's affair with Orlov ended, she planned to replace him with Potemkin but, after swearing his loyalty, Potemkin retired to a monastery. He refused to return to court until Catherine had sent away all her other favourites.

For two years they had an intense affair. However, these activities gave him an enormous appetite. He put on weight which turned the Empress off. However, Potemkin retained his position at court by selecting young men for her pleasure.

Although Potemkin was referred to as 'husband' by Catherine, he hand-picked handsome cavalry officers in their 20s for her. Candidates were first examined by Catherine's personal physician for symptoms of syphilis. Then their virility was tested by one of Catherine's ladies-in-waiting. When Ivan Rimsky-Korsakov, the grandfather of the composer, returned to Countess Bruce for extra tests, she was sacked and a more elderly virility tester was employed.

At least 13 officers passed this exhaustive selection procedure. News spread across Europe, and when Casanova heard of it he set off for Russia. But he was not even considered and contented himself by exchanging 'tokens of the tenderest friendship', swearing 'eternal love' to the beautiful and androgynous Lieutenant Lunin.

Aleksandr Dmitriev-Mamonov had to be excused duty, despite having passed the tests with flying colours. He had made one of the ladies of the court pregnant and had to marry her. This sent Catherine into a sulk, but she still favoured them with an expensive wedding present.

Those who had successfully passed through all the hoops were installed in special apartments below Catherine's, connected to hers by a private staircase. One thousand roubles would be waiting for them there. If a candidate proved satisfactory and a repeat performance was required, the 'Emperor of the night' would be promoted to the rank of adjutant-general and given a salary of 12,000 roubles a month, plus expenses. One of her lovers said that they considered themselves 'kept girls'. When she was finished with a lover, he would receive a handsome golden handshake which in one case amounted to an estate with 4,000 serfs. This was a bit heavy on the public purse, but no one complained. Catherine was an autocrat.

Catherine continued this way until she was 60. Then she fell in love with 22-year-old Platon Zubov. This put Potemkin's nose out of joint as the ambitious Zubov became a rival for power.

The myth has come down that Catherine died when she declared that no man could satisfy her and she tried sex with a horse. The horse, it was said, was lowered onto her by crane. The crane broke and she was crushed to death. There is, however, no evidence to support this scandalous tale. She died at the age of 67, two days after suffering a massive stroke. No equine involvement was suspected.

Catherine the Great was succeeded by her son, Paul, who it seems suffered a mental illness. He was fearful of his mother and, during her reign, built up his own private army. Even after his own coronation in 1796, his paranoia did not disappear. He cut Russia off from the rest of the world, preventing citizens travelling abroad and banning all foreign music and books. Even the wearing of French hats, boots or coats was outlawed.

Failing to kneel before the Tsar's palaces, even if you

were on horseback or in a carriage, was an offence punishable by banishment. By the end of his reign, the suspicion of harbouring 'nefarious thoughts' led to a long term in Siberia. Four years after taking the throne, he was murdered by his courtiers, and his son, Alexander, who was one of the conspirators, was installed in his place.

The last of the Romanov Tsars, Nicholas II, was happily married to Queen Victoria's favourite granddaughter, Princess Alix of Hesse. She had already turned down a proposal from the future Edward VII's son, Prince Eddy, heir to the British throne, as she had been madly in love with Nicholas since she first saw him when she was 12. With Victoria's blessing, Alix changed her name to Alexandra when she went to Russia to marry her Tsar.

Their marriage was blissful until they discovered that the Tsarevich, their eldest son Alexsei, was a haemophiliac. In their desperation, they turned to a strolling Siberian priest named Rasputin, who brought scandal to the Romanovs by trading his seemingly magical powers over the Tsarevich's condition for political influence.

Rasputin was a pretty scandalous character from his beginnings in the Siberian village of Pokrovskoye. He was born Grigory Yefimovich Novykh in about 1872, only becoming Rasputin later – the name means 'the debauched one' in Russian. It was not wholly his fault. The local children would bathe naked in the pond and the young girls of the village apparently quickly picked him out for special attention because of his 13in penis. A further initiation into the world of sex came at the hands of Irina Danilov Kubasova, the pretty wife of a Russian general. She lured him into her bedroom where she and six of her maids seduced him.

After that, he joined a sect of flagellants named the Khlist, who believed that true mortification of the flesh came through sexual exhaustion. At 20, he married the long-suffering Praskovia Feodorovna who gave him four children. However, he was soon expelled from his village by a respectable priest and he took to the road with his wife and Dunia Bekyeshova, one of Irina Danilov Kubasova's maids, who became his life-long mistress. Together they wandered around Russia with Rasputin initiating hordes of other women into the rites of the Khlist in unrestrained orgies. His wife was not fazed by his numerous mistresses.

'He has enough to go around,' she said.

His doctrine of redemption through sexual release attracted numerous respectable guilt-ridden women, allowing many converts to enjoy sex for the first time. His unkempt appearance and peasant manners added to his attraction as a 'holy satyr'. As his biographer, Robert Massie, said: 'Making love to the unwashed peasant with his dirty beard and filthy hands was a new and thrilling sensation.' In fact, many of his lovers dowsed themselves in perfume beforehand as his body odour was so powerful.

By the time he reached St Petersburg, he had a powerful reputation as a mystic, a healer and a clairvoyant. In 1905, he was introduced at court. Soon after, he was called on to tend the Tsarevich. It was found that he could successfully ease the child's condition – perhaps due to hypnosis.

While Rasputin remained a paragon of chastity and humility at court, outside he continued his scandalous ways. Women gathered in his apartment, eager for an invitation to visit his bedroom or the 'holy of holies' as he called it. Usually, he would be found in the dining-room, surrounded by female disciples who took turns to sit on his lap while he instructed them on the mysteries of the resurrection. On one occasion, he gave a graphic description of the sex life of horses, then grabbed one of his distinguished guests by the hair and pulled her towards his bedroom, saying: 'Come, my lovely mare.'

He would often sing and they would dance wildly, collapsing in a swoon on being taken into the 'holy of holies' for a personal glimpse of paradise. One disciple, an opera singer, was so devoted to him that she would phone him to sing him his favourite songs. Attendance at his gatherings became so fashionable that cuckolded husbands would boast that their wives belonged to Rasputin.

People who tried to convey details of this scandalous behaviour to the Tsar's ears found themselves banished. But, in 1911, Nicholas could ignore the rumours no longer when his Prime Minister drew up a long bill of Rasputin's offences. The Tsar expelled Rasputin from court, but he was soon recalled by the Tsarina, who feared for her son's life.

During World War I, Tsar Nicholas took personal command of his troops, leaving all other government business in the hands of the Tsarina and her personal adviser, Rasputin, who began making disastrous appointments. Rasputin also meddled in military affairs to catastrophic effect. To save Russia from his malign influence, several attempts were made on Rasputin's life.

His enemies were finally successful on 30 December 1916. A gang of conservative noblemen fed him poisoned cake and wine. As he fell into a coma, one of the assassins, Prince Felix Yussupov, a homosexual who had been rebuffed by Rasputin several times, took this opportunity to sexually abuse him. Then he shot him four times. While Rasputin was still alive, a second assassin pulled out a knife and castrated him, throwing his severed penis across the room. It was recovered later by a servant who gave it to a maid. (In 1968, she was still alive, living in Paris, and possessed a polished wooden box in which she kept what looked like 'a blackened, overripe banana, about a foot long'.) Rasputin was then tied up and thrown into the icy Neva river, where he finally drowned.

His assassination redoubled Alexandra's belief in autocracy. She cracked down hard on the Russian people, but within weeks of the death of the mad monk the Romanovs were swept from power by the Russian Revolution.

Scandinavian Scandals

As well as getting on with it themselves, the British royal family have also been good at exporting scandal. A case in point was George III's sister, Princess Caroline Matilda, who was married at the age of 15 to King Christian VII of Denmark. Once ensconced in Copenhagen, she discovered that her husband was debauched and slowly going round the bend. So she took a lover and caused such a scandal that she had to be rescued by the Royal Navy.

It is not surprising that Christian went mad when you consider his upbringing. He was born in 1749. His father, Frederick the Good, was an alcoholic and incoherently drunk throughout most of his reign. Christian's mother, Queen Louisa, who was a daughter of Britain's George II, died when he was three. Frederick married again, but his wife, Princess Juliana Maria of Brunswick-Wolfenbuttel, loathed her stepson. This was counter-balanced somewhat by Frederick who doted on the child, but only when he was sober enough to recognize him.

A fearsome martinet, Count Reventlow, was appointed as his tutor. He beat the boy unmercifully. Christian's one ambition was to finish his schooling so that he could travel around Europe and be as debauched as all the other Crown Princes. He almost made it, but his father drank himself into an early grave when Christian was just 17.

Ruefully, he took up the reins of state. His first act as King was to appoint Count Reventlow as his chamberlain. By that time he had become emotionally dependent on his tormentor.

Frederick the Good had already set up the marriage with Princess Caroline Matilda. Christian liked her portrait well enough, but he was in no hurry to marry. He was keen to sow a few wild oats. But when he started chasing ladies-in-waiting and chambermaids, his courtiers took fright. They were afraid that Christian might go off the rails like his father.

They sent for Princess Caroline Matilda. When Christian saw her in the flesh, he was impressed. She had a pretty face and an inviting figure, and he quickly forgot his objections to marriage.

But, even though he had a Queen, he was a King and he thought he should spread himself around a bit among his subjects. He and a few close friends began enjoying nights on the tiles in Copenhagen, when not a few pretty young women felt obliged to do their patriotic duty and give their all for King and country.

As well as indulging in wild bouts of womanizing, Christian began to drink heavily. He scandalized Denmark with his relationship with a notorious prostitute who worked under the name 'Milady'. The King would ditch his royal regalia and go out on the town with Milady. During their drunken sprees Christian liked to indulge himself in senseless vandalism and would hurl the grossest insults at anyone who tried to stop him. On more than one occasion he was beaten up. One night he and Milady wrecked a rival brothel; on another, he was pursued by a baying mob to the gates of the palace.

Things got worse when Christian furnished Milady with a mansion and created her Baroness. Something had to be done, so the courtiers forced the King to banish her to Hamburg, where she was kept under guard.

That put an end to one scandal, but those in the inner circles of court feared that another, worse, one was about to follow. Christian had learned Reventlow's lessons too well. Ugly rumours were now in circulation that the King was paying pageboys to beat him; whoever beat him the hardest got the most money. In one bizarre rite, Christian submitted himself to being 'broken on the wheel' with a royal favourite dressed as an executioner standing beside him reading his death warrant.

There was just one thing to be done. The King had to be sent abroad. His ministers though he might sate himself discreetly in the courts of Europe while they got on with the business of government. To keep an eye on Christian, they sent with him a Dr Johann Struensee as his personal physician.

To ensure the maximum discretion – and the maximum fun – Christian travelled under a number of pseudonyms. His first stop was Germany, when he moved on through the low countries to Calais, where the royal yacht was waiting to carry him to England.

The moralistic George III did not fully grasp the purpose of the trip. As Christian travelled from Dover to London, George laid on a reception at Canterbury hosted by the Archbishop. Christian remarked that the last time a Danish king had entered Canterbury he had burned it to the ground.

In London, Christian adopted the pseuyonym Mr Frederickson and set about bedding as many whores as he could. In the 18th century, London was full of prostitutes and a man could get anything he wanted for a few pence. Mr Frederickson would dangle purses full of bright golden guineas in front of them. There was no way Struensee could restrain him.

The Dowager Princess of Wales, Caroline Matilda's mother, was shocked. So was George III. After a hugely expensive two-month orgy in London, George and Struensee persuaded Christian to leave.

Next stop was Paris, where Christian threw himself into another round of sexual excess. But it was soon clear that the exertion was telling on his health, particularly his mental health.

After six months on the road, Struensee managed to pry him away from the pleasures of Paris. When Christian returned home he seemed a changed man. He held himself with more dignity and bearing and he was kind and considerate to the Queen. His ministers were relieved that the rest cure had worked.

It did not last long. Under the influence of his old friends, he began drinking and womanizing again. But this time it was worse. He refused to attend to any matters of state and it was clear that he was slipping into idiocy.

Struensee saw his chance. He managed to persuade his mistress, Madame de Gabell, to seduce Christian. That way, he thought, he would be able to control the King. Unfortunately, Madame de Gabell was a moral woman. The ethical dilemma that this arrangement put her in was too much for her and she died.

Cursing his luck, Struensee suddenly spotted a better opportunity. He seduced Queen Caroline Matilda. Together with the Queen Mother, they relieved Christian of the bothersome business of government, leaving him free to give himself up to his pleasures full-time.

All went swimmingly until Caroline Matilda started appearing in public dressed in men's clothing. Tongues began wagging as to who was wearing the pants in the royal household. But it was Struensee who made the fatal mistake. Unusually for a usurper, he was basically a modern liberal. He instituted much-needed municipal and judicial reform, but foolishly he also established freedom of press. The first thing the papers started printing was stories about the scandal in the palace.

The Dowager Princess of Wales, Caroline Matilda's mother, arrived in Copenhagen and tried to persuade her daughter to flee to England. Caroline Matilda pretended that she did not speak English and refused. The Dowager Princess left empty-handed.

As the scandal grew, Denmark became dangerously politically unstable. The nobility, particularly, objected to Struensee, a humble doctor, setting himself up as a backroom monarch. But the Queen Mother knew which side her bread was buttered on. One night in January 1772, while Struensee and Caroline Matilda were out dancing, Juliana Maria went to see Christian. She persuaded him that his wife and Struensee planned to kill him and got the feeble-minded King to sign a warrant for their arrest.

They were seized and Struensee was tortured to death. Caroline Matilda was tried for adultery and found guilty. Her marriage was annulled and she was imprisoned. George III sent a British fleet to rescue her. Fearful of letting the scandal reach the shores of Britain, the already unpopular King George had her taken to Hanover, where she died three years later, at the age of 23.

Christian ruled, in name at least, for another 16 years, first as the puppet of the Queen Mother, Juliana Maria. Then, after ten years of her less-than-benevolent rule, Christian's teenage son, Frederick, staged a palace coup and installed himself as regent.

Not that the Scandinavians were not up to creating royal scandals of their own. In the 17th century, Sweden produced the brilliant and vivacious Queen Christina, who liked to wear men's clothes, refused to marry, gave up the throne and gallivanted around Europe getting into all manner of trouble.

When she was born on 8 December 1626, she was so hairy and cried in such a deep voice that her father King Gustavus was told that she was a boy. Gustavus was killed in battle in 1632 when Christina was six. Her mother withdrew to a room hung in black and slept with Gustavus's shroud at her side, under a gold casket containing his heart. This left the young monarch in the hands of five regents and surrounded by male courtiers, who supervised her education. She had no opportunity to develop an interest in feminine pursuits and instead loved to hunt reindeer on horseback in the snow. She rode at such a pace that no one could keep up with her, and she would often stay out in the biting cold for up to ten hours at a time.

At the age of 18, she took the oath as King of Sweden.

There had never been a reigning Queen before. She quickly mastered the art of statesmanship. She also had a great thirst for knowledge. Sleeping only four hours a night, she spent a little time on her toilette and dressed in Hungarian riding outfits of a distinctly masculine cut.

Christina developed a passion for her lady-in-waiting, the beautiful Ebba Sparre, but she married Count Jacob de la Gardie, leaving Christina seething with jealousy. Just when everyone had concluded that she was a lesbian, Christina fell in love with the Count's brother. She heaped honours on him and everyone assumed they were lovers. Eventually, however, she sent him away.

Other suitable suitors were suggested, but Christina fell out with her government over her refusal to marry.

'Marriage would entail many things to which I cannot become accustomed,' she told them. 'I really cannot say when I will overcome this inhibition.'

To make things worse, she was planning to convert to Catholicism. The French, she had concluded, had much more fun than dour Scandinavian Protestants. To that end, she abdicated in favour of her cousin who became Charles X. The abdication did not just take the form of signing a legal document resigning the position of monarch. There was a bizarre ceremony where she was stripped of her coronation robe and royal insignia. Then she had to lift the crown from her own head.

Christina had already stripped the palace in Stockholm of its furniture, which she had sent to Rome where she intended to settle. She set off via Denmark, dressed as a man and calling herself Count Dohna. In tow was the lovely Ebba Sparre. In Brussels, Christina declared herself a Catholic and threw herself into a round of parties. The scandal sheets happily chronicled her sexual misadventures which grew so outrageous that she was dubbed the 'Queen of Sodom', and the Swedish Government threatened to cut off her pension.

In 1655, Christina was welcomed in Rome by Pope Alexander VII as a prize convert. But Christina soon became an embarrassment. She had converted for fun, not piety. She made fun of the Church's holy relics and spoke to her friends in a loud voice during Mass.

Settling in the Palazzo Farnese, she hung the walls with extremely indelicate pictures and had the fig leaves removed from all the statues. She introduced Ebba as her 'bedfellow' and told everyone that her mind was as beautiful as her body.

However, in the evenings, Christina would change out of men's clothing and into more alluring attire to entertain leading churchmen. Cardinal Colonna fell in love with her and the Pope had to send him away from Rome to avoid a public scandal. Christina herself was in love with Cardinal Azzolino, although they managed to be more discreet.

She began dabbling in politics, which quickly made her unpopular, so she quit Rome for France where she received a royal welcome. She stayed at Fontainebleau with her two Italian courtiers, the Marquis Monaldesco, her chief equerry, and Count Santinelli, captain of her guard. The two men loathed each other and vied with each other for the favour of the Queen.

Monaldesco had discovered that Santinelli had swindled Christina over a property deal in Rome. To bring this to her attention, he forged a series of letters, which also made reference to her affair with Cardinal Azzolino and her intention of taking the throne of Naples.

However, Christina recognized his handwriting and summoned Monaldesco. She asked him what he thought the punishment for treachery should be. Thinking that she had been convinced by the forgeries and that the forfeit would be paid by Santinelli, he said 'Death'.

She agreed. On 10 November 1657, Monaldesco was summoned to the Galerie de Cerfs in Fontainebleau and asked to read the letters. As he did so, he found the door barred behind him. Santinelli and two guards entered with daggers in their hands. Realizing he had been rumbled, Monaldesco threw himself to his knees and begged Christina for mercy. She merely asked Father Lebel, a prior who had been summoned from the nearby Mathurin Monastery, to prepare Monaldesco for his death. Lebel also begged her to show mercy, as did Santinelli. He said that the case should be taken before the Royal Courts of France. Christina refused and told him to make haste and do his duty, as she strode from the gallery. For the next 15 minutes, she heard Monaldesco's screams as they hacked him to death.

The French were appalled at what they saw as an act of barbarity. Christina's host, Cardinal Mazarin, advised her to make herself scarce so she fled back to Rome. She was little more popular there and the Pope asked her to live outside the Papal See. As a sweetener, he offered her an annuity and an adviser to oversee her financial affairs – one Cardinal Azzolino.

Meanwhile, a woman named Gyldener was passing herself off as Christina in Sweden. She got away with it for several months. When she was unmasked as a fraud, Christina demanded that she be put to death. Charles X was more merciful and jailed her for a month on a ration of bread and water.

As if Queen Christina had not caused enough royal scandals, she now decided to interfere in European politics. First, she called for the Christian nations to unite to smash Turkey. Then she called on France to help her drive the Spanish out of Sicily, as part of her plan to seize the throne of Naples. Nobody took any notice.

Then Charles X died and Christina thought it was time to return to Sweden. When she reached Hamburg, she received a letter making it plain that she was not welcome in her homeland. She took no notice. In Stockholm, the government had no option but to greet her with due respect and house her in the royal apartments. They even allowed her to use one of the royal estates. But, when the locals complained that she was celebrating Mass there, the government had to ask her to leave.

Christina spent the rest of her life wandering aimlessly around Europe, growing fat, unpleasant and eccentric. She put herself up for the vacant throne of Poland but, reviewing her CV, the people of Poland chose the Duke of Lithuania for their monarch instead.

As her health began to fail, she returned to Rome where she died on 19 April 1689, with her faithful Cardinal Azzolino by her side.

The Sophie Tapes

On a September evening in 1993, at an exclusive rackets club near the Queen's residence at Windsor Castle, a little known 28-year-old public-relations executive called Sophie Rhys-Jones committed a breach of royal etiquette which was to lead her to marrying a prince.

Prince Edward, then 29, had spent the day hosting a charity fund-raiser at the Royal Berkshire Tennis Club in Holyport. Sophie Rhys-Jones was one of a large team promoting the event. She had met His Royal Highness for the first time a only few months before, over coffee and croissants at a Buckingham Palace breakfast meeting. That evening, as the event drew to a close, Sophie strolled across the court towards her host. Racket in hand, she smiled and said: 'I'd love to have a hit.'

The Prince, the youngest and most pampered of the Queen's children, was unaccustomed to such a proposal. He liked to choose his tennis partners himself. Indeed, after 12 hours of playing a royal version called real tennis, he had changed into a blue blazer, neatly pressed chino jeans and moccasins, hardly attire for a game. But he donned his whites and led Sophie onto the court.

Five years later, on 6 January 1999, the couple appeared at St James's Palace to announce their engagement. Sophie's family background was considered a virtue. Unlike the aristocratic Lady Diana Spencer and Sarah Ferguson, whose troubled family histories the Windsors blamed for their elder sons' failed marriages, Edward's new companion, though middle-class, came from an unbroken home. Sophie Helen Rhys-Jones was born in Oxford on 20 January 1965 to Christopher Bournes Rhys-Jones, a salesman of car tyres, and Mary O'Sullivan, a charity worker.

Business was important to Sophie from an early age. At 16, she enrolled in a two-year secretarial course at West Kent College in Tonbridge, working part-time as a barmaid at her local pub, the Halfway House. At 18 she left for London to pursue a career in public relations. At the age of 31 she set up her own business, R-JH Public Relations, based in Mayfair, with business partner Murray Harkin.

However, on 14 March 2001 her business world was to take a hard knock. The Countess of Wessex gave an astonishing insight into her most private thoughts during a secretly taped conversation with a bogus Arab sheik, over lunch at the Dorchester Hotel. She attacked politicians – the Blairs, William Hague and John Major in particular – in a series of indiscreet and unguarded comments. She gave away intimate and controversial secrets about members of the royal family which are likely to haunt her for many years to come. The tapes between Sophie, her business partner and the bogus sheik (a *News of the World* Investigations Editor), were among the most devastating revelations from within the royal family to come out in recent years. It was her thoughts on the roles of Charles, Camilla and the late Princess of Wales that proved to be the most embarrassing within the royal circle.

Harkin made matters even worse by boasting that he could arrange sex tours and orgies for the clients of their company R-JH, and how Prince Edward's wife's royal status could be used as a promotional tool. He also revealed how he used cocaine and had taken Ecstasy.

Following the drama of the 'Sophie tapes' she had no option but to step down as chairman of her company. Her business partner, Murray Harkin, also resigned. The Queen intervened on the insistence of Prince Charles and Princess Anne when it became clear that the tabloid concerned was to print taped conversations in which both the Countess and Harkin indicated that her royal staus helped promote their business.

Sophie's statement at the end of the scandal was: 'This has been a difficult time for me. I take very seriously the issues raised and, naturally, regret any embarrassment above all to the Queen. I am grateful for Her Majesty's support both on a personal level and for my being able to pursue a working career . . .'

Mysteries

Amelia Earhart

When aviation pioneer Amelia Earhart roared off into the skies on 1 June 1937, she may have carried a guilty secret with her. The darling girl of the air, who had become the first woman to fly solo across the Atlantic and the first pilot ever to fly solo from Hawaii to California, was determined to add one more flying record to her list of achievements.

Amelia was willing to risk her life to make the first flight around the world by the longest possible route – the closest course to the Equator, a distance of 27,000 miles. She was confident that she had the flying skill to make the gruelling journey and that her twin-engined Lockheed Electra 10-E aircraft was mechanically tough and reliable enough to carry her through the worst of the weather the Earth's tropics would throw at her.

But determined and self-sufficient though she was, Amelia Earhart could not hope to smash the world record again on initiative and guts alone. She needed help from friends in high places to make her record attempt possible.

There were certainly many powerful and important people who saw that co-operation with Amelia Earhart could pay dividends to suit all parties. Earhart would have to enlist the aid of the best technical experts at the Lockheed aircraft-builders and the vast resources of the United States navy for her enterprise. Without them, the project was doomed to failure.

Normally, the American aircraft-builders would have been only too willing to promote and sponsor any move by Earhart to get herself in the record books once more. Her exploits of daring marathon flights had captured the headlines and the country's imagination, and had helped to convince a hesitant public that travel by commercial airline was becoming a safe and commonplace event. They helped to sell hundreds of small airliners to more and more new operators each year.

But, in 1937, the plane-makers had different priorities. Their production lines were producing fewer civilian aircraft and were being increasingly committed to turning out combat planes for the US Army Air Corps and the US navy. Washington was nervously eyeing the expansion of Japanese military ambitions in the Pacific and they had themselves begun a growing programme of rearming and updating the squadrons of America's own flying forces.

During World War I, Japan had occupied the Marshall, Caroline and Mariana Islands and had managed to retain these under a League of Nations mandate. In 1934, the Japanese began isolating the islands from their Pacific neighbours. Both America and Japan had agreed, at the Naval Treaty Conference in Washington in 1923, that military construction of the Pacific islands occupied by either side should be strictly banned. Now American strategists believed the Japanese were secretly preparing their captive islands as giant munitions dumps, communications bases and airfields for an attack on the US controlled Pacific islands – or even the American mainland – in defiance of all the guarantees they had given the League of Nations.

The Americans themselves had launched a defensive military build-up in the Pacific, aimed mainly at developing radio facilities to control a series of direction-finding stations strung out across the ocean to detect any large movements of aircraft. The War Department had entered into a secret partnership with Pan American Airways to build a series of direction-finding bases on Midway and Wake Island, under the guise of providing navigation facilities for the airline's transoceanic flights across the Pacific.

The years of hidden preparation by the Japanese were to climax in 1941, with their surprise attack on Pearl Harbor. Even by 1937, the troubled skies over the Pacific were no place for amateur pilots to tax strained diplomatic relations by making trail-blazing publicity stunts in their aircraft. Amelia Earhart, however, was no unknown amateur. She had served as a lecturer and counsellor at the Purdue Research Foundation at Purdue University in Lafayette, Indiana; and the Foundation openly admitted its aims were to conduct aviation research 'with particular reference to National Defence'. The research unit was also in receipt of government grants backed by the US War Department, and the Foundation also openly admitted it was providing the money to buy the Lockheed Electra for Earhart, for the scientific purpose of testing and improving radio direction-finding equipment.

In her eagerness to claim the glory for new achievements in flying history, Amelia had originally wanted to go one step further. She planned to fly the Pacific from east to west and carry out the first mid-air refuelling, using specially adapted US navy planes. But the War Department ruled out her plan as too risky. Instead, they proposed an alternative, which would provide them with a strategic military bonus.

Amelia, they suggested, should be provided with a safe landing and refuelling stop in the middle of the vast ocean. The place they chose was remote Howland Island, only a few degrees north of the Equator and less than 600 miles from the Japanese-controlled Marshall Islands. Work began immediately on the construction of an airstrip and fuel dump, while suspicious Japanese warships patrolled around Howland on spying missions. Any muted protests from the Japanese were countered with outraged indignation on the part of the Americans, who explained that the airbase on the tiny speck of land, only three-quarters of a mile long and half a mile wide, was essential for the safety of the daring woman air pioneer.

In the mean time, Amelia continued with the preparations for her record-breaking flight and her aircraft was flown to Lockheed's private factory for special modifications. Amelia's technical supervisor, Paul Mantz, tried to monitor all the changes, but even he was unaware that Lockheed's chief specialist in its latest top-secret radio gear, Joseph Gurr, was detailed to fit experimental direction-finding equipment inside the plane.

On 17 March, Amelia set out on the first leg of the trip. But this proved only to be a disastrous false start after the first 2,410 miles, from San Francisco to Honolulu, had been covered. On take-off from Honolulu, overburdened with the weight of 1,100 US gallons of fuel and two navigators, the Electra crashed and its undercarriage collapsed.

Amelia sat down to an urgent conference with her technical advisors and her husband, George Palmer Putnam, and changed her plans completely. The flight would circumnavigate the globe from west to east. With the help of prevailing winds on the new route, she would be able to dispense with the weight of one navigator and give herself some margin of safety. (The delay in her plans also gave the US navy and the Army Air Corps a valuable breathing space in which to install more and more secret defence equipment on Howland Island.)

On 1 June, Earhart started again from scratch. By this time her aircraft was bristling with a bewildering array of low- and high-frequency radio equipment and direction-finders.

There can be little doubt that, as she took off, Amelia may have realized that she had already become a pawn in the deadly mock war games the US military chiefs were planning in the Pacific. But, for Amelia, her one goal was the successful achievement of her round-the-world trip. If her plane was being used as some kind of military flying test bed, it was a small price to pay for the chance to circle the globe. The flight was publicized every step of the way, with cheering crowds to greet her as she touched down, rested, refuelled and took off again from the various airfields in South America, Africa, Asia and Australia.

A month after her voyage had begun, her navigator, Captain Frederick Noonan, strapped himself into the cockpit behind her and the pair prepared to take off from Lae, in New Guinea, for the riskiest part of the flight. Their course was to go over a stretch of the Pacific never crossed by an aircraft before – the 2,556 miles from the coast of New Guinea to Howland Island. It was the major leg of the flight across open water. The next stop should have been Honolulu, then Oakland in San Francisco Bay and finally home in triumph to Lafayette, Indiana.

The flight plan between Lae and Howland Island was also the most crucial part of the journey for the US navy's warship *Ontario* and the coastguard cutter USS *Itasca*, supposedly acting as safety and rescue standby vessels, but secretly using Earhart's Electra as a 'target' plane to check and test their direction-finding equipment. As Amelia took off, the American radio operator in Lae, Harry Balfour, received a weather forecast on his radio and teleprinter from the US navy fleet base at Pearl Harbor. Although he called the information through to Earhart and her navigator several times, he received no reply.

Just five hours after his transmission, at 3pm, Balfour picked up Amelia's voice, clear and unflustered. All seemed to be going well. Two hours later the pilot radioed again, this time reporting that adverse weather conditions were forcing her to lose height and speed. But she was still unconcerned.

In mid-ocean, on board the warship *Ontario*, navigation officer Lieutenant Horace Blakeslee, who had estimated the plane should be overhead at 10pm, failed to make radio contact, although one of his deck officers thought he heard the sound of an aircraft overhead. The *Ontario*'s searchlights were switched on full, but heavy rainclouds had blotted out the sky. The warship, low on fuel supplies, was soon forced to return to base on a nearby island, and to leave the task of locating Amelia and her plane to the coastguard vessel *Itasca* almost 1,000 miles further along the course, off Howland Island. As the *Ontario* turned away, a land-based radio operator on Nauru Island to the north picked up a broadcast from her, reporting the words: 'A ship in sight ahead.'

In the early hours of the morning, at 2.45am, the radio room of the *Itasca* heard Amelia's voice on the radio again. The only part of the message they could understand was: 'Cloudy weather . . . cloudy.' On the island itself, a top-secret-frequency radio direction-finder failed to track the location of the transmissions.

An hour later Amelia broadcast again, forlornly reporting overcast weather and asking the coastguard ship to contact her on a new radio frequency. Again, they failed to locate her or raise her on the radio. Throughout the night they heard sporadic plaintive calls from Amelia Earhart, fragments of weary speech, but despite all their high-powered equipment they still could not reach her.

After 8.43am came Amelia's final message, frantic and desperate. She gave a confusing, wide-ranging compass position, which could have put her anywhere on a line stretching hundreds of miles both north or south of Howland Island. Then, all contact was lost for good, and soon the massive, but fruitless, search began.

President Franklin Roosevelt personally ordered the battleship USS *Colorado* from Hawaii to steam full-speed to the search area with its three catapult-launched spotter aircraft. The following day he instructed the aircraft carrier USS *Lexington* and three destroyers to set off on a ten-day voyage from the west coast of America to join the search.

Nervous US navy senior brass, who had secretly organized the seemingly innocent Earhart flight as an experimental trial, now began to complain they were 'spending millions of dollars and disrupting navy training schedules to search for a couple of stunt fliers'.

There was a spate of heartless and cruel hoax calls from American radio hams, claiming that they had picked up distress messages from Amelia. Some claimed she was 'injured but alive' and quoted her call sign – KHAQQ.

On 5 July newspaper stories reported that a radio message had been picked up from Amelia by the Pan American Airways bases on Midway and Wake Islands. The message indicated that Amelia had been forced down several miles southeast of Howland, near the Phoenix Islands. War Department chiefs rushed to deny the reports, afraid that the Japanese might learn of the existence and power of these covert radio installations. For two weeks, an entire task force of US warships and planes scoured more than 150,000 square miles of the Pacific, skirting the Japanese-held islands to the north.

Then, speculation erupted among the more sceptical and scandal-hungry Americans that Amelia Earhart had been on a mission for the government and had landed safely on Howland Island, in order to give the War Department an excuse to send warships and aircraft to spy on the Japanese war preparations in the Pacific. There were reports that US pilots, supposedly engaged in the search for their public heroine, had returned to base with aerial photographs of Japanese bases.

The rumours persisted for almost a year. One newspaper in Oakland, California, began a series of articles about Earhart's disappearance. Their first issue claimed that the woman pilot had been lost because the direction-finding equipment on Howland had been supplied with the wrong kind of batteries and had failed the moment it was switched on. But Washington soon put a stop to this, and no further articles were published.

Amelia Earhart and Captain Noonan were never seen again. Three years later, after the attack on Pearl Harbor and the overwhelming carnage of the war in the Pacific, the fate of the two fliers paled into insignificance until, as America fought back against the Japanese and began to drive them westward across the ocean, the mystery of Amelia Earhart slowly began to unravel.

Then it suddenly deepened again. In 1944, the victorious US forces captured the Marshall Islands from the Japanese. During routine interrogation, Vice-Admiral Edgar Cruise was told by a native interpreter that two American fliers, a man and a woman, had been brought to the islands by Japanese captors in 1937. The couple had been transferred to the grim Garapon Prison at Japanese military headquarters in Saipan in the Mariana Islands. The woman was dispirited and broken. After only a few months in the hellish conditions of the military torture centre, she died of dysentery. Her male companion, of no further use to his interrogators, was executed.

Twenty years later, in 1964, two former US Marines, who had served in the Pacific, announced publicly that they had recovered the remains of Amelia Earhart and Frederick Noonan from unmarked graves on Saipan in July 1944 and had transferred them back to the United States for burial. But the US Marine Corps still refuses to confirm or deny their stories.

And so the mystery remains. Was Amelia Earhart an intrepid espionage agent who gave her life to help her country develop its air defences? Did she die an unsung heroine with her brave navigator in the squalor of a Japanese prison camp? Is she buried in a secret grave back in her American homeland with the location of her final resting place known only to a handful of military intelligence officials? Or was she simply an enthusiastic amateur glory-seeker who didn't care who organized and subsidized her daring exploits, just as long as she made the headlines?

The unemotional answer may lie in a report in a small

Australian newspaper, published a year after her disappearance. The Sydney newspaper claimed that the United States had secretly informed the Australian Government, their Pacific ally, of their plans to monitor Amelia's last flight as cover for its preparations for war. The US War Department, which made great propaganda of the treachery of the Japanese sneak attack on Pearl Harbor, had refused to admit that it had duped her into a peacetime spying mission. The newspaper claimed the last distress signal had, in fact, come from the location of the Phoenix Islands, but the search squadrons used it as an excuse to turn north and spy on the potential enemy.

The paper concluded: 'Sentiment comes second to Secret Service.'

Madeleine Smith

The sensational trial of Madeleine Smith, which kept staid Edinburgh in a ferment for nine days in July 1857, has always divided people into two camps. There are those who believe that Madeleine was a cunning, cold-hearted poisoner who, once she had tired of her lover, killed him so that she could marry someone socially superior. And there are those who consider her a pathetic victim of blackmail, driven to despair by Emile L'Angelier, the man she once loved, but totally innocent of his death.

When the jury returned a verdict of 'not proven', Madeleine Smith, who throughout the trial had shown interest but no concern, was seen to sigh heavily, then smile. Wild cheering echoed through the court. But the fact remained that L'Angelier had died an agonizing death with 82 grains of arsenic in his stomach, enough to kill a dozen men, and nobody knew how it had got there.

Before having an opinion one way or the other it is necessary to know something about the background of this handsome, languid girl from a middle-class Victorian home and her suitor, an impoverished but dapper young packing clerk who desperately wanted position and respect and 'a lady' for his wife.

Madeleine was the elder daughter of a highly successful Scottish architect, James Smith, who was one of the pillars of Glasgow. He had offices in Vincent Street, a solid family house in India Street and a somewhat over-ornate country residence on the Clyde. She was not beautiful but her lustrous eyes, luxuriant brown curls and graceful carriage made her very attractive. Her father was a typical Victorian papa who provided a prosperous household with six servants for his family, but expected his word to be taken as law. She emerged in her finery most evenings to attend some function or other; but the days could be tedious with little to do but occupy herself with typical Victorian hobbies thought suitable for a young lady, such as painting on vellum, making feather flowers and creating pictures from seaweed. What no one knew, until she met Emile, was that behind the façade of demure respectability was a vibrant, sensual woman crying to be let out.

Emile L'Angelier was a total stranger to her sort of world. His father was a nurseryman in Jersey and he had been sent to Scotland to work with a firm of seedmen, with the object of improving his status. When Madeleine met him, however, he was still a packing clerk, earning very little, but with rather grandiose ideas about his future. However his employer seemed to consider him industrious, honest and sober and, if he was somewhat vain, perhaps that was because he was French.

She first saw him staring at her as she was strolling in Sauchiehall Street with a friend. Their eyes met, and he bowed. He discovered someone at his work who knew her and who promised he would introduce Emile at the first opportunity. When that moment came he took the opportunity of giving her a note, a billet doux, which expressed his feelings in flowery terms. Madeleine told him she had worn it next to her heart at the ball that night. So began the vast correspondence that was later to prove so damning. The letters showed that by April 1855 he had gained her affections but was not sure of them. Twice during the year she tried to break off their relationship but he was persistent. He made it clear he was not a man to be so easily dropped. In a copy of a letter, written as early as 19 July 1855, he showed what he was capable of. 'Think what your father would say if I sent him your letters for perusal . . .'

She had poured out all her suppressed sensuality on paper, writing him love letters that made people gasp with shock, for it was a period in which women were supposed to suffer sex, not enjoy it. Later, when L'Angelier's lodgings were searched, over 500 letters from Madeleine were discovered and 60 of them were read out in court.

Their go-between was a friend of Emile's called Mary Perry who seems to have been fond of him without expecting a relationship. She was perfectly satisfied to be a letter-carrier between her friend and this fine lady and let them use her house for their secret meetings.

Once they had declared their love for each other in fulsome romantic terms they became 'engaged' and obviously slept together. On 7 May 1856 Madeleine wrote him this letter:

> 'My own beloved husband:
> I trust to God you got home safe, and were not much the worse for being out. Thank you, my love, for coming so far to see your Mimi. It is truly a pleasure to see my Emile. If we did wrong last night, it must have been in the excitement of our love. I suppose we ought to have waited till we were married. Yes, beloved, I did truly love you with my soul. I was happy; it was a pleasure to be with you. Oh, if we

> could have remained, never more to have parted! Darling Emile, did I seem cold to you last night? Darling, I love you, my own Emile. I love you with all my heart and soul. Am I not your wife? Yes, I am; and you may rest assured that after what has passed I cannot be the wife of any other . . .'

Madeleine had obviously made up her mind to introduce Emile to her father, but James Smith had no intention of letting his daughter marry a penniless little foreigner. 'Do keep cool when you see him, I know his temper – every inch like my own,' she advised Emile. But the meeting never took place. Emile's pride was wounded and the hurt is reflected in a letter he wrote to his beloved in which he fumes and fusses about the treatment he received.

'Never fear, my own beloved husband,' she wrote to console him. 'I shall be quite ready whenever you fix our marriage day . . . I am quite sure when they hear we are married they will all give in.'

When the family moved down to Row, their country house on the Clyde, she asked for a ground-floor bedroom. This meant she just had to step out of her window to meet him. Throughout that summer of 1856 she abandoned herself to love. Emile seems to have accepted that they were betrothed and that they would eventually be married.

But he had also noticed that a certain name seemed to have crept into her conversation and her letters with a frequency that alarmed him. The name was William Minnoch. This gentleman had for some time admired Madeleine and wanted her for his wife. He was a short, fair-complexioned businessman in his 30s, well educated, successful and well liked by James Smith who considered him an ideal son-in-law. He began calling, with obvious intent, but Madeleine said she did not find him in the least attractive and was not interested in him. 'Don't give ear to any reports you may hear . . . there are several going about regarding me getting married . . . regard them not' she told Emile. But he was very disturbed and she did not help matters when she remarked in a letter she sent him towards the end of August: 'Minnoch was never so pleasant as he has been this last visit. He was very nice indeed.'

When the Smith family returned to Glasgow secret meetings were made more difficult than before. They moved to a different house and this time Madeleine's bedroom was in the basement with the bedroom window at street level covered by bars. There was no chance of her slipping out without being detected. They would sometimes have a whispered conversation through the bars but it was not very satisfactory. Emile began to feel depressed.

Still, nothing had prepared him for the shock which came in her next letter. She talked of their love as though it was in the past. 'We shall often talk over all our past performances – it really has been quite a small romance,' she said lightly. He was devastated. He began to see his dream of being someone of consequence fading rapidly as he woke to the reality of her increasing coldness towards him.

She had been seen in public with Minnoch and her letters to Emile became shorter and shorter and were signed simply 'Yours devotedly'. There was no doubt that she had enjoyed being escorted by someone as well regarded and socially acceptable as William, as she now called him, and on 28 January she made up her mind to accept his proposal of marriage.

First, she had to bring an end to her affair with the little Frenchman. Emile played into her hands by indulging in a petty little habit with which he showed her his displeasure. He returned one of her letters. Her response, considering the passionate abandon of her previous correspondence was brutal:

'This may astonish you, but you have more than once

> returned me my letters and my mind was made up that I should not stand the same thing again. And you also annoyed me much on Saturday by your conduct in coming so near to me. Altogether I think owing to coolness and indifference (nothing else) that we had better for the future consider ourselves as strangers. I trust to your honour as a gentleman that you will not reveal anything that has passed between us . . . I shall feel obliged by your bringing my letters and likeness . . . I trust you may yet be happy, and get one more worthy of you than I.'

It became evident that he would not give her up without a fight. Nor would he give up the letters and threatened to show them to her father. His friend Tom Kennedy, who was cashier at Huggins, where he worked, tried to persuade him to behave like a gentleman and let the whole affair come to an end. Weeping, Emile told him: 'No, I shan't; she shall never marry another man as long as I live . . .' He also said miserably: 'Tom, it's an infatuation; she shall be the death of me.'

When Madeleine realized that he was not going to return the letters and might, in his present state, pluck up the courage to show them to her father, she became frantic. 'Emile will you not spare me this – hate me, despise me – but do not expose me. I cannot write more. I feel ill tonight.'

She asked him to come to the house, where she could talk to him through the bedroom window. He kept the appointment on 11 February 1857 and she appears to have agreed to a wedding the following September.

On the morning of 20 February when Emile's landlady, Mrs Jenkins, went to call him for breakfast, she found him very ill. He said that on the evening before as he was returning home he was seized with violent spasms in the stomach and thought he was going to die before he could reach his bed. During the night he had been very sick.

Four days later Mrs Jenkins was wakened at 4am by groans and cries from his room. The symptoms were the same as on 20 February, but this time Emile was shivering and complained that he was cold and thirsty. The doctor who was fetched to see him decided it was a bilious attack and prescribed accordingly. He advised him to take a short holiday.

At about this time Madeleine had been shopping for arsenic in Sauchiehall Street. She went into a chemist and asked for sixpence worth of poison. Asked for what purpose she needed it, she replied: 'For the garden and for rats at our country house.' The arsenic was sold to her mixed with soot according to the law and she seemed concerned about the colour of it. The chemist admitted afterwards he did wonder why if she was only giving it to rats.

She had written to Emile showing concern about his bilious attacks, addressing him as 'My dear, sweet Emile' and sending him love and kisses. She assured him she loved no one else in the world but him. Emile, by now wary of her passionate outpourings, asked her to give some plain answers to his questions. Nevertheless, he signed himself 'your ever affectionate husband – Emile L'Angelier'.

Emile was feeling a little better and went to see his friend and go-between, Miss Perry. He told her he had seen Madeleine, then remarked: 'I can't think why I was so unwell after getting coffee and chocolate from her on the two occasions we met.' He even went as far as to say he thought the drinks might have been poisoned, but obviously did not consider that had anything to do with the woman he loved.

She was very much occupied elsewhere. She had gone up to Bridge of Allan in Stirlingshire to make arrangements for her marriage to William Minnoch. She seems to have forgotten that she had promised to marry Emile in September. Before she left Glasgow she had been shopping again. This time she asked for an ounce of arsenic 'for rats in Blythwood

Square' (their Glasgow home). But Christina Haggart, the Smiths' maid, swore she had never seen a rat in that house.

Madeleine continued to write Emile affectionate letters: 'I long to see you, to miss and embrace you, my own, only sweet love. Miss me my sweet one – my love, my own dear sweet little pet.' Why she insisted on sending him these sugary epistles while demanding the return of her other letters is hard to guess.

Emile got leave from work and caught the train to Bridge of Allan, hoping to catch Madeleine, but she had already returned to Glasgow. He had missed a letter she had written asking him to meet her on 19 March and another letter containing an urgent summons was sent on to him by his landlady. He read the note eagerly: 'Why, my beloved, did you not come to me. Oh beloved are you ill? Come to me sweet one. I waited and waited for you, but you care not. I shall wait again tomorrow night same hour and arrangement. Do come sweet love, my own dear love of a sweetheart . . .' He caught the first train back.

When he arrived back at his lodgings in Franklin Place on the evening of 22 March he told his landlady that he would be very late that night. He went out, presumably to see Madeleine. He did not return until 2.30am and rang the bell violently. Mrs Jenkins found him doubled up with pain on the doorstep. He told her all the old symptoms had returned and she helped him to his room where he again vomited a greenish substance. By 4am he was so bad Mrs Jenkins herself ran out to fetch the doctor, who said he would visit him in the morning, meanwhile she was to give him a few drops of laudanum and a mustard plaster. But two hours later in response to urgent pleas from Mrs Jenkins the doctor stirred himself and hurried round to Franklin Place to give his patient a morphine injection.

When Mrs Jenkins drew back the curtains in Emile's room at 9am the next morning he looked so pale that she asked if he would care to see anybody. He asked for his friend, Miss Perry, but before she could be fetched the doctor arrived. When he lifted Emile's head from the pillow, it fell back limply. He was dead.

When they came to look through his belongings they found a letter which began: 'Why, my beloved, did you not come to me? . . .'

Nothing now could stop the relentless stream of inquiries and of course they led straight to Madeleine, to her love affair with Emile and to the letters she had written him. An autopsy had revealed that Emile's stomach had contained enough arsenic to kill 40 men and the position of the poison in his body showed that it had been administered more than once.

One morning when the maidservant went to waken Madeleine she found her bed empty. It was thought that she had probably gone to their country house and Minnoch set off with one of her brothers to fetch her back. They caught up with her on the Clyde steamer but the tactful husband-to-be asked for no explanations.

On Tuesday 31 March Madeleine, showing great composure, made a statement to the Sheriff of Lanarkshire telling the whole story of her relationship with Emile L'Angelier and even admitting that they had plans to marry. But she insisted the last time she saw him was three weeks before his death.

When the trial began on 30 June all eyes were fixed on the trapdoor leading down to the cells. There was a gasp from the public gallery as the prisoner came up and moved towards the dock. She was tall, elegantly dressed with a fashionable bonnet, and exuded an air of nonchalance that some observers thought indecent. She was veiled and carried a lace-edged handkerchief and a bottle of smelling salts. She rose, threw back her veil and in a clear voice declared herself 'not guilty'.

She was asked why she had bought arsenic and, contrary

to what she had told the chemist, she explained to the court that it was purely for cosmetic purposes, to soften her hands and improve her complexion. Victorian women often did this, though it was obviously unwise. Madeleine said she had diluted it with water and used it on her face, neck and arms. The prosecution made a great deal of the fact that she had given one reason for purchasing arsenic to the Glasgow chemist but quite a different one to the court. It was however essential to show that she had arsenic at the right time and also the opportunity for administering it at that time. Could she have laced the coffee and cocoa she handed to Emile through her bedroom window? It was very hard to prove.

On the fifth day of her trial the letters were produced and read out in a thin voice by the aged clerk. The Lord Advocate ordered that passages that were particularly offensive should be omitted. She did not show a scrap of emotion as she heard evidence of her passionate love for a dead man.

When it came to the summing-up the Lord Advocate, for the prosecution, said he would show that Madeleine had got herself into such a position that murder was the only solution. She had, he said, the means, the opportunity, the motive and the cool character that was perfectly compatible with murder. But Dean Inglis of the Faculty of Advocates, for the defence, put Madeleine's case in a masterly speech. He presented Emile as vain, pretentious and conceited, a seducer who had corrupted an innocent girl. He had also at one time boasted of being an arsenic eater and there was evidence he had been a frequent sufferer from stomach ailments. 'Think you,' the Dean demanded, 'that without temptation, without evil teaching, a poor girl falls into such depths of degradation? No! Influence from without – most corrupting influence – can alone account for such a fall.' He appealed to the noblest instincts of all those listening to consider the awful fate of this girl if found guilty.

The jury was out for 25 minutes before bringing in their 'not proven' verdict. It may have been popular with the crowds but it was noticed that the usually courteous Dean Inglis left the courtroom without so much as a glance at his client. Only when it was all over did they begin to think of her total lack of emotion. One newspaper commented that she had demeaned herself as if L'Angelier had never had a place in her affections. 'If it had been a trial for poisoning a dog, the indifference could not have been greater.'

Her indifference towards William Minnoch was equally noticeable. The whole business had made him ill with grief but when told he had been ill she commented: 'My friend I know nothing of it. I have not seen him. I hear he has been ill, which I don't much care.' Minnoch had had to make a very brief appearance as a witness for the prosecution and was never forgiven.

The 'not proven' verdict was not a comfortable one to live with in Scotland. It really meant that some parts of the evidence were too doubtful to risk a conviction. Madeleine moved to London where she married an artist, bore him three children and lived an interesting life. Her last days were spent in America where she died at the great age of 91, protesting her innocence to the end.

Lucrezia Borgia

Lucrezia Borgia is, of course, the name on everyone's lips when you mention the subject of wicked women. She belonged to one of the most feared and hated families in history and the unspeakable crimes laid at her door include incest, not only with her brother, Cesare, but with her father, Pope Alexander VI.

The Borgias were certainly a terrible brood, but does Lucrezia herself deserve the reputation she has gained over the centuries?

Those who have written about her in modern times have come to the conclusion that she was used as a pawn by the brilliant, ruthless, Borgia men and sacrificed to their terrible ambition. It was under their influence and through their actions that she became 'the most execrated woman of her age'.

She lived in a world in which the concepts of decency and morality were very different from our own. The fact that her father, the libertine Rodrigo Borgia, could become head of the Catholic Church was evidence of that. But, says the historian Gregorovius, who is the most quoted authority on Lucrezia: 'She was neither better nor worse than the women of her time. She was thoughtless and filled with the joy of living.'

If she had not been the daughter of Alexander VI and the sister of Cesare Borgia she would have been unnoticed by the historians of her age, or at most would have been mentioned only as one of the many charming women who constituted the society of Rome. In the hands of her father and her brother, however, she became the tool and also the victim of their political machinations, against which she had not the strength to make any resistance.

Chroniclers of the day using scandal, innuendo and rumour, and the very real hatred felt for the Borgias, turned Lucrezia into a legendary monster and that is the picture that has endured.

Her family, Spanish in origin, had a meteoric rise from obscurity because within a relatively short span of time it produced a number of brilliant men, distinguished by their sensual beauty, force of intellect and ruthless ambition. One of these was Cardinal Rodrigo Borgia whose mistress, a Roman beauty called Vannozza, bore him several children including Lucrezia and the infamous Cesare.

Lucrezia was born on 18 April 1480. She was brought up in her mother's house on the Piazza Pizzo di Merlo, only a few steps away from the Cardinal's Palace. Rodrigo did not acknowledge the children as his own until he had been made Pope and was absolutely sure of his power.

Before she was 11 years old the first suitor had made a bid for Lucrezia's hand. Two months later another appeared and was favourably considered, but both were swept away as too insignificant when Rodrigo took the Triple Crown and desired a prestigious match for his lovely daughter.

He put her into the care of the two women who were closest to him, his cousin and confidante Adriana di Mila, who was married to an Orsini, and her daughter-in-law Giulia Farnese, an exquisite woman, said to be a poem in gold and ivory, who became Rodrigo's most famous mistress. These two tended the darling of the Borgia family like a hot-house orchid, keeping her apart in the splendour of the Palazzo of Santa Maria until she was prepared for her first marriage.

At 13 Lucrezia was golden-haired and graceful, with a slender white neck and teeth like pearls; a delectable morsel to offer to the handsome Giovanni Sforza, Lord of Pesare. They were married in a magnificent ceremony to which half of Rome was invited.

The marriage was not to last long. The Borgias saw to that. They soon realized they had underplayed their hand in marrying Lucrezia to Sforza when they could have used her to gain entrance to the powerful house of Aragon. They made up their minds to get rid of the unfortunate bridegroom.

Their method could not have been more humiliating. They announced to the world that Sforza had proved impotent and that his wife was still a virgin. The greviously insulted Lord of Pesaro called upon all the saints in the calendar to bear witness that he was a full man and had 'known his wife carnally on countless occasions'. Ripped from the arms of the child-wife he loved, he swore vengeance on the Borgias. But their power was too great. They forced him to sign a confession admitting his impotence and he fled Rome before anything worse could happen to him.

Although Lucrezia had not been averse to this first husband, she accepted the family decision without protest and retired to the convent of San Sisto on the Via Appia to enhance her virginal image in preparation for another marriage. When she left the convent the nuns were said to have been loathe to see her go for she had turned the convent into a place of sophistication and fashionable pleasure.

Towards the end of February 1498 news spread through Rome that Lucrezia was pregnant. Her lover, it was said, was a Spanish gentleman at the Papal Court: Pedro Calderon, known generally as Perotto. A man of immense charm, he was certainly guilty of desiring her, if not actually seducing her. Cesare Borgia had Perotto thrown into prison and soon after his corpse was found in the river Tiber.

From this affair stemmed most of the stories of incest that hung like a foul miasma about the Borgias for ever after. Cesare, a dazzling man, handsome, hard and pitiless, certainly loved his sister with an intensity that seemed abnormal and could have been incestuous in motive although there is no evidence that her affection for him was of the same nature. Rumours began to spread that the child Lucrezia was said to be expecting was the result of incest. Sforza seized upon the gossip to get his own back and accused Lucrezia of sleeping not only with her brother but also with her father, the Pope.

Whatever the truth – and Perotto was the most likely father – a child called Giovanni, who was later created Duke of Nepi, was born in Rome in March 1498. He grew up at Lucrezia's side but she always referred to him as her little brother. By others he was referred enigmatically as 'The Roman Infante'. He remained a mystery.

The next match arranged for Lucrezia was, like the first, for political reasons. Alfonso, nephew of the King of Naples who created him Duke of Bisceglie for the alliance, was, however, of far more use to the Borgias than poor Sforza. Through him Cesare hoped to gain entrance by marriage to the house of Aragon.

Alfonso promised to stay in Rome with Lucrezia for one year before carrying her off to his lands near the sea, and all seemed well until the bloodthirsty Cesare started his political intriguing once again. Before long he and the young bridegroom were at daggers drawn. Many in Rome saw the terrible signs of Cesare's jealousy and said prayers for the Duke of Bisceglie.

One evening Alfonso visited the Vatican. When he set out from there to make his way home to the Palace of Santa Maria, across the Piazza of St Peter's, he was brutally attacked. His friends carried him home half-dead with a split skull and terrible wounds to his body and legs. When Lucrezia saw him she nearly fainted. She nursed Alfonso back to health with great devotion but Cesare was determined to finish the job that had been so badly bungled.

One evening Alfonso rested at home, a gang of ruffians broke into his room and one of them, a professional garrotter, killed him before he could cry for help. The affair marked a new phase in Cesare's career in ruthlessness and no one heeded his protests that the Duke of Bisceglie had threatened him.

Lucrezia was sent away from Rome to the Castle of Nepi where, for a time, she cried bitterly over the loss of her beautiful young husband. But she was a Borgia and, in spite of her tenderness for the dead Alfonso, she dried her tears and waited to see what her father and brothers had in store for her next.

Recalled to the Vatican by her father, Lucrezia tried to amuse herself, in spite of being a widow. Lurid accounts were printed of parties which Cesare gave to distract her. At one of these he was said to have strewn hot chestnuts over the floor of the Pope's apartment and forced naked courtesans to crawl along lighted candles to retrieve them. Other accounts of parties at which prizes were awarded in fertility contests and obscene theatricals were performed reminded many people of earlier Roman orgies.

There is no record of Lucrezia ever taking part, however. Indeed about this time she began to be better known for her piety and gentleness.

She was about to be introduced to her third husband. The Borgias had chosen an alliance with the ancient and noble family of d'Este but negotiations had not gone as smoothly as they wished. Their prospective bridegroom, Alfonso d'Esta, the Duke of Ferrara's son, balked at the prospect of taking to his bed a lady of such notoriety. He was also worried that he might suffer the same fate as her previous husband. His father, furious that his plans for the allegiance were in jeopardy, warned his son that he would marry Lucrezia himself if necessary.

The two families argued and bargained and eventually the Pope settled a fabulous dowry on his daughter. Even so, it was only half of that demanded. Lucrezia was married for the third time in great splendour and at her wedding was seen to dance radiantly with the brother who had made her a widow.

She took leave of her father for the last time and set out with her new husband and a priceless trousseau including magnificent clothes, great works of art, jewellery and rare furniture to spend the rest of her days with the great Prince of Ferrara. He took her to the family's vast medieval castle at Vecchio where she continued to amaze him with her charm, grace and modesty.

For a time she continued to be a subject of gossip and speculation. Her name was linked with that of the poet Pietro Bembo. Did she become his mistress or not? His poetry was widely believed to have been written in memory of the passionate hours he had spent in her arms. More dangerous was the friendship she cultivated with Ercole Strozzi, a fervent, elegant young poet who did not bother to hide his feelings for her.

There was a terrible scandal when Strozzi was found dead in the street, wrapped in a cloak, his body a mass of dagger wounds. Those who hated the very name of Borgia said she had organized the killing out of jealousy because the poet was about to take a wife. Others hinted that Strozzi knew too much and she had feared he might talk about the favours bestowed upon himself and Bembo by the Prince of Ferrara's wife.

Time passed, she became Duchess of Ferrara and poets and men of letters began to superimpose another image of Lucrezia, that of a supremely virtuous woman, flawless, perfect and an angel of mercy. It was probably just as exaggerated as the one she had left behind in Rome.

All we do know for certain is that when she died of childbirth in June 1519 she was regarded with admiration and esteem by those who knew her. She was deeply mourned by the Duke of Ferrara who called her 'my dearest wife'.

Trials

'A Dingo Has Got My Baby!'

Shortly before nightfall on the evening of 17 August 1980, a group of campers were enjoying a barbecue near Ayers Rock in the Australian outback. Suddenly there was a shout.

'A dingo has got my baby!' called Mrs Lindy Chamberlain. In horror, her husband and other campers ran back to the Chamberlains' tent to find the baby girl's basket empty. 'All I could see was a horrible, lonely whiteness in that basket,' the father told police some time later. But other witnesses remembered traces of blood around the tent. And, about a week later, the child's torn and blood-stained jumpsuit, singlet and nappy were found near the base of Ayers Rock. Of nine-week-old Azaria Chamberlain, however, there was no trace. She had vanished, never to be seen again.

It seemed a horrific tragedy, made all the nightmarish by the looming presence of Ayers Rock – one of the weirdest things on Earth. The vast red platform rises abruptly to more than 1,000ft above the outback of the Northern Territory, forming the largest monolith in the world. Chameleon-like, its colour changes according to atmospheric conditions and the sun's position. The Aborigines have always regarded it as a magical place and the site of many strange happenings.

The baby's mysterious disappearance prompted a flood of gossip and speculation. Lindy and Michael Chamberlain, both in their 30s, were members of the Seventh Day Adventist Church, he being a minister. It was rumoured that the baby's name, Azaria, meant 'sacrifice in the wilderness'; had the little girl really been taken by a wild dog? How was it that the clothing had been found, while the baby's body had completely vanished? Many people came to regard the circumstances as suspicious, and the case won nationwide attention.

In February 1981 the coroner at Alice Springs delivered his verdict on the missing child. Taking the unprecedented step of reading his finding (a 13-page document) before television cameras, he informed an estimated viewing audience of two million people that the parents were entirely blameless. Azaria Chantal Loren Chamberlain had met her death while being attacked by a wild dingo; in trying to make off with the baby, 'the dingo would have caused severe crushing to the base of the skull and neck and lacerations to the throat and neck'. The body had been disposed of by a person or persons unknown, and neither the parents nor their sons Aidan (7) and Reagan (4), who had been camping with them at the time, were in any degree responsible. Moreover, 'I find that the name Azaria does not mean and never has meant "sacrifice in the wilderness".'

The coroner expressed sympathy for the bereaved parents: 'You have not only suffered the loss of your beloved child in the most tragic circumstances, but you have all been subjected to months of innuendoes, suspicion and probably the most malicious gossip ever witnessed in this country.' He declared that he had permitted TV coverage to stop the rumours in the most direct way possible.

It was a very emphatic performance – but the case simply would not die. A year later, in February 1982, a second inquest was called on the basis of new forensic evidence. On this occasion a forensic expert testified that traces of blood had been found on the clasp of a camera bag belonging to the parents. It was foetal blood – that is, the blood of a baby less than six months old – and with it was found baby hair. Blood had also been cleaned from conspicuous areas in the couple's car, but it had not been eradicated completely: there were traces in all sorts of nooks and crannies such as the door handles, the door hinge and places under the dashboard. The evidence was consistent with what was to become the prosecution's extraordinary allegation – that Mrs Chamberlain had taken the baby from the tent to the front seat of the car and there cut her throat. Afterwards, it was alleged, the body had been buried at the campsite, but dug up again. Azaria's clothing had been removed and placed at the spot where it was found several days later.

The coroner decided that there was a case for Mrs Chamberlain being sent to trial for murder, and her husband as an accessory in seeking to cover the act up. The accused parents were clearly stunned by the finding, and Michael Chamberlain remained for some time with his head buried in his hands, visibly distressed.

The 'Dingo Case' had now acquired a worldwide audience, and Lindy Chamberlain went into hiding before the trial. When proceedings opened on Monday 13 September, the world learned of a new twist in the drama. Mrs Chamberlain, 34, was seven months' pregnant – she might well give birth to another child during the trial.

The Supreme Court at Darwin was packed. So great was foreign interest that a separate room had to be set aside for the news media, with its own closed-circuit TV system linking up with proceedings in the court. The judge warned the jury not to allow anything they might have read to prejudice their verdict, while acknowledging that the publicity was 'without precedent in our lifetime'.

Mr Ian Barker QC, opening for the prosecution, said the foetal blood found in the car exploded the dingo story, which was no more than a 'fanciful lie to conceal the truth'. The prosecution would not try to establish Mrs Chamberlain's motive. But the evidence, he said, pointed conclusively to the fact that she had murdered her baby, entering the tent afterwards to leave the smears of blood that were found there later. The body was probably placed in the camera bag in the car prior to its eventual disposal.

In the weeks that followed, powerful evidence was

marshalled to support the case. For example, Professor Malcolm Chaikin, head of textile technology at New South Wales University, declared that the baby's clothing had not been torn by a dingo's teeth but cut with some fairly sharp scissors; moreover, he claimed to have found some fragments of the material in Mrs Chamberlain's camera bag. James Malcolm Cameron, professor of forensic medicine, was flown in from the London Hospital medical college and also denied the likelihood of a wild dog's involvement. Asked what the clothing evidence pointed to, he said: 'It suggests that there was an incised wound of the neck. In other words, a cut throat.' The wound was caused by 'a cutting instrument across or around the neck held by a human element'.

The human story which emerged from campsite witnesses was, however, generally favourable to the defence. A Mrs Lowe was asked if anything in Lindy's behaviour prior to the disappearance had suggested that murder was on her mind. 'No, exactly the opposite,' replied the woman. 'She had a "new mum" glow about her.'

There was sobbing from the parents in the dock when another witness described how Lindy Chamberlain told her she had called her baby Azaria because it meant 'Blessed of God'.

Mrs Alice Amy Whittaker said she had seen a dingo emerging from the bush while she was washing up at the campsite. It was skirting the lighted area and seemed to be moving towards the Chamberlains' tent. This was only 20 minutes before Michael Chamberlain rushed up to her and begged her and her husband to pray for Azaria because she had been taken by a dingo. Later that night Mrs Whittaker had comforted Lindy Chamberlain by saying that what had happened was God's will. Lindy tried to resign herself: 'It says, doesn't it, that at the Second Coming babies will be restored back to their mothers' arms?' But she was distressed and seemed particularly agitated by the idea that the searchers might be looking in the wrong place: 'I will have to live with this for the rest of my life. I don't want to have to if my baby simply died because I did not look in the right place.'

Some controversy surrounded the issue of dingoes' general habits. Was such an attack – with the removal of the prey – consistent with the wild dogs' known behaviour? Mr Leslie Harris, president of the Dingo Foundation, testified for the defence, asserting that a dingo might well regard a sleeping baby as prey and would be capable of carrying one off. A dingo, he said, might close its jaws over the entire head and make off with it so as not to lose its meal to other dingoes.

Several other witnesses testified to dingo attacks in the Ayers Rock area. One man described how his four-year-old son had been attacked by a wild dog at the same campsite only a month before Azaria's disappearance.

What of the bloodstains in the car? In June 1979 – a year before the event – the Chamberlains had picked up a man injured in a road accident. The victim testified in court that he had been bleeding profusely from the head. Of course, his was not the foetal blood, but the damning evidence of this issue was challenged by the defence's own forensic witness, who claimed that the foetal blood-test results were not reliable.

At one stage, the whole court travelled 800 miles to study the scene of the disappearance. Lindy Chamberlain was permitted to stay in Darwin, for she was by now eight months' pregnant. But she did give evidence when the court returned, in the fifth week of the trial.

Her version of events was already embodied in a statement made to police. She claimed that she had put Azaria to bed while her husband was at the barbecue, and afterwards came back to the cooking place to prepare a meal for her oldest son, Aidan. A baby's cry was heard from somewhere near the tent, and Lindy went back to check that all was well. As she walked towards the tent she saw a youngish dingo coming out of it; she yelled and briefly gave chase. Then, thinking only that her baby might have been bitten, she hurried into the tent.

In the box, Lindy Chamberlain was often emotional. She broke down in tears when asked to examine her baby's bloodstained clothing. When the judge asked if she was all right she said that she was – but two of the three women on the jury began crying and the trial had to be temporarily adjourned.

Lindy Chamberlain wept again that day when the prosecution's allegations were repeated. 'It's not true,' she declared through stifled sobs. The next day she broke down again, complaining to the prosecutor that 'you are talking about my baby, not some object'. And, when it was alleged that she deliberately smeared the family tent with blood, she replied fiercely: 'No, that's pure fabrication.'

Summing up for the defence, her counsel asserted that there was no conceivable motive for the killing. Ten independent witnesses had been brought forward to testify that Lindy was a loving and caring mother to Azaria. The prosecution's whole story would be 'laughable if it was not such a horribly serious matter'.

What was the jury to make of it all? From the Press reports, the forensic evidence did not appear conclusive either way, while the problem of motive was tormenting. Why should Lindy Chamberlain murder her baby? Was there anything in the rumour of a sacrifice? Or had she suffered from post-natal depression? Then again, if she was innocent, what on earth had happened to the body? Why were no bones or other human relics found? The fact of the matter was that, to many outsiders, both the dingo and murder stories seemed improbable.

The jury of nine men and three women had, however, observed all the long and complex proceedings. And on Friday 29 October, after deliberating for six hours, they returned unanimous verdicts of guilty: Lindy Chamberlain of murdering her baby and Michael Chamberlain of being an accessory after the fact. The trial judge, Mr Justice James Muirhead, passed the mandatory sentence of life imprisonment with hard labour on the convicted woman.

She received the sentence impassively, but was tear-stained when driven from the court to Berrimah Prison on the outskirts of Darwin. Her husband, subsequently given an 18-month suspended sentence, was released on a promise of good behaviour, and immediately attended a church service with his sons.

A verdict had been reached on the missing baby – but what of the one to be born? On 17 November, under guard at a Darwin hospital, Lindy Chamberlain gave birth to a second girl. But she was not permitted to keep the child in prison, and Kahlia, as the baby was called, was taken from her mother only hours after the delivery. Australian justice was so cruel, though, as to enforce a permanent separation. Two days later, Lindy Chamberlain was freed on bail pending an appeal; out of concern for the baby's welfare the mother was permitted to retire to an Adventist Church college with her family while awaiting the Appeal Court's ruling.

The judgement came in April 1983, when the Chamberlains' joint appeals were dismissed by the Federal Court in Sydney. The judges referred to the importance of seeing and hearing scientific witnesses in order to evaluate their testimony. As for the couple's credibility: 'If the jury disbelieved them, as they must have done, we are quite unable to say that they were wrong.'

Lindy Chamberlain was returned to jail, and all attempts to obtain her release failed until sensational new forensic evidence, including a baby's jacket, was found at Ayers Rock in January 1986. Yet another inquiry was ordered: Lindy Chamberlain was freed pending its outcome – and officials declared that whatever the result she would not be sent back to jail.

The Arsenic-eater's Wife: Mrs Maybrick

In 1884 an extraordinary murder case was reported from Liverpool. Two women, Mrs Flanagan and Mrs Higgins, confessed to killing Mr Higgins by poison which they had obtained by soaking arsenic out of flypapers. Since the women came from the working class, the case never quite became a classic. But only five years later another flypaper poison drama hit the headlines in Liverpool, and this one unfolded in a comfortable middle-class setting. Moreover, it featured a delicious cocktail of arsenic mixed with adultery – and culminated in one of the most controversial trial verdicts ever reached in an English court. The Maybrick Mystery was one of the grand Victorian crime blockbusters, and more than 30 years after the trial the name of the leading lady was still well remembered. When James Joyce wrote his novel *Ulysses* (1922) he had Molly soliloquize at length about the case in a passage beginning 'take that Mrs Maybrick that poisoned her husband . . . white Arsenic she put in his tea off flypaper . . .' But did she?

Born Florence Elizabeth Chandler, the future Mrs Maybrick was a Southern belle from Mobile, Alabama, who was educated partly in Europe. In 1881, at the age of only 18, she married James Maybrick, a wealthy English cotton broker of 42. Three years later the couple settled down at Battlecrease House in Liverpool, where Mrs Maybrick bore her husband two children, a boy and a girl. And their family life seems to have been happy enough until, in 1887, Florence discovered that her husband had a mistress in Liverpool. James had sired no fewer than five children by the woman – two of them since his wedding.

It is clear that, afterwards, something froze between Mr and Mrs Maybrick. While keeping up outward appearances, they stopped sleeping together as man and wife. Increasingly, Florence looked for pleasure in the company of Alfred Brierley, a handsome young friend of her husband, while James continued to visit his mistress and indulge his favourite pastime – of eating arsenic.

It may sound incredible, but the people of Styria and the Tyrol had long practised arsenic-eating for therapeutic purposes; James Maybrick was a hypochondriac who took the substance both as a tonic and as an aphrodisiac. The Victorians were more cavalier with their medicines than we are today, and Maybrick also took a host of other potentially lethal preparations, including strychnine. But arsenic seems to have been his favourite. 'It is meat and liquor to me,' he once told a friend. 'I don't tell everybody. I take it when I can get it, but the doctors won't put any into my medicine except now and then. That only tantalizes me.' To another acquaintance he confided as he added some grey powder to a dish of food: 'You would be horrified, I dare say, if you knew what this is – it is arsenic. We all take some poison more or less. For instance, I am now taking arsenic enough to kill you.'

Mrs Maybrick knew something of her husband's addiction to medicines, and in March of 1889 she mentioned to the family doctor that James sometimes took a white powder which she thought might be strychnine. What was the likely result? The doctor replied that her husband ought to take care, because he could die. Then he joked: 'Well, if he should ever die suddenly, call me, and I can say you have had some conversation with me about it.'

Not long after this exchange, Mrs Maybrick for the first time spent an illicit weekend in London with Brierley. Her husband grew suspicious and on 29 March the Maybricks were seen quarrelling openly at the Grand National. There was a furious row at home, too, that evening, in which Maybrick beat his wife and dragged her around the bedroom. The following day, when the doctor treated her black eye, Mrs Maybrick told him that she intended to seek a separation.

Mrs Maybrick did not, in fact, open legal proceedings. But the row simmered on through April, and it was at the end of the month that Florence made a soon-to-be-notorious trip to a local chemist, where she bought a dozen arsenic-coated flypapers. Soon afterwards, the papers were seen by servants to be soaking in a washstand in Mrs Maybrick's bedroom.

On 25 April, James Maybrick drew up a new will leaving almost everything in trust for his children – and almost nothing to Florence.

On 28 April, James Maybrick was taken violently sick after eating a lunch that his wife had prepared for him. It was not the first time he had felt unwell – he had long suffered from dyspepsia, and complained of headaches and stiffness of the limbs. But that night he was dazed, vomiting, and practically numb in the legs. He recovered somewhat the next day, but in the week that followed he relapsed repeatedly. During this period Mrs Maybrick visited another local chemist – and bought another two dozen flypapers.

On 7 May, Maybrick collapsed, vomiting so severely that he could keep practically no food down. His tongue was badly furred and he experienced the tormenting and persistent sensation that he had a hair in his throat. The servants had never much liked Florence, and neither had Maybrick's family; nor had the flypaper poisonings of Mrs Flanagan and Mrs Higgins been forgotten in Liverpool. It was Alice Yapp, the children's nurse, who first voiced her suspicions, declaring to a family friend: 'Thank God, Mrs Briggs, you have come, for the mistress is poisoning the master.'

Was she? None of the doctors concerned with the case had suspected poisoning before; but now nurses, family and servants all started watching Mrs Maybrick with keen interest. And one evening Florence was seen furtively removing a bottle of meat juice from the sick man's bedroom table; equally furtively, she brought it back two minutes later. Had she tampered with the contents? The bottle was quietly removed by a doctor, pending chemical analysis.

On other occasions, curious fragments of conversation were overheard from the sick room. Once, for example, Mrs Maybrick tried to get her husband to take some medicine. Maybrick flatly refused and said: 'Don't give me the wrong medicine again.'

'What are you talking about?' Mrs Maybrick replied. 'You never had the wrong medicine.'

James Maybrick died at 8.40pm on Saturday 11 May. And almost immediately his brothers Edwin and Michael locked Florence up while a search of the house was made. Hidden in a trunk in a linen cupboard was a packet labelled 'Arsenic – Poison for Cats'. Analysis confirmed that the bottle of meat juice, handled by Florence, had contained arsenic. And, when arsenic was found in the dead man's stomach, Mrs Maybrick was formally arrested.

The trial opened on Wednesday 31 July 1889 amid the most intense public interest. The Press had got hold of all the key details and had effectively found the prisoner guilty already, so that the black van which conducted her to the Liverpool courthouse was booed and jeered by a vast crowd. Nevertheless, Mrs Maybrick – who wore black crepe in the dock – replied with a clear 'not guilty' when charged with murder, and the trial did not go entirely as the papers had anticipated.

The prosecutor's case was straightforward. He described the adulterous meeting with Brierley in London; the subsequent quarrel; the buying of flypapers and the sudden onset of the dead man's illness. There was the bottle of meat juice treated with arsenic, the packet of 'Arsenic –

Poison for Cats'; a handkerchief had also been found soaked in arsenic, and arsenic was even found soaked into the pocket of a dressing gown worn by Mrs Maybrick. To cap it all, nurse Yapp had intercepted a letter written by Mrs Maybrick to Brierley, and this was read out at the trial. It had been composed during the early stages of Maybrick's illness, and to the Victorian court it was a thoroughly shocking document. While writing of her husband being 'sick unto death', Florence had seemed chiefly concerned to reassure her lover ('my own darling') that the details of their liaison were safe. Moreover, the doctors at that stage did not suspect that Maybrick's illness might be fatal – how did Florence know that he was 'sick unto death'?

But Mrs Maybrick was powerfully represented by a brilliant defence counsel in Sir Charles Russell, who had an answer for every suspicious circumstance. Take the famous flypapers, for example. Mrs Maybrick had from the moment of her arrest maintained that she bought and soaked these in order to prepare an arsenical face-wash to treat her complexion. Arsenic was in fact widely used in cosmetics at the time, and, as Sir Charles pointed out, Mrs Maybrick bought the papers quite openly at shops where she was well known. Would she do so if she had any malign purpose? The papers, were, moreover, left soaking all day for the servants to see.

The cosmetic face-wash explained the stained handkerchief and dressing-gown pocket. But what of the poisoned meat juice? Again, Mrs Maybrick had kept nothing back. She had candidly stated on arrest that throughout that particular evening her husband had been nagging her to give him one of the powders which he habitually took. She at first refused, but he begged her so piteously to put some in his food that in the end she agreed. But she had no idea that the substance concerned was arsenic – it was just one of James's 'powders'. As for the expression 'sick unto death' which had been used apparently prematurely, it was merely a Southern figure of speech meaning gravely – not necessarily fatally – ill.

Ultimately, the strength of the defence case lay in the medical evidence. Only a small quantity of arsenic was found in James Maybrick's stomach at the post mortem; there were traces of strychnine, hyoscine and morphine too. The hypochondriac had badly abused his stomach and had died from an acute inflammation which, the defence alleged, might have been provoked by almost anything. The distinguished Dr Tidy, one of the nation's leading forensic experts, testified for the defence and was quite unshakeable in his refusal to diagnose arsenic poisoning – or poisoning of any kind:

Prosecutor: He died from gastro-enteritis caused by an irritant?

Dr Tidy: Yes.

Prosecutor: It was some strong irritant, probably poison?

Dr Tidy: Some substance which to him acted as an irritant.

Prosecutor: Which was poisonous enough to kill him?

Dr Tidy: Which to him acted as an irritant.

Prosecutor: Can you suggest to us what it was?

Dr Tidy: No, I cannot.

This exchange continued for some time before the prosecutor retired defeated. The climax of the trial came when Mrs Maybrick herself was permitted, by the judge, to make a brief statement. (Under the law of the time, she was not allowed to give evidence and submit to questioning. This was changed in 1898 with the introduction of the Criminal Evidence Act.) Halting and tearful, she described how she prepared her arsenical face-wash; how she had mixed the powder into her husband's meat juice; and how, on the day before he died, she had fully confessed her adultery and received 'his entire forgiveness for the fearful wrong I had done him'.

Mrs Maybrick collapsed after speaking, and had to be revived with smelling salts. By now the court, the Press and the public were all firmly on her side and an acquittal seemed almost certain. After all, it had not been conclusively proved that Maybrick died from arsenic at all – let alone that the prisoner had poisoned him. And if he *did* die of arsenic, it might well have been self-administered.

However, throughout the trial the judge, Mr Justice Stephen, had shown a certain lack of grip on the proceedings. He had recently suffered a stroke (and was soon to be admitted to an asylum) and in summing up he repeatedly blundered over the facts in a way detrimental to Mrs Maybrick's cause. To everyone's astonishment the jury found the prisoner guilty of murder, and while she sobbed and protested in the dock, sentence of death was passed upon her.

There was an immediate public outcry. The prosecution's witnesses were hissed and jostled as they left the court; nationwide petitions were raised; questions were asked in parliament while, at the gaol where Mrs Maybrick was being held, flowers arrived by the cartload. In fact, Mrs Maybrick received several offers of marriage as the day of her execution drew nearer. Then, at the last minute, with her scaffold already built, the Home Secretary bowed to public pressure and commuted the sentence to life imprisonment.

Florence Maybrick served 15 years as a model prisoner before, in 1904, she was released. She went back to the United States, where she lectured for some time on the need for penal reform, always including her declaration 'I swear to you I am innocent'. Eventually she disappeared from the public eye to live out her life as a recluse dependent chiefly on the charity of friends. She died in South Kent, Connecticut, in 1941 at the age of 76.

Did she do it? All who have studied the case agree that she should never have been convicted on the evidence.

'The element of doubt existed and it should have been resolved in her favour, because that is the law. . . . She was entitled to an acquittal,' wrote thriller-writer Raymond Chandler, a keen student of the case. He was fascinated not only by the mystery but by the coincidence that Mrs Maybrick's maiden name, Florence Chandler, was the same as his mother's. In fact, Chandler at one time planned a history of the affair, and took the trouble to itemize all the points for and against Mrs Maybrick's case.

What did the creator of private eye Philip Marlowe make of it all? 'I am pretty well convinced the dame was guilty,' Chandler wrote to a friend. But that was only one man's verdict – the fact is, nobody knows.

Death of a Playboy Prince: Madame Fahmy

The public in the 1920s was fascinated by the mysterious East: it was the decade when Valentino was *The Sheik* and Fairbanks was *The Thief of Baghdad*; when Tutankhamun's tomb was opened and when, throughout the Western world, crop-haired jazz girls daubed their eyelids with Egyptian kohl. And in 1923 there occurred a sensational murder trial to match the taste of the period. In a sumptuous suite at the Savoy Hotel, Madame Marie-Marguérite Fahmy shot dead her Egyptian playboy husband, Prince Ali Kamel Fahmy Bey. He had treated her, it seemed, like an Oriental beast. To the case's exotic mixture of sex, luxury and blood were added the talents of Sir Edward Marshall Hall, the most flamboyant defence counsel of the age. Small wonder that the Savoy Shooting stole the front-page headlines.

Madame Fahmy, the accused, was a glamorous Parisian brunette aged 32 at the time of the trial. The Prince, ten years younger, was a wealthy Egyptian and attaché at the French Legation in Cairo. The couple had met in Paris during May of 1922, at which time she was a divorcee. And she progressed quickly from becoming the Prince's mistress to becoming his wife; the pair were married in December of that year. Madame Fahmy accepted the Moslem faith for the purpose of the wedding, but insisted on her right to wear Western clothes. She also stipulated that she retain the right of divorce, but this was not acknowledged by her husband. Prince Fahmy considered his wife bound to him under Moslem law: he possessed the sole right of divorce (as well as the right to take three more wives should he wish to do so).

The marriage was disastrous. Whatever infatuation was present at the outset, the couple quarrelled wherever they lived as man and wife: in Paris, Cairo and in London, to which they came in July of 1923. Often Prince Fahmy beat his wife, once so severely that her jaw was dislocated. On another occasion he kept her locked up for three days on his yacht; on yet another he swore an oath on the Koran that one day he would kill her. This was done with such solemnity that the frightened woman wrote formally to her lawyer accusing her husband if she should ever disappear: 'Yesterday, January 21, 1923, at three o'clock in the afternoon, he took his Bible or Koran – I do not know how it is called – kissed it, put his hand on it, and swore to avenge himself upon me tomorrow, in eight days, a month, three months, but I must disappear in his hands. This oath was taken without any reason, neither jealousy, nor a scene on my part.' As for the Prince, he really does seem to have regarded his wife as a creature to be mastered by force. 'Just now I am engaged in training her,' he once wrote. 'With women one must be severe – no bad habits.'

They had been at the Savoy for barely a week when the fatal row broke out. On the evening of 9 July, the couple quarrelled violently in the hotel restaurant, and Madame Fahmy, it was to be said at the trial, shouted in French: 'You shut up. I will smash this bottle over your head.' Asked by the band leader if she wanted anything special played, she answered: 'I don't want any music – my husband has threatened to kill me tonight.' Upstairs, at about 1.30am, the quarrel was still going on. A porter saw Prince Fahmy burst from his room in his pyjamas, a flushed mark on his cheek. 'Look at my face!' he fumed. 'Look what she has done!' Then Madame Fahmy came out too, still in her white, beaded evening dress, and shouted furiously in French.

The porter ushered them back into their suite, and walked on down the corridor. Moments later, three shots detonated. Rushing back to the suite, the porter saw Madame Fahmy toss down a .32 Browning automatic. The Prince lay bleeding from headwounds, and died not long after in hospital.

Charged with murder, Madame Fahmy was brought to trial at the Old Bailey in September 1923. Her cause inevitably stirred up a lot of public sympathy, but sympathy alone does not win court cases. Madame Fahmy had manifestly shot her husband dead at point-blank range in the heat of a domestic quarrel. And it would need all the talents of her defence counsel, Marshall Hall, to get her off the hook.

He gave the case everything he had got. Handsome, and flamboyant in style, the advocate was famed for theatrical effects which have disappeared from the modern lawyer's repertoire. But they still swayed juries in the 1920s, and Marshall Hall was their leading exponent.

Of course, he dwelled on Prince Fahmy's cruelty, cataloguing the beatings and humiliations endured by his wife. But there was more to be said against the dead man. Marshall Hall suggested that he was a homosexual who enjoyed a compromising relationship with his male secretary. Madame Fahmy, it was alleged, had been made to submit to a nameless but nauseating sexual indignity (presumably anal intercourse), and suffered painful illness in consequence. In fact, that illness was what provoked the quarrel on the fateful night. She had asked for money to pay for an operation in Paris, and he told her that she could only have it if she agreed to indulge his whim. 'I will if you do something for me,' he had said, before starting to tear off her dress.

When Madame Fahmy refused, he half-strangled her. 'He seized me suddenly and brutally by the throat with his left hand,' she testified in French. (All of her statements were made in her native tongue and delivered to the court through an interpreter.) 'His thumb was on my windpipe and his fingers were pressing on my neck. I pushed him away but he crouched to spring on me, and said "I will kill you!"'

'I lifted my arm in front of me and without looking pulled the trigger. The next moment I saw him on the ground before me. I do not know how many times the revolver went off.' She had thought that the gun was empty of cartridges. 'I thought the sight of the pistol might frighten him,' she sobbed under cross-examination.

Marshall Hall's final speech to the jury was regarded as the most dramatic of his brilliant career. Having cast the Prince as an Oriental monster of depravity, he impersonated him, stalking across the court in emulation of his advance on his wife. Then, pistol in hand, the advocate took the part of his client: 'As he crouched for the last time, crouched like an animal, retired for the last time to get a bound forward – she turned the pistol and put it to his face.'

Suddenly, Marshall Hall levelled the gun at the foreman of the jury. He paused for a moment. 'And to her horror the thing went off!'

All eyes were fixed on the tableau. The court was in total silence. And then Marshall Hall released the gun, which clattered to the floor – exactly as Madame Fahmy had dropped it.

It was a spellbinding moment, and the advocate had further touches of courtroom magic in store. Concluding his address, he referred to the Oriental darkness into which the prisoner had been plunged by her marriage. 'I ask you to open the gate and let this Western woman go back into the light of God's great Western sun,' he ended, extending a prophetic arm high up on the Old Bailey skylight. A shaft of sun came through – right on cue.

In no time at all, the jury had found Madame Fahmy not guilty of murder; not guilty of manslaughter either. Such volcanic cheers erupted with the verdict that the judge ordered the public benches to be cleared and it was in an emptied court that Madame Fahmy sobbed her gratitude as she was released from custody, a free woman.

The whole case had become a triumph for 'Western light' over 'Oriental darkness' in an almost offensive manner. In fact, Marshall Hall received a formal complaint from the leader of the Egyptian Bar, accusing him of castigating all Egypt and indeed the entire East in order to save his client. The truth is that the fictional ideal of *The Sheik* had met a horribly flawed counterpart in Prince Fahmy. Marshall Hall had merely toyed with the conventions of his day, reversing the romantic image to make the dead playboy an archetype of evil.

Red Empress: Jiang Qing

She loved orchids and kept pet monkeys; in her private jet were silken bedsheets. The daughter of a concubine, a Shanghai film starlet in her youth, Jiang Qing hardly presented the obvious picture of a left-wing revolutionary. And yet she was a key figure in the gigantic human upheaval of China's Cultural Revolution. And as wife to

Chairman Mao she helped to shape the lives of well over 800 million people.

It has been said that Jiang Qing always resented men, despite her widely rumoured promiscuity. Born in Shadong province in 1912, both she and her mother were mistreated by her father, and she grew up an outcast in the houses of wealthy male clients. By the age of 19, she had already been through two marriages and was the subject of lewd gossip when she made a film career under the name of Lan Ping (Blue Apple). But Jiang Qing had a vein of deep seriousness. In 1938 she met Mao Tse-tung, leader of the Chinese communists, and became his fourth wife – despite furious opposition from within the Party. In fact the marriage provoked a serious internal crisis, and only went ahead on the agreement that the former starlet would play no part in politics whatsoever.

For many years, Madame Mao honoured that promise. But it was broken in the early 1960s when she began radically reforming cultural life in Shanghai, especially in adapting traditional Chinese opera to make it serve modern revolutionary themes. Under a left-wing party boss, Shanghai was becoming a hotbed of reinvigorated revolutionism – and it was here, in 1966, that the first salvoes of the Cultural Revolution were fired.

The Great Proletarian Cultural Revolution was a massive onslaught, launched by Mao against traditional attitudes and bureaucracy which had been creeping back into Chinese life since the People's Republic was formed in 1949. Young people especially were mobilized as Red Guards to rekindle revolutionary zeal; many universities were closed and thousands of professors and party officials were hounded from their jobs to face persecution and disgrace. Several of the most prominent figures in Chinese life were publicly humiliated, and people all over the world became familiar with propaganda images of young Chinese, massed in their thousands, chanting loyalty to Mao and spouting his 'thoughts', which were encapsulated in the Little Red Book, which they waved.

Ferment was most intense during the years 1966–8, but the Cultural Revolution did not end definitively until Mao's death in September 1976. In that sense, it lasted a full decade, and throughout the period Jiang Qing belonged to the central group directing change: she was at the epicentre of the earthquake.

On Mao's death a power struggle broke out between the radical and moderate factions in China. Jiang Qing with three close associates in the leadership – Yao Wenyuan, Zhang Chunqiao and Wang Hongwen – represented the extreme leftist tendency, and, nicknamed the Gang of Four, they tried to seize the reins of government. They failed. Arrested in October 1976, they were held for four years pending trial.

The Gang of Four had pursued its own ends with vindictive fury in its day. Now that the tables had turned, it was inevitable that there should be a grand reckoning. And few can have savoured the situation more than the new Vice-Premier, Deng Xiao-ping. Twice disgraced under the Cultural Revolution, he had at one time been forced to work in a kitchen. But Deng was rapidly becoming the effective head of government and leading a dramatic programme of liberalization. He did not mince words about Mao's widow; she was a woman 'so evil, not enough evil can be said about her'.

The trial opened in November 1980 at the Public Security Headquarters in Peking. The crowd outside was bitterly hostile to the accused, who were brought in by the back entrance. Inside the building, before an audience of some 800 handpicked 'members of the public,' a welter of charges was read out against the Gang of Four inciting them and six other defendants with ultimate responsibility for the persecution of exactly 729,511 people under the Cultural Revolution – of whom 34,800 died. On the bench sat a panel of 30 judges, and the session was opened by Chief Justice Jiang Hua – himself a victim of the Red Guards.

Jiang Qing's three associates looked pale and dispirited as they entered the iron-railed dock. In fact, little was heard from them in the days which followed; two collaborated fully with the new authorities in hope of lenient treatment, while the third, Zhang Chunqiao, refused to co-operate in any way – he did not utter a single word during the entire trial. So, from the outset, Mao's widow held all the limelight. Pouchy-cheeked and bespectacled, the 67-year-old woman no longer looked a ravishing beauty. But she walked with pride and confidence into the dock – she was the star without question.

Defiance was the keynote of her performance. It was even reported that in a preliminary hearing Jiang Qing complained of the heat. When nothing was done, she stripped naked before the judges – only putting her clothes back on when officials turned off the heating. (The story may be true in its essentials; but it is unlikely that she got any further in undressing than undoing a tunic button or two.)

It was a remarkable trial. The authorities clearly took some trouble to project the image of fair and just proceedings, televized extracts were shown throughout China, as well as broadcast worldwide by satellite. Yet no foreign journalists were allowed to attend the hearings, and there are startling gaps in the record of precisely what went on.

Nevertheless the world saw plenty of Jiang Qing. On 26 November two young women from her earlier entourage came forward as witnesses to describe how, in 1974, Jiang had told them to poison Mao's mind against certain veteran communists. Mao's widow could be seen leaning nonchalantly against the rim of the dock and refusing to answer questions about the conspiracies of the late Marshal Lin Biao. Looking nonchalant was just one of her tricks; at other moments in the trial she would pointedly remove her hearing aid, as if indifferent to what was being said.

A whole range of charges was brought against her. One of the most persistent was that she had persecuted China's many ethnic minorities by, for example, suppressing the national costumes of Tibetans, Koreans and Mongols in favour of the familiar Maoist boiler suit (for herself, Madame Mao was known to detest the boiler suit, preferring to wear long black dresses of her own design). She had also forced Moslems to breed pigs, against their religion, further damaging race relations.

It was also heard how she had persecuted past acquaintances who had known her before her marriage to Mao. Allusions were made to her supposedly lurid private life, and it was said that she had organized raids on people's homes to recover compromising letters and documents.

Some of the most damaging evidence related to the framing of President Liu Shao-qi, who had been condemned as a reactionary during the Cultural Revolution and died mysteriously in prison. Mao's widow seems to have been particularly jealous of Liu's elegant US-born wife, who spent 11 years in prison. In court, Jiang Qing claimed to remember nothing about ordering her arrest on the trumped-up charge that she was a secret agent of the United States, Japan and Taiwan. Then a document ordering the arrest was produced and shown to bear Jiang Qing's signature. 'Yes, it's my handwriting,' Mao's widow admitted almost contemptuously. 'I recognize it.'

She also admitted to signing arrest orders for 11 other people connected with Liu, one of whom was to die under torture. Even Liu's cook had been arrested on the grounds that the excellence of his cooking had corrupted his employer. The unhappy man's skill had been a recipe for disaster. He appeared in court to testify that he'd been imprisoned for more than six years on the promise of an early release if he helped seal the fates of Liu and his wife.

It seems that Jiang Qing considered these and similar actions 'justifiable' in the battle against revisionism. But her replies were carefully edited, so that the whole truth is not known. For example, the main thrust of her defence seems to have been that she did everything with Mao's full consent, and was 'only obeying orders'. This was not a line that the new leadership wanted explored at length. In 1980, the cult of Mao was still very much alive, and, although unprecedented official criticisms of him did emerge at the time of the trial, they came only in muted tones. Nor was there any official mention of the brief collaboration between the Gang of Four and Mao's nominal successor, Chairman Hua Guo-feng. Yet it was reliably reported that Jiang Qing did incriminate him for his actions in 1976; certainly, his fall from power rapidly accelerated during the trial and he was forced to resign. (This suited Vice-Chairman Deng very nicely: it has even been suggested that the whole trial was stage-managed to incriminate Hua.)

But the authorities did not censor Jiang Qing's extraordinary outbursts, which made the proceedings utterly compelling as a human drama. For example, on 12 December, Liao Mosha, an eminent essayist, described in the witness box how he had been condemned to eight years in gaol at the behest of Mao's wife. While giving testimony about the ordeal he appeared to break down, wiping his eyes. This clearly infuriated Jiang Qing. In sneering tones she hurled abuse at the man, shouting out that he was an 'enemy agent'. Twice the bench tried to call her to silence by ringing an electric bell; Jiang replied by rounding on the judges calling them 'renegades'. Eventually, she was grabbed by two burly young policewomen who hustled her from the court; the trial was suspended.

It was not the last time that the choleric widow had to be forcibly restrained. Similarly angry outbursts recurred later, when she was accused of persecuting another writer.

Jiang denied the charge until a tape-recording from 1970 was played, in which she could be heard demanding evidence against her victim – even though she was told that none existed. Jiang Qing then acknowledged that the voice was her own, and tried to justify her position. The court, however, did not want to hear any justifications – she was shouted down by a woman prosecutor and again dragged from the court.

On 29 December, as proceedings drew to an end, the chief prosecutor called for the death sentence, which was carried out in China by a single bullet in the back of the head. In her own final statement, Jiang Qing lambasted her accusers, calling the new regime one of 'reactionaries', 'counter-revolutionaries' and 'Fascists'. With ill-concealed emotion she proclaimed that 'arresting me and bringing me to trial is a defamation of Chairman Mao Tse-tung', while 'trying me is tantamount to vilifying the people in their hundreds of millions'. How, she wanted to know, could the court take it upon itself to sentence Mao's spouse of nearly 40 years? She shouted Maoist slogans: 'It is right to rebel!'; 'Making revolution is no crime!' And once again she was dragged from the court, this time yelling defiantly: 'You just want my head. I am prepared to die!'

Many in the new leadership probably believed that, for propaganda purposes, an execution should be avoided. But Mao's widow was making it very hard for them by her contemptuous defiance. Of course, she and her co-defendants were found guilty. But there was a considerable delay before sentence was passed – a delay marked by leftist bombings in Shanghai – the Gang of Four's power base.

Finally, on 25 January 1981, the court came up with a compromise not uncommon in China. Jiang Qing was given a suspended death sentence. Under Chinese law it provided for the prisoner to be gaoled for two years and then executed – if there was no sign of any repentance. The same sentence was passed on the still silent Zhang Chunqiao, while Wang received life and Yao was given a sentence of 20 years.

Mao's widow seemed unusually tense and subdued before sentence was passed. But immediately afterwards she began loudly protesting, and, forcibly handcuffed, she was removed from the courtroom for the last time, shouting Maoist slogans.

The whole trial had been remarkable – stage-managed, certainly, but nevertheless opening up windows into the soul of revolutionary China with its cliques, tensions and rivalries. It was Jiang Qing who, single-handedly, turned what might have been a farce into a compulsive drama. Vituperative, defiant – and cruelly indifferent to the fate of her own victims – Mao's widow, the 'Red Empress', was also electrifying for her courage and conviction.

Two years after sentence was passed, the death penalty was lifted and life imprisonment substituted. But it was hard to believe that she had really repented. The newspapers reported only that she was being held in a high-security prison and understood to be kept in solitary confinement. It was said, too, that she passed the time in making little dolls, which earned her pocket money for small prison purchases.

The Strange Case of the Scottish Nanny: Carol Compton

When 21-year-old Carol Compton entered the Livorno courtroom, the Pressmen seemed to go mad. Journalists vaulted across the tables and surged past police in attempts to reach the girl as she was led, wearing jeans and a crucifix, into the cage built for terrorists which served as her dock. The court had banned photographers, but still the cameras clicked and whirred, registering the pale, bewildered face of the accused. In the case she chewed gum incessantly. Her mother snatched a kiss through the bars, calling, 'You're not scared, are you? I have been waiting for this for a long time. Get up and give them what for.'

It was December 1983, and this was no ordinary case. For 16 months, young Carol Compton from Aberdeen had been held on charges of arson and attempted murder. But what fascinated Press and public alike were the allegations, loudly aired in the Italian media, that she was a witch.

She had been held since August 1982, when she had been arrested on the island of Elba. Carol had worked there as a nanny for an Italian family, and it was alleged that shortly after her arrival two suspicious fires broke out – one of them threatening the life of a three-year-old child named Agnese. Before coming to Elba, Carol had worked for a household in the northern town of Ortosel. Three suspicious fires were said to have broken out there too. But it wasn't just the fires that captured the Press's attention. It had been reported that all kinds of paranormal events occurred when Carol was around.

The case was heard by two professional and six lay judges, and from the outset the proceedings were chaotic. Apart from the antics of the Pressmen, the courtroom acoustics were poor and Carol's thick Scottish accent presented problems for the interpreter. For example, she spoke on one occasion of a baby's 'cot'; it sounded like 'coat', and was translated as 'blanket'. She spoke of noises making her 'nervous'; the word was translated as *nervosa*, which means irritable. Complaints were made by a British Embassy official about the competence of the interpreter. At one point Carol abandoned translation and spoke directly to the bench in what little Italian she had picked up while in gaol.

Despite the problems, the trial went ahead and the issue of witchcraft soon came up. In early testimony, Carol's first employer had described how her maid in Rome spoke of a vase that had inexplicably fallen to the floor in Carol's presence; a picture of the Madonna had done so too. In court, the employer now admitted that the events could be explained in terms of normal accident. But the paranormal would not go away: a forensic expert from Pisa University claimed that the two fires he had investigated were 'phenomenal': they seemed to burn *downward* instead of up, and 'they were created by an intense sort of heat, but not by flames'.

Later, the grandmother of little Agnese testified that strange things had happened at her home on Elba after Carol's arrival. A plate and a cake dish fell to the floor without apparently being touched. 'Good heavens, there are spirits in our home,' she claimed to have said at the time.

All very spooky – but not really very substantial. Throughout the trial the prosecutor himself tried to keep sorcery out of the case. Carol Compton, he said, was not being tried as a witch but on five counts of arson and one of attempted murder. There was nothing inexplicable about the fires, he said: Carol Compton had started them. He could not be positive about the motive, but strongly suggested as a likely explanation that Carol might have lit the fires so that she could return to her boyfriend in Rome. In summing up he asked for a seven-year sentence, and criticized the media's impact on the proceedings. 'We have talked more fully about falling vases,' he complained, 'than about the baby she is accused of trying to murder.'

The main defence counsel was similarly dismissive about the so-called paranormal element. And in the end no ducking stools or *autos da fé* were invoked. Carol Compton was found not guilty of attempted murder, and acquitted of one of the five arson charges. But she was found guilty on the four others (two of them being reduced to attempted arson). The Scottish nanny was sentenced to two years in prison, meaning immediate release because of the long time she had already spent in pre-trial detention.

Carol Compton left Italy for home as soon as the trial was over. The judges subsequently issued a written explanation of her verdict, confirming that there was nothing paranormal about the case. In November 1984, an appeal on Carol's behalf failed, the Italian court holding the original conviction.

Artificial Insemination – a Test Case: Corinne Parpalaix

Sperm banks, womb-leasing, artificial insemination . . . the advances of modern medicine have created a wealth of new legal as well as moral problems. One of the most extraordinary cases to come before the courts was that of Madame Corinne Parpalaix, a Frenchwoman who desperately wanted a child by her husband. The problem was that her husband was dead.

Corinne had first met Alain in August 1981. He was a police officer who, shortly after they met, discovered that he had a serious illness. Told that he would require an operation which might leave him sterile, he decided first to make a deposit in a sperm bank known as Cecos – the Centre for the Study and Conservation of Sperm.

Alain's condition worsened afterwards. The couple married in hospital on 23 December 1983, but only two days later, on Christmas Day, he died.

Alain had left no written instruction about who was to inherit his sperm. But both his wife and his parents insisted that shortly before he died he had expressed a last wish to have a baby by Corinne. The sperm bank, however, refused to release his deposit without formal instructions from the Ministry of Health. And the Ministry declared that, since the whole subject of artificial insemination was under review, no such instructions could be issued.

Corinne had recourse to the law, and in August 1984 a court at Creteil, just outside Paris, ruled that the sperm bank must hand the deposit over. Madame Parpalaix wept with relief when she heard the judgement. Thanking the court and her lawyers, she declared: 'This judgement makes me a happy woman.'

The case had made legal history. But, sadly for Madame Parpalaix, her husband's illness had left him with sperm of very poor quality. Doctors decided that for the maximum chance of conception they must inseminate her with the whole deposit at once – and in January 1985 it was announced that the attempt had failed.

As a sidelight on the legal complexities, it might be added that a baby would have been illegitimate. Under French law, a child must be born within 300 days of a husband's demise if paternity is to be acknowledged.

The *Lady Chatterley* Trial

There are 13 episodes of sexual intercourse in D.H. Lawrence's novel *Lady Chatterley's Lover*. We know, because the prosecutor at the book's famous trial carefully counted them for the benefit of the jury. Lawrence, he complained, went further than to describe mere bedroom scenes:

> 'One starts in my lady's boudoir, in her husband's house, one goes to the floor of a hut in the forest with a blanket laid down as a bed; we see them do it again

in the undergrowth of the forest, amongst the shrubbery, and not only in the undergrowth of the forest, in the pouring rain, both of them stark naked and dripping with raindrops.'

Oh horrible, most horrible. *Stark naked and dripping with raindrops!* But worse was to come. The prosecuting counsel, Mr Mervyn Griffith-Jones, invited the jury to consider the sorry arithmetic: 'The word *fuck* or *fucking* occurs no less than 30 times. I have added them all up. *Cunt* 14 times; *balls* 13 times; *shit* and *arse* six times apiece; *cock* four times; *piss* three times, and so on.'

These words were at the root of the problem. An expurgated version of Lawrence's novel had been available in Britain since 1928, but in 1960, when Penguin Books tried to publish the first full English edition, the Director of Public Prosecutions took action. Penguin was brought to trial under the Obscene Publications Act and 200,000 copies, priced at 3s 6d, were held back from sale pending the court's decision.

Today, *Lady Chatterley's Lover* is generally agreed to be the worst novel Lawrence ever wrote; embarrassing not for its sexual explicitness but for weakness of plot and characterization. Lady Chatterley, the heroine, is feebly drawn while Mellors, her gamekeeper lover, is a grotesquely implausible creation. Nevertheless, for free-thinking men and women at the threshold of the Swinging Sixties, the book's defence became a cause célèbre, and scores of prominent intellectuals offered to testify on its behalf.

The trial opened, amid intense public interest, on 20 October 1960. The Clerk of the Court referred to Penguin Books Ltd as the 'prisoner at the Bar', despite the fact that the great panelled dock at the Old Bailey's Court No. 1 was empty. Prosecution was brought under the Obscene Publications Act of 1959 which, only recently introduced, stated that a book might be considered obscene if its effect 'if taken as a whole is such as to tend to deprave or corrupt'. However, section 4 of the Act provided immunity for noted artworks: a person should not be convicted of an offence if the published material was 'for the public good on the ground that it is in the interests of science, literature, art, or learning, or of other objects of general concern'.

The prosecution had its work cut out: even if the book were proved to be obscene, it could be excused on grounds of artistic merit.

Mr Mervyn Griffith-Jones, in opening, totted up his arithmetic of obscenity and went on to allege that the central characters were little more than 'bodies – bodies which continuously have sexual intercourse'. Was it, he asked, a book suitable for schoolchildren? 'Is it a book that is published at £5 a time as perhaps a historical document, being part of the works of a great writer, or is it, on the other hand, a book which is widely distributed at a price that the merest infant can afford?'

Perhaps a hint of snobbery, out of tune with the times, was betrayed by the line of argument. Clearly, the prosecution's worry had much to do with the fact that the book was going out as a cheap paperback, accessible to millions. And Mr Griffith-Jones showed his hand calamitously when he posed his now-celebrated question: 'Is it a book that you would have lying around the house? *Is it a book that you would even wish your wife or your servants to read?'*

It was an extraordinary blunder, suggesting that the jury – and indeed the whole reading public – consisted of wealthy gentlemen employing a sizeable domestic staff. Yet this was 1960, and three people on the jury were demonstrably women themselves. Perhaps the whole prosecution case was sunk irreparably by the gaffe: certainly, the jury members were visibly amused by the remark, which perfectly typecast Lady Chatterley's enemies as blimpish and fuddy-duddy.

The defence, in contrast, opened by establishing

Lawrence's prominent place among the great writers of the 20th century. Far from tending to deprave or corrupt, said Mr Gerald Gardiner, the book was moral in purpose, enshrining the author's faith in physical tenderness between people as an alternative to the public worship of money and what Lawrence called the 'bitch-goddess, Success'. Explicitness about the body and its functions was essential to the author's purpose – the book was in no way obscene.

Before the trial could go further, the jury had to read the book itself. Where was this to be done? In the comfort of home, or in the jury room at the Old Bailey? The defence pressed for the former, urging: 'The jury rooms are jolly uncomfortable places. There are hard wooden seats, and anything more unnatural than 12 men and women sitting round a table on hard wooden chairs with a book is hard to imagine.'

The judge arrived at a compromise, ruling that the jury must read the book at the Old Bailey, but ordering that a special room be fitted out with deep leather armchairs. It took the slowest reader among the jury three days to finish the task – after that, witnesses could be called.

In all, 35 public figures came forward to speak for the defence: critics, theologians, teachers, writers and editors among them. It was the first time that defendants were permitted to bring witnesses on the literary and moral qualities of a book in an obscenity case, and many household names appeared before the court: Dame Rebecca West, E.M. Forster, Dilys Powell, Cecil Day Lewis, the Bishop of Woolwich and others. Less well known – but just as important to the defence – were figures such as Miss Sarah Beryl Jones, Classics Mistress at Keighley Girls Grammar School, who testified that *Lady Chatterley* was fit to be read by her charges.

Norman St John-Stevas, then a practising barrister and author of *Obscenity and the Law*, acknowledged: 'I would not say it was the best book Lawrence ever wrote', but continued 'I think it is a very well-written book and is a contribution of considerable value to English literature'. A Catholic, he added: 'This is undoubtedly a moral book.'

Another prominent politician of the future, Mr Roy Jenkins MP had been chief sponsor of the Obscene Publications Bill during its difficult progress through parliament. He made it clear, before being cut off by the judge, that the prosecution was against the intention of the Act. He was asked if he considered the book literature:

> *Jenkins:* Yes, it most certainly is. Indeed, if I may add, it did not occur to me in the five years' work I did on the Bill . . .
> *The judge:* I really don't think we want to go into that.
> *Jenkins* (beaming): I am so sorry, my Lord.

Sorry or not, the point had been made.

Against the 35 witnesses called by the defence, the prosecution brought not one. In a masterful summing-up, Mr Gerald Gardiner submitted that the book would not deprave or corrupt anyone in real life, neither young people nor 'with deference to my friend I should add, not even your wives or servants'. Members of the jury smiled at that – and at 2.35pm on the last day of the trial they found in favour of Penguin Books, returning a verdict of not guilty.

It was never quite clear whether the jury had judged that the book was not obscene, or that it *was* obscene but redeemed by artistic merit. What is certain is that the verdict revolutionized views on what was fit to publish – and helped in a new era of permissiveness in society.

Marie Stopes

A hundred years ago, the subject of birth control was taboo. In Victorian novels, for example, you might come across discreet allusions to sexual activity; you might read of children born out of wedlock. But you could plough through a whole fiction library without discovering that unwanted pregnancies were preventable. This was remarkable, since overpopulation had long been considered a pressing problem, and forms of contraception had been accessible to the public since 1823. The fact was that talking about the issue was not considered very nice. Good heavens, the *ladies* might overhear.

In the event, it was the ladies who broke the silence. There was Annie Besant, tried and acquitted in 1877 on an immorality charge for publishing a family-planning tract. There was Margaret Sanger, who first coined the term 'birth control' in her magazine *The Woman Rebel*, in 1914. And then there was Dr Marie Stopes.

Born in 1880, Marie Charlotte Carmichael Stopes was a quite extraordinary woman. Energetic, intelligent and compassionate, she also managed to be wilful, humourless and entirely lacking in tact. She had worked as a botanist at Manchester University until the failure of her first marriage in 1916 started her thinking about marital problems. Two years later she published her notorious *Married Love* – a study of happiness in married couples.

It was not primarily a book about sex or birth control. But since the subjects were germane to her theme she weighed in with confidence. Sex, she argued, should not just be something for men to enjoy; women should also take pleasure in it to the benefit of a loving marriage. The reason why women often failed to find happiness was through fear of unwanted pregnancies. And so she advocated contraception.

Outrage! *The Times* refused to carry advertisements for the book, which proved a marvellous publicity boost. Over 2,000 copies were sold in a fortnight and the volume swiftly ran through a phenomenal 26 editions. Marie Stopes used the proceeds to set up a birth-control clinic, which opened at Holloway in north London in March 1921. There, a fully qualified nursing staff gave free advice and fitting of contraceptives to poor mothers. The favoured method was the rubber check pessary – issued at cost price.

The clinic proved a roaring success among the careworn women of London's teeming slums. But many leading churchmen and doctors took exception to Marie Stopes's crusade. In particular, a Dr Halliday Gibson Sutherland from Edinburgh University decided to take up cudgels; learning that a certain Professor McIlroy considered the check pessary dangerous, and being a devout Catholic, Sutherland produced his own book on the subject of birth control. The publication contained provocative passages about Marie Stopes. Sutherland complained of 'exposing the poor to experiment,' and wrote:

> 'In the midst of a London slum, a woman who is a Doctor of *German* Philosophy has opened a birth-control clinic where women are instructed in a method of contraception described by Professor McIlroy as "the most harmful method of which I have had experience". It is truly amazing that this monstrous campaign should be tolerated by the Home Secretary.'

Dauntlessly, Marie Stopes took up the challenge, suing Sutherland for libel and defamation of character.

The nine-day trial opened at the High Court on 21 February 1921, and battalions of distinguished medics were conscripted as witnesses by both sides. In the end, the conflicting medical evidence probably nullified itself, but there were some heated exchanges with the Bench. The presiding judge, through his interventions, came down clearly on the side of Halliday Sutherland and exhibited an obvious distaste for the whole subject.

'What possible good would it do to young persons to learn about check pessaries?' he fumed at a witness at one point.

Dr Meredith Young, for Marie Stopes, replied: 'If they do not learn it in a cleanly and proper manner, they will learn it in a dirty and sordid manner.'

'Why should they?' the Lord Chief Justice persisted, and embarked on a diatribe to the effect that millions of people breeze serenely through life without knowing the first thing about these blasted check pessaries. In a case bristling with gynaecological talk, his exasperation was perhaps understandable. But it was a male exasperation – these things were women's matters of no concern to a gentleman. And that, in a sense, was the point: unwanted pregnancies might be of no concern to gentlemen but they were of intimate concern to the mothers involved.

Marie Stopes herself counterpoised 'wise scientific prevention' with the 'horrible criminal abortion' so frequently practised in slumland. *Experimenting* on the poor? But the rubber pessary had been in use for more than 40 years – what was experimental about it? And in the end she received a mixed verdict from the all-male jury. After deliberating for four hours, they decided that the libel was substantially true but that it did not amount to fair comment, and £100 damages were awarded to her.

Marie Stopes subsequently won a full victory in the Appeal Court – but lost when Dr Sutherland took his case on to the House of Lords. Ordered to return the damages and repay very substantial costs, she ended up legally and financially the loser. But Marie Stopes had won a prize far more valuable in terms of mass publicity. The great taboo had been lifted – and lifted definitively.

The Bigamous Countess of Bristol: Elizabeth Chudleigh

An hour before midnight on 14 August 1744, Elizabeth Chudleigh, Maid of Honour to the Princess of Wales, secretly married Augustus John Hervey, son of the Earl of Bristol. The ceremony took place at the chapel of Lainston House near Winchester, by the light of a single wax taper stuck in the hat of one of the witnesses. There were only five people present besides the couple: two male witnesses for him; two women for her; and the parson, the Reverend Thomas Amis. The affair had to be kept secret for at that time the couple had poor prospects: he was no more than a junior naval officer, and she would sacrifice her £400 annual income from her court position if she openly lost her status as a Maid. The marriage made no financial sense – the likeliest explanation is that the two were much in love and wanted to consummate their passion legally.

Afterwards, the couple spent four days and nights together before Hervey was called to set sail for the West Indies, and Elizabeth returned to court. Subsequently, the couple saw precious little of one another. It has been speculated that Hervey was a poor sexual performer – or that he suffered from syphilis and infected her – either way, Elizabeth's ardent feelings for him died. She lived very happily on her own at her mother's house in Conduit Street and when Hervey returned on shore leave in January 1747 she only admitted him under protest. After an episode of what amounted to legal rape, she secretly bore him a son later that year. But the child died after only a few months and the relationship was over.

Elizabeth had her life to live, and she lived it to the full. The ravishing daughter of a Devonshire colonel, Miss Chudleigh (as she was still known) was a notorious figure at court and her favours were eagerly sought by many a noble lord. 'She breathed in an atmosphere of sighs,' it is reported. 'Every butterfly fluttered around her.' If the gossip is to be believed she was even wooed and won by George II; certainly, she made herself notorious at a masquerade in Somerset House, where she appeared as Iphigenia – virtually in the nude. 'Miss Chudleigh's dress, or rather undress, was remarkable,' wrote Mrs Elizabeth Montagu, continuing that even the other Maids of Honour (by no means maids in the strictest sense) refused to speak to her. Elizabeth was also rebuked by her royal mistress, who threw a shawl over her in the ballroom. But the gallant Miss Chudleigh was indifferent to all criticism and continued to behave as scandalously as ever. Practically no one at this stage knew about her secret marriage.

Twelve years passed after the death of her child and the break with Augustus John Hervey. She turned down offers of marriage from figures as eminent as the Duke of Hamilton and the Duke of Ancaster. But a hankering for title and secure wealth seems to have stayed with her. In 1759, it was reported that the Earl of Bristol was mortally sick. If he died, and her marriage were made public, she would become Countess of Bristol, commanding a fortune of £100,000. Elizabeth hastened to Hampshire and the aged Reverend Amis, demanding documentation of the marriage. With the aid of a lawyer, she persuaded the parson to backdate the church register to include an entry for her secret wedding.

All that she needed now was for the old Earl to die – unfortunately for her, he recovered from his illness and lived on for almost ten years more!

Elizabeth must have gnashed her teeth at this unwanted turn of events. But a more glittering prospect began to beckon. For some time she lived more or less openly as mistress to the very wealthy Duke of Kingston, a veteran of Culloden. And when the Duke offered her his hand in marriage she was ready, at last, to accept. The trouble was that the tables had turned: the secret marriage, which she had earlier been so eager to have certified, now stood in the way of her hopes.

Hervey also wanted to extricate himself from any marital obligation, and suggested a divorce in which Elizabeth should appear as the guilty party. Elizabeth was outraged and replied with a very rude letter to the effect that she refused 'to prove herself a whore' for his sake. No, on legal advice she chose a different course, deciding to sue her husband in a Church court for the offence of jactitation of marriage (falsely claiming a marriage to have taken place). The suit began in November 1768, and by February of the next year an ecclesiastical Church granted a favourable decree. On 8 March 1769, Miss Elizabeth Chudleigh married the Duke of Kingston, and nobody raised any just cause or impediment.

For four years the couple lived together as man and wife, the Duchess giving lavish fêtes and balls as befitted her high position in society. And when the Duke died, childless, on 23 September 1773, she was set to inherit practically the whole of his fortune, for she had seen to it that his second will was very favourable: it left almost everything to her and nothing to the Duke's surviving sister, wife of a man named Meadows, or the Meadows children.

Meadows immediately started Chancery proceedings, claiming that the Duchess had exercised undue influence over the will. And it was during these proceedings that the questions arose: was Elizabeth really the Duchess of Kingston? Or was she the Countess of Bristol (for the old Earl had at last died)?

Formally charged with bigamy, Elizabeth came back from a trip to Europe to stand trial in the House of Lords.

Proceedings opened on 15 April 1776, at Westminster Hall, amid gorgeous pomp and ceremony. The Queen,

Prince of Wales and Princess Royal were all in attendance, along with practically the whole of London society. 'All the world, great and small, are gone to Westminster Hall,' wrote a Mrs Delany, referring to the worries about getting tickets. There was also 'the distress of rising early to be in time enough for a place, the anxiety about hairdressers (poor souls hurried out of their lives), mortifications that feathers and flying lappets should be laid aside for that day as they would obstruct the view from those who sit behind', and much more. Another contemporary spoke of the trial as a sight which for 'beauty and magnificence' rivalled a coronation.

Against the resplendent setting, with the peers in crimson velvet and white ermine, the Duchess appeared a sober figure. Led in by Black Rod, she was dressed in deep mourning, hooded in black, with black gauze, black ruffles, black cape and black gloves: the perfect image of a grieving widow – except that nobody quite believed it. At different points she pretended to scribble and pretended to be taken ill 'but performed it badly'. When her own turn came to give evidence she spoke for three-quarters of an hour – all to no avail. The evidence of her secret wedding was too strong: one of the two female witnesses turned up to testify about it. And, when the trial closed on 22 April, the peers were almost unanimous in their verdict.

One after another they found against her, declaring: 'Guilty, upon my honour'. The only exception was the Duke of Newcastle, who found: 'Guilty erroneously, but not intentionally, upon my honour'. No penalty was imposed, out of deference to Elizabeth's nobility (a commoner would have been burned on the hand), but she was warned that if she offended again she risked capital punishment.

She had entered the Hall as Duchess of Kingston; she left as the Countess of Bristol. But if her opponent, Meadows, thought he could now sue for the Kingston estate, he had reckoned without the cunning of the middle-aged adventuress.

On the night after the trial ended, she organized a great party for her friends. But she did not turn up herself; instead, having got her cousin to ride around London posing in her carriage, she quietly slipped away from the capital, attained Dover and escaped by packet to Calais. Thereafter she toured the courts of Europe – still calling herself Duchess of Kingston – and lived to enjoy a scandalous old age abroad. She died in 1788 of a burst blood vessel.

Palimony – Billie Jean King

The most sensational case regarding palimony revolved around the tennis star Billie Jean King.

Mrs King had been married for 16 years to sports promoter Larry King. Yet in April 1981 an astonished public learned that she was to be sued by her former secretary – a woman – who alleged that she and Mrs King had lived together for many years in a lesbian relationship. There had never yet been a homosexual palimony case, and the issue could hardly have found a more famous protagonist than the six-times Wimbledon singles champion.

Marilyn Barnett, 33, a one-time hairdresser, had filed a 13-page suit seeking lifetime support and title to a beach house in Malibu which she claimed Mrs King had promised her. She claimed that in or about May 1972 she and Mrs King met and began dating on a regular basis. Sexual intimacy had begun some six months after the first date and Ms Barnett claimed that she gave up her hairdressing career to become Billie Jean's secretary, abandoning 'all other things so that King's energy could be totally directed towards tennis'. In 1979, Ms Barnett claimed, Mrs King breached an oral contract by demanding that she move out of the Malibu house so that it could be sold.

Some months before the suit was filed, Marilyn Barnett had fallen from the balcony of a building; she was now a paraplegic.

Initially, Mrs King was reported to have denied the homosexual relationship, saying: 'I am completely shocked and disappointed by the action Miss Barnett has taken.' She added that the woman had indeed worked as her secretary in the 1970s, but had been 'phased out' when Mrs King started to reduce her business activities in order to concentrate on tennis.

The next day, however, the tennis star called a press conference in Los Angeles and, against the advice of her lawyers, admitted: 'I did have an affair with Marilyn Barnett.'

Billie Jean's husband and parents were at the conference and gave her full support as she addressed the journalists. 'I've always been honest,' she said, 'I've decided to talk with you as I've always talked – from my heart.' Of her former lover, she said: 'I am very disappointed and shocked that Marilyn has done this, not only to herself – a very self-destructive thing – but to other people who care for her.' Though the affair had been over for some time, she admitted: 'I made a mistake. I will assume that responsibility. I discussed it with Larry – in some ways I think we're much closer today than we've ever been, and our marriage is stronger.'

As for Ms Barnett's property claims, Mrs King denied the promise of lifetime support, the beach house or any other financial arrangement. And she declined to comment on Press stories that Marilyn Barnett had become a paraplegic in a suicide leap – rather than a fall – from a balcony.

Not long afterwards, Mrs King tendered her resignation as president of the Women's Tennis Association. That resignation was rejected by WTA authorities, and in general the public response was overwhelmingly favourable toward the beleaguered tennis star. Letters and telegrams of support came to her by the sackful, and sympathy only increased when it was alleged that a national tabloid was offering $25,000 for some 100 love letters written by her to her former secretary. (Those letters were not, in fact, to be publicized; lawyers acting for the two women made a joint agreement to keep their contents secret.)

When the case came to court, it came in two parts. The first suit, heard in December 1981, was in fact brought by Mrs King and her husband to force Marilyn Barnett to leave their beach home. The former hairdresser hobbled with a walking stick into the Superior Court at Los Angeles, wearing a long grey skirt to hide her leg braces. In the witness stand she was asked by Mrs King's counsel what she had done for his client.

'I gave up my career, my identity, my pride and my home,' replied Ms Barnett. She said that she had hoped her relationship with Billie Jean would last for life and, asked if she felt that the tennis star owed her something, she replied firmly 'Yes'.

Nobody could deny that a deep human drama underlay the courtroom wranglings. But Mrs King, who watched arm in arm with her husband, was granted the decision, winning the right to evict her former lover from the disputed beach house. The judge had ruled that Ms Barnett had come close to trying to extort money from the tennis star; it appeared that Billie Jean and her husband had offered her £125,000 to get her to leave the house. Ms Barnett had refused, according to the judge, because she felt that she could get more money.

Almost a year later, in November 1982, a judge dismissed Marilyn Barnett's remaining claims. The suit had created immense public interest and helped to cement an important legal principle. But, in practice, a plea for palimony had failed.

Cranks and Crackpots

'Queen' of the Jews: Lady Hester Stanhope

Shut away from the world in an isolated monastery in the hills of Lebanon, one of the most remarkable women of the 19th century waited to become Queen of the Jews.

Lady Hester Stanhope, once a glamorous figure in London society, had been told by fortune-tellers and self-styled prophets that this was to be her destiny.

The predictions had started long ago in England. They were repeated again in the East. Passages from scriptures and lines from ancient Arab manuscripts had been shown to her to prove she was to become the long-awaited bride of a new Messiah.

Transformed by years of exotic wanderings in Syria, Palestine and Lebanon, her life as an English aristocrat a thing of the past, Lady Hester began to believe the predictions.

How else could one explain her strange life?

Curious travellers from Europe called to pay their respects at the home she created for herself from the half-ruined and abandoned monastery of Mar Elias. Stories had filtered back to England of how this daughter of the great Chatham family had abandoned her life as a European and had become a legend in the Middle East.

Visitors found a statuesque, commanding woman, nearly 6ft tall, dressed like a male Turk in voluminous trousers, her head shaved and covered by a turban. As her guests talked, she filled the room with smoke, puffing continually at her Turkish chibouk.

They could hardly believe that this was the niece of William Pitt the Younger, one of the greatest of British Prime Ministers. She had been famous as his hostess at Walmer Castle – a lady of fashion and an ornament of the

London drawing rooms.

Now they discovered her absorbed by the East and obsessed with mysticism and astrology. She had power and influence among the Arabs and many of the ruling sheiks regarded her with awe. They had never met an English woman – indeed, any woman – quite like her before.

It was in 1810, when she was 33 years old, that life in England turned sour for Lady Hester. First came the death of her beloved uncle, Pitt, then that of her favourite brother, Charles. This was crowned by a bitter disappointment in love.

She decided to take a long sea voyage to revive her sad spirits. Accompanied by a small group of admirers – including her physician, Dr Charles Meryon, and a young man called Michael Bruce, who was to become her lover – she set out to forget her troubles and see the world.

She was never to return.

With her friends, time passed pleasantly enough. They reached Athens, where the poet Byron was said to have dived into the sea off Piraeus to greet her, and then went on to Constantinople. Cairo was to be their next destination.

They set sail, ran into terrible storms, and were shipwrecked off the island of Rhodes, losing all their possessions. No European clothes could be found on the island, so the whole party had to dress in Eastern costume.

Lady Hester refused to wear the veil or dress of the Eastern woman. Instead, she wore Turkish male clothes: a long robe, turban and yellow slippers. And this was how she dressed for the rest of her life.

When she eventually reached Cairo on board a British frigate which had called to rescue the shipwrecked travellers, she bought a new outfit so that she could appear before the Pasha in style.

In his memoirs, Dr Meryon said she purchased a robe of purple velvet encrusted with gold embroidery (cost unknown), two cashmere shawls at £50 each, embroidered trousers at £40, waistcoat and jacket – another £50. Her sabre cost £20 and her saddle £35. It still took another £100 to complete her outfit. She looked so impressive that when she entered his palace the Pasha rose to greet her.

Regardless of expense, she then set out on a series of spectacular journeys through the Middle East, riding on a magnificent Egyptian saddle of crimson velvet embroidered with gold, her lavish costume covered with a white hooded cloak.

She was received with great wonder and awe by many of the sheiks who took her to be some strange English Princess of fabulous wealth. Many people warned her that it would be unwise to enter a city unveiled but she ignored them. Even in Damascus, then the most fanatical of Moslem cities, where Christians were despised, she rode side-saddle with her proud profile exposed for all to see.

Some took her for a young man whose beard had not grown. But those who realized she was a woman were bemused. They did not know what to make of her. Fortunately, they were cautious and treated her with respect, pouring coffee before her horse as she rode by.

In Jerusalem she was formally received by the governor. When it was known that she was on her way to the Church of the Holy Sepulchre, the doors were first closed in her face, then flung wide open to allow her to enter – a mark of great respect.

Increasingly, Lady Hester began to see herself as an exotic heroine with a mystical destiny. Her friends jokingly called her Queen Hester and she began to take them seriously.

Her loyal English retinue dwindled as the cost of her travelling rose, but she was still attended by the indomitable Mrs Anne Fry, who was as English as muffins and must have hated every minute of it.

The greatest journey was yet to come. Lady Hester was

passionately determined to visit the ruins of the great city of Palmyra in the Arabian Desert. Until then, only three Englishmen had reached it. The route across the sands was infested with tribes of fierce Bedouin who would rob and kill without mercy.

She dressed as a Bedouin and set out with a fantastic caravan which included 22 camels and mountains of luggage. A black slave armed with an axe guarded her tent at night. Sheiks came from all parts of the desert to see this extraordinary woman 'with the courage of a lion and the eyes of an eagle'.

Her reputation preceded her. When she reached Palmyra she was received like a Queen of the desert and crowned in a celebration pageant. It must have seemed as though the prophecies were coming true.

By 1814 she had had enough of wandering and found the disused monastery of Mar Elias on a hilltop overlooking the sea near Sidon in Lebanon. She created a beautiful garden there and conducted her household strictly in the Turkish manner.

From Mar Elias she wielded considerable influence over her Arab neighbours, refusing to be cowed by local rulers and offering sanctuary to refugees whenever there were religious wars. She sheltered hundreds of them over the years. Feeding them alone cost her a fortune.

When Mar Elias became too small to house her refugees and when the faithful Dr Meryon returned home at last, she moved to Djoun, another ruined monastery farther into the mountains with not even a nearby village.

From there she kept up correspondence with some of the greatest names of her day. Travellers to whom the name of Hester Stanhope had become a legend would go out of their way to visit her. Many reported that her brilliant mind was being wasted. She could keep up a conversation for eight or nine hours at a stretch, hypnotizing her listeners.

She continued to be lavishly generous, partly to maintain her importance in the eyes of the Arabs, partly because she had no money sense whatsoever.

Assuming that the British Government would foot the bill, she mounted an extravagant expedition to search for buried treasure in the ancient city of Ascalon. The expedition was a flop and the British Government was not even remotely interested.

Financially it was the last straw. She was deeply in debt and the pension she relied on from England was stopped to pay off her foreign creditors. She became involved in an interminable wrangle with Lord Palmerston, Queen Victoria's Prime Minister, who had given the order to cut off her money.

Furious, she wrote to the Queen upbraiding her for allowing Palmerston to behave in such a high-handed manner. 'There is no trifling with those who have Pitt blood in their veins,' she informed Her Majesty.

As the years went by, she became more eccentric. She would not receive visitors until it was dark. Then, folding a cashmere turban over her now-shaven head, she would sit so that the light fell only on her hands and face, which still retained some of their former beauty.

Her roof leaked. Her servants stole everything of value. After Palmerston's action, she sealed up all the entrances to the monastery, leaving only one door for cattle to pass to and fro.

No one called her Queen Hester any more.

She died peacefully at Djoun in June 1839, at the age of 63. When the British consul from Beirut arrived at the monastery to deal with her affairs, he found that 35 rooms had been sealed up to prevent robbery.

He opened them expecting to find treasure. But they were full of rubbish – old books and papers, rotting Arab saddles and empty medicine bottles.

The Princess and the Pirates

One April evening in 1817 a clergyman in the village of Almondsbury, Gloucestershire, opened his cottage door to find a young woman outside. She was modestly dressed in a plain black frock with a high, ruffled neck but her hair was swathed in a black turban and she babbled incoherently in a language he did not understand.

Since she was obviously exhausted, he let her rest for a while before sending for the village overseer, who dealt with all the waifs and strays who turned up in the parish. He too was completely baffled.

Eventually the two men bundled her into a carriage and set off for Knole Park, home of local magistrate and landowner Samuel Worrall.

At the sight of the fine mansion, the strange girl became terrified and only after a fierce struggle could she be persuaded to go inside. It was Mrs Worrall, a kind, motherly woman, who eventually managed to calm the stranger.

She was an enchanting creature, her head small and neat, her eyes black and limpid. When she smiled her soft, full lips parted to show dazzling white teeth and, when she became excited, a rosy flush spread over her dusky skin. Her hands were delicate and apparently unaccustomed to hard work. She appeared to be about 25 years old.

It was decided to send her, with a maid, to sleep for the night in the village inn. Supper was laid on a table, but she refused to touch it. When the landlord brought tea, however, she seized the cup greedily, covered her eyes and gabbled some kind of prayer.

When the landlord's wife took her to her room, she stubbornly refused to get into bed and indicated that she would rather curl up on the floor. It was only when the landlord's small daughter bounced encouragingly up and down on the feather mattress that she at last consented to lie down and go to sleep.

The following morning Mrs Worrall arrived at the inn to find the young woman sitting disconsolately by the fire. She jumped up, greeted her with joy and clung to her hand possessively. There seemed no alternative but to take her back to Knole Park, where breakfast was laid. It was Good Friday and freshly baked hot cross buns were on the table. The girl reached out and took one, then to everyone's amazement cut off the cross with a knife and stuffed it in the bodice of her dress. Could she be a Christian?

When Mrs Worrall later returned from church, she marched up to her 'guest', looked her in the eye and said: 'My good young woman, I very much fear that you are imposing on me and that you can understand and answer me in my own language . . .'

The girl gazed back, uncomprehending.

'If so,' she went on, 'and distress has driven you to this, make a friend of me. I will give you money and clothes and put you on your journey without disclosing your conduct to anyone – but it must be on condition that you speak the truth.'

Still there was no sign of understanding.

Suddenly Mrs Worrall had a brainwave. Thumping herself on the chest, she called out 'Worrall! Worrall!' After several repeats of this performance the girl grinned from ear to ear and pointing to herself shouted 'Caraboo! Caraboo!'

For the next ten weeks Caraboo ruled the roost. The Worralls were besieged by curious friends and acquaintances, many of them bringing foreign visitors. Among them was a Portuguese from Malaya, who triumphantly announced that Caraboo was a Princess. She had been kidnapped by pirates and brought to England against her will. Her language was a mixture of dialects used on the coast of Sumatra!

Her admirers were enormously impressed. But it was another widely travelled friend of the Worralls who, using signs, gestures and a smattering of the words she seemed to know, finally extracted her remarkable, vividly detailed story. She came, he said, from the island of Javasu in the East Indies. Her father, Jessu Mandu, was a high-caste Chinese of such awesome authority that people had to make obeisance to him on both knees. He was carried about on the shoulders of macratoos (common men) in a kind of sedan chair and wore a nugget of gold with three peacock feathers in his headdress. He had four wives, and Caraboo's mother, the favourite, was a beautiful Malay who blackened her teeth and wore jewels in her nose.

Caraboo had been walking in the garden one day with three sammen (serving maids) when she was seized by the crew of a pirate ship. Her father swam after the marauding party, but after a fight the raiders won the day; she was bound hand and foot and carried off to sea.

After 11 days, the pirate chief sold her to the captain of a brig named Tappa Boo, a terrifying man with black whiskers, greasy black hair worn in a plait and an evil eye. His perpetual smile scared her out of her wits.

After several months at sea, the brig reached northern waters and skirted the coast of England. One night, in desperation, Caraboo jumped overboard and swam for shore.

At the time she had been wearing a dress of finest silk worked with gold. She dried it in the sun and soon after, meeting a village girl in the fields, exchanged it for a simple black frock and shawl, which she wound round her head like a turban. For six weeks she roamed the countryside, begging for food and sleeping in barns and hayricks until, one night, she reached Almondsbury.

Deeply impressed, the Worrall household settled down to living with their royal guest.

She cut the most unlikely figure on the lawns of an

English country house. From a length of calico she made herself a dress with sleeves so wide and long they trailed on the ground. Her feet were bare and her head was decorated with feathers and flowers.

Sometimes she carried a gong which she struck loudly and often, and sometimes she would bang on a tambourine. Armed with a bow and arrow, she would stalk about the place like Diana, goddess of the hunt.

They allowed her to prepare her own food. She was particularly fond of rice and hot vegetable curries, but ate little meat and drank only water and tea. She refused to eat pigeon cooked in the kitchen, but picked up a live one, cut off its head, burying this in the ground, then roasted and ate the rest of it.

She seemed strongly religious. When shown a drawing of an idol from the South Seas she threw it to the ground and made it clear that she worshipped Allah-Tallah – the true God. She said her prayers night and morning, made a temple in the shrubbery and every Tuesday perched on the steep roof at Knole, praying until sunset.

As the weeks went by the Worralls' nerves became a little ragged. No one knew quite what she would do next. Passionately fond of bathing, she once plunged into the lake fully dressed. She would also wash her face in the fish pond.

Then, suddenly, it was all over. One June night Caraboo stole away. She did not take a pin that did not belong to her. All her gifts and trinkets were left in a neat pile in her room.

Weeks went by. After inquiries Mrs Worrall learned that her protégée had turned up in Bath, and set off in pursuit.

Hearing that Caraboo had been taken up by a fashionable society woman, she burst into a tea party and found the girl being courted by a horde of elegant admirers. When she saw Mrs Worrall she sank gracefully to her knees, begging forgiveness, saying she had run away to find someone who would help her return to her homeland.

The determined Mrs Worrall took her back to Gloucestershire. But the bubble was about to burst.

Glowing descriptions of the exotic stranger began to appear in various newspapers, including the *Bristol Journal*. A lodging-house keeper called Mrs Neale, coming across the story of the Princess from Javasu, decided it rang a bell. Caraboo sounded very much like a fanciful young woman who had stayed with her some months before . . . very much like her.

Mrs Neale was eventually brought face to face with Caraboo in Mrs Worrall's presence. Without hesitation, she exclaimed: 'That's Mary Baker!'

Caraboo burst into tears. She admitted that she was in fact the daughter of a poor Devon cobbler and had never in her life set foot in a foreign country.

Her story is told in a slender pamphlet published in 1817 under the title *Caraboo – a Narrative of a Singular Imposition Practised Upon the Benevolence of a Lady*. It draws a picture of a delightful eccentric.

Caraboo was born Mary Wilcocks in the village of Witheridge, near Crediton, Devonshire, in 1791. Her parents were poor, respectable people with too many children. She received little education and ran wild until she was eight years old, when she was taught spinning.

At 16 her parents found her a steady job at a nearby farmhouse, looking after the farmer's children and doing manual work. But her head was full of dreams. On her days off she pretended to be a Spanish or French woman. Once she dressed up as a gypsy and looked so authentic her employers did not recognize her.

After two years of earning ten pence a week she asked for a rise. The farmer refused to pay her any more so she went back home. Her furious father thrashed her with a leather strap. It was more than her wild spirit could take.

She ran away.

Once, between jobs, she lived with a tribe of gypsies, slept in barns and begged for food. The rough life did not suit her. She became desperately ill and was taken to St Giles Hospital, London, where she almost died.

After recovering, she found a good position with a Mr Matthews and his wife who lived in a handsome house in Clapham Place. Her employer taught her to read properly and to write, allowing her to use his library. She spent all her leisure time devouring books that described life in far-off lands, exotic customs and romantic adventures.

After three years she was dismissed and became a vagabond again. For a time she protected herself from the robbers and murderers who roamed the heaths around London by dressing in male breeches and jacket, cutting off her hair and passing herself off as a young man.

Back in petticoats, she became a servant to a fishmonger's wife in Dark House Lane, Billingsgate. Only one thing made the job bearable; she was sent out regularly on errands. In a bookshop she caught the eye of a well-dressed foreigner. Introducing himself as Herr Bakerstendht (which she shortened to Baker), he told her he had travelled widely in the East and soon declared his love for her. After two months she went through a form of marriage with him. Soon he told her he had to travel to Calais on business and would send for her later. Of course she never saw him again.

From then on she retired into her fantasy world: eventually she became Princess Caraboo of Javasu.

There were red faces when the truth became known. But people admitted she was a remarkable young woman and were curious to meet her. She was visited by all sorts of people, including linguists, who were dying to know how she had kept up the deception.

Her 'language' had been made up mostly of Malay and Arabic words which she had learned from 'Mr Baker', plus a smattering of Romany picked up from the gypsies; and her knowledge of life in the East had come only from books.

When the good-hearted Mrs Worrall had got over her shock she agreed to help the Devonshire 'Princess'. Mary longed to go to America. The magistrate's wife fitted her out with clothes, gave her some money and booked her passage on board a ship leaving Bristol, putting her in charge of a group of missionaries.

That is not quite the end of the story. The *Bristol Journal* of 13 September 1817, carried a letter from Sir Hudson Lowe, governor of Napoleon's prison island, St Helena.

Apparently, one day during a storm, Sir Hudson saw a ship tacking offshore. The wind proved too strong and he watched it bear away to the northwest. Shortly afterwards a small boat, bobbing like a cork, was seen entering the harbour. Sir Hudson went down to the beach and watched a 'female of interesting appearance' scramble ashore. It was Mary Baker.

She had felt, she explained, an 'ardent desire' to see Napoleon. When she realized they were not going to land at St Helena, she cut loose a lifeboat and rowed for the shore.

Sir Hudson introduced her to Napoleon as Princess Caraboo and apparently she carried on her performance as though there had been no interval. Napoleon was completely captivated and asked that she might be allowed an apartment in his house . . .

Mary Baker clearly had a genius for making men believe what they wanted to believe. How her affair with Napoleon ended we do not know. That was the last heard of her. But there was a rumour, years later, that she had been seen in London, selling leeches.

The Outrageous Mrs Satan

As the model of a gracious, if slightly imperious, lady of the manor, nobody could beat Mrs John Biddulph Martin, whose banker husband, when he died, had left her Bredon's Norton in Worcestershire. She opened flower shops, turned her tithe barn into a village hall, took a proper interest in the education of local children and entertained the Prince of Wales, who sent her a basket of grouse.

Who could have guessed that this grande dame with the fine profile had once been dubbed 'Mrs Satan' for her outspoken ideas on free love, and had taken the extraordinary step of suing the British Museum when she realized that two documents on its shelves would shatter her new image?

Indeed, Mrs John Biddulph Martin was once considered the most outrageous woman in America, an eccentric who kept all her lovers under one roof and then had the nerve to put her name forward as a Presidential candidate. She was a visionary who claimed that Demosthenes, the ancient Greek orator, had guided her life, a fervent suffragette who told women to enjoy their sex life and take as many lovers as they wanted, a medium who gave spirit-world advice on stocks and shares to Vanderbilt himself. As a beautiful woman conducting a personal revolt against convention, Mrs Biddulph Martin, formerly Victoria Woodhull, shocked America for a decade.

She was fond of describing her birthplace as a picturesque cottage, painted white with a porch running round it and a garden in front. In fact, Victoria Woodhull was born on 23 September 1838 in a broken-down old shack full of noisy, brawling children out in the dusty frontier town of Homer, Ohio. Her father, Buck Claflin, ran a grist mill. Her mother, Roxanna, told fortunes and doctored her ten children by hypnotism. Victoria started talking to spirits when she was three and said that her only friends in childhood were angels. Now and then she saw the devil.

One hot summer night the Claflin mill burned down in suspicious circumstances and Victoria's father, suspected of arson, was asked to leave town. The neighbours raised a subscription fund to send his family after him. For years the whole tribe wandered from town to town selling patent medicines and a complexion oil they concocted from vegetable juices. But it was when Victoria's youngest sister, Tennessee, announced that she too heard spirit voices that Buck Claflin thought of a marvellous idea for making money. He set both girls to work holding séances. People at the boarding houses where they stayed often complained about the shrieks and weird noises. But the money rolled in. Victoria and her sister had found a career.

Victoria's wide blue eyes and rose-petal skin attracted men wherever she went. Before she was 16, she was married. Her husband was a young doctor called Canning Woodhull who mistakenly thought she was going to settle down. She bore him two children, a boy called Byron and a girl bizarrely named Zulu Maud, then decided Ohio was too small for her. She persuaded him to give up his practice and take her to California; then, missing her family, they moved on to join her sister, Tennie, in Cincinnati, where the two girls advertized themselves as clairvoyants. They usually gave rather noisy séances at a dollar a head. When they added fortune-telling and magnetic healing the customers piled in – especially the men.

Poor Woodhull had not realized that marrying Victoria meant marrying the whole Claflin tribe. Soon he gave up the struggle and became a drunkard and a woman-chaser.

Victoria looked to Demosthenes for her next move. Apparently he turned up every now and then in a snow-white toga, pointing her in the right direction and consoling her with the promise that one day she would be wealthy.

Moving on to St Louis, she fell dramatically in love with a handsome young man sporting side whiskers, who called to seek her advice as a spiritualist. As soon as she saw him she wanted him. Her method was unique. She went into a trance, crying out that their destinies were linked. They were to be joined in marriage. The fact that both the caller, Colonel James Harvey Blood, and Victoria herself were already married did not come into it at all. She told him they had been betrothed 'by the powers of the air'. Blood, an upstanding man and city auditor, looked into Victoria's blue eyes and succumbed. He left his wife and children and went off with her in a wagon.

After their spiritual betrothal they lived together as lovers; their house became a meeting place for radical thinkers and Victoria took to the lecture platform to practise what she preached.

But Demosthenes had promised her wealth and presumably it was he who led her to Cornelius Vanderbilt, the richest man in America. Vanderbilt was an ailing man and had lost patience with orthodox medicine. When Victoria and her sister were introduced to him as miracle healers from the West, he decided to give them a chance. The fact that they were both very attractive women probably had something to do with it. Victoria became his good friend – Tennie became his mistress.

Sometimes Vanderbilt asked Victoria for advice about the stock market from the spirit world, but he soon realized that his own instincts were better than advice from 'beyond'. Instead *he* gave *her* tips about stocks and shares. Victoria and her sister opened a brokerage office, the first to be run by women in the history of Wall Street, at the start of 1870. Business flourished, with Colonel Blood in the back office doing most of the actual work, and Victoria was able to fulfil her ambition; she rented a mansion and filled it with little gold chairs, gilt mirrors and servants!

Not three months after the sisters had astonished New

York with their appearance in Wall Street, Victoria dropped the biggest bombshell of all. She announced herself as a candidate for the Presidency. With her suffragette hackles rising, she said she had proved herself in business to be the equal of men, so she reckoned she could act for the unfranchised women of the country. To promote her campaign she spoke on lecture platforms all over the country and launched a newspaper called *Woodhull and Claflin's Weekly* in which she lashed out at everybody who didn't agree with her and wrote articles supporting free love, abortion, birth control, legalized prostitution, vegetarianism, magnetic healing and easier divorce laws. It was a runaway success and achieved national distribution. Everybody wanted to hear what that dreadful Woodhull woman was saying.

Her household arrangements were, as usual, chaotic; full of over-ripe loves and hates. She had obtained a divorce and married Colonel Blood; then, to her horror, her first husband turned up on her doorstep, a pathetic wreck, ruined by drink and morphine. He had nowhere to go, so she took him in. Her mother, who hated Blood and was insanely jealous, chose this moment to bring a court case, swearing that Blood had assaulted her, and revealing that her daughter now had two husbands under one roof, if not in the same bed.

The Press had a field day speculating on the love life of the Presidential candidate. But they didn't know half. Just about this time, Stephen Pearl Andrews appeared on the scene. He was the great intellectual in her life who knew 30 languages and had written a book in Chinese. He, too, joined the household. Then there was Theodore Tilton. 'He slept every night for three months in my arms,' she told the world. Whatever Colonel Blood *thought*, he made no complaints.

Tilton was one of the figures in a huge scandal that rocked America and put Victoria Woodhull behind bars.

His wife had been seduced by the Reverend Henry Ward Beecher, the most famous preacher in America, believed by everyone to be the nearest thing to a saint. In fact, between sermons, Beecher had been making love to every pretty parishioner he could lay his hands on. Victoria was incensed that her honesty about free love had condemned her as a wicked woman, while Beecher was protected by a wall of hypocrisy.

She tried to force him into the open, met him, and even, so she claimed later, slept with him. But, when she tried to blackmail him into supporting her on a public platform, he burst into tears and begged to be left off the hook.

What turned out to be her most famous appearance in public was booked at the Steinway Hall. Beecher had refused to introduce her as promised, and she went on stage in a fine passion.

'My judges preach against free love openly, and practise it secretly,' she stormed.

'Are you a free lover?' someone shouted.

'Yes,' she cried. 'Yes, I am a free lover.'

The audience burst into an uproar of cheers, hisses, boos and catcalls, but Victoria swept on, her voice rising above the din. 'I have an inalienable, constitutional and natural right to love whom I may, to love for as long or as short a period as I can, to change that love every day if I please! And with that right neither you nor any law you can frame have any right to interfere!'

Bedlam followed and was fully reported next day. The 'Free Love' speech, combined with her violent reactions and almost unprintable answers to questions, proved too much. She was asked to leave the splendid mansion she rented and spent a night on the pavement before she could persuade a boarding-house keeper to take her family in. The brokerage business suffered, advertising disappeared from their newspaper and Vanderbilt gently withdrew his support. The suffragettes stood staunchly by her.

It was too unfair. Victoria decided it was time the whole truth was known about the Beecher-Tilton scandal. First of all she was seized by 'a great gust of inspiration' and told all she knew to an audience of spiritualists. Then she and her sister, Tennie, brought out a special edition of *Woodhull and Claflin's Weekly* on 2 November 1872, revealing the whole story. It was a sensation. Primly dressed in dark-blue suits, they were both arrested for having circulated 'an obscene and indecent publication' and thrown into jail. They spent six months behind bars before a technical point gained them a verdict of 'not guilty'. The Beecher scandal dragged on for years. To some he remained a hero. Others branded him 'a dunghill covered with flowers'. His reputation never recovered.

The scandal did little to help Victoria in her bid for the Presidency. When Grant swept into office, she received only a few popular votes. Her private life, too, was in turmoil. Though she herself was having an affair with a 19-year-old college boy who helped to manage her lecture tours, she was furious to discover that Colonel Blood had also been seeking consolation. Outraged by his infidelity, she asked him to leave!

With his departure her fiery enthusiasm somehow seemed to wane. She took to religion. Then in 1877 Vanderbilt died and Victoria made it known that the old man owed her 100,000 dollars. His heir took the hint. He paid up with the proviso that both Victoria and Tennessee removed themselves from American soil until the business of the will was settled. With a new wardrobe, servants and six first-class state rooms, the sisters sailed for England.

Victoria decided to become a new woman. She had divorced Blood for infidelity. It was the first time that most people realized they had ever been legally married, for she had never taken his name. Free love was obviously on the scrap heap and when she lectured in England – she could never keep off a public platform for long – she chose subjects such as the sanctity of marriage and 'The Human Body, the Temple of God'.

Sitting in the audience at one of these lectures was a charming, highly respectable banker, John Biddulph Martin. He was a partner in Martin's Bank, the family firm, and 36 years old. Charmed by Victoria's 'high intellect' and fascinated by her personality, he determined to make her his wife. Martin's parents were appalled by his choice. They had read all about Victoria in the newspapers. So, the one-time free lover, certain that Demosthenes had led her to her destiny, set about to obliterate her past and present herself as a noble and much-wronged woman. After six years they gave in and Victoria became Mrs John Biddulph Martin on 31 October 1883. She was 45 and proved herself, as to the manner born, perfect mistress of her husband's dignified mansion in Hyde Park Gate, London. For the next 18 years they lived happily together, the respectable banker thoroughly enjoying his extraordinary wife's company.

She never quite lived down her eccentric past and spent the rest of her life denying the outrageous things she was supposed to have said and done. Two documents on the shelves of the British Museum Library nearly gave her a heart attack. They were pamphlets on the Beecher-Tilton scandal, with ample reference to the part she played in it. She begged her husband to act, and the trustees of the British Museum were astounded to find themselves sued for libel. The trial, without precedent, lasted for five days and Victoria listened to it all with the air of a martyr, answering questions with such charming evasion that nobody quite understood what all the fuss was about. In the end the jury decided libel had been committed, but with no attempt to injure, and awarded her £1 damages!

When John Biddulph Martin died of pneumonia in 1879, Victoria sold her Hyde Park Gate house and moved into her husband's country manor at Bredon's Norton, there to live the life of a respected dowager of the English shires. Tennessee had also done well for herself. She became the wife of Sir Francis Cook.

But the old Victoria would not quite lie down. At the age of 63 she suddenly got bored with being respectable. She gave up part of her estate for emancipated young women to learn farming, opened a school for progressive education, took up her old passion for spiritualism and involved herself in dozens of other things.

In her old age she refused to go to bed, always sleeping in a chair because she thought she could cheat death that way. For four years she slept upright, but on the morning of 9 June 1927 she was found to have drifted off in her sleep. One can't help hoping that it was Demosthenes who came for her.

High-class Kleptomania

Plump, vivacious Lady Cork, wife of the seventh Earl of Cork and Orrery, was an immensely popular woman who even enchanted that grumpy literary giant Dr Johnson. But she had one little failing that drove her friends to distraction. This was the unfortunate habit of collecting things that did not belong to her.

So well known was her 'tendency' that when she went out to dinner her hosts would put away their silver and leave out pewter spoons and forms which would be scooped up and hidden in her muff. If she visited friends in the country, her maid, on their return home, would have to gather together all the things she knew did not belong to her mistress and send them back to the house where she had been staying – with humble apologies.

Nobody knew quite when it all started. Throughout her long life – she lived to be 94 – she loved good company, and, as one of London's most famous hostesses, seemed content with collecting literary lions. As her more unorthodox collections became well known, however, a society wit was prompted to quip that heaven would be rather boring for poor Lady Cork, because there would be nothing to pinch.

Before marrying Lord Cork in 1786 she was plain Mary Monckton. Her early taste for literature made people think she was going to be something of a blue stocking, but she turned out to be a sparkling wit. She often entertained Dr Johnson at her mother's house in Charles Street, Berkeley Square, and he was, by all accounts, very fond of her.

Fanny Burney, who wrote vivid accounts of 18th-century characters, described her as being: 'very short, very fat but handsome, splendidly and fantastically dressed, rouged not unbecomingly yet evidently and palpably desirous of gaining notice and admiration . . . '

She certainly gained the admiration of Lord Cork and became his second wife when she was 40. With marriage, her passion for entertaining increased and all the famous people of her day came to her dinners and receptions, among them Lord Byron, Sir Walter Scott, Sheridan and the Prince Regent himself. She went on entertaining in style until well past her 90th birthday.

Her drawing rooms, where the famous gathered, were furnished in rather a peculiar manner. There was nothing else in them apart from dozens of large, handsome armchairs lined up against the walls and made fast in some way, so that it was impossible to move them. It was laughingly suggested that as she herself had difficulty distinguishing between 'mine' and 'thine' she perhaps thought her guests had the same problem.

When Lady Cork went shopping, London tradesmen would never allow their goods to be taken to her carriage for approval, as was the custom with people of wealth and position. They always insisted she went inside the shop and, once there, an assistant was appointed to follow her while she was making purchases.

Once she even stole a hedgehog. It belonged to one of the porters at the hotel where she was staying. Being a pet, and quite tame, it was allowed to run about the entrance hall and caused a lot of amusement. Lady Cork could not resist it. As she was leaving she bent down and whipped it into her handbag. But after only a few miles travelling with the disgruntled, prickly little creature she realized she had made a mistake. At the first stop for refreshment – at a village bakery – she managed to exchange it for a sponge cake. She had convinced the baker that hedgehogs were marvellous for keeping down black beetles, and said she knew bakeries were inundated with such pests!

On another occasion, when leaving a party, she made off with another guest's carriage and kept it for half a day before the irate owner turned up for it. Lady Cork did not apologize but complained that the high steps of the vehicle did not suit her short legs.

She was very proud of her remarkable memory and in her 80s could recite half a book at a time. When she suspected it was beginning to fail she kept a young companion by her side who was referred to simply as 'my memory'.

Sir Joshua Reynolds painted Lady Cork when she was young and dashing, but a sketch of her made by a niece, which still exists, sums up her irrepressible, unrepentant nature far better. Under it is written:

'Look at me
I'm ninety-three
And all my faculties I keep
Eat, drink and laugh and soundly sleep.'

Riches to Rags

Every morning when the Seaboard National Bank in New York opened its front doors, a grim-faced woman wearing ancient, rusty black clothes, ten years out of fashion, stalked in and seated herself behind a desk in the foyer.

She greeted no one but was soon immersed in wheeling and dealing, apparently conducting her business from a pile of cheap trunks and suitcases strewn around the floor.

Nobody got too near her. She stank. But everyone treated her with respect, even awe. For one thing, she had a foul temper. For another, she happened to be Mrs Hetty Green, one of the richest women in the world – and one of the meanest.

So mean was Hetty that she would spend half the night looking for a lost 2-cent postage stamp; she wouldn't pay rent for an office and she rode around in a carriage that had once been considered too derelict for anything but a henhouse. Yet at the end of the 19th century her annual income was seven million dollars, and she even managed to evade the 3 per cent tax that was due!

She was born Hetty Howland Robinson on 21 November 1835, and came from a long line of Quakers with money-making in the blood. The building of their immense fortune started when a Howland ancestor bought 'one black cow' in Plymouth, Massachusetts, in 1624. From then on, through generations of farming, land sales, slave trafficking and whaling, the millions piled up.

Her father, Edward Mott Robinson, was a tough, ruthless Philadelphian who had married for money and looked forward to setting up his own dynasty. He was appalled when his wife announced she could have no more children and he realized his only heir was a bad-tempered little girl.

But little Hetty soon won him over. By the age of six she

was reading the financial pages in the daily papers. She would sit on his knee and listen to him quote from the stock-market report. Her aggressiveness and understanding of money made him feel he had a son after all.

When he died he left her a fortune worth six million dollars in liquid assets. That would have been more than enough for most women, but not Hetty. She learned that her Aunt Sylvia, a Howland, had made a will distributing her two-million-dollar fortune to charity. She wanted that as well and fully intended to get it. Her plotting and scheming was the talk of the decade, but she failed after contesting the will with an apparently forged document.

To everyone's astonishment, Hetty became a bride at the age of 33. She was by no means an unattractive woman in her prime, having a fine figure, peach-coloured complexion and ice-blue eyes. Her husband, Edward Henry Green, member of a wealthy Vermont family, fell in love with her at first sight. Perhaps love blinded him – he seemed to have made no protest when his adored one made him renounce all rights to her fortune before the wedding!

For a time they lived in the bridegroom's splendid Manhattan apartment, but when news reached Hetty that her Howland cousins were seeking ways to bring her to court for forgery in connection with another of her interminable financial battles, she showed fright for the first time in her life and, with Edward, fled to London.

For the next eight years they lived at the exclusive Langham Hotel, where her two children, Ned and Sylvia, were born. Hetty didn't mind. She wasn't footing the bills.

On their return to America she soon tired of domesticity and being a wife. She quarrelled about every penny with her in-laws, her husband and her servants. Every shopkeeper in the neighbourhood detested her. Her only real interest was increasing her investments. She couldn't even be bothered to wash, and the hands that dealt in millions of dollars were usually dirty with black-rimmed nails.

When her marriage ended after 14 years and Edward Green decided to retire to the peace of his club, Hetty moved into a shabby furnished apartment in a seedy part of Brooklyn with her two unfortunate children in tow. She never turned on the heat even in the coldest weather and insisted there was nothing wrong with cold water for washing and bathing, if you went in for that sort of thing.

Most of the time she wore an ancient black dress which had turned a queer shade of green over underclothes that were never changed until they fell to pieces. Her shabby handbag was always stuffed with cheap broken biscuits bought from a corner store so that she need never buy a meal in a restaurant.

Her meanness even extended to her children – though she was genuinely fond of them – and they were dominated by her till the day she died. Her son Ned never had proper medical attention for a deformed leg and ended up with a cork one. It didn't stop him having a colourful public career and a somewhat lurid private life. Away from his mother, he lived lavishly, ran up enormous bills and sometimes hadn't a cent in his pocket. Her daughter Sylvia was a pathetic, drab young woman who wore outmoded clothes and couldn't dance because she had hammer toes. Hetty discouraged all Sylvia's suitors, saying they were only after the family fortune. When she did finally give her consent it was only after her future son-in-law had promised to waive all rights to her property and money!

Once her children had left 'home', Hetty decided her apartment was too spacious for her requirements. She moved to two shabby furnished rooms on the fifth floor of an apartment house. She would have preferred to make do with one, but much of her business was done in the evening when brokers and prospective borrowers called – she was primarily a money-lender with foresight that amounted to genius – and modesty prevented her from receiving them in a room with a bed in it.

She insisted on handling everything herself and would journey thousands of miles to collect a forgotten debt of a few hundred dollars – always travelling in the cheapest possible way and taking her own food.

Restaurants were anathema to Hetty – unless someone else was paying the bill. When she worked at her desk in the bank she always brought her own lunch – not sandwiches like normal people, but a tin of oatmeal which she heated on the office radiators. She ate a huge bowl of it every day – bone dry. She said it gave her strength to fight 'the wolves of Wall Street'. And of course it only cost her a fraction of a cent.

As she grew older she became even more formidable. Her mouth set in a thin line and her jaw jutted with grim determination. But even Hetty's determination couldn't fend off ill health. She began to get discomfort from a particularly bad hernia – probably caused by hauling heavy account books from the bank vaults to her desk – and decided, whatever it cost her, to see a doctor.

When told she should have an operation, she demanded to know how much it would cost. The doctor, knowing her reputation, swallowed hard: 'My fee will be 150 dollars, hospital charges extra.' There was a moment's silence, then Hetty shrieked: 'You're all alike. A bunch of robbers.' Although the doctor had every right to be angry, he found the situation comical. When he asked for his 15-dollar examination fee he thought 'she would have produced it from her handbag which was tied round her waist with string!'

As Hetty's fortune grew and grew she became obsessed with the idea that she was marked out to be kidnapped or robbed and went to great trouble to throw her would-be 'attackers' off the scent. She would take circuitous routes, double back on her tracks and even hide in doorways. She even began to think that her father and aunt had been poisoned by their enemies.

She died after a stroke when she was 80, leaving behind one of the greatest fortunes in the world. Nobody knew for sure *exactly* how much she was worth. Wall Street made a low estimate of 100 million dollars, though admitted it could be nearer 200 million. Within 40 years it had all been dispersed – and because she gave not a cent to charity, no hospital, college or library perpetuates her memory – only those stories of her incredible meanness.

Butterflies and Beaux

Miss Margaret Fountaine was a fascinating English spinster who spent all her life falling in love and chasing butterflies. Wearing a pair of plimsolls and a rather large cork sun helmet, she climbed mountains, tramped through jungles, slept in flea-ridden huts from Damascus to Tibet in the hope of snaring prize specimens for her collection, and, while trekking through some of the world's most dangerous territory armed with nothing more legal than a butterfly net, she managed to capture both lepidoptera and men!

She was one of that bumper crop of determined and eccentric lady travellers produced by the vicarages of Victorian England, but the full story of her intrepid travels and equally intrepid love affairs only came to light many years later.

Her magnificent collection of 22,000 butterflies, mounted in ten great mahogany cases, was bequeathed to the Castle Museum, Norwich, in 1940, on condition that the curator also accepted a sealed black metal box, which was not to be opened until 15 April 1978.

No one had the faintest idea what was inside, but when the seals were broken it was found to contain 12 volumes of her diaries – 3,000 pages of vivid prose written in a neat, sloping hand, along with photographs, drawings, postcards and pressed flowers. (Some were edited and published in book form by W.F. Cater, an assistant editor of *The Sunday Times*, who had already fallen under her spell.)

Existing photographs of this rather prim, doleful-looking lady convey no idea of the passionate creature she undoubtedly was – especially when wearing her butterfly-hunting costume. This consisted of a man's check shirt with several extra canvas pockets sewn on, a striped cotton skirt with more pockets, cotton gloves with the fingertips cut off, the large cork helmet and the inevitable plimsolls. Her chest was festooned with various bits of equipment including a heavy black chain with a compass on one end.

She spent so long in the sunny places of the world that she dreaded going home to England. But, whenever she did return, she would shop for clothes. She bought half-a-dozen pairs of plimsolls at a time, and was especially fond of the top people's London store, Harrods. Once, when going out to India, she decided to buy some dresses as she had been invited to stay with the Viceroy. She chose silk ones, perfectly suitable for Viceregal garden parties. The dressmaker was horrified when Miss Fountaine told her to slit open the side seams and insert two large canvas pockets. 'They'll hang all right for the party,' she explained. 'Then I'll fill them with butterfly boxes afterwards.' She saw nothing in the least peculiar about wearing a Harrods dress with plimsolls for scrambling round in the dust after butterflies.

For a time she had a studio in Hampstead as her base camp in England. It was starkly simple. She would stay just long enough to deal with her affairs then suddenly decide to go on another expedition. Up she would jump from the breakfast table, throw a few things into a bag and set off for the other end of the world, leaving the remains of her meal on the table. Her accountant, obviously an understanding man, would go in and clear up, knowing that she might not be back for years.

Margaret Fountaine was the eldest daughter of a Norfolk country clergyman, the Reverend John Fountaine, rector of South Acre, a hamlet 20 miles from Norwich. She was born in 1862 and grew up, with seven brothers and sisters, in a world dominated by maids, governesses and nannies.

In her teens she went to church regularly and just as regularly fell in love with the curates. But it was her passionate infatuation for an Irish chorister called Septimus Hewson that really changed her life. Septimus was a cad and a drunk, though she would never admit it. She fell in love with him as he sang in Norwich Cathedral choir, pursued him round the cloisters in a most unladylike fashion and even wrote letters begging him to take pity on her. Septimus gave in for a time and they were almost engaged, but then he abandoned her for drink and another woman.

To mend her broken heart, Miss Fountaine decided to travel. Her uncle had just left her a modest income of £100 a year – enough, she reckoned, to enable her to see the world. With her sister as companion, she set out for Switzerland, then on to the hills of Tuscany, the Italian lakes and Rome, all the time chasing butterflies and being chased by men. She was, by all accounts, far more attractive than the stiff Victorian portraits convey, and a typical entry in her diary reads: 'I spent most of my time with the Baron . . . as I might have expected, he too ended by making me an improper proposition.'

Butterfly-chasing had started as a pastime but quickly became an all-consuming passion. It was not in her nature to do things by halves. She cycled hundreds of miles through Italy, often to some straggling dirty village full of goats and chickens, spending hours scrambling over rocks and tangled undergrowth in pursuit of some elusive beauty. It was really an extraordinary feat when one remembers the appalling roads of those days, not to mention the cumbersome ankle-length skirts.

From Italy on to Corsica where in the rugged mountains she met up with bandits, including the infamous Jacques Bellacoscia, a Corsican hero who had started his career by shooting the mayor of Ajaccio. 'I drink with Jacques,' she wrote, 'and sometimes in the quieter walks of life, I love to look back upon that wild mountain scene, the outlaw and his clan, the savage dogs who prowled about among the grey rocks and the purple heather . . .' So impressed was she by Jacques that she kept a piece of Corsican heather in her diary.

She remained on the island for a while, in pursuit of butterflies which she knew existed nowhere else. As for men, her method of dealing with tough-looking customers likely to have guns hidden under their velvet jackets was to swear at them for all she was worth. However, on one expedition 'a wild, gypsy-looking fellow' insisted on carrying her equipment. 'So intense was my keenness in pursuit of entomology that I felt no fear whatsoever to wander out into the country quite alone with this man,' she wrote naïvely. In the end she escaped from his clutches by leaping over a ditch in her plimsolls.

Nothing could stop her now. In Hungary she was greeted with open arms by the Budapest entomologists (and a little too warmly by a certain Dr Popovitch). She accompanied them on their annual outing into the mountains, went on an expedition with a certain tall, fair Herr Torok for whom she felt a rising passion, and would sometimes trek for nearly 12 hours with nothing more than two pieces of bread and a mug of sheep's milk to sustain her. Inhabitants of the small Hungarian villages thought she was a harmless lunatic!

But it was in Damascus that Miss Fountaine was to meet the love of her life. She was 39 when she engaged a 24-

year-old Syrian courier called Khalil Neimy to escort her through the Middle East. He was fair for an Arab, wore his tarboosh jauntily on the back of his head and spoke in a strong American accent. He fell madly in love with her at first sight, offered to be her servant for nothing more than his keep, and smothered her hands and arms with passionate kisses. The Norfolk parson's daughter bristled with indignation at first, and then succumbed.

She discovered later that he already had a wife and two children, but his story was a sad one and she forgave him. He was her devoted lover and companion for 28 years, until his death, and she insisted that her magnificent collection of butterflies should be named the Fountaine-Neimy Collection so that his name would be remembered.

Together they travelled through some of the wildest places in the world, frequently where no white woman had been seen before. Conditions were often appalling: 'I passed a terrible night on the floor – the place was infested with fleas and vermin,' she wrote after staying in some filthy little village in order to capture a beautiful white butterfly.

After a particularly bad dose of malaria in North Africa she started to bathe in diluted creosote to deter leeches and other pests. It turned her to a darker shade of brown.

Still highly susceptible to men, she admitted that on a trip to Crete she was 'consoled' by the flattering though highly improper suggestions of an Egyptian ship's officer. Travelling to the tropics, where butterfly after butterfly was popped into specially made, white, ant-resistant boxes, she found the African bush frightening but a proposal of marriage by a Frenchman flattering. Poor Khalil once had to pretend he was her brother to preserve the status quo.

Eventually an ecstatic Miss Fountaine reached Sikkim, the butterfly-collector's paradise, and, hiring a sturdy Tibetan pony, rode over hair-raising precipitous paths through the 'cloud land of the Himalayas, a world of wild winds and bitter cold and strange, curious faces'. Her childhood dreams were realized as she stood looking down into Tibet, but she was only to have a glimpse of that mysterious country. A huge, unmelted mass of snow and ice blocked the Chumbi Valley and they had to turn back.

She never stopped travelling. There are stories of her being lost in the African jungle, caught in an earthquake in Cuba, chasing exotic specimens in Fiji. When she visited her relations in America she earned money by collecting spiders' nests at four dollars a dozen and accepting orders for butterflies off the Californian hills. She surprised her young nephew by playing a skilled game of pool. Her energy was prodigious. When she was nearly 70 she rode 45 miles a day on a butterfly expedition, most of it at the gallop.

But she was most incorrigible when it came to mixing love and butterflies. On one journey, when she set out to explore the regions along the great rivers of South America, she was pursued relentlessly by an amorous Brazilian. At a crucial point in their relationship, the Norfolk parson's daughter wrote: 'It forced itself upon my unsuspecting brain that very soon he would be *out* of his pyjamas . . . it reminded me of the days of long ago.'

Her travels ended on a dusty road in Trinidad one day in 1940. She had collapsed in the heat and, when a kindly monk, Brother Bruno, found her, she was already dying of a heart attack. Her beloved butterfly net lay just out of reach beside her.

Secrets and Spies

Mata Hari

Mata Hari was the most famous of all women spies, using beauty, seduction and sexuality to squeeze secrets from men who might have withstood any torture, save that inflicted by a lovely woman's charms.

Mata Hari was born in the Dutch town of Leeuwarden on 7 August 1876 as Margaretha Geertruida Zelle. She led an ordinary childhood, was an ordinary student and made the same moans that most teenagers do when they long to do more exciting things. For her that excitement meant moving to a teacher's college near Amsterdam when she was 18.

But Margaretha quickly tired of studying and, a year later, married an army officer who took her off to Java. It was here that she first heard the native name 'Mata Hari' – meaning 'eye of the day' – the name under which she would sell military secrets and the name under which she would die.

For the next seven years of her marriage, Margaretha lived the life of an upper-class colonial woman. But she was a woman acutely aware of her own beauty. In Java she started the dalliances which proved to her that her seductive charms could win her anything she wanted. Her husband found out about her affairs but played the part of a cuckolded husband well. He tolerated Margaretha's infidelity for a number of years before taking her back to Holland where they separated and later divorced.

Margaretha found herself with little money in 1902 and so decided to take up the one thing that had been attractive to her as a teenage girl – dancing. She was a very provocative professional and the dancing was strictly for men only. However, Paris was the place to be in cabaret so, in 1905, she moved to the French capital to continue her dancing – and her affairs.

It was there that she adopted the name Mata Hari, that she had first heard used in Java. History is blurred on her days in Paris, but papers released by French authorities recently showed she had many lovers, most of them military officers. Such dalliances were to damn her when the Great War arrived and the world was divided into armed camps. She stayed in Paris for two years after 1914, as the Kaiser's forces were locked in stalemate with the Allied armies on a broad front stretching from the Channel ports to the frontier of Switzerland.

In 1916 Mata Hari moved back to The Hague, in neutral Holland – and it was there that she moved into espionage. She fell into the bed of a German diplomat who asked her for details of the French armies in two vital sectors; one was the Somme front where an Anglo-French offensive was expected. The other was at Verdun, which had been heavily fortified and ringed by steel and concrete constructions. The diplomat promised her cash.

The French were later to allege that Mata Hari gleaned the secrets of the French strengths from her lovers in the French army. What is known is that she was betrayed to the French authorities in 1917 after she had gone to Paris to pass on some intelligence about French battle plans to a Prussian officer. In a war which was bleeding France, she was tried, sentenced to death by a military court and executed on 15 October 1917 by a firing squad.

What were the secrets that she had passed on? Certainly news of Verdun and the Somme offensive could be deemed to be damaging to the war effort of the Allied nations. But European capitals were full of agents, and the Somme offensive was certainly no secret to the Germans who knew about it months before it began. Who was it who betrayed Mata Hari?

Since 1917 historians have been puzzled about the whole affair – particularly the French Government's refusal to allow public scrutiny of papers sealed in 1917 about Mata Hari. But in 1985 a US journalist, Russell Warren Howe, claimed he was shown the secret papers of the spy lady Mata Hari at the Chateau de Vincennes – the very place where she was executed. He claims that the papers show she was not a German agent, but a freelance 'operative' whose sole espionage effort was in Madrid working for the French. Howe says she seduced a German military attaché there and spent three days in bed with him, but the information she got was stale or inaccurate.

Howe claims she did accept money from German intelligence, but all she gave them were easily culled newspaper reports and old gossip. But France in the Great War was rife with anti-foreign sentiments and had suffered appalling losses which at one time threatened to break the army. Inept generals were to blame, but a scapegoat in the form of a conniving woman seemed a far better bet, argues Howe. At her trial she was charged with peddling secrets which cost the lives of hundreds of thousands of Allied servicemen. And the Germans – who believed that Mata Hari had cheated them as a double agent – sent messages in a code which they knew the French had broken implicating her in the espionage charges.

Whichever story is true – that she was a German spy, a French spy or both – Mata Hari broke the ground rules of espionage in that she was indiscreet and naïve enough to think that her bed-hopping would not alert informers. Who actually informed on her is, to this day, still a secret.

Cynthia: the Spy They Couldn't Resist

The night-watchman at the French embassy in Washington was wary. He did not trust the couple who pleaded to be allowed to spend nights of passion inside the building.

The man said he was married, and had nowhere else to pursue his affair. He always gave generous bribes. But, two days earlier, the champagne with which they plied the watchman had made him strangely drowsy. He had slept like a baby all night. Now they were back again. The watchman decided to check what they were really up to. He crept to the door of the room where they were. Gingerly he peeped inside – then backed away. The girl, a green-eyed, auburn-haired beauty, was completely naked, stretched seductively across a couch. Little did the guard at the Vichy French mission realize that his eyes had just feasted on the body of the most successful sex spy of World War II, a woman whose espionage exploits made those of Mata Hari pale into insignificance.

Amy Elizabeth Thorpe was American-born, but had married British diplomat Arthur Pack during the 1930s. He was a dry, pompous man, completely unsuitable for a girl with her looks and spirit of adventure, but she stuck with him as his work took him to Chile, Spain and finally Poland. There she was at last given the chance of some excitement. In 1937, British intelligence invited her to become an agent. She accepted readily.

Soon Amy – codenamed Cynthia during the war – was the mistress of a well-placed official at the Polish Foreign Ministry in Warsaw. He told her of developments in Germany and Czechoslovakia, useful inside information for the British. But, more importantly, she learned of Polish engineers working on a version of the German Enigma cypher machine. It was the first step in an operation which led to Britain acquiring the code which cracked Hitler's secret communications.

By 1941, Cynthia was in New York, the prize agent in the star-studded pack at British Security Coordination. William Stephenson needed someone to lure secrets from the embassies of the Italians and Vichy French. Cynthia's successes in Poland made her ideal. She was established in a comfortable home in Washington, and joined the cocktail-party circuit in the American capital, renewing acquaintance with an old flame, Admiral Alberto Lais, then Mussolini's naval attaché in the USA.

Unlike later sex spies, Cynthia made no secret of her intentions. She blatantly told Lais she needed Italian codes and cyphers to help Allied intelligence in the war effort against his country. He was so besotted by her beauty that he provided them for copying. Even BSC veterans were stunned. One said: 'It seems fantastic that a man of his experience and seniority, who was by instinct, training and conviction a patriotic officer, should have been so enfeebled by passion.' The Italian codes helped the outnumbered British fleet outwit Axis ships in the Mediterranean, and were of priceless value in the Allied invasions of North Africa. But, once Lais had served his purpose, Cynthia threw him over. She told the FBI about his knowledge of sabotage in American ports, and he was sent home as an undesirable.

Her next target was the embassy of Vichy France, the pro-Nazi puppet government set up after Hitler's occupation of the country. Captain Charles Brousse, a former naval pilot, was the ambassador's press officer. He had worked with British intelligence before the war, but was sickened when British ships attacked the French navy at Oran in 1940 to prevent the fleet being used by the Germans. He was also no friend of Americans, believing them vulgar, with no understanding of the political realities of his country.

Slowly, seductively, Cynthia won him over. She was as smart mentally as she was attractive physically, and Brousse was captivated. He even agreed to her moving into the hotel where he lived with his third wife. He told her about a cache of French gold hidden on the Caribbean island of Martinique. BSC sent agents to locate it and prevent it falling into Nazi hands. Stephenson then cheekily used control of the gold as security in negotiations for badly needed loans from America for the British war effort. Cynthia also learned of more Nazi plots against Allied shipping. And she was told of German agents in North and South America funded via the French Legation. Then came a difficult order – get hold of new French naval codes.

These were locked in a strongroom at Vichy France's embassy in Washington. Even Brousse had no access to them. Together they planned their love tryst deception of the night watchman. Generous tips and the 'nowhere to go' sob story made their faces familiar. Then came the night when they brought the bottles of champagne. The watchman's suspicions were correct. While he slept off drugs in the booze, Cynthia and Brousse let an expert locksmith in through a side door to study the vault where the codes were kept, and on the night the watchman peeped at naked Cynthia BSC experts were at the vault copying the vital cyphers.

Like Cynthia's work on Enigma and the Italian codes, it was an espionage coup that changed the course of the war. In 1945, official BSC papers said the powerful and intoxicating hold Cynthia established over worldly-wise men 'opened the way back into France and ultimately into Germany'. And when H. Montgomery Hyde, Stephenson's official biographer, asked Cynthia years later whether she was a little ashamed of her sexual antics she replied: 'Ashamed? Not in the least. My superiors told me that my work saved thousands of British and American lives.'

Cynthia volunteered for further service in Europe. She wanted to be parachuted behind the German lines as a secret assassin. Though she had taken risks before, this time spymasters ruled it was too dangerous. After 1945, Brousse divorced his wife, and Cynthia's husband Arthur Pack was found shot dead in Argentina. He had been in poor health. The way was clear for Cynthia to marry Brousse, which she did. They lived in a castle in the South of France until 1963, when the world's most successful amorous agent died of cancer. Brousse died ten years later.

The King and Mrs Simpson

Edward VIII nurtured the secret close to his heart for months. He had fallen for a woman that his position as monarch would never allow him to marry. And yet, hopelessly and obsessively, he could not end the affair – preferring instead to abandon his throne in order to keep the affections of Wallis Simpson. But, for the British people, the love affair was kept secret. While abroad people snickered over the weak Edward's little-boy-lost love for the divorced Simpson, censors and the British establishment combined to keep the very people he reigned over in the dark about the King's lover. It was a calculated move designed to keep an entire nation cut off from reality. It was hardly surprising, therefore, that once the secret was out it engulfed Edward, Wallis, the establishment and the monarchy like a tidal wave.

Edward VIII was King of Great Britain for 326 days before he abdicated for the woman he loved. But he had been blindly in love for nearly three years with Wallis Simpson. The object of His Majesty's desire in 1936 was the lady he had met in 1931, a witty but rather plain 34-year-old American, who had had a childhood and upbringing just about as far as one could get from the House of Windsor. Her father, a businessman from Maryland, had died when she was just five months old and she had been raised in Baltimore by her mother. She married a navy pilot in 1916, confessing that she found the combination of uniform and derring-do a thrilling one. But the union with Earl Winfield Spencer was short-lived and they were separated in 1922. Her second marriage came in 1928 to Ernest Simpson, a respectable businessman, half British, half American, who headed the London Office of his family's shipping company. It was his arrival in Britain in 1929 that thrust Wallis Simpson onto the London social scene. It had always been an ambition of her mother's that Wallis should elevate herself within society, leaving behind the low social order and poverty of her upbringing. With marriage to Ernest she seemed to have accomplished her goal and established a reputation among the rich and privileged set of the time as something of an amusing and competent hostess. She moved among diplomats, lords and ladies – and loved it. However, as Wallis began to enjoy the London social whirl more and more, she began to find her husband staid, dull and uninteresting.

It was in December 1930 that the new first secretary at the American Embassy, Benjamin Thaw, was invited to dinner at the Simpsons. He came with his wife Consuelo, and her sister Thelma, Viscountess Furness. Lady Furness, a vampish beauty with affected Hollywood starlet looks and manners, had her own secret; she was mistress to the Prince of Wales. A friendship burgeoned between the three women, with Thelma confiding to Wallis about her secret love. Eventually, the Simpsons dined with the Prince and were soon regular visitors to his country retreat. He too dined at the Simpsons' flat off Oxford Street. In January 1934 the Viscountess, at a dinner party, discreetly said to Wallis Simpson: 'I am making a trip to the United States. Please would you look after the Prince to make sure he isn't lonely?' Wallis looked after him all right, rather a little too well for Thelma's liking. By the time she returned in the spring, Wallis and the Prince were lovers.

The secret of the relationship was shared by a small elite group. In the 1930s the Press was far more conservative and did not employ the kind of professional 'royal watchers' whose sole tasks are reporting trivia and intimate details of the House of Windsor. Conversely, Edward was being sucked into an emotional vortex which would run directly contrary to his responsibilities as the future King of Great Britain. The secret love letters, which were released after Wallis Simpson's death at the age of 89 in 1986, showed the bizarre mother-son relationship which the couple shared – even though Wallis was in fact two years younger than the Prince. His letters are full of infantile pleading, a need to be reassured and cosseted, adoring in his affections for her. Hers are admonishing, stern, sensible, possessive.

The privileged group of friends who in the early days witnessed them together say that he was completely captivated by her. She, slender, sophisticated, poised, elegant and witty, was the exact opposite of the rather boyish would-be King of Great Britain.

It is not known at which exact date the Prince told the royal family of his love for Wallis Simpson – but they could well have learned from the Prince's indiscreet flaunting of his new mistress on trips to Paris, the French Riviera, Budapest, Berlin and Italy. The foreign Press had a field day. Detailed accounts of their trysts in romantic hotels were published in every language from French to Finnish and even the American Press came in on the act – they called Wallis 'Queen Wally'! Amazingly, Fleet Street printed not a word. The newspapers were then owned by the powerful Press barons, men like Rothermere and Beaverbrook, who saw it as their duty to preserve the façade of the British monarchy – even if their future King was behaving like a playboy. Newspapers coming into the country from overseas had references to the liaison removed and the British public remained ignorant of Edward's behaviour with a twice-divorced woman. The US Press in particular went to town with photographs and a story about the couple's visits to Yugoslavia, Greece and Turkey.

Edward became King Edward VIII in December 1935. The affair was at its height and the love letters from Edward to Wallis became ever more sloppy and infantile. But Edward still had the British establishment on his side – that curious creature which is capable of so much indiscretion as long as it is discreet. For Edward and Wallis that turning point was reached when the secret was out on 3 December 1936. Some weeks before then Wallis had finally received a divorce from her husband. Prime Minister Stanley Baldwin, who knew then of the entanglement that Edward had with Wallis, asked the King to persuade Wallis not to go through with the divorce. But Edward told him: 'I have no right to interfere with the affairs of an individual. It would be wrong were I to attempt to influence Mrs Simpson just because she happens to be a friend of the king.' Secretly, it was what he wished and conspired for – knowing that in six months' time, before his coronation, he would be free to wed her.

The conspiracy of silence ended when the Bishop of Bradford, Dr Blunt, publicly chastised Edward for his carefree lifestyle which he said was incongruous with a man who was the head of the British Empire. The newspaper construed that the Bishop's outburst was aimed directly at the relationship between the King and Wallis Simpson. The secret was out. Edward was swamped by the public reaction to his affair and naïvely believed that the establishment and the people would understand his affair of the heart. But there would be no sympathetic tears shed for his blighted love. Queen Mary, his mother, was outraged and sent for Baldwin to attend Buckingham Palace. Edward had hoped to move Baldwin into accepting Wallis as his bride and, therefore, as the future Queen. Edward had not yet had his coronation and he believed his popularity with the British people would win through and he would be allowed to marry Wallis. Baldwin told him: 'We will not have it sir. People are talking about you and this American woman. I have had so many nasty letters from people who respected your father and who do not appreciate the way you are going on.'

In the eight days between revelation and abdication, Wallis was subjected to a fearful hate campaign. Stones were hurled through the window of her London home and she received hurtful letters. The children were later to sing in the streets: 'Hark the herald angels sing, Mrs Simpson's pinched our King.' Wallis fled to the south of France while Edward battled against the established order and his own feelings. He was told to ditch Wallis and to assume the responsibilities to which his whole life had been leading like a man. He tried to sway various influential politicians and Press barons, but without much success. One in whom he found an ally was Winston Churchill who, at a lunch with playwright Noël Coward remarked: 'Why shouldn't the King marry his cutie?' 'Because,' remarked Coward, 'England does not want a Queen Cutie.' Finally Edward approached the publisher of the *Daily Mail*, Esmond Harmsworth, who suggested a morganatic marriage – once popular in German royal states – whereby Wallis could become his bride, but would not assume the title of Queen. Her children similarly would have no rights to the throne of Great Britain. Wallis begrudgingly accepted the idea, but it was to no avail; the cabinet would not entertain the idea. If Edward were to remain as King, it would be without Wallis Simpson at his side.

The King, hopelessly, blindly in love with Wallis, decided to abdicate and resolve the constitutional crisis looming over Britain. When Wallis heard that he had stepped down from the throne on 11 December, and broadcast his message to the British people the following night, she wept. Later in her memoirs she wrote: 'I was lying on the sofa with my hands over my eyes, trying to hide my tears.' The King had told the nation that he could not rule without the woman he loved by his side. Edward then left for France, never again to set foot on the shores of his beloved Great Britain.

The couple lived in a splendid white château on the outskirts of Paris for which they paid a peppercorn rent. They married in the Loire Valley and remained as distant outcasts from the royal family until their deaths – he in May 1972 aged 77, she 14 years later.

Only at Edward's funeral at St George's Chapel, Windsor, did Wallis come to see the members of the royal family that she so wished to join. She spent one night in Buckingham Palace before returning to her exile in Paris. She ended her days lonely, bedridden, a sad figure whose secret affair burgeoned into one of the classic romantic tragedies of the 20th century. On her dressing-room table she kept a framed message penned by Edward, who assumed the title of Duke of Windsor after his abdication. The touching lines read: 'My friend, with thee to live alone, methinks were better than to own, a crown, a sceptre and a throne.'

Baby Love

In 1986 scandal split the Anglican Church in the United States. It was in the shape of a little bundle of joy called Evan. Evan is now a healthy little girl who plays happily in the garden of her home without a care in the world – and she certainly has no inkling that her birth took place in a storm of publicity. For Evan was born to an unmarried woman priest – a priest, moreover, who conceived her baby not just out of wedlock but from artificial insemination, from not one but three donors! Now the Church hierarchy is threatening that if the mother does not reveal the father's identity she will face excommunication.

The Reverend Lesley Northup was brought up in a religious family in Washington. From her earliest days she attended Sunday school and was fascinated both by the ritual of the Church and the values which its message of love and compassion instilled in her. Lesley Northup's mind was firmly made up; she was going to spread the word of the Lord when she grew up. In 1981 she was ordained by the Bishop of New York, the Right Reverend Paul Moore. He announced to the assembled congregation that Lesley Northup had the 'qualities and dignity' of a woman well suited to the calling of Christ.

But Reverend Northup had another, equally strong calling – to become a mother. She said: 'I knew that my life was devoted to God and I didn't want a husband because I was so devoted to the Church. But there were feelings within me that I would like to be a mother. To give life, to nurture it and watch it grow. That seemed important to me and did not veer from the teachings of the Bible. I know that the pathway I was considering was not a very romantic one, but it was morally correct. I have no regrets.'

What Lesley did was to enlist the help of two fellow sympathetic male priests and another Church worker. They each agreed to provide sperm for artificial insemination. 'I chose them because they were healthy and relatively stable,' said Lesley. 'Good looks didn't count and there was no adultery because they were all single. I was determined that no one, including myself, should know the identity of the father. So on three consecutive nights at my home I artificially inseminated myself. The results are to be found in the beautiful form of my baby daughter.'

Lesley did not foresee the strength of protest and indignation that rose up to meet her when Evan was born. Aside from Church outrage, she was the target of a vicious and prolonged campaign of abuse from the public. Her home was the target of vandals and one letter to her read: 'You have sinned against the Lord. You are an abomination to the Church you claim to represent, whore! You will fry in hell.'

Lesley was stunned by the public reaction. She said: 'I did nothing wrong and yet this was happening to me. I didn't want a baby to be the result of a promiscuous act and I didn't want anyone to think that. People said to me: "If you want a baby so badly why don't you just get married?" But you don't just wake up one day and say: "I'll go to the supermarket today and get a husband." And you don't get married just to have a baby. When I got pregnant I didn't want any of the donors to feel responsible individually, but when Evan was born I received christening gifts from all of them. Judging by her looks I have no idea who her father is. She had the bad taste – but the good sense – to resemble a small clone of her mother, so both the donor anonymity and my exclusive parental rights have been protected.'

'Now if I happen to meet one of them, they ask how she is, but that is all. I couldn't have done this without men but I would point out I am not a radical feminist. I have gone out with men, I have had relationships with men. I have no anti-male bias whatsoever. I have a quiet, middle-class life and I really am rather conservative in my politics. I chose artificial insemination because it would have been dishonest to get married just to have a baby – plus I devote too much time to God.'

Lesley admits that finding the men for the undertaking was a tricky business – especially as she stipulated that they were not to have any involvement in the child's upbringing. But the greatest problems facing her stem from the Church establishment in the United States. She has been the subject of countless debates and the latest dictate from her Bishops demand that she reveal the father before they move on to decide what is to become of her. But Lesley is adamant – the secret of the donors will stay just that. Even the local Bishop who ordained her has gone against Church thinking to declare his support for her. He said: 'There was no adultery and there were no grounds to depose her. So I came out and said: "OK, I am right behind you." I have no intention of criticizing her or condemning her. I couldn't tell her not to have the baby. When you get down to it, she wanted to bring up her own child and I felt she could do a great job. I looked over the Ten Commandments and I didn't see that she had broken any of them.'

But his view is not shared by many more orthodox, right-wing clerics in the Church hierarchy. One of her most outspoken critics, the Reverend John Yates of Vermont, said: 'Her decision to produce a child through artificial insemination is another indicator of the discouraging, dehumanizing drift in our society's perceptions of parenthood and family life. Many in the church do not think she belongs in the cloth and I would support that view.'

Lesley continues to show that she is a force to be reckoned with, declaring: 'I am so proud of what I have done I won't even keep the truth from Evan. How it's phrased will depend on when she asks, but certainly she'll get the whole truth. And she may have a brother or sister as well – because I would certainly have no qualms about doing it again.'

Eric Clapton and the Chambermaid

For months the gossip columns had been filled with the news that buzzed across the Atlantic. Eric Clapton, legendary guitarist, musician extraordinaire, a man who beat heroin and booze addictions to produce some of the best rock music ever, was to be a father again. That fact alone wasn't so startling – it was *who* was going to be the mother. Clapton had already raised more than a few music-world eyebrows when his beautiful Italian mistress Lory Del Santo gave birth at the age of 26 to the singer's son Conor in August 1986. Patti Boyd, 38, who left ex-Beatle George Harrison for Clapton in 1974, and who married him in 1979, named Lory in her divorce petition. When the rumours started buzzing towards the end of the summer of 1987 that Clapton was going to be a father again, the thoughts were not of *when* but of *who* was carrying his child.

As it turned out, neither Lory nor Patty was pregnant by Clapton. But out of the shadows of New York's clubland came a part-time singer, part-time chambermaid, with a definite bulge under her dress. Alina Moreni, who was aged 27, was carrying Eric Clapton's love child – or so she said.

Fleet Street went mad for her story. The bouncy beauty had an amazing yarn to tell of her secret affair. In both British and American newspapers she boasted how fairy-tale love had blossomed when she met Clapton at a club in Manhattan one night. She said that she lived in one of New York's smartest streets, Park Avenue, with her wealthy mother, and was an Italian Baroness in a self-imposed exile of luxury in the most exciting city she knew. Her life, she sighed, was a tidal wave of champagne and roses, played out against the backdrop of exciting New York. Her story was the stuff of romantic novels. In one interview she said: 'I knew when I fell in love with Eric Clapton that it was never going to be easy. He has a beautiful heart, but not much brains. He thinks with the most intimate part of his body. But underneath all that he's just a playful, insecure child. That's why I have always liked him – and that's one of the things he always liked about me: my honesty.'

Alina's honesty in her interviews was quite breath-taking. She revealed how she and Clapton had a mad passionate fling which resulted in her pregnancy. She said it was a matter of time before Eric made a statement about their love, and also about the matter of paying maintenance for the child which was due to be born in April 1988.

The publicity was certainly paying off for Alina. She was booked to sing in some of the better-known New York nightclubs and boasted proudly of a hurried love-call to Eric every time she was offstage. 'He makes my heart beat with desire,' she gushed in a New York newspaper. 'He is just waiting for the day we can be together for ever. He, me and our baby. It will be perfect.' Even though she was heavily pregnant, Alina managed to draw the kind of publicity usually reserved for more shapely aspiring crooners. She was snapped by the paparazzi as she left clubs, snapped as she went in, and droned on about the 'special magic' she shared with Eric. 'I am only revealing the secret of our love because he is soon to break the news to Lory,' said Alina. But the real secret was something quite different indeed . . .

Day by day Alina was getting bigger until she resembled a matronly Italian housewife, clasping her hands in front of her to help hold the burden she was carrying. And then one day her manager, Lynne Robinson, who was helping to promote her singing career, noticed that the 'pregnancy lump' seemed to move! 'I have seen pregnant women before,' said Lynne, 'and this seemed most odd. The lump definitely shifted – and when I saw her again it seemed to have moved once again.' There was no comment from the Clapton camp about the singer's entangled love life. His management refused to be drawn into the star's personal life.

Then in May, when Alina looked fit to burst, she 'went into hospital to give birth to our darling child'. But while she was away newspaper reporters from both sides of the Atlantic began sniffing around what looked like being a very fishy tale indeed. It turned out that Alina was no Italian Baroness. She was a full-time, hard-up maid who last year cleaned the apartment of Eric Clapton. There was no crime in rich and poor getting together in a union of passion, however. Friends rushed to her side to say that the Italian Baroness story was concocted merely to give Eric's friends in the pop world a more favourable impression of his latest love.

But then other cracks began appearing in the saga; Robinson told how she tried to reach out to touch pregnant Alina's stomach, and 'she winced away as if in pain'. She added: 'She wouldn't let me near her. That was when I was convinced that she was a faker and that the whole thing was some kind of calculated sting against Clapton. I said to her: "You are a very, very sick girl and need help." I am a mother of three children and I know how people behave when they are pregnant. There was no way that this woman was carrying anything other than a pillow up her dress.'

Alina's other close friend Rose Genero, who had known her for six years, said Alina telephoned her from a New York hospital on 8 May to say she had given birth to a bouncing baby girl, and that she was going to call her Rosa Lina Clapton. Eric had been on the telephone from London, she told Rose, and everything was fine. 'But I checked back with the hospital and there was no record of her being there or indeed of a baby girl being born that night,' said Rose. 'I think I knew then that the real secret was not her fling with a pop star, but the fact that she had embarked on a Walter Mitty exercise that had only one ending. She was bound to be found out sooner or later. Maybe she did have a fling with Clapton but she sure as hell wasn't carrying his baby.'

With pressure from the media building up, Alina went into hiding with her 'baby' – she still insisted that she had given birth and that Eric was on his way to see her. But then two days later she confessed sobbing to Fleet Street reporters: 'I did not have his baby. I had an abortion because I saw the way he was treating me. When I saw his attitude towards me I knew that he had changed. But I am a woman and I am proud. That is why I pretended for so long that I was carrying his child. It was a very upsetting time all round and now I need lots of therapy for my condition.'

A psychiatrist, John Felton, noted in a US magazine: 'Many girls build up secret love affairs with famous people. They take the pin-up poster adulation one step further and create entire lives and love affairs around them until they finally believe that they are having a relationship with that person. For someone to pretend that they are pregnant is merely taking it just one stage further. The excitement comes from the person who is smitten believing that it is their "secret" – something private and dark and mysterious. Once that illusion is shattered there is nothing left.'

Clapton still refuses to comment on the entire affair. The last word, however, went to Alina who said: 'Dear Eric, I shall always love him . . .'

The Princess and the Captain

One way or another, when it comes to affairs of the heart, the House of Windsor has had more than its fair share of anguish and pain. The Prince of Wales, who went on to become King Edward VII, scandalized society with his fling with the exquisite Lillie Langtry. A later successor to his title abandoned the throne for divorcee Wallis Simpson. In more modern times the dalliance between His Royal Highness Prince Andrew and a former soft-porn film star named Koo Stark caused more than just a little concern. But perhaps the saddest secret affair was that between Princess Margaret and Group Captain Peter Townsend; their modern-day love story rivalled anything that Shakespeare could dream up and was eventually to lead to heartbreak for them and strife within the royal family. It started as a schoolgirl crush but went on to become a deeply passionate affair which was kept secret – until a knowing glance gave them away. To this day, there are many people who think Princess Margaret was the hardest done-by royal of all.

She was just an innocent 14-year-old schoolgirl when she met the debonair Townsend in 1944. The 29-year-old tall war hero, who had distinguished himself in the Battle of Britain, came to Buckingham Palace as an Equerry to King George VI. The appeal for Margaret was instant: Townsend was good-looking, charming, distinguished – and a war hero. For a young woman, increasingly aware of her own blossoming sexuality, he was an incomparable idol. He was also unattainable – married to a pretty wife called Rosemary. He was given a house in the grounds of Windsor Castle and assigned to his duties. Margaret adored him and sought him out for – allegedly – fatherly advice and friendship. There was never any question that he would be hers – yet. But in 1947 the King took Margaret and her sister, the Princess Elizabeth, on a three-month tour of southern Africa. The voyage was planned as a test of the love that Prince Philip of Greece held for Princess Elizabeth. Philip had been courting her for some while and the King thought that a long separation would test the feelings of both. Elizabeth's sadness, however, at being parted from Philip was made up for in feelings of pure joy for Margaret – for it meant the royal party were accompanied by Group Captain Townsend – while Rosemary stayed at home. Old newsreels of the time testify to the happiness and warmth that the 17-year-old Margaret radiated on the visit while she was near to the man she loved. On the visit she stayed up late into the warm African nights, listening to the cultured, witty humour and gentle views of Townsend.

For Margaret, it is almost as if she had a sixth-sense that

she would one day be in his arms. She stayed away from the many suitors in society who were attracted to her, waiting for the chance to become Townsend's love. That chance occurred in 1951 when he and Rosemary parted. Their long separations due to his royal tours and other duties put a strain on the union that was too great to bear. She was unfaithful to him and in August 1951, just days after the Princess had celebrated her 21st birthday, Townsend told the Princess: 'The marriage is over. We married in wartime and were not right for each other.' The pair were horseriding in the grounds of Balmoral and it was there that Margaret told him for the first time of the burning passion she held for him. It was the start of the affair.

Like her predecessors within the House of Windsor, Margaret underestimated both public interest and her own family's reaction to her 'deep friendship'. The couple were once caught by the King himself as Townsend was carrying Princess Margaret up the stairs as if she were his bride and he were taking her over the threshold! 'I told him to do it papa, I ordered him,' blurted the embarrassed Margaret who had not breathed a word of her feelings to her father. By this time Townsend was the Deputy Master of the Royal Household and, as such, had ample opportunity to plan his time around seeing the Princess. They arranged cosy weekends at the homes of discreet friends – a practice later adopted by Prince Andrew when he was seeing Koo Stark – and made sure never to show displays of public affection when the eyes of Britain's Press were upon them. They drove away from the Palace in plain cars, Margaret often down in her seat so she would not be spotted by the curious tourists who thronged at the iron railings, craning their necks to catch a glimpse of the inhabitants. Her love for Townsend was deep, genuine – and doomed. Like all secrets, they could never keep it completely and were the subject of a vicious whispering campaign within the establishment. Townsend was accused of being a 'cradle-snatcher' and Margaret of having foolish child-like emotions that she could neither control nor understand. One of the most severe critics of the burgeoning relationship was Prince Philip, who had married Princess Elizabeth. He thought that a divorced 'employee' of the 'family firm' was not a fitting candidate to romance the Queen's sister. But Margaret was determined to share her life with Townsend – even going to see Sir Alan Lascelles, the Queen's private secretary, to enquire whether a divorce on Townsend's part – and for admitted adultery by his wife – would stand in the way of their future happiness together. Lascelles, an independent thinker, said he could see no problems as long as a respectable period of time elapsed before the couple contemplated marriage. Margaret said they were thinking of a period over a year away, and he replied: 'Then I can foresee no problems.' The whole of the royal family now knew that Townsend was courting the Princess as their liaison became less secret. The British public did not. They learned about it when the couple themselves broke their cardinal rule about public displays of affection. The game was up when, shortly after the Westminster Abbey coronation ceremony for Queen Elizabeth, Princess Margaret was observed by a Fleet Street reporter leaning forward to brush a speck of dirt from Townsend's blue RAF uniform. It was interpreted for what it was – the act of a woman in love, making sure her man looks his best. Captain Townsend's glance into her eyes gave Fleet Street sensational headlines for the next day: 'Princess Margaret's Love for RAF Hero' being one of the more reserved statements.

The couple were treated to a prime display of what Britain excels at – hypocrisy. It was 1953, the divorce rate was soaring and women were on the pathway to determining their own futures. But the establishment balked at what it felt was a constitutional crisis to rival that of the Edward and Wallis Simpson affair of the 1930s. In her role as head of state, the Queen is also the head of the Church of England, defender of the faith and the symbol of all that is sacrosanct in moral behaviour. The idea of her sister first cavorting with, and then marrying, a divorced man, was just too much to bear. Churchill was Prime Minister and was under great pressure to separate the couple. There were none of the kind words that the young Princess had received from Sir Alan; only a cold warning that their love could never be. Townsend was packed off to Brussels as the air attaché to the British Embassy, and Margaret was sent on a tour of Rhodesia with her mother.

The Princess, still nurturing her belief that they would be allowed to marry, called Townsend on booked international calls twice a day. The lovers plotted future trysts, secret meetings, away from both the pressure of the Palace – where Prince Philip was emerging as a major figure in mustering anti-Townsend sympathies – and the Press which had unleashed the news of the couple's love to the world. Remarkably, their romance survived. For the three years that Group Captain Townsend was posted to Brussels their affair was played out in snatched meetings and all-too-brief rendezvous at secret addresses. But, shortly before her 25th birthday, Margaret was summoned by her sister, the Queen, and told that Winston Churchill had communicated to her that parliament would never sanction a marriage to Townsend. She could renounce her royal status, and go into exile like the Duke of Windsor, but there could be no 'acceptance' into the royal family.

In October 1955 came the last week that the couple were to spend together. They dined at the home of friends in London and at country houses, Margaret nurturing a last-ditch hope that parliament would relent, Townsend, the wider, elder man, knowing their affair was doomed and on its last lap. After consultations with the Archbishop of Canterbury, Margaret met with Queen Elizabeth and told her that she and Townsend had decided to call the whole thing off. On Monday 31 October, a week after crowds outside Clarence House had yelled slogans like 'marry him, marry him!', a statement from Margaret was released to the Press. The moving statement said: 'I would like it to be known that I have decided not to marry Group Captain Peter Townsend. I have been aware that subject to my renouncing my rights of succession it might have been possible for me to contract a civil marriage. But mindful of the Church's teaching that a Christian marriage is indissoluble, and conscious of my duty to the Commonwealth, I have resolved to put these considerations before any others. I have reached the decision entirely alone, and in doing so I have been strengthened by the unfailing support and devotion of Group Captain Townsend.'

It was over. Princess Margaret went on to marry Anthony Armstrong-Jones, later Lord Snowdon. The initially blissful marriage foundered and in 1978 they were finally divorced. Friends of Margaret say that her heart had never healed from the days of that heady affair with the man who was probably her only true love.

Thelma Todd – the Ice Cream Blonde

On the night of Sunday 15 December 1935, bubbly comedienne Thelma Todd attended a lavish party at a swish Hollywood nightclub, the Trocadero. It was one of the hottest tickets in town and, fittingly, the beautiful comic star was the guest of honour – however, this was to be the last party the so-called Ice Cream Blonde would ever attend. The next time her friends would see her there would be no laughter, no Christmas cheer, no clinking of cocktail glasses . . . only the quiet murmurs of sadness as they filed past her coffin.

What actually happened in the eight hours between the time the effervescent Thelma left the party and the time her limp body was discovered in her garage one can only guess. There were many clues and contradictory stories, as well as whispers of drug-trafficking, gambling and even the possible involvement of Charles 'Lucky' Luciano, the first Godfather of organized crime, and a man feared by studio bosses and politicians alike. Yet the case of the Ice Cream Blonde remains shrouded in mystery. It is a mystery Hollywood never solved – or forgot.

According to initial police investigations at the time, Thelma was chauffeured home following the swinging evening at the Trocadero. She had walked up the long stairway to the apartment she shared with her lover, director Roland West, while her driver watched to make sure she entered safely. The next time anyone saw her for certain – apart from the killer – she was slumped behind the wheel of her chocolate-coloured Lincoln convertible, blood dripping from her mouth onto her silver-and-blue evening gown and expensive mink coat. The ignition switch was on, but the motor was dead. So too was the delicious comedienne, whose flowing blonde locks and light-headed antics in film comedies with such superstars as the Marx Brothers and Laurel and Hardy had won her a legion of fans. She was just 30 years old.

Following a lengthy police inquiry, which uncovered a baffling array of contradictory evidence, the grand jury which investigated the death delivered a curious verdict – death by asphyxiation due to carbon monoxide poisoning. The conclusion, which left many questions unanswered, suggested that Thelma may have committed suicide. Yet why would Thelma want to kill herself? She had everything to live for – a successful career, scores of friends, money. In fact, actress Ida Lupino, a close friend who had been at the fateful Trocadero party, said Thelma seemed on top of the world that night, even gleefully telling her closest friends that she had taken a new lover, a San Francisco businessman, behind West's back. And, if she had committed suicide, as implausible as that was, why was blood found on her mouth and clothes? And, strangest of all, why had several credible eye-witnesses claimed to have seen Thelma very much alive driving through Hollywood with an unidentified man beside her, after the party? Who was this dark stranger? Could it have been West, or maybe even the murderer? Were they the same person? Where were he and Thelma going at such a late hour? None of these questions was ever fully answered, despite the grand-jury investigation and the lengthy police inquiry.

However, later it was revealed that West, who together with Thelma co-owned a smart neighbourhood restaurant favoured by movie stars, did eventually admit to the authorities – but only after a lengthy grilling – that he and the actress had a blazing row after she returned home from the party. But West told investigators he threw Thelma out of the apartment, and did not kill her. Other residents in the neighbourhood backed up West's story. They told police they heard a screaming Thelma pounding and kicking on the front door of the apartment – leaving fresh kick marks which were later verified – before storming off into the night. West, it seemed, had an airtight alibi. But amateur sleuths always suspected that the director had staged the whole scene – just like one of his movies. According to them, West used a look-alike Thelma to play out the row in front of startled neighbours – while inside he quietly knocked out the real Thelma before stuffing her in the car and turning on the ignition. Supporters of this scenario claim West had long wanted to end the often-stormy affair, and keep the prized restaurant for himself. Alas, like all the other theories, it was never proven, though in 1976, Pat Di Cicco, the once-powerful Hollywood agent and Thelma's former husband, said that he always believed West was behind the killing. (West was never to make another picture and died a forgotten man in 1952.) Meanwhile, not long after Thelma had been laid to rest amid much publicity, her lawyer was demanding a second inquest which he claimed would prove what he always suspected: that the happy-go-lucky comedienne had been bumped off by professional hit-men working under orders from 'Lucky' Luciano. Luciano, the most powerful New York gangster of his day, had been expanding his empire into bars, clubs and restaurants up and down the Californian coast, setting up illegal gambling dens in back rooms. And it was no secret that emissaries from the evil Luciano had once approached Thelma seeking her permission to open a casino on the top floor of her restaurant. Luciano believed Thelma's rich, carefree friends would flock to the den. She refused, however, and Luciano was not known for giving people second chances. According to the lawyer, the moment Thelma turned 'Lucky' down she became a marked woman, and it was only a matter of time before she was killed. As plausible as this theory was, the Luciano connection hardly saw the light of day, let alone the inside of a courtroom. Before any real inquiry had begun, the investigation was unceremoniously dropped. It seems the studio bosses, who wisely feared the all-powerful mobster and his ties to the film industry, eventually persuaded the lawyer to let the matter rest in peace.

And so the investigations into the mysterious death of Thelma Todd, the one-time grammar-school teacher who found fame and fortune among the bright lights of Hollywood, were consigned to the massive scrap heap of criminal history.

It was a sad ending for the vivacious woman with the

turquoise blue eyes who had thrilled movie-goers in films as warm-hearted, vital and happy as she herself had been.

Mary Astor's Diary

Unlike so many of her contemporaries, actress Mary Astor not only survived the public airing of some of her most intimate secrets but she actually fared much better after her love life had been exposed. Such are the vagaries of a fickle public.

Mary, the fluttery-eyed murderess in the 1941 mystery classic, *The Maltese Falcon,* had one life-long friend – her diary, in which she faithfully confided every day. Now this may be a harmless hobby for a starry-eyed young girl growing up in the wheat fields of Illinois, but for a lust-filled screen siren it could, and would, prove to be dynamic. Newspapers of the day didn't call it 'the little blue book' because of its colourful binding, and its contents became 'must reading' in tabloids across the nation. The public just couldn't get enough and, as its revelations came tumbling out, newspaper circulation managers reached heights of ecstasy not unlike those Mary wrote about.

Eventually, the diary would become the most talked-about book of its time, causing a delicious uproar from Hollywood to New York. Guessing the likely 'stars' of Mary's prose became a national pastime, as did filling in the asterisks which covered Mary's sometimes 'colourful' language.

But the identities of all but two men remain secret to this day – and so does the whereabouts of the diary itself, which has become as elusive as the legendary Maltese Falcon. Yet, if it hadn't been for a pair of misplaced cufflinks, the world might never have even known about the diary's existence, let alone its incredible contents.

It was 1935, and Mary, a delicate beauty with a sophisticated grace, was involved in a torrid extramarital affair with playwright George S. Kaufman, whom she had met during a trip to New York. Following every one of their encounters, Mary would rush home to her diary and begin writing furiously about that day's love-making in rhapsodic detail.

Despite its explicit contents, however, Mary inexplicably took no pains to hide the book, and instead kept it in a drawer of her bedroom – the bedroom she sometimes shared with her husband, Dr Franklyn Thorpe. It was a careless mistake Mary would come to rue dearly.

One day, as the good doctor was looking around for his errant cufflinks, he came across the diary and, being the inquisitive type, decided to take a peek at his wife's innermost secrets. The contents wounded what hurt most – his pride. It didn't take Dr Thorpe long to realize that he was not the Casanova being written about. As he continued reading, he discovered the superman to be none other than Kaufman, a witty, though otherwise bland, New Yorker. One can imagine how the poor physician felt as he sat on his bed, poring over Mary's exquisite memories.

In one very descriptive passage, Thorpe learned that his wife's affair with Kaufman had continued even after Mary got home to Hollywood from the visit to New York. Kaufman, not wanting to be far from the action, had conveniently set up his winter headquarters in nearby Palm Springs, and Thorpe soon found that all those trips Mary had made to the studio for 'costume fittings' were actually ruses to meet with her lover.

Dr Thorpe soon discovered that Mary's affair with Kaufman had been bubbling away merrily for over a year. But there were other names in the book as well, including a list of the best lovers in Hollywood – a list Mary had compiled from personal experience – including screen legend John Barrymore. Just who else was included on the list was never revealed, but it sent shock waves throughout the movie industry and allegedly sent some very prominent actors running for cover.

Of course, to Dr Thorpe, one name was more than enough to send him into a frenzied jealousy. He demanded Mary end the affair, but the defiant actress, unable to do without Kaufman's considerable charms, promptly told him what he could do with his suggestion. Not surprisingly, the doctor, who had wisely held on to the diary, demanded and was granted a divorce. He then went after custody of their four-year-old daughter, Marylyn. While Mary may not have contested the divorce proceedings too strongly, she was prepared to fight all out to retain custody of the child.

In the down-and-dirty struggle which ensued, Dr Thorpe began leaking selected passages of the saucy diary to the Press, while Mary sat on the witness stand in tears. The public was agog, but Astor's lovers were aghast lest they be named. Kaufman's friends reported that he tore his hair out and cried that he was being crucified as the revelations about him and Mary came tumbling out, while John Barrymore vanished into an asylum. In addition, a deputation of Hollywood tycoons, some of them rumoured to be in the book, visited Astor and begged her to withdraw her claim to Marylyn.

Astor refused, risking her reputation and career, and so the scandal continued, as Thorpe leaked more and more pages, until Judge 'Goody' Knight, who was presiding over the whole custody battle, ordered the diary impounded as 'pornography'. The public, to say nothing of the newspaper editors, was dismayed.

But, with his most explosive ammunition now in the hands of the court, Thorpe, whose own philandering was no secret in Hollywood, was fighting a losing battle. Indeed, his maid testified that on four successive nights he had four different showgirls share his bed. The court, which by now had had about all it could take of bedroom antics, decided that Thorpe was no saint himself, and ordered that the child spend nine months of the year with Mary, and the three-month summer vacation with her father. However, much to Mary's dismay, the judge steadfastly refused to return her beloved diary.

What actually became of the diary is still a mystery. In 1952, it was reportedly burned, but stories persist to this day that it still exists, as phantom-like as the Maltese Falcon.

According to the late New York journalist Howard Teichmann, the diary was never destroyed as reported by the wire services, but was locked in an underground vault of the *Daily News* newspaper which mysteriously acquired it many years ago. After Mary's death in 1987, a team of reporters from the newspaper scoured the files looking for the lost legend, but found only some correspondence between editors of the paper and Astor's ex-husband. Unfortunately, the editors who might have had first-hand knowledge of the diary's whereabouts and therefore be able to shed some light on one of Hollywood's most enduring mysteries are now dead.

The diary's final resting place, and the identities of Mary's many lovers, remain among Hollywood's most vexing mysteries.

Wealthy Losers

Gloria Vanderbilt

As a neglected innocent in a world which put wealth, privilege and pleasure before anything else, Gloria Vanderbilt became one of the most haunting figures of the 1930s. She was only ten years old, and heiress to a fortune, when she made front-page news in a scandal-ridden tug-of-war between her beautiful but feckless young mother, Gloria Morgan Vanderbilt, and her powerful millionaire aunt, Gertrude Vanderbilt Whitney. To everyone she became known as the 'poor little rich girl'.

The scandal broke at the time of the great Depression in America, when poverty, misery, hunger and broken dreams were the order of the day. But the plight of little Gloria struck a chord that transcended class barriers. Despite the fact that one day she would inherit the Vanderbilt millions, no one envied her. The public eagerly lapped up the more bizarre details of life with the upper crust when the battle for her custody came to court, but they had nothing but sympathy for the round-faced child trying desperately to smile through her ordeal.

Little Gloria, it appeared, had been shunted around the world like an unwanted parcel, too often neglected and forgotten in a world of rich adults pursuing their own pleasure. While they spooned up caviar, she was found to be undernourished; while they dripped with sables and mink, her clothes were often shabby and her shoes scuffed. In later, happier life Gloria wrote that one of her earliest memories was of her mother 'wearing a crystal spangled white gown, looking more fragile and pale than any moonflower and disappearing down an endless hotel corridor'. She remembered longing to take her hand, but did not dare for fear of disturbing the perfect symmetry of long white fingers and scarlet nails. More than anything, she wanted this beautiful creature to take her in her arms and hug her.

Ever since she had been born, on 20 February 1924, little Gloria had had to content herself with being on the fringe of her mother's life. Before her marriage to Reggie Vanderbilt, Gloria Morgan and her twin, Thelma, had been known as 'the Magnificent Morgans'. With their dark hair, magnolia skin and delicate sensuality, they were the rage of American society when they emerged as social butterflies in the season of 1922. They came from a good family, but had no fortune, and their object was to find one. Thelma crossed the Atlantic to become Lady Furness and mistress of the Prince of Wales. Gloria met and married Reggie Vanderbilt.

At 43, Reggie was a hopeless alcoholic who had managed to get through 25 million dollars of his fortune in 14 years. He was short, stout, addicted to gambling and pornography, but still regarded as a brilliant catch by the Morgans. The incredible Vanderbilt palace on Fifth Avenue, where Reggie's mother, Alice, reigned supreme, was enough to convince any girl that she was marrying well. Its 137 rooms included a vast white-and-gold ballroom and a dining-room where 200 guests sat down to ten-course banquets served on the Vanderbilt solid-gold service.

During their courtship Reggie behaved like any other rich suitor, buying Gloria mountains of orchids and diamonds from Tiffany's. She did not take in the hard fact that he had spent every cent of his personal fortune and was living on the income of a 5-million-dollar trust established by his father. He could give her the great Vanderbilt name, but her only chance of financial security would be to have a child who would eventually inherit from the trust fund.

After their wedding, Reggie still spent money with abandon, denying himself and his bride nothing. They were constantly on the move, forever entertaining and seldom in bed before dawn. When Gloria gave birth to a $7^3/_4$lb baby girl by Caesarean section, Reggie was so delighted with the new experience of being a father that he slipped a diamond-and-emerald bracelet over his daughter's tiny wrist.

However, once mother and baby had recovered, the new arrival made no difference to her parents' lifestyle. Though reported to be enormously fond of her, they followed the usual pattern of their kind and left her to be cared for by others. From the moment she was born, little Gloria was in the hands of two dominant, unbalanced women. One was her maternal grandmother, Laura Morgan, always referred to as Mamma Morgan, a crazed, hysterical woman who put terrifying ideas into her granddaughter's head; the other was hired nurse Emma Keislich, who became devoted to her charge but obsessively protective. Little Gloria called the latter 'Dodo', looked to her for mother-love and nearly died of grief when she was sacked.

Gloria Morgan had been married to Reggie for two years when his drinking finally caught up with him and he died a horrible death through multiple haemorrhages. She was left in the unbelievable position of being a Mrs Vanderbilt without money. Reggie had not only got through his fortune, but had left enormous debts. It was her baby daughter who would one day become an heiress under a trust fund set up by her ancestor Cornelius Vanderbilt II. And nobody could touch that money until she was 21 years old.

Fortunately, Gloria had a meeting with Surrogate Foley of the New York County Surrogates Court. He realized the position she was in, had the power to act and made her a handsome stopgap allowance for the 'support and education of her daughter'. In fact, for a time it was the only money she had to live on. But the rich are never as broke as they think they are, and gradually she received enough from various Vanderbilt sources to leave New York, where she was expected to don widow's weeds, and head, instead, for Paris.

As Mrs Vanderbilt, Gloria had grown used to living in luxury and she didn't intend to change her ways. She shipped her entire household to Paris, where she proceeded to buy a new wardrobe from the top couturiers. Little Gloria was carted around Europe in the wake of her restless, remote, untouchable mother. Years later, she would remember: 'I lived from hotel to hotel until I was eight-and-a-half years old . . .' During one year alone, her schedule was breathtaking. In January she was taken to the Sherry-Netherland Hotel in New York where the Vanderbilts had a luxurious suite, and was left there with her nurse while her mother went to California. In March she was sent back to Paris while her mother went to England. A month later, she was sent for and taken to England, to stay first at a hotel in Maidenhead, then at her aunt Lady Furness's country house, Burrough Court, at Melton Mowbray. In May she was hustled off to nearby Gaddesby Hall, where all the people were strangers and she saw no one but Dodo. In June she returned to Paris, where she was put to bed with scarlet fever. Shaky, but recovered, in July she was packed off to the Hotel Victoria in Glion. In August she actually spent two weeks with her mother in Monte Carlo. 'But I saw very little of her,' she wrote in her later autobiography. 'She was beautiful and exquisite . . . she was mysterious, remote and unattainable to me . . . the ropes of pearls against the soft velvet of her yellow dress . . . how could I ever reach out and be part of her?'

In the autumn of 1926, the beautiful widow booked a passage for herself and her brother Harry on the *Leviathan*, sailing for New York with Queen Marie of Romania and her nephew Gottfield, Prince Hohenloe. A romance developed, for Gloria always had a weakness for famous names, and when she returned to Paris she hinted to her mother that she might become Princess of Hohenloe-Langenburg. Mamma Morgan became hysterical. She knew the Prince had no money and became convinced that he wanted to marry Gloria for one reason only – to get his hands on her granddaughter's inheritance.

All her children, including Gloria, thought that Laura Morgan was crazy. She looked weird, with her face powdered white, her hair dyed ginger-blonde and half-moon pencil lines replacing her shaven eyebrows. Little Gloria loved her because she gave her affection, but the old lady became quite obsessed about the child's safety and, eventually, was convinced that her daughter intended to kill her. Once Prince Hohenloe came on the scene she transferred her mad venom and her fears towards him. She came to believe that, once married to her daughter, the Prince would murder little Gloria for her money. Her daughter, she said, would weep 'like a Magdalen', but the child's millions would be hers. These accusations were made with alarming frequency. No one could keep Mamma Morgan quiet. Something of their content must have been passed on to three-year-old Gloria. She became nervous, hyperactive and increasingly hypochondriac.

On the one hand was Mamma Morgan with her crazy fears, on the other Dodo with her smothering, protective nature, continually calling doctors and describing her charge as 'delicate'. Between them, as the years went by, they set up a genuine fear in little Gloria's mind that, somehow or other, she was going to die before she was much older.

When she was eight, the first signs of bitterness crept into the sweet, childish letters she wrote to 'Dear Momey'. Suddenly, she seemed to realize that all the times she was alone her mother was in lively company, laughing with somebody else. Sometimes she would disappear for cruises or visits for weeks on end. Mamma Morgan had been sent home to New York, but she still wrote to her granddaughter and Gloria answered with touching letters addressed to 'Dear Naney'. In one she wrote: 'My mother said not to write to you but I will not pay any attention to her. She is a rare bease (sic). Well, I will be in dear old New York soon . . .'

It had been agreed that little Gloria should be educated in America, and a school had already been chosen for her. The Vanderbilt trustees began putting pressure on Gloria to bring her home. She was furious at the inconvenience. The child had already spoiled her life by wrecking her chances with Prince Hohenloe, who had gone off to marry Princess Margarita of Greece and Denmark. Now she was being asked to give up her wonderful life in Europe for her daughter's sake.

But in March 1932 they did return, to an America suffering from the effects of the 1929 Wall Street Crash. Bread lines were forming in the streets of New York, thousands of desperate people had committed suicide, and crime was getting out of hand. Since 1929, more than 2,000 people had been kidnapped for ransom. Just seven days after the Vanderbilts arrived in New York, the 21-month-old baby son of aviation pioneer Colonel Charles Lindbergh was kidnapped and later found in a shallow grave. Everyone was talking about the case.

One morning, an anonymous letter arrived at the Sherry-Hilton Hotel where the Vanderbilts were staying. It contained a threat to kidnap little Gloria. Mamma Morgan feared the worst and told her daughter she must hire detectives immediately. There had been so much publicity about their return and the Vanderbilt name was associated with such vast wealth that kidnapping was a very real possibility. Gloria called an agency and guards were posted. But she, herself, had no intention of spending the summer in New York. With the excuse that she had to close up her Paris house, she left her child in the care of Mamma Morgan, Dodo and the detectives and returned to Europe.

The old lady was appalled by her granddaughter's condition. She was thin, pale and drawn; she stammered and had a nervous twitch on one side of her face. There were shadows under her eyes. Doctors concluded that her tonsils needed removing; but, before any operation, she had to be brought back to full health.

One evening in May, news came through that the Lindbergh baby had been found buried in woods near Princeton, killed by a blow to the head. Little Gloria heard everything. Later that night she was found writhing on her bed with terrible stomach pains. The doctor, called in to see her, remembered her anguish long afterwards as she pleaded: 'Don't let me die.' He concluded she was in a state of mortal terror, not helped by the two women left to care for her whose constant fears for her safety, expressed aloud, increased her vulnerability.

This was the state little Gloria was in when she was taken to dinner with her aunt, Gertrude Vanderbilt Whitney, a formidable and impressive lady.

Gertrude was the châtelaine of great estates, a wealthy society matron, sculptor and founder of the Whitney Museum of Modern Art. She seemed, to the world at large, cold and patrician but, nevertheless, a woman who would do her duty. In a detailed account of the Vanderbilt-Whitney affair, *Little Gloria – Happy at Last*, Barbara Goldsmith reveals that Gertrude had another self, known only to a few. This other self was 'a bohemian, a hedonist, a sophisticate who accepted bizarre behaviour . . . she was a woman who took lover after lover and gloried in the pleasure they gave her; a woman of immense vanity who created herself as a seductive, exotic, unique personality'.

This complex woman, herself the mother of three children, was disturbed, as others had been, to see how pale, thin and nervous her niece had become. She had not seen a great deal of little Gloria since her brother Reggie had died, and she knew nothing of the child's secret fears, but the maternal instinct in her came to the fore. She arranged for her own doctor to perform the tonsillectomy and promised Mamma Morgan that she would approach Gloria to ask if the child could stay with her in the country until she regained her health.

Gloria had returned from Europe just in time for her daughter's operation, and was delighted by the offer. She intended to return to Paris as soon as possible and the arrangement suited her perfectly.

The day after Gloria sailed, her daughter was driven to the magnificent Whitney estate, Wheatley Hills in Old Westbury, with Dodo and a bodyguard for company. There, Gertrude was waiting for her in the Venetian-style mansion with an indoor gymnasium, swimming-pool and tennis court, fine stables and acres of parkland. She was shown the stables, where she could have her own pony, and the bedroom Gertrude had furnished specially for her, next to her own.

After six weeks in the country, little Gloria had gained weight, her colour was better and she caught cold less easily, and Gertrude asked Gloria to let the child stay with her till Christmas. Then the visit was protracted even further, and soon the trustees, doctors, lawyers and even Mamma Morgan were urging her to leave little Gloria in Gertrude's care. Slowly it dawned on Gloria that she might never get her daughter back.

Gloria took a house on 72nd Street and hoped that would convince people she intended to provide a home. But, at the same time, the newspapers were full of pictures of her out on the town with millionaire promoter 'Blumie' Blumenthal, flamboyant son of a kosher butcher. He was married, and of dubious character. Vanderbilt guardian and trustee Tom Gilchrist warned that the publicity was not good for her. Gloria wept. She could not get her allowance of $4,000 a month unless little Gloria lived with her. How on earth was she going to manage?

Gloria made an attempt to win back her daughter in June 1934, offering to take her to New York, but little

Gloria turned white and began to shake. She did not want to live with her mother; she wanted to stay with Aunt Ger. Eventually, the 'don't want' turned to fear – fear that her own mother might kidnap her. Gloria was certain that the child's mind had been poisoned against her. There was only one way she could get her back. She would have to go to court.

The preliminary hearing of the Vanderbilt-Whitney custody case was scheduled for Friday 28 September 1934. Ten-year-old Gloria arrived at the Supreme Court Chambers with clenched hands, grinning nervously. She could only barely understand the fight that had arisen between her mother and Aunt Ger. The two protagonists appeared in black and their best furs, diamonds glittering. For the next six weeks the papers were full of nothing but the Vanderbilt-Whitney trial, laid bare, in mouth-watering detail, the lives of two women who represented the upper, upper crust in America and who bore two of its most famous names.

Day after day, Gloria took the stand to justify her way of life and protest her love for her child. She was the public's favourite. Each day she arrived in court on the arm of her nurse and was portrayed by the Press as a beautiful, pathetic, loving, if somewhat wayward, mother. Gertrude, on the other hand, emerged as the tough, powerful older woman who thought that her money could buy anything – 'a haughty matriarch of iron whim'. And between them there was little Gloria, forced to face questioning that no child should have endured. She was made to testify for two-and-half hours and, afterwards, curled up like a foetus in the arms of her bodyguard.

Little Gloria made it quite plain to the court that she wanted to stay with Aunt Ger, that she loved Aunt Ger and did not like living with her mother. In the end it was judged that the life led by little Gloria from the death of her father until June 1932 was 'in every way unsuitable, unfit, improper, calculated to destroy her health and neglectful of her moral, spiritual and mental education . . .'

Custody was given to Gertrude Vanderbilt Whitney. Gloria was led from the court in a state of collapse and little Gloria emerged from the trial a celebrity.

Gloria's new life on the Whitney estate included a black pony of her own, six servants to look after her every need, bodyguards and private detectives, but not her beloved Dodo. The nurse's influence was considered claustrophobic, making the child fearful and neurotic.

But, now the trial was over, was her happiness assured? It seems not. She could not be consoled for the loss of Dodo and blamed her mother for her removal, though she was not responsible. The aunt she loved so much, having won the case, was seldom there. She began spending the week in the city and returned to Wheatley Hills only at the weekend when little Gloria was visiting her mother. She was not a woman who could express affection. Gloria's cousin and closest friend, Gerta, recalled: 'No one cared about her, no one. After that trial everyone simply forgot about Gloria – they let her grow up like a barbarian!'

When she was 16, she made a decision that proved how emotionally complicated this whole affair had been. She moved to California to live with her mother. Now a most attractive young woman, it was not long before she was seen around town with famous Hollywood escorts, including Franchot Tone, Errol Flynn and Van Heflin. Obviously attracted to older men, she had an intense love affair with Howard Hughes. While still only 17 she fell in love with a handsome Hollywood playboy, Pat di Cicco, son of a Long Island farmer, and they were married on 28 December 1941. But she soon regretted having been so impulsive. Pat di Cicco, in spite of his good looks, expensive clothes and charm, turned out to be a bully and an appalling husband.

Gertrude Whitney, who had violently disapproved of

the match, died four months after the wedding. In her will she left her niece a diamond-and-pearl bracelet, known to have been her favourite, and therefore seen as a token of her love.

At 21, Gloria came into her Vanderbilt millions, obtained a divorce from di Cicco and, in a blaze of publicity, married famous conductor Leopold Stokowsky, who was 42 years older than herself. That marriage, too, would end.

There would be other marriages, and there would also be fulfilment of a different kind. Gloria Vanderbilt began to use her talent as a designer and businesswoman and has since made a huge success in both fields. She also began to write, and produced two magical volumes of autobiography. The relationship with her mother was to remain a stormy one, and there were periods of estrangement. But, on her 60th birthday, she gave her mother a diamond bracelet. All had been forgiven. Little Gloria was 'happy at last'.

Barbara Hutton

When she was a child, Woolworth heiress Barbara Hutton's favourite game was make-believe. She wanted to be a Princess and she wanted to be loved for herself alone. She never outgrew this longing and eventually married seven times, searching for the man who would fulfil her dreams, her valiant Prince in shining armour.

Three of her husbands *were* Princes and another made her a Countess, but each marital encounter ended in disaster. Eventually her life fell into a pattern. She would fall desperately in love, often with someone who was otherwise engaged; having captured and married him, disappointment would set in and her interest begin to fade. He would be replaced. Her search for this elusive consort lasted a lifetime, so that even when she was 60 she was capable of losing her heart to a fortune-hunter if he treated her like a Princess.

In the end, despite her massive wealth, she was just a vulnerable, sick woman riddled with loneliness. 'I inherited everything but love,' she told her friend and biographer, Philip Van Rensselaer. 'I've always been searching for it, because I didn't know what it was.'

Barbara Hutton was born in New York City on 14 November 1912, to the sort of wealth that most of us find hard to imagine. The money was made, prosaically enough, by her grandfather, Frank Winfield Woolworth, who had launched the 'dime stores' in America that later spread throughout the world. By the time Barbara was born, he was already a multi-millionaire. Her first memory was of the 60-roomed white marble mansion of Glen Clove on the North Shore of Long Island, where she used to visit the old gentleman she called 'Woolly'. He adored her. She was a chubby, golden-haired child with wide blue eyes and porcelain skin. To please her, he would join in her make-believe and call her 'Princess', ordering the chauffeur to treat her like royalty.

Her parents were an ill-matched pair who did not seem to have much idea of what to do with her. Her mother, Edna, F.W. Woolworth's youngest daughter, was a homely, shy woman who never got used to being rich. When Barbara was only five, she was found dead in her luxurious suite at the Plaza Hotel, New York, and there was talk of suicide. Frank Hutton, her father, was on the other hand a brash, energetic man, a Wall Street broker who drank heavily, gambled and womanized. He showered his daughter with gifts, but plainly found her boring.

Barbara was eventually sent off to a select girls' school to be educated in the social graces. She went on several pre-arranged dates with Yale undergraduates, but was not generally sought after. She blamed it on her plumpness.

Most of the fashionable young girls of the time were as slender as blades of grass. Barbara, though pleasing to look at with her fair, shining hair and lovely eyes, was obviously too well padded. She started the first of the endless dieting regimes that, in the end, destroyed her health. She finally became determined to be thin when she met her first Prince . . .

They were introduced to each other by a mutual friend. Prince Alexis Mdivani was already well known on the international social scene. The 16-year-old schoolgirl found him devastatingly attractive. He was one of three brothers from Tiflis, in Georgia, who had arrived in Paris just before World War I with their father, Colonel Zakharias Mdivani. They all became associated with famous beauties. Alexis was an unusual-looking man with a wide, Slavic face, deep greyish-green eyes and sandy-coloured hair. A great deal of his attraction lay in his voice, which was heavily accented, throaty and seductive. Like his brothers, he had acquired his title somewhat mysteriously. 'Where they come from anyone with three sheep is considered royalty,' quipped one society wit.

The Prince's first amorous experience was said to have been with the legendary French cabaret star Mistinguett, and this was followed by a tempestuous affair with the raven-haired American actress Kay Francis. Sixteen-year-old Barbara, desperately trying to lose weight on a diet of black coffee and crackers, was hardly in the same league. He was sympathetic, but unimpressed. She wiped away secret tears and tried not to think about him.

In December 1930, Frank Hutton gave his daughter a coming-out party that would be remembered for decades. Most people were still reeling from the effects of the Wall Street Crash but the Hutton family had emerged almost unscathed, its enormous wealth was so widely and wisely invested. Newspapers recorded the party with acid comment. The celebrations began with a tea for 500 socialites, followed by a dinner for another 500. The main event was on 21 December, when the entire ballroom suite of the Ritz Carlton Hotel was taken over for a ball estimated to have cost 60,000 dollars. Four orchestras played, while 1,000 guests drank 2,000 bottles of champagne in a setting decorated with 10,000 roses, 20,000 bunches of white violets and a forest of silver birch trees. In the streets outside, people were queuing for handouts of bread and soup.

Having launched his daughter in society, Frank Hutton considered she was now ready to receive offers of marriage from men of distinction and wealth. Prince Mdivani was not quite what he had in mind.

Barbara had met Alexis again at a party given by Paris designer Jean Patou in Biarritz. He saw at once that she was no longer the lovelorn schoolgirl, but a sophisticated young woman of considerable style. There was something about them when they were together that alerted the sensitive antennae of party-giver and gossip columnist Elsa Maxwell.

The Prince, however, met and married Barbara's friend, heiress Louise Van Alen. That made him even more desirable as far as Barbara was concerned. She stayed in Europe, hung around with the high-flying Mdivani set, and within 18 months had achieved her end: one day, Louise walked in and found her husband in bed with Barbara. By the end of November 1932, their marriage had been terminated in the divorce court, and when Barbara returned to New York Alexis went with her.

Frank Hutton gave Alexis a very cool reception when he called to pay his respects. Barbara was still under 21, and he made it clear he did not consider a divorced Russian emigré a suitable bridegroom for his daughter. When he saw the determined glint in her eye, however, he gave in, called an army of lawyers to safeguard her fortune and arranged for Alexis to receive a dowry of one million dollars plus a substantial annual allowance. Considering the Prince had just received a million-dollar divorce settlement from Louise Van Alen, he seemed to be doing very nicely from his various romantic attachments.

Barbara insisted on being married in Paris. Huge crowds gathered outside the Russian cathedral of St Alexander Nevsky to see her arrive, icily calm and beautiful in ivory satin with a train 8ft long. When she emerged as Princess Mdivani, it seemed to her that a childhood dream had come true. It was soon to be shattered.

They left for their honeymoon on the overnight train from Paris in a blaze of publicity and with 70 pieces of luggage between them, everything embossed with a gold crown and Mdivani initials. Their destination was Lake Como, then on to Venice, where they had booked the royal suite at the Excelsior Hotel on the Lido. As the train rushed through the night, the Mdivanis retired to their luxurious sleeping compartment. Barbara slipped into an exquisite chiffon nightdress and turned to Alexis to be admired. Taking a very cool look at her somewhat generous figure, he blurted out: 'Barbara, you're too damn fat!' Then he pulled her to her feet and roughly kissed her lips. 'Come on,' he said coldly, 'let's get down to business.'

Barbara was desperately hurt. Her awareness of her weight problem made his brutal frankness even more painful. Next day, she went on a crash diet that consisted of nothing but three cups of coffee a day and a few crackers. She maintained this punishment of her body for three weeks at a stretch, until she had lost 40lb within the first few months of her marriage. Sometimes she looked tired and ill, but as the pounds dropped off her she also achieved a more refined beauty.

On 14 November 1933, Barbara celebrated her 21st birthday and came into full and unrestricted control of her immense fortune. It was estimated that if she spent 10,000 dollars a day for the next ten years she would still only have made a small dent in her bank account.

That winter, the Mdivanis decided to take a second honeymoon and slipped off with a few friends for an extended spending spree in Japan, China and India. Barbara was fascinated by the Orient and immersed herself in sightseeing. Alexis was bored by her enthusiasm – his taste was for night-life, polo, dinner parties and shopping. He dozed off on a bench while she toured the Imperial Palace in Peking, and went into a black mood when she tried to drag him round a Buddhist monastery. He began to have temper tantrums, in which he hurled himself to the floor and screamed when things were not going the way he wanted. Then there was his vanity. Indoors he usually walked around naked, to show off his bronzed, muscular figure; and he bought almost as much jewellery as she did. By the time they returned to her suite at the Ritz in Paris she was writing in her diary: 'I feel bored, bored with Alexis. I feel tired, I feel tired of Alexis.'

It was obvious to those around them that something had gone wrong with the marriage. As rumours spread that the Mdivanis were 'finished' Barbara gave a party to celebrate her 22nd birthday. The huge Regency ballroom of the Ritz and a series of adjoining rooms were magically converted to look like a street in Casablanca, and 2,200 guests danced the night away to the sound of popping champagne corks. Among the guests with a seat of honour at the Mdivanis' table was a remarkably good-looking aristocrat named Count Curt Haugwitz-Reventlow, a Prussian-born Dane seldom seen on the international party circuit. When the music started he asked Barbara to dance, and as the orchestra played on they became completely absorbed in each other. Alexis stood on the sidelines fuming, for he recognized the signs of mutual attraction. Barbara had met her second husband.

Frank Hutton decided this time that he would have the foreigner's background thoroughly checked. He was impressed by what he discovered. The Count was a bachelor, whose ancestors had been Danish noblemen for 800 years. He was a fine athlete, brilliant on the ski slopes, but most of his time was spent running the family farm in Denmark. No one could produce a scrap of gossip about him, even though he was considered one of the handsomest men in Europe.

In March 1935, Barbara told Alexis she wanted a divorce and after some tempestuous scenes she set off for Reno, Nevada, to establish six weeks' residence while Count Reventlow went home to Denmark for an audience with King Christian. As a feudal landowner he was expected to seek his monarch's approval before entering into a matrimonial contract.

They were married in a short and simple ceremony which took place at a small, quiet resort overlooking Lake Tahoe. Thirty policemen, special deputies and private detectives were called in to keep the public at a distance. Barbara, looking tense but dewy-eyed, wore a plain yellow print dress with a matching straw hat and carried a nosegay of wild flowers gathered for her by her bridegroom. Reventlow was quiet and withdrawn.

The first nights of their marriage were spent in San Francisco, where Barbara managed to throw an impromptu party for 500 people. After a week, Reventlow complained that they never seemed to be alone and wondered if it was going to be like this from now on. He decided they must leave for their honeymoon in Denmark right away. En route, Barbara learned that Prince Mdivani had been killed in a car crash near Perpignan. Although Barbara remained utterly composed at the news, the Count said afterwards that a shadow seemed to pass across her eyes.

The newlyweds stayed at the Reventlow family's Hardenberg Castle on the stark, misty island of Lolland. Everyone hoped that Barbara would settle down there, but she hated it from the start. The only occasion she remembered with pleasure was a dinner party at which Curt's brother, Heinrich, presented her with an emerald bracelet made specially for her at Tiffany's in New York. She was touched by his thoughtfulness and treasured the gift. But nothing could change her mind. She hated the climate, could not understand the language and became increasingly restless. The honeymoon was cut short and it wasn't long before they were back in Paris at the Ritz Hotel.

Count Reventlow soon became aware of his wife's almost morbid dread of food. Most days were spent fasting. She would smoke incessantly and drink cup after cup of black coffee, but only toy with the food on her plate. When she stepped on the scales and found she had gained a few ounces, she would burst into tears. The Count found that her reluctance to eat affected him, and even he no longer enjoyed his meals. He suggested she should visit a dietician, but the problem was deeper than he thought.

By mid-September, Barbara found she was pregnant. Her figure would now increase whether she liked it or not. Once she got over her irritation at not being able to wear the latest Chanel gowns for a while, she confessed to close friends she was hoping for a son.

She decided to have the baby in England, which, at that time, seemed to her a place which represented peace and strength. On 23 February 1936, Countess Reventlow was delivered of a baby boy, Lance, in the bedroom of her rented Regency house in Hyde Park Gardens. The bedroom was equipped like a top London clinic. There were serious complications to the Caesarean birth, and it was a few days before she was able to sit up, smiling wanly on her pillows of white satin and old lace.

After the tragedy of the Lindbergh kidnapping in America in 1932, the thought that the same thing could happen to her baby was always present in her mind. She asked her husband to find them somewhere safer to live.

The Count heard that St Dunstan's Lodge, an elegant

castle located in the centre of London, off the outer circle of Regent's Park, had come up for sale. Barbara loved it, but as the house itself had been damaged by fire she decided to tear it down and build a neo-Georgian mansion in its place. She would call it Winfield House in memory of her grandfather.

Reventlow was staggered by the amount of money Barbara poured into the project. He never got used to her casual attitude towards spending millions. She changed her mind so often during construction that the estimated one million dollars rose to 3 million and finally to 4 million. Half as much again was spent on furnishings. The third floor was turned into a nursery suite for Lance, with walls lined with pink calfskin. All this was placed behind a 10ft spiked steel fence.

Nobody knows quite when the bickering began. The Reventlows had one furious row over the dismissal of a servant, which ended in a physical struggle, after which Barbara booked herself into a nursing home. She tried hard to achieve a domestic lifestyle for the sake of their son, but was defeated by her own restlessness. The Count preferred a strictly regulated life, in which the same thing happened day after day. She became bored, fed up with his lack of humour, his bursts of anger and lack of tenderness. All the romance of their first encounter had gone.

Reventlow still loved his wife, however. He reacted jealously and violently when she became infatuated with Prince Friedrich of Prussia, son of Kaiser Wilhelm II, a tall blond young aristocrat who was in London to learn English by working at Schroeder's Bank. She was slipping away from him, and eventually Reventlow moved into the nearby Bath Club. One day, he received a visit from the family solicitor, who told him that Barbara was anxious to bring the marriage to an end without rancour or ill feeling.

Her next choice of husband, actor Cary Grant, surprised everybody. He was considered a rank outsider in the

Hutton stakes. Barbara first met him quite casually aboard the liner *Normandie*. They later encountered each other at social gatherings in London, Paris, New York and Palm Beach. Grant was one of the film industry's highest-paid stars, a matinée idol with stunning good looks. To the first hint of any romance with him Barbara reacted sharply: 'He is just a good friend, nothing more.'

By 1941, the couple could not hide the fact that they were in love. Barbara threw a party, ostensibly for just a few friends, but really to give notice to females hovering around the star that, from now on, he was out of circulation. They made an incredibly handsome couple – Barbara sleek and blonde, shimmering with emeralds, and Cary Grant smooth, tanned, flashing his familiar, shy smile.

They were married quietly on 7 July 1942, in a six-minute ceremony at a summerhouse retreat on the shores of Lake Arrowhead in the San Bernadino mountains. The omens were good.

At first, Barbara enjoyed being married to Cary Grant. They socialized, gave fabulous parties and seemed very much in love. But soon her old restlessness was apparent. She had won the prize; soon, no doubt, she would be bored. Cary Grant began to resent the constant social buzz; it seemed as though *she* could not live without it. He was up early, worked hard at the studios all day, and when he came home in the evening was not always in the mood to play host or to go out. Sometimes he played up at dinner parties to embarrass her. Friends could see the problem. He was a dedicated professional, and she was just an extremely rich lady with nothing much to do.

There was another problem. Gradually Barbara's wealth and her compulsion to spend began to get on his nerves. Why, he asked her, did they have to have such a huge staff? He could not get used to the staggering bills they had to pay even for such basics as electricity, food and toiletries. Soon, his nagging began to get on Barbara's nerves. She used her insomnia as an excuse to sleep in a separate bedroom.

The marriage ended on 30 August 1945. There was no bitterness and Cary Grant blamed himself for not being more sensitive to her needs. Years afterwards, when they were still friends, he said: 'We know each other better now than when we were married.'

To console herself, Barbara bought a Moorish palace in Tangier – and found herself another Prince. Compared with most of the people in her circle Prince Igor Troubetzkoy was poor, but his title, as far as she was concerned, was beyond price. He was the youngest son of Prince Nicholas Troubetzkoy, a favourite of the former Tzar, and his line went back to the 14th century. Soon after their first encounter, Barbara invited him to her suite at the Ritz for dinner. She was in her liveliest mood, and he was enchanted. She found herself terribly attracted by his lean, athletic figure, twinkling green eyes and sensitive mouth. Prince Igor, looking back on that night, said: 'She phoned – we dined – and my word, how fast!'

Prince Troubetzkoy became a regular visitor at the flower-filled suite at the Ritz and, as a connoisseur of art, was overwhelmed by the treasures he saw there: exquisite Chinese porcelain and jade, paintings by Cezanne, a Botticelli, antique-gold snuffboxes and incredible jewels. And as for Barbara – she could hardly wait to become a Princess again.

Anxious to avoid the Press, they married in the tiny Swiss village of Chur. But on the journey back to Paris the Press caught up with them and Barbara reported: 'I've never been happier. We will be on our honeymoon for 30 or 40 more years.'

Brave words, but Prince Igor realized how little they meant when they arrived at the Ritz. Once in her suite, Barbara brought him down to earth by stating that they would occupy separate bedrooms: his bedroom was down the hall.

Her new husband was soon made acutely aware of her diet problems, which by now amounted to anorexia. She still drank black coffee, smoked incessantly and would only eat tiny morsels of food. Formal meals were rarely served in her suite and Troubetzkoy had no alternative but to take himself off to restaurants.

Barbara also suffered from terrible insomnia and often spent the night hours telephoning friends in New York, London, Los Angeles and Tangier. All too often, it seemed, she was phoning one Baron Gottfried von Cramm, a German tennis ace. She refused to talk to Prince Igor about her relationship with the Baron; he had actually been in and out of her life for years and was always ready to offer her a shoulder to cry on.

The Troubetzkoys had not been married three months when the Prince began to notice a worrying change in Barbara. She became gaunt and hollow-eyed, her legs were like sticks and her skin was grey. Her doctors blamed her life of semi-starvation and insomnia. She seemed to improve after a summer on the Riviera and in Switzerland, but soon relapsed. Her husband called in one of the world's greatest urologists and he diagnosed serious kidney malfunction brought on by self-neglect.

For a time, Barbara's life was in the balance. She asked her doctor to send a telegram to von Cramm telling him to come at once. Prince Igor began to feel he must have failed her as a husband, yet he loved her very much. Just what did this German tennis player mean to her? Troubetzkoy did not know it, but in a moment of delirium she had confessed her unrequited love for the German. She was already beginning to weary of her fourth husband.

During the two years they were married, Prince Igor spent most of his time pacing up and down hospital corridors, waiting to be summoned. Even when she recovered, he was kept at arm's length. He would sometimes escape from the impersonal luxury of the Ritz and have a sandwich and a glass of beer in a bistro – anything to touch reality. He tried hard to understand her, but in the end had to admit defeat. Thus, there was yet another divorce, and a bitter one, for Troubetzkoy was deeply hurt.

Barbara continued moving restlessly around the world and was seen on more than one occasion with von Cramm. But her friends were staggered when they realized that the new man in her life was international playboy Porfirio Rubirosa. They knew that he had just been dismissed from his post as Dominican ambassador for amorous misconduct and, without salary or expense account, needed financial backing. It was also generally known that he was crazy about the Hungarian actress Zsa Zsa Gabor.

Barbara was impervious to all this. She had decided to marry Rubirosa and even phone calls and telegrams from Cary Grant and Gottfried von Cramm, begging her to think again, had no effect. The marriage took place at the Park Avenue home of the Dominican consul in New York on 30 December 1953. Under her wide picture hat she looked strained and tired, and she admitted: 'I'm so tired, I could die.' In fact, she collapsed and had to go to bed before the wedding party had ended. That night 'Rubi' went out on the town and returned in the early hours with a showgirl on his arm.

Barbara knew from the start that this marriage wouldn't work, that she should never have gone into it. She wasn't in love with Rubirosa; she had just wanted to prove she could get any man she wanted.

The second night after the wedding, Barbara slipped on the bathroom floor and broke her ankle. While she was confined to a wheelchair, her husband was courting Miss Gabor by telephone as though the marriage had never taken place. After just 73 days it ended, and Barbara fled to the peace of the Moorish palace, with its fountains and sun-filled rooms.

At some time during her brief marriage to Rubirosa, friends had heard her say wistfully: 'I was in love with him for 17 years, then he told me he didn't love me.'

'Who?' a friend asked in surprise.

'My tennis player – von Cramm!'

With the wreck of five marriages behind her, she asked von Cramm to stay with her for the rest of the summer of 1955. The spell of Tangier worked wonders. Barbara seemed to regain her looks and vitality, and when she returned to Paris in the autumn it was to plan their wedding.

On a day of heavy wind and rain, Barbara married her Baron in a civil ceremony at Versailles City Hall. Von Cramm was a nervous bridegroom, but Barbara looked radiant in a blue Balenciaga suit and pearls. 'We should have married 18 years ago. It would have saved me many heartaches,' Barbara told the Press. But even this dream was doomed to be short-lived.

Their first dilemma came when Gottfried tried to get a visa at the American Embassy so that he could spend the winter with Barbara at Palm Beach. The application was rejected. No reason was given, but there had been past indications that the Baron had homosexual tendencies. He was a decent, kind and honourable man but, as far as the American authorities of that time were concerned, unacceptable.

In his biography of Barbara Hutton, C. David Heymann says that Gottfried von Cramm's inability to relate to her at any kind of sexual level created a deep schism. She took it personally, and the dilemma drove them apart. Von Cramm began making long business trips to Germany, and Barbara occupied herself by having dinner parties. Although they did not divorce until 1957, they began to go their separate ways. The collapse of the dream of an idyllic love which she had nurtured for years made her so ill that she lost weight without dieting.

It had all ended so quickly she could hardly believe it. She began to drink heavily and, for a time, mixed with an international crowd that did the same. But, in spite of her disastrous experiences with matrimony, she did not feel happy as a single woman. Before long, she entered into her seventh, and most exotic, marriage.

Barbara met Raymond Doan, a Vietnamese artist who had been educated in France, on a motoring tour of Morocco. He was married. When he invited the whole of Barbara's party to his house for tea, she bought one of his paintings. A few weeks later, arrangements were made for him to have a one-man show in Tangier. When Barbara, fascinated, attended the opening, he showed her an oil painting he had done of her palace, Sidi Hosni. She bought not only this canvas but the whole of his exhibition.

Her friends were not surprised when Raymond Doan moved into the palace. They had seen how this slim, dark-skinned artist had awakened her interest. There was a stillness about him that intrigued her and, besides, she had always been in love with the East.

One day she went to the Laotian Embassy in Rabat. She had heard titles could be bought there and she wanted one for Raymond Doan. They explained she must have been mistaken; they did not go in for selling titles; but an old man on the premises claimed to have one, and she could probably make a deal with him. The deal was struck. Raymond Doan the artist was now Prince Raymond Doan Vinh Na Champassak. The reason was simple. Barbara wanted to marry him, and she wanted to be a Princess once more.

The wedding to her seventh husband took place in Mexico in April 1964. After a civil service there was a Buddhist ceremony, for which Barbara dressed in a green kaftan trimmed with gold; there were gold rings on each of her big toes and bells round her ankles. Doan wore a white suit with a brilliant swathe of silk over one shoulder. Barbara's friends could see that she was living out a fantasy and wondered how long it would last.

The years that followed were difficult for Doan, a gentle, considerate man. Barbara, increasingly frail and wasted from her lifelong neglect of her health, broke bones easily and suffered from various illnesses. Doan was always there when she wanted him, but she seemed to be drifting further and further away from reality. Eventually, in April 1971, she began to make inquiries about the purchase of an Italian palazzo. She wanted it, she explained, as a going-away present for Doan. Those who knew her well realized this meant the marriage was over, and the palazzo a souvenir.

She did not want another divorce. Pathetically, she explained she wanted to keep her purchased title. Raymond Doan's only public statement after the final separation was gallant: 'She gave me much more than money, she gave me love.'

But had she really known what love was? The story of her last years is a story of slow disintegration. She tried for a while to console herself, with an exciting young matador called Angel Teruel, but the liaison did not last long. Her last appearance in public showed an emaciated, frail woman, dripping with jewels, her eyes hidden behind enormous sunglasses. When she died on 11 May 1979, aged 66, there were friends at her bedside – but no husband.

Henrietta Guinness

During the Swinging Sixties, Lady Henrietta Guinness was one of the bright young hopes of the famous Anglo-Irish brewing family and heiress to millions of pounds. It came, therefore, as a great shock to her brother, Lord Iveagh, head of the Guinness clan, when she blurted out: 'I hate the rich man's attitude to life. I'm tired of snobbery. I want to be with real people.'

She threw herself wildly into the classless, rootless life of King's Road, Chelsea, where young London aristocrats in search of a thrill mingled with the 1960s elite – hairdressers, models, photographers, struggling artists and the so-called 'beautiful people'. It quickly became known that Henrietta cared so little for her money that she was trying to *give* it away. Family lawyers frantically tried to prevent her from dispersing her fortune to all and sundry, but with little effect.

Struggling to free herself from a dynasty that had evolved over nine generations into a formidable social force, its name synonymous with wealth, glamour and privilege, she told her friends: 'If I had been poor, I would have been happy.' But her search for something to replace the rich man's way of life ended tragically when, in 1978, at the age of 35, she committed suicide by throwing herself from an aqueduct in the Italian town of Spoleto.

Henrietta was not the first Guinness to try to break away. The family history is full of eccentrics, missionaries, adventurers, ranchers and sheep-farmers. One generation alone produced a pop singer, a champion amateur jockey, a lady who modelled topless for Andy Warhol and two professional authors. Nor has the family escaped its share of tragedy, notably by losing several of its young heirs in a series of fatal car accidents. But there was something especially poignant about the life and death of Henrietta.

For 250 years her forbears had been building up the fortune that is now estimated in hundreds of millions. Their origins were humble enough. It was late in the 17th century when a poor young soldier called Richard Guinness was sent from England to Ireland in the course of duty. He married, left the army and became butler to the Protestant Archbishop of Cashel. One of his duties was to brew beer, a rich dark brew very much like the strong porter favoured by working men in those days. Legend has it that the water of Dublin's river, the Liffey, gave the beer its special character. Whatever the secret, it was passed down to Richard's son, Arthur, who in 1756, set up a brewery at Leixip, just across the boundary of County Kildare, with a legacy of £100 left him by the Archbishop. He called the brew 'Guinness', and from him has descended the generations of the great Guinness family. In 1867 a Baronetage was conferred, and in 1919 the head of the family was created Earl of Iveagh.

Henrietta was the daughter of Arthur Onslow Guinness, Viscount Elveden, great-great-great-great-grandson of the founder of the Guinness dynasty and heir to the second Lord Iveagh. Her mother was Lady Elizabeth Hare, daughter of the Earl of Listowel. She never knew her father. Arthur was killed in action in Holland in 1945 at the end of World War II. He was only 33 and Henrietta was barely two and a half. His widow was left to bring up his son, Ben, who became the present Lord Iveagh, and his two small daughters, Henrietta and Elizabeth.

Henrietta's childhood was that of a super-rich little girl with servants at her beck and call, wanting for nothing. Her mother married again, this time Rory More O'Ferrall of the celebrated family of Irish bloodstock breeders and trainers. From then on, the three children were shuttled between great estates in England and the family's much-loved Dublin seat, Farmleigh.

Most of her memories were of the Elveden Estate in East Anglia, which her grandfather had bought from the Maharaja of Lahore and which had been turned into a palatial country house to which Kings, dukes and foreign nobility were invited. It had passed the days of its greatest glory and Henrietta was relieved when her mother told her that the family would live in the comfortable Old Rectory in the grounds, only opening the vast 100-roomed mansion for special events. She preferred the beautiful Pyrford Court near Woking in Surrey with its view from the upper storey across 2,000 acres of pine trees and gorse.

But whether it was at Elveden, at Pyrford, at the family's handsome London house, Gloucester Lodge in Regent's Park, or at Farmleigh, there was always an army of servants to cater for every whim.

Henrietta received the classic education befitting a wealthy heiress, including a spell at finishing school. She emerged from the process at 19 as a delightful girl who had sparkle, zest for living and a generosity of spirit that was utterly genuine. She was pleasant-looking, but no beauty. Short in stature and inclined to plumpness, she also had the blonde, blue-eyed family colouring and an infectious laugh.

At first, she took part in all the rituals of upper-crust life: balls, champagne parties, weekends at vast country houses, point-to-points. But she showed no interest in the Old Etonians and Harrovians who escorted her, and before long she did not even try to hide her boredom. This was when she told a close friend that she hated the way she was living: 'I'm tired of snobbery and I want to be with real people.'

Leaving behind the life she considered 'meaningless', she sought companionship in the trendy *demi-monde* of Chelsea, where her friends were other free-wheeling young aristocrats, waiters, actors, hairdressers, models and the new wave tinkering with the hippy culture. Her generosity was soon legendary. Never mind how many bottles of champagne they drank, no matter how fantastic the bill, Henrietta would pay. The horrified Guinnesses slowly began to realize that Henrietta was throwing her fortune away. She had a hard core of genuine friends, but there were too many one-night acquaintances and hangers-on.

From the beginning, she seemed fated to have love affairs that brought her nothing but unhappiness. In 1963, she ran off with well-known man-about-Chelsea, 26-year-old Michael Beeby. Nothing came of the affair, but on their return from the south of France they crashed in her red Aston Martin. Both were badly injured, Henrietta nearly losing her life. The effects of that crash, both mental and physical, kept her in and out of nursing homes and clinics for the next two and a half years.

Nothing seemed to go right for her during that period. While in hospital she learned that her closest and best friend, Sara D'Avigdor Goldsmid, had been drowned. The severity of the loss can be judged from the fact that, years later, she named her baby daughter Sara in her memory.

From this time on she was to suffer bouts of depression, but if she found happiness anywhere it was among the trendy Chelsea characters who flocked around her on her return to London life. Overweight and insecure, she grasped at straws for companionship and comfort, always keeping up the façade of 'good old Henrietta'.

Henrietta continued to spend her money wildly and recklessly. Her brother, Lord Iveagh, and the trustees of the Iveagh Estate tried to reason with her. In the end, out of concern for her future and trying to protect her £5,000,000 inheritance, they prevailed upon her to sign it all into an unbreakable lifetime trust. Frederic Mullally, who tells the whole story of the Guinness family in his book *The Silver Salver*, says: 'A portion of it bore regular interest which Henrietta dispersed virtually as soon as – and sometimes before – it reached her bank. It went either in outright gifts, or in hospitality to the mixed company of freeloaders and fair-weather friends who, together with the more genuine variety, made up her court.' At this time, he says, she was smoking 'pot' like the rest of the gang and being ripped off by some of the Chelsea restaurateurs who were happy to pad out her nightly bills in compensation for the behaviour of her retinue.

One restaurant owner who kept a fatherly eye on Henrietta was Alvaro Maccioni. His place at 124 King's Road was considered one of the 'in' restaurants at that time and was always full to the doors. He protected her, as far as he could, and kept her from inviting every Tom, Dick and Harry off the streets for her wildly gregarious suppers.

In 1973, when she was 25, Henrietta fell in love with one of Alvaro's chefs, a tall, handsome young Italian called Benito Chericato. From the moment she set eyes on him she would do anything to be near him. Alvaro could not keep her out of his kitchen. She would wash dishes, polish glasses, chop vegetables, anything to be near Benito. The young chef was flattered, but placed in a most difficult position. Henrietta made no bones about the fact that she wanted to marry him, but Benito already had a girl in his life and they had children.

As a Guinness, Henrietta was used to getting what she wanted. The quiet, unassuming young Italian was bowled over and totally confused. She persuaded him to take her to Italy to meet his parents and even turned Catholic to make herself more acceptable to them. After they were married, she said, she would buy them a hotel-restaurant in northern Italy. They would have the biggest hotel on Lake Garda. 'I don't want him to be a cook all his life,' she told friends. 'He will receive guests, and I will do the housekeeping.'

Henrietta's plans might just have been the answer to the aching void in her life and would have given her existence real meaning. But Benito was not prepared to marry her and the affair fizzled out around 1969. They remained friends, and she set him up in his own restaurant in Belgravia at the reported cost of £28,000.

Ever since her teens, Henrietta's hairdresser had been Stewart Hiscock, a good-natured man in his 30s who proved to be one of her genuine friends. He would often take her home to supper with his wife. They were both very concerned about her and especially about the fact that, in spite of her wealth, she did not have a place of her own. She lived like a gypsy. After a discussion one night she promised to find somewhere, but ended up taking 'a terrible bedsitter' in Rutland Gate, Knightsbridge.

The Iveagh trustees finally agreed to buy her a modest mews house in Belgravia. She took little interest in furnishing it, however, and adorned her windowsills with posies of flowers stuck in milk bottles. But, for a time, she was happy there. She had switched her enthusiasm from the Chelsea scene to London's art galleries and studios, where she enjoyed the company of modern painters and sculptors, bought works by Hockney and Nolan, but had to be restrained from buying up whole collections when she took a fancy to the work of an unknown artist.

In 1976 Labour Chancellor of the Exchequer, Denis Healey, announced his policy to 'soak the rich', and the Iveagh trustees pressed Henrietta to go into tax exile to save her fortune. Though she claimed she cared little for her money, they pointed out she really had no alternative. Her almost manic generosity, together with the annual tax burden on her unearned income, had ruled out any chance of her accumulating any savings. The trustees clamped down on the release of further chunks of her capital.

Henrietta's trustees finally suggested she go on a world tour – but her heart was really in Italy. She loved the Italian people and made up her mind to go to Rome. She could live happily on her income there and might persuade the guardians of her wealth to allow her enough capital to buy a small house. Her friends could then fly out to join her for weekends.

Before she left for Italy, Henrietta made another of her stunningly generous gestures. A year after buying the Belgravia restaurant for Benito Chericato, she had gone into partnership with Stewart Hiscock, setting him up on his own in an elegant hair salon just off Kensington High Street. He thrived, numbering among his clients Mrs Michael Heseltine, Rex Harrison's wife, Elizabeth, and the

Countess of Normanton. Her last act before leaving England was to hand over her share of the £70,000 business to the astounded Hiscock.

A Lady in her own right since her brother had become the third Lord Iveagh, Henrietta was more than ever a rebel against the Tatler lifestyle enjoyed by most of the Guinness clan. But she had not really found another answer and was prone to bouts of illness and depression. When she set off for Rome, she took with her only the things she prized the most. One of her most valued possessions was her favourite Porsche car. She had a few Hockney and Nolan paintings, which she took with her wrapped in Irish linen sheets. There was a silver kettle, a valuable necklace her grandfather had left to her and some pearls, which she valued highly because her brother Ben, Lord Iveagh, had given them to her for her 21st birthday. But she took very little money.

When she first arrived in Italy, Henrietta suffered one of her periods of depression. Friends in Rome, not understanding how delicate was her mental health – a legacy of that awful car crash in the Ssouth of France – arranged parties to welcome her into the smart set. It was the last thing she wanted. She took herself off to a quiet, backstreet hotel where she could be alone and think about the future.

When she had been in Italy for about a year, she heard about a famous Arts Festival held annually in the lovely old town of Spoleto, about 75 miles north of Rome. She decided to spend a few days there.

Among the thousands who attended the Festival, Henrietta had eyes for only one. He was a tall, good-looking, quietly spoken Italian called Luigi Marinori, an ex-medical student who had a temporary job as a waiter at the Festival. Henrietta spoke fluent Italian. She was attracted by him and made no secret of it. They arranged to see each other again and were soon deeply in love.

Henrietta abandoned Rome so that she could be with Luigi, and before long moved in with his family. This meant living with Luigi's father, who was a metal mechanic, his mother, who worked as a chambermaid, his brother and his grandmother. The Guinness heiress seemed very happy at last. The Marinori house was a shabbily built modern villa with green shutters in a dowdy section of Spoleto overshadowed by towering council blocks. But there were bright red pelargoniums in pots outside the door and the six rooms of the house were sparkling clean and full of life. She behaved like any other Italian girl living at home, helping Luigi's mother with the washing, shopping and making pasta.

For a long time, Luigi said nothing to his parents about Henrietta's background. They were completely unaware that she was an heiress with a title of her own and a fortune accumulating year by year. He didn't seem at all interested in her money. In 1977, when she was 35, she gave birth to Luigi's child, a beautiful little girl whom she called Sara. Three months after the birth, they were married, quietly, in a civil ceremony at Spoleto Town Hall.

Henrietta tried hard to remain anonymous in Spoleto. She dressed simply, helped her mother-in-law with the housework and seemed to be a devoted wife and mother. The only thing that distinguished her from the other Italian women in that part of town was that she drove around in a brand-new blue Fiat. But when her mother, Lady Elizabeth, turned up in a chauffeur-driven car to see her new granddaughter, tongues began to wag. Luigi, they realized, was a very, very lucky fellow.

After the birth of Sara, Henrietta suffered a fresh bout of depression and she entered a local clinic for treatment. Once she was well again, the future seemed to hold a great deal of promise. Luigi had a job as a truck driver. She had persuaded the trustees to give her £26,000 of her capital to buy a crumbling old monastery on the outskirts of Spoleto and she planned to turn it into a comfortable home for herself, Luigi and Sara. All she wanted was a peaceful, tranquil life.

One beautiful May morning in 1978, Luigi took the wheel of the Fiat and drove Henrietta to see her dentist, Signor Giorgio Mastropiero, promising to pick her up later. When he returned she had already left, and the dentist said she seemed to be in a confused state.

Some dark force inside her led Henrietta to the 14th-century Bridge of Towers, which looms over an old Roman aqueduct and the Tessino River. A young couple saw her, wearing a dark blouse, white skirt and knee-high boots, but she had plunged to her death before they could reach her. She left her handbag behind. It contained a photograph of her baby, a bank book showing a £400 deposit, an address book full of English names and a letter from a friend.

The tragedy brought the families of Guinness and Marinori together in grief. At the funeral, Lady Elizabeth was seen to be trying to comfort the baby's Italian grandmother. There was a simple funeral service at Spoleto's 1,500-year-old San Salvatore Church and the burial took place in the adjoining cemetery. Luigi Marinori was too stricken to speak. He had cared nothing for his wife's fortune, said his family. He had loved her. But not even he had been able to give her peace of mind.

Everyone expected a legal wrangle, with an ugly tug-of-war over little Sara Marinori, but matters were arranged quietly and decently. The Guinness family agreed to Sara being brought up by her father in Spoleto until the time came for her to inherit her mother's fortune. She was only six months old when Henrietta fell to her death. At the time the inheritance was worth in the region of £5,000,000, but it is estimated the money was worth nearer £25,000,000 by the time Sara was 21.

What does it mean to her? What *can* it mean to her?

Brought up in a simple, loving family where a new bicycle is a thing to be looked forward to and treasured, money on this scale may be hard for her to grasp. But she too is a Guinness heiress. In London, a friend of Henrietta was quoted as saying: 'I only hope her inheritance will bring her more happiness than it brought her mother.'

Evalyn Walsh McClean

Washington hostess Evalyn Walsh McClean had such a passion for diamonds that, in 1911, she begged her millionaire husband to buy her one of the most infamous gemstones in the world. It was the Hope diamond, often more aptly called the Diamond of Despair.

Mrs McClean, a renowned collector who already owned the fabulous 100-carat Star of the East, refused to believe there was anything sinister about the Hope diamond, anything that could bring her bad luck. She was quite undaunted by the trail of tragedy that had followed the diamond for three centuries like some foul miasma; she only saw its beauty.

When the diamond was first shown to her by jeweller Pierre Cartier, Evalyn did not like the setting but confessed she was mesmerized by its strange deep-blue light. Her husband, Edward McClean, the newspaper tycoon, agreed to buy it for a price said to be in the region of £60,000. He had it re-set and hung on a thick diamond-studded chain.

Since Evalyn McClean was one of the richest and most famous society hostesses of her day, the purchase of the Hope diamond made front-page news. So, too, did the tragic events that followed. Her only son was killed in a motor accident. The marriage to Edward McClean went wrong and they were divorced – he was later admitted to a mental home, where he died penniless. Her daughter died from an overdose of sleeping drugs and two women friends who borrowed the diamond also died sudden and unexpected deaths. Evalyn herself ended life in a haze of drink and drugs, with much of her great fortune gone.

Even before the Hope diamond appeared in her life, Evalyn Walsh McClean's story was one of incredible wealth tainted by disaster.

She was the daughter of an Irish immigrant carpenter, Tom Walsh, who had left Clonmel, Tipperary, to escape the famine of the 1850s and struck gold in the mountains of southwestern Colorado. On arrival in the New World, Tom had found work on the Colorado Central Railroad. But he soon succumbed to the gold fever that was in the air and joined thousands of others prospecting in the Black Hills with varying luck. He married, turned his hand to hotel-keeping in Leadville, then began prospecting again. This time, he went out to a remote, desolate area behind Red Mountain, where no one had ever prospected before. He found a vast fissure of tellurium gold, where only silver lead carbonates had been found previously. Within a year, Tom Walsh's Camp Bird Mine was one of the greatest gold producers in the western hemisphere.

Evalyn was born on 1 August 1886. She was 12 years old when she began to realize that her parents were rich beyond most people's wildest dreams. Tom Walsh was making money at a stupendous rate and had no desire to hide his light under a bushel in Leadville, Colorado, or even Denver for that matter. He rented a vast suite of rooms at the old Cochran Hotel in Washington for the season and fitted out his womenfolk in appropriate style. Mrs Walsh, refined and ladylike, was draped in furs that made other women faint with envy. Little Evalyn asked for, and got, a blue Victoria carriage of her own, drawn by a pair of sleek sorrels and accompanied by a coachman in livery.

Politically astute, Tom Walsh set out to make sure he

knew the right people. He and his wife entertained lavishly, in great style, and contributed to all the right charities. President McKinley could not help but be impressed, and in 1899 he sent Tom Walsh to Paris to be a commissioner at the Paris Exposition. Little Evalyn went too, and fell in love with France, its sophistication, luxury and style. She was most impressed by the private train in which she and her parents travelled to visit King Leopold of the Belgians. Each carriage was as big as a room, hung with costly paintings, the floors strewn with rare oriental rugs. Liveried servants were constantly at her elbow offering delicacies of the most expensive kind. She made a vow that she would travel in splendour until the day she died.

On their return to Washington, Tom Walsh decided to build a house that would reflect his fantastic success, and a five-million-dollar mansion was commissioned on the luxurious Massachusetts Avenue. As a teenager, Evalyn drifted about the 60-roomed house, which had a grand staircase guarded by marble nymphs, a theatre, a ballroom and a spectacular reception hall with a well that soared four floors upwards to a dome of coloured glass.

She was sent to a finishing school in Paris with a letter of credit from her father which, besides allowing her $10,000 for basic expenses, also gave her credit at all the best shops, including Cartier the jewellers. After a few months, however, Tom Walsh heard that his daughter was spending a good deal too much time among aspiring young artists on the Left Bank and had promised many of them financial backing. Evalyn was ordered home. Before leaving Paris she went shopping and arrived home with eight trunks full of dresses from Worth and Paquin and some magnificent furs, including a sable coat with matching scarf and muff.

The next time Evalyn visited Europe, this time Italy, her father went along as chaperone. High-spirited, wilful and attractive, Evalyn was much sought after by handsome young Italians from families with high-sounding titles but no money. When a flirtation with an Italian Prince looked as though it might get out of hand, Tom Walsh made a bargain with his daughter. If she would get rid of the Prince, he would buy her a car.

Like all the young rich at that time, Evalyn was mad about cars and happily clinched the deal with her father, choosing a smart, red Mercedes roadster. At the time it seemed such a delightful toy. Little did she realize that the pretty red car was the first fateful link in a lifetime chain of disasters.

In 1905, back home in America, Tom Walsh decided to establish a family residence in Newport, which at that time, according to Lucius Beebe, who has recorded the affairs of the super-rich in *The Big Spenders*, was the 'ultimate citadel of New York society'. He bought a house which had once belonged to William Waldorf Astor and was popularly supposed to 'reek with bad luck'. The Walshes didn't believe in such things and launched their new lives there on a sea of champagne.

One fine summer's day, Evalyn set out from the Astor house to attend a clam bake in her precious red Mercedes. Her chauffeur took the wheel and a crowd of young people, full of fun and high spirits, clambered in the back. On the return journey, her brother Vinson sat beside the chauffeur and she rode in the back with a couple of boy-friends. As they were crossing a wooden railed bridge, the Mercedes blew a tyre, ploughed through the rails and crashed upside-down in the stream below. Evalyn, trapped in her seat, was nearly drowned before passers-by managed to pull her free. But her brother Vinson was dead, his body pierced by an enormous splinter that had been sheared off by the bridge on impact.

Evalyn never fully recovered from the effects of that appalling day. Her leg was badly fractured and never properly set. She was in such agony that morphine was prescribed and she became addicted to it. After a series of highly delicate operations she was left a nervous wreck. Some of her hair fell out and a patch at the back remained quite bald. For the rest of her life she had to wear a succession of wigs and take drugs whenever the pain in her leg became too bad.

The Astor house at Newport held nothing but painful memories. Once Evalyn began to walk around, it was felt that perhaps a move back to Colorado might be a good idea. Tom Walsh bought an estate south of Denver, named it Clonmel, after his birthplace in Ireland, and again gave a huge party to declare his faith in the future. But even he began to have doubts when he was nearly killed in a railway accident on his way to inspect new gold diggings in the Colorado mountains.

In July 1908, Evalyn caused a sensation by her marriage to Edward Beale McClean. His family owned the *Washington Post* and were considered aristocrats, a cut above the 'new rich'. They had first met as teenagers, when their parents sent them to dancing class, and had kept up a mild flirtation ever since. Ned McClean had proposed to Evalyn at regular intervals, but she did not take him seriously until that summer of 1908. Both were spoiled children, brought up in unbelievable luxury, but Tom Walsh had made some attempt to make Evalyn aware of the rest of the world. Ned's mother, on the other hand, had ruined him, even paying his friends to let him win at games. She was looking forward to seeing her boy married at a wedding of 'cosmic proportions', says Lucius Beebe. But the two young people had other ideas. Out driving one day, Ned begged Evalyn to marry him without delay, by special licence. A few phone calls to influential people and the ceremony was arranged at St Mark's Episcopal Church in Denver. Evalyn could not even remember the name of the clergyman who tied the knot.

Both families were furious, but once the dust had

settled arrangements were made to send them on honeymoon in style. The father of the bride and the father of the bridegroom each produced letters of credit for $100,000. The combined sum today would be worth about one million dollars. The happy couple set sail for Europe, where they spent the whole lot in two months.

Seldom can a couple have celebrated with such abandon. They had shipped Ned's favourite yellow Packard roadster from the States with them, but in Paris acquired an additional Mercedes, and later, considering one Mercedes insufficient, bought another. They had a chauffeur, a valet, and a personal maid for Evalyn as well as a mountain of luggage. Evalyn added to the mountain as she purchased furs and couture dresses by the score. Ned had bought her a travelling case fitted out in solid gold, but it had been forgotten, left behind, only to be discovered years later in a cupboard thick with dust.

Part of their honeymoon was spent in the Middle East, and while in Turkey they asked the US ambassador to introduce them to Sultan Abdul Hamid. A meeting was arranged, with all the necessary courtesies, and Evalyn was taken to the harem to be entertained by the Sultan's favourite, Salma Zubayaba. As they drank dark, pungent Turkish coffee out of gold filigree cups, Evalyn's eyes were fixed on Zubayaba's throat. Against the dusky skin lay a fabulous gemstone, deep blue in colour and of the greatest brilliance and purity. It was the Hope diamond.

'I'd give the world to have it, Ned,' Evalyn said as they left the palace. But several deaths had yet to take place before it came into her hands.

The doting young husband whisked her off to Cartier's in Paris to buy her another diamond instead. She was lucky. Just at that moment, a pear-shaped diamond, known to experts all over the world as the Star of the East, had come up for sale and, at 600,000 francs, was waiting for a rich collector. The McCleans did not have enough money with them to pay for it, so it was charged to Tom Walsh's account. There is no record of what he said when he got the bill, but Evalyn was convinced he would understand she just had to have it.

After the honeymoon the McCleans settled down in Massachusetts Avenue, Washington, for a short spell of domesticity. Their son, Vinson, was born in 1909 and placed in a gold crib sent by King Leopold of Belgium. Nurses and bodyguards watched over the child day and night in case of kidnap, for there had been several threats. But the lull in their frantic social life was short-lived. When her father died of cancer, Evalyn was freed from parental restraint and took off with Ned on a binge around Europe. They were seen at all the fashionable places, spending money like it was going out of fashion.

One of their escapades shocked even the most blasé of their rich friends. Evalyn had been exceptionally lucky at the Casino in Monte Carlo and wanted to return to Paris immediately to spend her winnings. Ned said he would drive her there in his yellow Fiat. The chauffeur could sit in the back. He took on a bet that he could get there before the Blue Train, at that time one of the fastest trains in Europe. He won the bet, arriving in Paris ten minutes before the scheduled express. Celebrations were muted however; the chauffeur had had a heart attack and was found dead in the back of the car. Ned's driving had proved too much for him.

Next morning, as the McCleans were at breakfast in their suite at the Bristol Hotel, Pierre Cartier, the jeweller, asked to see him. In his hand was a small package sealed with red wax. It contained the Hope diamond. Its last owner, the Sultan who had received the McCleans in Constantinople, had shot dead his favourite wife in a fit of rage and had, himself, been deposed. The diamond went to a Greek broker, who was killed with his wife and child when his horse and carriage bolted over a precipice. Now it was in Paris in the hands of Cartier. Though he warned Evalyn of its terrible history she answered with a laugh: 'Bad-luck objects are lucky for me. Anyway, I don't believe there is such a thing as a jinx.'

The fantastic blue diamond had first been discovered in 1642 by French explorer Jean Baptiste Tavernier. Some accounts say he bought it in the rough from a mine on the banks of the Kistna River in India, but the more romantic version of its discovery says he stole it from a Burmese temple where it was embedded in the forehead of the god Rama-Sita. However he came by it, it did him no good. After selling it to the French Bourbon King, Louis XIV, he died penniless, disgraced and in exile.

The stone was then passed down to Louis XVI who gave it to his Queen, Marie Antoinette. Both of them died on the guillotine. Marie Antoinette's friend, the Princess de Lamballe, who had worn it on occasions, was torn to pieces by the mob.

The diamond turned up next around 1800 in the possession of a Dutch diamond-cutter named Fals, who shaped it into its present form. Fals's son stole it and the cutter died of grief. In remorse, the son killed himself.

Eventually, the stone was bought by Henry Thomas Hope, an English banker, who gave it its name. Henry Hope escaped any evil consequences but his grandson, Sir Francis Hope, had a disastrous marriage and died destitute. The next owner, a French financier, went mad and eventually committed suicide.

So the terrible toll went on, until more than 20 people associated with the stone had met with disaster. In 1908, the diamond was sold to a Russian nobleman, Prince Kanitovski. He gave it to his mistress, Mademoiselle Ladue, one of the stars of the Folies Bergère. She was shot in the theatre by a spurned lover and, two days later, the Prince himself was stabbed to death in a Paris street. The jewel eventually came into the hands of Sultan Abdul

Hamid and then, through Cartier, to Evalyn Walsh McClean.

To celebrate the acquisition of the Hope diamond, Evalyn gave a dinner party at the house in Massachusetts Avenue, which was talked about for years afterwards. It was said even *she* was startled by the size of the bill. There were 48 for dinner, which was served on gold plates with 4,000 yellow lilies from England decorating the table. The champagne glasses had stems 12in high.

For the next period of their lives the McCleans lived liked royalty. They bought country estates and town houses as casually as an ordinary person would buy a pair of gloves. Their favourite country residence, Black Point Farm at Newport, had a staff of 30 for the house and as many more for the grounds and stables. At home in Massachusetts Avenue, Evalyn had commandeered the whole top floor – a space as big as a park – for her personal wardrobe. Her ballgowns and furs alone took up the space of an ordinary-sized room.

But things had started to go wrong.

Evalyn adored her first son Vinson, whom she had named after her brother killed in the wooden-bridge accident. Nothing was too good for him and the American Press referred to him as the 'one million dollar baby'. Entire performances of the Ringling Brothers circus were bought out so that he might be the only one in the audience and have all the acts performed just for him. Dressed in ermine, cossetted and pampered, he still could not escape his fate. Soon after the purchase of the Hope diamond, Vinson was killed in a car accident.

Nothing was more therapeutic, as far as Evalyn was concerned, than spending money. After Vinson's death she lived more flamboyantly than ever, though friends knew she had suffered greatly. She never went to bed, if she could help it, before six or seven in the morning and hated to be alone. On a visit to New York, for instance, she would take a suite at the Waldorf, invite 100 people in for cocktails then take them all to a championship boxing match.

Her marriage to Ned McClean had entered stormy waters. He was constantly being hounded by his creditors, and eventually he gave up trying to cope with life any longer and was admitted to a mental institution, where he later died.

As she grew older, Evalyn had to face the fact that she had spent a vast fortune in her lifetime and the well was beginning to run dry. Although the Depression of the 1930s made her feel miserable, she did not really understand the financial problems of ordinary people. When depressed, she knew of only one way to make herself feel better. Once, she took a train to New York, where her old friend Pierre Cartier, who happened to be over from Paris, promised to find something to cheer her up. Like a magician, he produced a dazzling ruby-and-emerald bracelet with a 16-carat diamond, known as the Star of the South, as its centrepiece. 'I felt like a new woman the moment he put it on,' she recalled in her memoirs. 'There's nothing like spending money as a cure for not having it.'

By 1947, Evalyn's health was beginning to show signs of strain and she took painkillers as a matter of course. However, nothing could deaden the agony of what happened that summer, when her daughter Evalyn Beale McClean, who had married Senator Robert R. Reynolds of North Carolina, a man much older than herself, was found dead after taking an overdose of sleeping pills.

Not long afterwards, at the comparatively early age of 61 Evalyn herself died of pneumonia. She had always predicted that she would die bankrupt, and almost did, as her estate was probated at a mere $606,000.

The Hope diamond was left jointly to her six grandchildren, but they were never allowed to touch it. Meanwhile, it remained one of the most wanted gems in the world. The Russian Government was said to have opened negotiations for it, but the deal fell through and the stone was sold to Harry Winston, famous New York diamond dealer. In 1958 he gave it to the Smithsonian Institute in Washington to form the basis of what he hoped would become a famous collection.

No doubt the McClean family thought the Hope diamond and its sinister legend was out of their lives for ever. But, in December 1967, 25-year-old Evalyn McClean, lovely young granddaughter of Evalyn Walsh McClean, was found dead at her home in a suburb of Dallas, Texas, where she lived alone. There was no sign of violence. Neighbours broke into the house after seeing no activity for several days, and found her dressed in jeans and a sweater on the bed . . .

Queen Soraya

Two moments were unforgettable in the life of Soraya Esfandiary. Once was when she stood by the side of His Imperial Majesty the Shah of Iran at the age of 18 and became his Empress. The other was the day she stood on the steps of the plane taking her to Europe and out of his life for ever.

Only seven years stretched between the joy of the first and the anguish of the second; seven years at the end of which she lost the man she loved, her country and her crown. And all for one reason alone – she could not give the Shah the son and heir he wanted.

The story of Queen Soraya and the Shah is one of the most poignant in modern history. Everyone presumed the marriage to be one of convenience. Everything depended on whether she could provide an heir for the Peacock Throne. What no one had taken into account was the fact that the two people concerned would fall deeply in love.

Soraya, a ravishingly beautiful young woman, was the daughter of an Iranian father and a German mother. She had silky raven-black hair, high cheekbones, huge, dreamy green eyes and full red lips. Only a fraction of that beauty was evident when, one day in 1950, the Shah saw some rather fuzzy snapshots of her taken in St Moritz. But they were enough to rouse his interest.

Officials at the Iranian court had begun to despair of the Shah ever taking serious interest in what they considered to be a marriageable girl. None of the aristocratic young women they paraded before him at receptions and balls seemed to have touched his heart. Mohammed Reza Pahlevi was now 31 years old, imperiously handsome, a fine sportsman and fabulously rich. But he was also a lonely and unhappy man. His first marriage to Princess Fawzia, sister of King Farouk of Egypt, had ended in divorce. Their only child was a daughter, Princess Shahnaz. He knew it was his duty to marry again to secure the Pahlevi dynasty, but he was modern in his thinking and wanted to do so, if possible, for love.

He was sitting alone one night when one of his mother's ladies-in-waiting, and an old friend of the royal family, showed him pictures of her niece on the ski slopes in Switzerland. She told him her name was Soraya. 'She seems very pretty,' he admitted. 'What a pity the photographs are not clearer.' His obvious interest stirred her to action. She telephoned to London, where Soraya was studying, and ordered more pictures to be taken immediately and sent to her at the palace in Tehran.

A few days later, the Shah was presented with clear pictures of the stunning 18-year-old girl, laughing among the gold-tinted autumn leaves in St James's Park, London. There was also a studio portrait, serious, dignified, showing the beauty of her slightly Oriental features. He studied her face carefully, then said, with a laugh: 'Well, perhaps this is the one . . .' There was a bustle among the rather formidable women in the Shah's family. His mother, the Dowager Empress, told her daughter, Princess Shams: 'Fly to London and have a look at this girl.'

Soraya Esfandiary was the daughter of a Persian diplomat and his German-born wife. Her father, Khalil Esfandiary, belonged to the clan of the Baktiari, feuding nomads whose ancestry could be traced back to the 12th century. Soraya was born at Isfahan on 22 June 1932, spent part of her childhood in Europe but returned to her birthplace during World War II. Once hostilities were over, her mother sent her to finishing schools in Switzerland so that she could absorb the European tradition rather than that of the submissive female behind the veil. She loved Switzerland and considered the years she spent at school there among the happiest in her life.

She was already receiving proposals of marriage. All the suitors came from old Iranian families who visited her parents at their house in Zurich and asked for her hand. She was told not to take the proposals too seriously; her studies came first. To emphasize the point, she was sent to London in the summer of 1950 to perfect her English.

That autumn her cousin, Gudars Bakriari, who was studying at the same language school, asked her if he could take photographs of her. They were, he said, for his mother to show to the Dowager Empress. She was intrigued and puzzled. When her father wrote to say the Shah had asked for her to be presented at court, she began to have premonitions that her life was about to change.

Premonition turned to certainty when the Shah's eldest sister, Princess Shams, arrived in London, took her to dinner at the Iranian Embassy and suggested they flew to Paris together to do some shopping. But the visit to Paris turned out to be far more than a simple shopping expedition. Soraya was schooled in some of the formal protocol and etiquette demanded at court in Tehran. She was taking her first steps towards ascending the Peacock Throne.

Accompanied by her father and Princess Shams, Soraya took the night flight to Tehran on 7 October. She had scarcely unpacked her suitcase when a call came through from the palace: the Dowager Empress had arranged a small dinner at which only the innermost family circle would be present. Though she was tired, she slipped into one of her new Paris dresses and made herself ready.

The formidable old lady was waiting for her, seated in a deep chair covered in yellow silk. Members of the Royal Family were grouped around her. They welcomed her amiably and for 15 minutes questioned her lengthily about her health and the health of her relatives, a mark of good manners in Iranian society.

A servant entered the room and announced: 'His Majesty the Shah!'

The Shah was strikingly handsome in the dress uniform of a general of the Iranian Air Force. Soraya trembled a little when she was presented to him, but managed to bow with dignity. Rather stiffly, he led her to the dining table and beckoned her to sit next to him. Throughout the meal he gave her his whole attention, questioning her about her studies in Switzerland and England. He, too, had been to boarding school in Switzerland and knew the country around Montreux and Lausanne. As the evening went on, the strong attraction between the two of them began to be very noticeable.

As they left the palace Soraya's father asked her: 'Well, what do you think of him?'

'I like him,' she replied.

'Are you willing to marry him?'

'Do I have to make up my mind at once?'

'It would be better,' her father replied. 'The Shah requested just now that I ask you for your answer this evening.'

This was all hastier than she had expected. But in her autobiography Soraya says: 'My sensation of pleasure did not leave room either for surprise or confusion . . . without a second's hesitation I agreed to marry him.'

Next morning her photograph was in the world's newspapers. Three days later, the official celebrations to mark their engagement took place in the Imperial Palace. The wedding was announced for 27 December.

Every day for the next three weeks the young couple went horseriding, driving into the country for picnics and flying in the Shah's private plane. By the end of October, however, Tehran was in the grip of a typhoid epidemic. Soraya returned from one of her outings with a high colour, abnormally bright eyes and her body shaking with fever. The court doctor was called and confirmed that she, too, was a victim.

For days her temperature raged around 106 degrees and her life hung by a thread. When the crisis had passed she was confined to bed for three months as she fought her way back to health and strength. It was during this period that Soraya and Shah fell deeply in love. Each day he spent hours at her bedside; he brought her flowers and gifts and, when she began to feel better, had a record-player and film-projector fixed up in her room. He was tender and kind and now she *really* knew she wanted to marry him.

The wedding had been postponed until 12 February 1951. Soraya was still weak, and when the great day dawned, and she woke to find Tehran in deep snow, the doctor insisted she wore thick white woollen stockings underneath her wedding dress. And what a dress! Designed by Christian Dior it was a breathtaking creation of silver brocade, tulle and floating ostrich feathers. The train was 12 yards long and the whole concoction weighed 40lb. During the ceremony Soraya nearly fainted. The Shah saw her distress and after the ceremony asked a lady-in-waiting to cut away part of the incredible skirt to lessen the weight. It was so full that nobody even noticed.

At the great reception that night Soraya wore some of the Pahlevi Crown Jewels for the first time. Her tiara sparkled with diamonds; round her neck were rows of emeralds; great emerald drops hung from her ears and one flawless green jewel on her finger caught the light. Everyone was talking about the wedding presents. The Russian dictator, Stalin, had sent the Shah a writing set studded with black diamonds, and for Soraya there was a snow-white Russian mink coat.

After a two-week honeymoon in a villa on the shores of the Caspian Sea, the couple were forced to return to Tehran where a political crisis threatened. They had only been back three days when the Prime Minister of Iran was shot by fanatics while attending divine service in a mosque. His place was taken by Dr Mohamed Mossadeq, a virulent anti-monarchist whose ambition was to make himself dictator. The antics of this dangerous, emotionally unstable man threw Iran into chaos for the next two and a half years and involved the Shah in a bitter row with Britain over the supply of Iranian oil.

Under the influence of Mossadeq, Iran slid towards ruin and anarchy. The situation became so dangerous, as Mossadeq's hysterical supporters yelled for the execution of the entire royal family, that in August 1953 the Shah and Soraya fled to Rome. Mossadeq was finally ousted by the loyal General Zahedi who gathered the support of the army. Once the situation had settled down, the royal couple returned to a jubilant welcome from the Iranian people.

Trouble had brought the Shah and Soraya to an even deeper understanding. After the Mossadeq crisis there were to be others, equally frightening. Iran was in a constant state of ferment, but there followed a period in which the royal couple were able to settle down to a more regular married life, to carry out their various social duties and to visit ordinary Iranians in their villages and homes.

Both the Shah and Soraya loved sports. They swam, rode and sailed together, played volleyball and learned to water-ski. Like any other young couple they enjoyed parties, fancy-dress balls, private film shows and picnics. Late in 1954 they set out on a series of state visits to Britain, Germany and the United States. Everywhere, Soraya was admired and photographed, and everywhere people were asking the same question: when was she going to give the Shah the son and heir he desperately needed?

There could be no official coronation of the Empress until a Crown Prince had been born. After four years of marriage, the cradle remained empty. To show his faith in her, Mohammed Reza told Soraya that he intended to have a crown specially designed for his Empress. One day he took her to the Melli Bank, the national bank where the crown jewels are kept, and helped her to choose the precious stones to go in it.

Soraya comforted herself with the thought that her own mother had to wait six years for her arrival. Doctors she consulted assured her that it was quite possible that this kind of thing ran in families. She must be patient. Worry would only make matters worse.

But the Shah, ruling over such a volatile country and with many jealous and ambitious men around him, could not afford to wait. At 35, after 15 years and two marriages, he still had no heir to the throne. He gently suggested to his Queen that they should both undergo medical examinations. She agreed, and on 8 December 1954 they were booked into the Presbyterian Medical Center in New York. For three days they were both given a thorough check-up. All tests proved that they were perfectly normal. The doctors saw no reason why they should not have children. Queen Soraya was told to go home and be patient.

For some time the Shah did not refer to the subject of his heir. They threw themselves into good works and charitable causes hoping the problem would resolve itself. On 3 April 1957, he appointed a new Prime Minister, Dr Manachur Eghbal, a university professor of whom great things were expected. He was full of new ideas.

A few days after his appointment, Dr Eghbal asked for an audience with the Shah. He spoke quietly but firmly: 'Your Majesty, if I am to undertake reform in your name, you own authority must be unassailable. Either the Empress must present you with an heir in the near future, or the dynasty's future must be assured in some other way.'

Soraya, by this time, had given up hope. She knew that if she was to hold onto her marriage she would have to suggest a solution. At first she thought of Princess Shahnaz, the Shah's daughter. Could she be nominated Crown Princess? There was also the possibility of choosing one of the Shah's half-brothers.

Haggard and distraught at the thought of losing her, the Shah decided to call his Council of Wise Men to discuss what could be done. He advised Soraya to await the outcome of discussions, which were held in Europe so that she would not be around to be hurt. She agreed to go skiing at St Moritz.

Thus, on 13 February 1958, almost seven years to the day since their wedding, Queen Soraya kissed her husband goodbye, walked through a guard of honour to the waiting plane and turned for one last look. They were never to meet again.

Day after day, Soraya waited in Switzerland to see what the outcome of the Wise Men's discussion would be. She spoke to the Shah on the telephone, but it was no consolation. He sounded so forlorn. After a month, three emissaries from Tehran arrived to see her. The only glimmer of hope they gave her was that she could remain Empress if she agreed to the Shah taking a second wife who would give him an heir. He was entitled to do this under Islamic law. Would she agree? Soraya gazed at the three anxious faces, her eyes filled with tears and she shook her head.

A few days later the Shah announced the divorce 'with great sorrow'. There was no doubting the Shah's grief. He looked as if his heart was breaking. Soraya, inconsolable for a time, threw herself madly into the mainstream of jet-set life. She was seen with film stars and playboys, her name was linked with Princes and millionaires. She was always on the move and never seemed to smile. She would never speak of the past.

Eighteen months after they had parted, the Shah married Farah Diba and she gave him the heir he longed for. But, as fate would have it, they, too, eventually were forced into a bitter exile when the Ayatollah overthrew the Shah, leaving the Peacock Throne unoccupied.

Nina Dyer

Nina Dyer was not a raving beauty. She was a quiet, withdrawn, enigmatic young woman who earned her living as a not very successful model. But, within the space of a few years, she married *two* world-famous millionaires. One made her a Baroness, the other a Princess. Between them they showered her with jewels and bought her spectacular presents. Other women could only look on and wonder.

Somewhere, something went wrong with what appeared to be idyllic romances. The first marriage lasted ten months, the second three years. She spent the last years of her life as a lonely divorcee, drifting from one glittering party to another. Suddenly, the presents didn't matter to her any more. 'It reaches a point where a woman loved by a rich man only has to admire something in passing and it arrives on her doorstep, tied with blue ribbons,' she said in a voice of disillusion.

When Nina Dyer first started out as a model, the attractive, gregarious girls who worked with her felt she was not one of them, that she was not interested in casually dating young Mayfair men but was saving herself for someone special. The fact that she had been brought up in Ceylon, now Sri Lanka, made her 'different'. Born on 15 February 1930 she had always presumed her father to be Ceylon tea-planter Stanley Dyer, with whom her mother lived until she died in 1954. Years later William Aldrich, director of an electrical firm in Chaldon, Surrey, her mother's real husband, claimed Nina was his child.

Brought back to England, she became a drama student at Mrs Helen Ackerley's school of Speech, Drama and Deportment, in Liverpool. When she had finished the course Mrs Ackerley told her the brutal truth: that she would never make an actress. She advised her, instead, to try modelling.

Nina was a striking-looking girl with dark titian hair and a slender figure, but her features were too bold for real beauty. At first she tried modelling in London, where she lived in a very modest flat in South Kensington. She did not make a great impression among the leggy beauties of the day, but suddenly decided to try her luck in Paris, found work with the couturiers and developed a new, better poised, more soigné look.

At every opportunity, she went off to the Riviera with a bikini and a pair of Pekinese dogs. Photographers soon began to notice her and her picture appeared frequently in the newspapers. On one such holiday, when she was 22, she met and became romantically involved with Nicolas Franco, Spanish ambassador to Portugal and younger brother of the Spanish dictator. He offered to sponsor a film career for her in Spain, but she had other plans.

Back in Paris she had been taken up by rich and influential friends who took her to parties at some of the smartest homes in Paris. She now dressed superbly and attracted many admiring glances. One night, over the rim of a cocktail glass, her eyes met those of 33-year-old Baron Heinrich von Thyssen, one of the richest men in Europe.

The blond Baron, who had inherited a steel and shipping fortune from his uncle, Fritz von Thyssen, one of Hitler's great supporters, was an extremely attractive proposition. Though still married to Austrian-born Princess Theresa de Lippe, divorce was on its way. He was now a naturalized Swiss and would soon be free to look for a companion among Europe's loveliest women.

Nina, with her slight lisp, Riviera suntan and silken poise, intrigued him. Next day he telephoned. She saw no point in playing the old game of hard to get – 'From the minute he spoke to me, he was the only man in my life,' she said at the time. They were soon seen together at all the smart places. His first presents to her were two cars – a Ferrari sports and a Simca – both with gold ignition and door keys.

When they were eventually engaged, he gave her a £30,000 ring and a £20,000 brooch to match. They were married in Colombo, Ceylon, in December 1954. She was 24. A Paris-in-spring wedding had been planned, but when Nina's mother died in a road accident outside Colombo they decided to marry quietly at the island's register office. She wore a simple, low-necked white dress. He wore a shark-skin suit. And they looked very much in love.

Cruising in San San Bay off Jamaica on their honeymoon, they spotted an uninhabited, palm-fringed island with pure white sandy beaches. Nina turned to her husband, saying impulsively: 'Heini, I would *love* to live on that island!' Gazing into her lovely eyes he assured her: 'So you shall, my dear, so you shall.'

Thyssen bought Pellow Island for Nina without disclosing the cost. They planned to build a house there for holidays, decorating the rooms with French murals and installing an all-American modern kitchen.

He gave her so many spectacular presents. Among the jewels he bought was a necklace of huge black pearls and earrings and a black solitaire pearl ring to match. Wanting to give her a house of her own, he acquired the Château Midori, 15 miles from Paris, where she started a small menagerie. Being an animal lover she was over the moon when he presented her with a three-month-old black panther and a baby leopard. To make them feel at home, she installed a huge tropical climbing plant with vine-like branches in the middle of her drawing room. It began to take over and creep across the ceiling.

They had only been married ten months when Nina announced that they were to part. Divorce proceedings were to be heard at Lugano, Switzerland, where the Baron had his home. 'What went wrong? The truth is we didn't really get on together from the start,' Thyssen admitted to his surprised friends. 'There are many reasons. Partly, I think, we married too hastily.' Nina complained: 'He set a pace few marriages could survive. He had so many business interests he was seldom in the same place or country for more than a few days at a time. It was all high finance and high society.'

Nina settled down to wait for her divorce in her rambling, half-empty château in the French town of Garches. She had never got round to furnishing it and now asked for money to buy carpets and curtains. For company, she had a flock of pet parrots, ten dogs, two hummingbirds, her panther and her leopard. When the parting finally came, 'incompatibility' was given as the reason for the breakdown of the marriage. The Baron gave

Nina £1,000,000 and his best wishes. After the divorce he went on to marry 24-year-old beauty Fiona Campbell-Walter, another London model.

Nina continued to hobnob with the titled rich of Europe. She got to know playboy Prince Aly Khan, then escorting the famous French model Bettina. One night, Aly asked her to one of the champagne parties he always gave in Paris after the Grand Prix. He introduced her to his dark, handsome half-brother, Prince Sadruddin . . . and it was love at first sight for both of them.

At the time, it was thought that, when the old Aga Khan died, 24-year-old Sadruddin might become his successor as ruler of the Moslem Ismaelis. If that happened, his wife would become Begum. However, the Aga had already decided that his grandson, Karim, would take over on his death. Nevertheless, Sadruddin was a young man held in the highest esteem; he was more serious than Aly, more stable.

'Sadri', as everyone called him, was a student at Harvard. He was in Europe for a short time to see his father, who was ill. Since he was 17, his name had been linked with beautiful women, among them French ballerina Ethery Pageva, French actress Anouk, 17-year-old Princess Shahnaz, daughter of the Shah of Iran, and British socialite Doon Plunket, a member of the Guinness family. Now he began to woo Nina.

Unlike his brother, Aly, Sadri had no interest in racing but, like Nina, he loved animals. They also shared an interest in music and outdoor sports. She was fascinated by his hobby – collecting Persian miniatures of the 16th and 17th centuries. One thing pleased her: no one could accuse her of fortune-hunting; Baron von Thyssen's divorce settlement meant she had a fortune in her own right.

After he had proposed, only one thing worried Prince Sadruddin. The Aga Khan had made it plain that he wanted his son to marry an Asiatic girl; he thought there was too much European blood in the family. Sadri took Nina to meet his mother first. Princess Andree Khan was delighted with his choice. Then he went alone to confront his father. Fortunately, the old Aga was satisfied with his son's choice, especially when he heard that Nina was prepared to become a Moslem.

Once it was known that Nina was about to marry her second millionaire, she was besieged for interviews. She denied being a schemer; she said nothing was further from the truth; luck just seemed to come her way without her doing anything about it: 'It has been like that during most of my grown-up life.' Asked the secret of her success she sipped an orange juice and replied modestly: 'Be simple and dignified in your ways. Be natural. Be yourself. Don't put on airs. The very rich are often simple people with simple tastes.'

Nina and Prince Sadruddin were married in Geneva on a beautiful June day in 1957. She wore an exquisite short wedding dress of palest silver-grey organdie, designed by Dior. All her Thyssen jewels were left at home. Her ring was just a simple band of gold. Sadri wore one exactly the same. First a civil ceremony was performed by the Mayor. Then came the religious rites, in which two Imams officiated, at the Prince's magnificent château outside Geneva. The wedding was a strictly family affair with only 29 guests. Aly Khan was there with Bettina, and the bridesmaid was Sadri's young cousin. The bride changed her name to Princess Shirin, the word 'shirin' meaning sweetness.

For two years the marriage seemed to go well. The pair had made a touching pact on their wedding day, never to be seated apart at dinner tables or to dance with anyone else at receptions, balls and nightclubs. It was all the more noticeable, then, when they began to appear in public separately.

In material terms, Nina had scooped the pool again. The Prince had given her a £36,000 blue diamond ring and an expensive sports car, and made her a £50,000-a-year tax-free allowance. She lived in superb style at their château in Switzerland and their villa in the south of France. But she was lonely a great deal of the time.

Sadri became immersed in a project to save the Nubian monuments, which were threatened with submersion when the Egyptians built the Aswan Dam. He became absorbed in the diplomatic world and, by October 1960, was in New York a great deal of the time as an ambassador to the United Nations. The two of them had not been seen together for months. Nina was thought to be living quietly on Capri.

They parted in 1960 and were divorced two years later. The cause of the rift, again, was incompatibility.

Nina went back to her home in France and tried to make a social life for herself. Every evening she dressed carefully, chose jewels from her fabulous collection and went out. Sometimes she gave lavish parties, but it was obvious that she was a very lonely woman. A Portuguese couple were her only servants and she became very fond of their child, spoiling him with sweets and toys.

She arrived home at midnight on 3 July 1965, talked with her housekeeper for a few minutes, then, smiling sweetly, wished her goodnight. When her breakfast tray was taken to her bedroom next morning there was no reply. Eventually, the door was broken down and Nina was found dead. There was an empty tube of sleeping pills, but no note.

Both husbands attended her funeral at Garches cemetery, only a few hundred yards from her home. They covered her grave with hundreds of red roses. There was a card from the Baron, which said simply: 'From Heini to Nina.'

She left a will asking that her money should be used for the care of animals, but the Swiss court, for reasons not given, ruled it invalid. That was when William Aldrich of Surrey came forward to claim that he was her father. Her wonderful jewels were auctioned in Geneva and among the buyers rumoured to be interested were names like Elizabeth Taylor, Sophia Loren, Jackie Onassis and Maria Callas.

Nina was only 35 when she died. She had shot from comparative obscurity to be the wife of two very rich men within a very short time. But there is an old adage which says: 'From rags to riches, from riches to emptiness.' Perhaps she found it had come true.

Vivian Nicholson

Vivian Nicholson, a Yorkshire lass who still lives in Castleford where she was born, is remembered by people all over the country for one thing: when her husband Keith was lucky enough to come up on the Pools in 1961 she made no secret about what she was going to do with the money. 'I'm going to spend, spend, spend!' she shouted, joyously.

Who could blame her? All her life she had been so poor, then, suddenly, she was standing beneath the bright lights in one of London's top hotels holding a cheque for £152,300 18s 6d. She couldn't believe there was so much money in the world. And outside, in the shop windows, were all the things she'd never been able to afford.

She was 25 when it happened, a bright, perky blonde who had not had an easy time ever since she was born. Her father was a miner, but most of the time he was too ill to work. She went to the council school in Castleford and left when she was 15. Sometimes she daydreamed about going to art school but, with five children in the family, it just wasn't possible. As the eldest, she had to go out to work and 'bring a bit in'. First she worked in a sweet factory, then in a flour mill. She didn't like either, but when a chance came to work in the local cinema she thought it would be more exciting and became an usherette.

Vivian's first husband came along when she was 23, but the marriage was not a success and she was divorced seven months later. Soon after, she met a dark-haired, pleasant-faced young miner called Keith Nicholson. Though he was two years younger than she was, they hit it off immediately and their wedding took place in 1960.

They managed to get a council house in Kershaw Avenue, Airedale, near Castleford. Keith worked at nearby Wheldale Colliery and earned £14 a week. There was enough to get by on, but they often dreamed about what it would be like to win the Pools. Keith did them every Saturday, just a 4-shilling stake and no particular system. But on one particular weekend in 1961 he felt a chill go up his spine as he checked the results on TV. He knew he had six draws, then seven, but he wasn't *sure* whether he had the magical eight. Vivian's father called round. He checked them and said he *knew* they had eight. They hardly dared look at each other.

The Pools representatives turned up on the following Monday. Both Vivian and Keith had had sleepless nights since the discovery, and even when they were told officially they couldn't take it in. They still didn't know how much they had won, though they were assured it would be a sum worth having. All depended on how many other people had filled in eight draws.

For the next few weeks they could hardly sleep or eat. They did not find out that they were the *only* winners until just before they caught the train to London for the presentation. When they got off at the other end, the Press were waiting. 'What are you going to do with the money?' shouted reporters. 'I'm going to spend, spend, spend!' she laughed back.

They stayed at the Grosvenor Hotel in Park Lane, had a

memorable night out at the Pigalle and braced themselves for the presentation next day. Vivian had an idea that £75,000 was the most you could win on the Pools. When they told her the cheque was for more than £150,000, she felt as if the world had stopped turning.

While a bemused Keith tried to take in the advice that was being hurled at him by the finance men, Vivian went on her first shopping spree – to Harrods. She couldn't believe it was all real. Viv Nicholson from Castleford buying clothes for herself and the children, masses of toys, perfume, an 80-guinea watch – and buying them in the poshest store you could imagine! The hotel room was packed from floor to ceiling with Harrods parcels, and *still* it didn't seem *real*.

They flew back to Yorkshire feeling like film stars, with flashbulbs popping and the Press hanging on every word. Vivian, her arms full of flowers, was asked again and again if she'd really said she was going to 'spend, spend, spend'. All she could think of was getting back home and giving the children their toys.

That first night in Castleford was wonderful. They threw open the doors and invited everyone in for a drink. When the house was full they drank outside in the garden, even on the pavement. That was a party they'd never forget. But next day was different. Envy started to creep in. Envy and resentment. Why should the Nicholsons have all the luck? They were young, and there were older people who deserved it more. When they walked into their local pub for a drink, people fell silent and moved away. 'If I sit and talk to you, people will say I'm after something,' one neighbour explained curtly.

Now they were rich they could no longer stay in their council house. They bought a show house in Grange Avenue, Garforth, near Leeds . . . and regretted every minute they spent there. Vivian felt the chill as soon as she arrived. The neighbours, she said, ignored her; they would even cross the road to avoid speaking to her. She and her husband had been cold-shouldered out of Castleford because of the money; it was obvious they were not wanted here either.

Vivian found a way of getting her own back. After a night at the pub with Keith, she invited everybody back to the house for the loudest party she could manage. The record-player was on full blast and everyone was laughing and singing. Inevitably, the police came. But when she encountered frosty stares next morning she grinned to herself.

'We stayed there long enough for them to get really fed up with us and for us to really get mad and fed up with them,' Vivian told Stephen Smith and Peter Razzell, sociologists at London University who were conducting research on Pools winners. 'But they forced me into a lot of things; it isn't the Pools that change you, you know; it's the people around that change you,' she explained.

The couple found another house; a large bungalow on the Halbury Moor. It was expensive, but there was plenty of space for the children and their ponies, as well as the cars they had bought – Vivian had six cars in four years, and Keith changed his every two months. She went to the most expensive department stores in Leeds, and furnished the house exactly as she wanted it. Her favourite purchases were a £1,000 four-seater settee and an organ. She also bought herself a £1,000 diamond solitaire ring and £600 worth of clothes to cheer herself up.

Once the two older children had been sent to boarding school, both Vivian and Keith began to get bored. They had some good foreign holidays, including a trip to America, but at home they drank too much just to fill in time. When Viv began to feel ill and worried about becoming an alcoholic, Keith started going out drinking without her.

Keith was spending money like water, but he wouldn't discuss financial affairs; he wouldn't even go to the bank when the manager asked to see him. He was convinced the money would go on for ever. He had taken up fishing, shooting and golf, buying the most expensive equipment available. After taking up racing, he bought three race-horses and obviously had plans to gradually build up a stable. But, more than anything, Keith was mad about cars.

Whatever car he bought, he managed to smash it up within two months. He even had a crash on the way to his driving test. His latest car was a beautiful, shiny new Jaguar and he couldn't wait to get behind the wheel. One morning, he told Vivian he was going to see some new ponies for the children. His uncle was going along too. He was dying to show him how the car performed. On the way back, he ran off the road. By the time ambulancemen got Keith out, he was dead.

Vivian began to drink again. She felt lost without Keith, and she suddenly realized they had spent an awful lot of money. She was advised to sell the bungalow and buy something cheaper. The cars had to go and the children could not stay at boarding school. By the time the accountants had sorted out Viv's financial position, she found she had just £10 a week to live on; but she fought like a tigress to get a lump sum from the remaining money in Keith's estate, and won.

Once Viv had money in the bank again, she found the spending obsession was still with her. 'It's like being an alcoholic,' she claimed. Though she knew the capital she had could not last for more than five years, she couldn't resist buying a new car every now and then. She admitted she got depressed because, now, she knew what good living was like. She never wanted to go back to the sweet factory.

Since Keith died, Viv has had four more husbands, been widowed three times and divorced once. Now she lives in a modest terraced house in Victoria Street, Castleford, and has become a Jehovah's Witness. And the money? 'I don't think I'd want to win it again,' she admits.

Norah Docker

At the 1951 Motor Show in London the brightest, costliest exhibit was a huge 36-horsepower Daimler that not only glistened like gold but was actually *covered* in gold. It was a present from Daimler's chief, Sir Bernard Docker, to his wife, Norah. Twenty ounces of 18-carat gold plate covered the headlights, door handles, radiator, window edges, wheel discs and even the bumpers. Seven thousand gold stars were painted on the bodywork. It was fitted with a gold cocktail set and upholstered in yellow silk brocade. The coachwork was superb, and the workmanship splendid. But, people asked in whispers, wasn't it just a shade *vulgar*? 'Nonsense,' dismissed Lady Docker. 'Remember we do travel abroad a great deal and this will show people what England can do.'

If anyone was going to enjoy riding around in a gold-plated Daimler it would have to be Norah Docker. Her impulsive, extravagant behaviour made her the darling of the gossip columns for more than a decade. She managed to get herself and Sir Bernard banned from Monaco and the Côte d'Azur, banned from the royal enclosure at Ascot, banned even from their local public house when they went to live in Jersey.

Flaunting her wealth, creating scenes and making life difficult for the patient, good-natured husband who adored her were all par for the course as far as Lady Docker was concerned; but, in the end, it brought about Sir Bernard's business downfall and the loss of his position as Chairman and Managing Director of the Birmingham Small Arms (BSA) company which then owned Daimler.

Despite everything, Norah had en engaging personality

and was generous to a fault. It was just that she genuinely enjoyed kicking up a bit of a rumpus. She was usually forgiven, for she was a pretty woman with fair curly hair, wide hazel eyes and a peachy complexion. Her good looks enabled her to find no less than three rich husbands.

Life had not always been gold-plated for her. She was born Norah Turner in a flat above a butcher's shop in Derby. Her father was a car salesman who got into difficulties and committed suicide. For a time, her mother ran a public house. Norah's first job was as a trainee milliner at Bobby's Store in Southport, but she already had grand ideas even then. Nothing but the best, she decided, would do for her. The problem was how to get it.

Tossing aside her career in hats she went to London, intending to be an actress, but ending up as a dancing partner at the Café de Paris. Men found her very attractive, but she was only interested in the rich ones. In her autobiography she explained her strategy: 'When other girls would be satisfied with fur, I always demanded mink; when other girls would be satisfied with zircon, I would insist on a diamond. I always asked for champagne, and it had to be pink because I loved the colour.'

At the Café de Paris she met her first husband, Clement Callingham, Chairman of Henekey's the wine and spirit merchants, and a married man. They lived together before marriage and Callingham's wife cited her in a divorce action as co-respondent. When their son, Lance, was born in 1939 they celebrated the event with 500 bottles of champagne.

Clement Callingham died in 1945 and just over a year later, when she was 40, she married Sir William Collins, head of Cerebos Salt and Fortnum and Mason. Their union began inauspiciously with a row at Caxton Hall register office. He said something about her dress and she threw back at him the pearls he had given her as a wedding present. Things calmed down, but the marriage was never peaceful. After one tiff he cut her out of his will, leaving her a paltry £500. An illness softened his attitude and he restored her to favour. He died, however, when they had only been married for two years.

Now a rich widow with a fast-growing son, she decided she must find another husband quickly – 'Women can't bring up boys properly.' At the same time she was terrified of fortune-hunters. She decided if she could track down a man richer than herself, she could be sure of being married for love, not money. So she went husband-hunting and one night saw Sir Bernard Docker dancing at Ciro's. She knew immediately he was the man for her and admitted: 'I began to haunt him like the family ghost. Wherever he was, I turned up.' At last, he took her out to lunch. Going out together became a habit, but not a word of love was exchanged and she began to feel he was not interested. Just when she was about to give up, he was jolted into action.

Norah had gone off alone to Sweden on holiday. On the return journey her plane had to make a forced landing miles from anywhere. The passengers were stranded for 48 hours. No sooner was she back in London than Sir Bernard was on the phone: 'Thank God you're safe,' he shouted. 'Will you marry me?'

So, at 43, she became the wife of the most distinguished of all her husbands. Sir Bernard Docker was not only the Chairman of BSA but a senior director of the Midland Bank. He had interests in many other companies besides. She was particularly impressed by the fact that he owned one of the biggest and most luxurious yachts in the world, the 863-ton *Shemara,* and also had a fine country house at Stockbridge in Hampshire. He had been married once before, to actress Jeanne Stuart.

The Dockers flew the family flag from the masthead at Stockbridge and villagers referred to them jokingly as 'the King and Queen'. But a great deal of their leisure time was spent aboard the *Shemara*. It was often anchored in the harbour at Monaco while they played the tables in the casino at Monte Carlo.

Lady Docker had her first blazing row with the principality's officials in 1951. They had been invited to attend the annual Red Cross gala at the casino. Halfway through Norah began to protest in a loud voice that the cabaret was 'awful' and 'nothing better than a fashion parade'. There was a scuffle after the Casino Sporting Club President, Prince Jean-Louis Faucigny-Lucinge, told Sir Bernard: 'Take your wife away.' Lady Docker slapped a casino official across the face and exploded: 'How dare you! We will never come in here again!'

Despite this, the Dockers were invited to the wedding of Prince Rainier of Monaco and Grace Kelly in 1953 but, again, there was a row when they were refused admission to the casino later that night, and Lady Docker caused yet another scene.

Five years later came the worst row of all. The Dockers had been invited to the christening of Prince Rainier's son and heir, Prince Albert. As it was Lance's 19th birthday Norah took him along as well, only to be told that he could not attend the reception. This infuriated her Ladyship, who stomped off to have lunch at the Hôtel de Paris. On the table was a small flag in the Monaco colours. She snatched it up, tore it to bits and threw it on the floor. The action was taken very seriously. She was thereafter banned from the principality and, because of a certain treaty, that meant also from the Côte d'Azur. The Dockers' christening gifts were delivered back to their hotel in Cannes. Lady Docker said she didn't care; she'd always preferred Capri anyway.

The Dockers were regular attenders at Ascot and were usually welcomed in the royal enclosure. They were shocked, therefore, in 1953, to be told that the Duke of Norfolk was not going to issue them with the usual badge.

Someone, digging up the past, had suddenly realized that Norah had been the co-respondent in her first husband's divorce case. Lady Docker decided to put a brave face on it. She went badgeless to Ascot in her new sapphire mink with a sapphire silk dress and a hat made entirely of lacquered shells to match. Just as she had intended, she was the centre of attention. 'This year above all I was determined to get my picture in the papers,' she told everyone. She and Sir Bernard lunched at the Marlborough Club tent, then walked around with the other cash customers in the paddock. One or two loyalists came over from the enclosure to join them. At the end of the day Norah said she had never enjoyed Ascot so much before.

Her every move, her every whim, were reported. She twice became the world's women's marbles champion. She was elected Palm Beach Princess. She still created scenes. One night she walked out of the Café de Paris because Labour MP Bessie Braddock, famous for her ample and splendid girth, turned up in day clothes instead of evening glamour.

Just as people were getting tired of her tantrums she would do something that would restore her popularity. She and Sir Bernard went to visit miners down the pit at the Walter Haigh Colliery near Leeds. As a 'thank you' for the warm Yorkshire hospitality they had received, the Dockers invited the miners to join them for a day's outing on board the *Shemara*. Norah entertained them regally with roast chicken and champagne, and strawberries and cream. To loud cheers, she performed a lively version of the sailors' hornpipe.

Less well received was the news that leaked out in 1954. They had to issue a statement through their solicitors explaining their presence at a bizarre and much publicized party given in a Soho restaurant by Mr Billy Hill, a self-styled boss of London's underworld. The party had been arranged to celebrate the publication of Hill's autobiography. Among the guests were several CID officers and some well-known characters from London's underworld, including 'Johnny Up the Spout', 'Three Pints Rapid' and 'The Monkey'.

Lady Docker and Sir Bernard were seen sipping champagne and obviously enjoying themselves. At the end of the evening Billy Hill kissed her on the cheek as she thanked him for a most enjoyable time. Next day came their statement saying they had no idea Billy Hill was going to be their host; indeed, they had never heard of him; they had been misled into going to a party they would otherwise not have considered attending.

Gaffes such as this, and all the other publicity he had received since marrying the irrepressible Norah, had not helped Sir Bernard in his business life. Suddenly, in 1953, he resigned his directorship of the Midland Bank after a dispute with the board.

Three years later came trouble with BSA. The directors had not been very pleased about the publicity surrounding the gold Daimler Sir Bernard had built for his wife. They thought their product too dignified for such treatment. Nor did they appreciate the way in which Lady Docker made a habit of inspecting BSA factories and attending executive parties to which other wives were not invited.

When she heard of the boardroom move to depose Sir Bernard, Norah believed it was because they were jealous of her husband and, without his knowledge or consent, hired private detectives to investigate the activities of the other directors. It was to no avail. A resolution to sack him was carried by six votes to three at a board meeting in June 1956.

Norah sent a letter to 17,000 shareholders, pointing out to them the huge increase in BSA profits since he took over. Sir Bernard himself made an appeal on television. But, at an extraordinary meeting of the shareholders, the board's decision was upheld.

Norah was infuriated by one issue that had been given particular prominence in the affair. They had criticized her for presenting a bill for £7,910 for dresses worn at the Paris motor show to publicize the golden Daimler. She protested that she had gained enormous publicity for the company. 'In the end,' she said, ruefully, 'the old battle I lost was that against jealousy!'

The Dockers continued to enjoy country life in Hampshire and cruised around the world in the *Shemara*, but in 1959, the year after the row over the Monaco flag incident, something equally unpleasant happened. Lady Docker lost more than £100,000 worth of jewels.

Norah was in the habit of taking her valuables with her when she travelled. On 10 March 1959 they were staying at a hotel in Southampton. Their Rolls-Royce was left in the car park. The jewellery, including two sapphire and diamond necklaces, a sapphire bracelet, emerald bracelets and earrings and a solitaire diamond given to her by her second husband, Sir William Collins, was hidden in briefcases and covered with rugs. There were no visible signs that the locks had been tampered with. Lady Docker was in a state of near collapse. 'They've taken everything I've got,' she wailed.

Sir Bernard eventually resigned from most of his business interests, sold the *Shemara* and took his wife to live in the tax haven of Jersey. Norah was still sparking on all cylinders, however, and one day became involved in an argument with a popular singer of the day called Yana, whose husband kept a restaurant. Afterwards, she received a letter saying she was no longer welcome to dine there. The Dockers left for Palma, Majorca, with Norah calling the inhabitants of Jersey 'the most frightfully boring, dreadful people that have ever been born'.

In 1974, she was involved in a libel case after a Sunday newspaper suggested she had been thrown out of a Jersey hotel for using 'naughty words'. She was awarded damages of $^1/_2$p and ordered to pay her own costs.

After that, the sparkle seemed to leave Lady Docker. The champagne days were over and there was not the same amount of money to splash around. They had a pleasant life on Majorca for a while, but then Norah was forced to stay on in Majorca, because of the tax situation.

At 71 she was living alone in her rented apartment on Majorca while 81-year-old Sir Bernard gradually became bedridden and blind in a Bournemouth nursing home. She phoned him four times a week and visited him twice a year, at Christmas and in the summer. Their reunions were always affectionate and moving.

'When I telephone Sir Bernard I always put on my bright chat voice,' she told *Woman* magazine in an interview. 'But afterwards, when I put down the receiver, the truth hits me and I sit here and cry.'

Looking back over her remarkable life, Lady Docker admitted sadly: 'I never dreamed it would end like this. I thought the halcyon days would go on for ever. I thought Bernard was indestructible. I thought I was, too.'

Sir Bernard Docker died in May 1978. Five and a half years later, in December 1983, Lady Docker joined him. She was buried beside him in the tiny village churchyard at Stubbings, near Maidenhead in Berkshire. Only 29 people turned up for the funeral, including her son, Lance Callingham, and his family. But none of the 'friends' who had helped her drink the champagne in the 'halcyon days' were there. It was a quiet, tasteful end for such a glittering lady. As she said at the end of her autobiography: 'The party is over. On to the next one.'

Imelda Marcos

Imelda Marcos, wife of the deposed President of the Philippines, has been called everything from 'iron lady' to 'bloodsucker'. Out in the streets of New York, where she is expected to make an appearance in court facing fraud charges involving $268 million, Filipino expatriates chorus: 'Meldy, Meldy, you're a witch. You have stolen to get rich.' They are out for her blood.

With her innate sense of theatre, Madame Marcos turns up for the court hearing exquisitely groomed in a long blue dress with a low-cut neck, surrounded by solicitous supporters and with two nurses in attendance. Her husband is too ill to attend. She will take the burden on her shoulders. 'I have lost everything,' she cries. 'How can they do this to me!'

Back home in Malacanang Palace, where once she lived like a Queen, guards raiding the Marcoses' private quarters find some of the belongings she has left behind. There are 3,000 pairs of shoes, 35 racks of furs, 500 black brassières, 200 St Michael girdles, 1,500 handbags, perfume by the vat and hundreds of bars of expensive French soap.

Fleeing from the Philippines she simply didn't have time to pack the usual 400 pieces of luggage that would normally accompany her abroad. She had sent some on ahead, of course, but on the plane to Hawaii she carried only one piece of hand luggage into which she had managed to cram a great deal of money, a gold crown studded with diamonds, three tiaras, a million-pound emerald brooch, 60 pearl necklaces, 65 gold watches and 35 jewel-studded rings.

Imelda and her ailing 71-year-old husband Ferdinand started their exile in Hawaii humbly enough in a three-bedroomed house in which every inch of available space was occupied by faithful retainers, and filled with cardboard boxes and suitcases. Before long, they had been moved into a luxurious white-walled retreat overlooking Honolulu.

Called to appear before a New York court to have her fingerprints taken and to be charged with swindling on a gigantic scale, the ex-First Lady travelled by private jet with an entourage consisting of secretaries, two nurses, a publicist, a hairdresser, a priest, maids and lawyers.

In New York she occupies a richly carpeted suite at the Waldorf Astoria hotel, a suite with a formal dining-room, five marble bath tubs and a reception room banked with what must be thousands of dollars' worth of flowers, most of them rare and exotic.

But all is not as it seems. Madame Marcos still insists that she has lost everything; she and Ferdinand cannot get their hands on a single peso. It has been like that for two years. Their assets are completely frozen.

The simple fact is, explains a lawyer, that the Marcoses are living on borrowed funds and the love of well-wishers. The villa in Hawaii came about through an admirer, Doris Duke. The 75-year-old tobacco heiress lent Imelda her plane for the journey to New York, and the bill for the Waldorf Astoria, in the region of £1,200 a night, is also being picked up by friends. But now there are angry people outside the hotel, shouting: 'Meldy, Meldy . . . ', and, for once, Imelda dare not go shopping as she used to, when it was fun to pop into Gucci on Fifth Avenue for 50 pairs of shoes at a time.

According to her biographer, Carmen Bavarro, Imelda's father was a once-prosperous copra king who went bankrupt. Her mother, Remedios, had to make some sort of home for them in a garage. For years, Imelda dressed in ragged clothes and often went hungry. She grew into a beauty, however, and realized her looks could raise her from the poverty trap. Having won a beauty contest, partly by buttering up a local politician, she began to assess her chances in the political field. Her major coup was to marry Congressman Ferdinand Marcos.

Imelda came into her own just over 20 years ago, when her husband became President. Her looks, her poise, her clothes were all admired. No one realized that the Marcoses were embarking on a reign that was just an excuse for amassing a private fortune.

Ferdinand Marcos earned the equivalent of £5,000 a year, but he was already a wealthy man when he took over in the Philippines. His job conferred the ultimate benefit: immunity from prosecution. It also gave him the opportunity to establish great monopolies, to set up new enterprises conveniently controlled by relatives or associates and to hand out lucrative import licences. There were also, allegedly, huge handouts from grateful overseas firms who benefited from nuclear power and military contracts.

Imelda proved to be much more than a beauty queen. As First Lady she obviously enjoyed power and showed glimpses of a toughness that earned her the name 'iron butterfly'. She headed no fewer than 30 profitable government corporations and was a major contractor to the state. Having gained such power, she made sure her family benefited. Two of her brothers were given key jobs, one of them running the privately owned Manila Electric Company, the other being put in charge of the government-controlled gambling industry.

Her legendary extravagance abroad was apparently funded through the Philippine National Bank. Records recovered in the Philippines showed the bank was instructed to pay $26,000 for flowers ordered for her hotel suite, $800,000 for jewellery she had bought in New York in 1982 and $2 million as an advance for a trip abroad.

No wonder red carpets were laid out when she appeared. During one 90-day shopping binge in 1983, Imelda spent a staggering $6.5-million in New York and Europe. She has a very fine appreciation of her own beauty and does not care how much she spends trying to preserve and enhance it. Her dressing rooms at the gloomy Malacanang Palace contained enough furs, jewels, perfumes and cosmetics to stock a department store. Her collection of shoes was unique. One pair, meant for disco dancing, had dazzling lights in the high heels that ran off a little battery.

One of Imelda's favourite artists is Francis Bacon, whose often grotesque paintings depict the neurosis of modern man. She said she particularly appreciated him 'because the ugliness of his work makes you realize how beautiful you and your life are'. One thing she cannot forgive the new President of the Philippines, Mrs Cory Aquino, widow of one of Marcos's murdered opponents, is that 'she doesn't make up, doesn't do her nails'.

When the Marcoses first arrived at their cramped little house in Hawaii, the ex-President would complain about the unfaithfulness of their so-called friends. But Imelda, a devout Catholic, found some comfort. She firmly believed that both she and Ferdinand were divine beings: 'Only because of that have we been able to cope with all the ugliness that has happened to us.'

Murderous Women

Mary Ann Cotton

Welfare worker Thomas Riley walked briskly through the early-morning summer sunshine. It was 6am and he was on his way to another day's duties at the village workhouse in West Auckland. Times were hard for the people of County Durham, and Riley was kept busy trying to care for those who could not cope. As he turned into Front Street, he recalled the widow at No. 13. She had come to him only six days earlier, asking if he had room in the workhouse for her seven-year-old stepson, Charles Edward. 'It is hard to keep him when he is not my own, and he is stopping me from taking in a respectable lodger,' she said. Riley joked about the identity of the lodger. Was it the excise officer village gossips said she wanted to marry?' 'It may be so,' the woman had replied, 'but the boy is in the way.'

Now, as he walked to work, Riley noticed the widow in the doorway of her three-room stone cottage. She was clearly upset, and he crossed the road to ask why. He could not believe his ears at what she told him: 'My boy is dead.'

Riley went straight to the police and the local doctor. What he told them was the first step in an investigation that was to brand the widow, Mary Ann Cotton, the worst mass murderer Britain had ever seen.

Riley was suspicious about the death because the lad had seemed in perfect health when he saw him six days earlier. Dr Kilburn was also surprised to hear of the tragedy. He and his assistant Dr Chambers had seen the boy five times that week for what they thought were symptoms of gastro-enteritis, but they never thought the illness could be fatal. Dr Kilburn decided to withhold a death certificate and asked for permission to carry out a post-mortem examination. The coroner agreed to the request, and arranged an inquest for the following afternoon,

Saturday 13 July 1872.

The pressures of their practice meant the two doctors could not start their post-mortem until an hour before the hearing. After a cursory examination, Dr Kilburn told the jury in the Rose and Crown Inn, next to Cotton's house: 'I have found nothing to suggest poisoning. Death could have been from natural causes, possibly gastro-enteritis.' The jury returned a verdict of natural death, and Charles Edward was buried in a pauper's grave.

But Dr Kilburn had taken the precaution of preserving the contents of the boy's stomach in a bottle. On the following Wednesday he at last had time to put them to proper chemical tests. He went straight back to the police with the results. There were distinct traces of arsenic. Next morning, widow Cotton was arrested and charged with murder. The boy's body was dug up and sent to Leeds School of Medicine, where Dr Thomas Scattergood, lecturer in forensic medicine and toxicology, discovered more arsenic, in the bowels, liver, lungs, heart and kidneys.

Meanwhile, Thomas Riley was pointing out to the authorities that the death of Charles Edward was not the first in the family. In fact, there had been four in the two years since Mary Ann Cotton, a former nurse, had arrived in West Auckland. Her fourth husband, coalminer Frederick Cotton, died from 'gastric fever' on 19 September 1871, two days after their first wedding anniversary. He was 39. Then, between 10 March and 1 April 1872, ten-year-old Frederick, Cotton's son by a previous marriage, Robert, Mary Ann's 14-month-old son, and Mary Ann's former lover, Joseph Nattrass, who had moved in with her again, all died. Gastric fever was again the cause of death on their certificates, except for the baby, who died from 'teething convulsions'.

Those three bodies were exhumed while Mary Ann waited for her trial in Durham Jail, and Dr Scattergood found traces of arsenic in all of them. Newspapers began looking more closely at the life of the miner's daughter from the Durham pit village of Low Moorsley. They unearthed a horrifying dossier of an apparently kind, good-natured and devout Methodist who seemed to spread death wherever she went.

In 1852, aged 20, she had married a labourer called William Mowbray, and moved to Devon. She had five children there, but four died. The couple returned to the northeast, moving from house to house in the Sunderland area, while Mary Ann worked at the town's infirmary. They had three more children. All died. Then Mowbray died. Mary Ann married again. Her husband, an engineer called George Wood, died in October 1866, 14 months after the wedding.

A month later, Mary Ann moved in as housekeeper to widower James Robinson and his three children. She soon became pregnant and married Robinson. But within weeks of her arrival in the household Robinson's ten-month-old son John was dead. On 21 April 1867, Robinson's son James, six, went to his grave. Five days later, his sister Elizabeth, followed him. And, on 2 May, nine-year-old Isabella, the only survivor of Mary Ann's marriage to Mowbray, lost her life.

Mary Ann had two daughters by Robinson. The first died within days of birth. The second was given away to a friend when the marriage broke up. Robinson survived, possibly because he resisted his wife's pleas to take out insurance on his life. But others who knew Mary Ann were not so lucky. She went to visit her mother because she feared she 'might be about to die'. No one else was worried about the apparently sprightly 54-year-old, but within nine days she was dead. Mary Ann moved on, laden with clothes and bedlinen.

She met and became friends with Margaret Cotton, and was introduced to her brother Frederick. Mary Ann quickly became pregnant, and married her new lover bigamously – her third husband, Robinson, was still alive. The wedding was slightly marred by the unexpected death of Margaret, whose £60 bank account went to the newly-weds.

In all, 21 people close to Mary Ann lost their lives in less than 20 years. She had given birth to 11 children, yet only one survived – the girl she gave away. Small wonder, then, that on the morning of her trial, a local newspaper, unfettered by today's laws of libel and contempt, ran the headline 'The Great Poisoning Case At West Auckland – Horrible Revelations'. But, when she stepped into the courtroom at Durham Assizes shortly before 10am on 5 March 1873, she was charged only with one killing, that of her stepson, Charles Edward.

The prosecution, led by Sir Charles Russell, later to become Lord Chief Justice, alleged the 40-year-old widow had poisoned the boy because there was a Prudential Insurance policy on his life worth £8, and because he was an impediment to her marriage to her excise officer lover, a man called Quick-Manning, by whom she was already pregnant. 'She was badly off and Charles Edward was a tie and burden to her,' said Sir Charles.

Mary Ann Dodds, a former neighbour of the accused, told the court she had bought a mixer of arsenic and soft soap from one of the village's chemist's shops in May 1872, two months before the boy's death. 'The mixture was needed to remove bugs from a bed in Mary Ann's home,' she said. 'I rubbed most of it into the joints of the bed and the iron crosspieces underneath.'

Chemist John Townsend said the mixture would have contained about a course of arsenic – about 480g. Three grains were enough to kill an adult. He also thought it significant that his shop was not the closest chemist to widow Cotton's home.

Thomas Riley gave his evidence about Mary Ann's eagerness to get the boy off her hands, and Dr Kilburn explained the medical steps he had taken. It was then that controversy entered the trial. The prosecution wanted to introduce evidence of earlier deaths in the family. Defence lawyer Thomas Campbell Foster, appointed only two days before the trial because Cotton could not afford her own legal representation, protested that his client was charged with only one death, which he maintained was an accident caused by arsenic impregnation of some green floral wallpaper. To discuss the earlier deaths would prejudice a fair trial, he said.

But Judge Sir Thomas Archibald ruled against him, citing legal precedent. From that moment on, the verdict was a foregone conclusion. The defence introduced no witnesses, and at 6.50pm on the third day of the trial the jury returned after only an hour's deliberations to pronounce Mary Ann Cotton guilty of murder.

The judge donned his black cap to sentence her to death, saying: 'You seem to have given way to that most awful of all delusions, which sometimes takes possession of persons wanting in proper moral and religious sense, that you could carry out your wicked designs without detection. But while murder by poison is the most detestable of all crimes, and one at which human nature shudders, it is one the nature of which, in the order of God's providence, always leaves behind it complete and incontestable traces of guilt. Poisoning, as it were, in the very act of crime writes an indelible record of guilt.'

They were fine words, but not strictly true. The state of medical knowledge in the 1870s was a common killer, and overworked doctors could not examine every corpse without strong reasons. Though the final tolls of deaths in Mary Ann's circle was high, she avoided suspicion by moving house frequently, and always calling in local doctors when her victims began complaining of stomach pains. The fact that she had once been a nurse, and was well known for caring for sick neighbours, also made people trust her.

No one will ever know how many of the 21 unlucky people around her were poisoned for insurance money or possessions, or because they stood in the way of a new marriage. Most people put the number of murders at 14 or 15. But, despite the horror at what the *Newcastle Journal* newspaper described as 'a monster in human shape', many people had misgivings about her death sentence. There were doubts about hanging a woman, doubts about the way her defence in court had been organized, doubts about whether evidence of earlier deaths should have been allowed, doubts about the lack of any witness for the defence.

The *Newcastle Journal* admitted:

> 'Perhaps the most astounding thought of all is that a woman could act thus without becoming horrible and repulsive. Mary Ann Cotton, on the contrary, seems to have possessed the faculty of getting a new husband whenever she wanted one. To her other children and her lodger, even when she was deliberately poisoning them, she is said to have maintained a rather kindly manner.'

The paper felt instinctively that the earth should be rid of her, but added: 'Pity cannot be withheld, though it must be mingled with horror.'

Mary Ann spent her last few days in jail trying to win support for a petition for a reprieve. She gave birth to Quick-Manning's daughter, Margaret, and arranged for her to go to a married couple who could not have children. Five days before her execution, the baby was forcibly taken from her. On 24 March 1873, still maintaining her innocence, she went to the scaffold at Durham. It was three minutes before the convulsions of her body stopped.

Within eight days, a stage play, *The Life and Death of Mary Ann Cotton*, was being performed in theatres, labelled 'a great moral drama'. Mothers threatened recalcitrant children with the prospect of a visit from the West Auckland widow, and youngsters made up a skipping rhyme which began: 'Mary Ann Cotton, she's dead and rotten.' But she remains today one of the most enigmatic figures in the gallery of killers – a simple-minded mass murderer who evoked revulsion and sympathy in equal measures.

Lydia Sherman

Wherever Lydia Sherman went she found buildings infested with rats. Or at least that was the story she told the neighbourhood druggist from whom she bought her poison.

The arsenic soon eliminated the rats and, as it turned out, some of the human beings she considered a nuisance, too. As many as 42 people were believed to have died by Lydia's hand.

Married to patrolman Edward Struck of the New York Police Department, the sturdy but attractive housewife kept a low profile until 1864. Then Struck was sacked by the police for a shabby display of cowardice and promptly turned into an unemployed drunk. Lydia put him to bed one evening with a lethal snack of oatmeal gruel and rat poison.

Puzzled as to the manner of his death, the doctor blamed it on 'consumption' but made up his mind to ask for an official investigation. But Lydia had ensured her husband had a quick burial and the authorities saw no reason to intrude on her 'grief'.

One by one Lydia's children died – Mary Ann, Edward,

William, George, Ann Eliza, and finally the widow's namesake, tiny toddler Lydia. In every case she shrewdly called in a different doctor, all of whom obligingly took her word for the cause of death.

An ex-brother-in-law went to the authorities swearing Lydia was 'full of black evil' and demanding that the bodies be exhumed. But the bored bureaucrats refused to budge.

Lydia moved from one job to another. In 1868 she married an aging and rich widower named Dennis Hurlbut. With rat poison available at 10 cents a package, he was soon out of the way.

That left her free to marry Nelson Sherman, who took her with him to his Connecticut home. There she had problems, including a suspicious mother-in-law and the four Sherman children by a previous marriage.

Two of the children she disposed of at once. Mourning the death of his 14-year-old daughter, Addie, Nelson Sherman turned to alcohol and thus signed his own death warrant.

'I just wanted to lure him off the liquor habit,' Lydia said. A Connecticut doctor was suspicious and insisted that his stomach and liver be analysed. Toxicologists found enough arsenic to kill an army. The vital organs of the two children were also permeated with poison.

Pleading that she had murdered out of human compassion – 'all those people were sick, after all' – the fashionably dressed widow cut an impressive figure at her trial in New Haven, Connecticut. And, in a way, her luck held. Amazingly gentle with the not-so-gentle murderess, Judge Park instructed the jury to consider only charges of second-degree murder.

Sentenced to life in Weathersfield Prison, she vowed she would never die in jail. But there her luck did end – she was still behind bars when she died in 1878.

Jane Andrews

On 16 May 2001 Judge Michael Hyam sentenced 34-year-old Jane Andrews to life imprisonment, concluding that: 'In killing the man you loved, you ended his life and ruined your own. It is evident that you made your attack on him when you were consumed with anger and bitterness. Nothing could justify what you did.'

Jane Andrews was a social climber, anxious to leave the days of her modest northeast upbringing far behind her. From her early 20s, she craved acceptance into the wealthy London social set and would lie and deceive with effortless skill.

At 21, shortly after completing a course in fashion and design at Grimsby College of Art, she applied to an anonymous advert in *The Lady* magazine for a dresser. Within months she had been employed in the royal household. Andrews became a royal aide for the Duchess of York, initially as her dresser, but the role developed into assistant, shopper, style advisor, confidante and travel companion all merged into one.

During her years serving the royal family, Andrews made the most of her position to find a wealthy husband for herself. Her attempts to lure a suitable husband into her grasp seemed glaringly apparent to the people she surrounded herself with, the 'Sloane set' as she called them. In 1990 she married Christopher Dunn-Butler, but her numerous flings eventually brought the marriage to an end five years later. A string of failed relationships (many of which involved acquaintances of the Duchess) followed until 1998 when she met, and fell in love with, Tommy Cressman.

An intense and often difficult character, Andrews desperately wanted to make Tommy Cressman fall in love with her. In actual fact, Cressman felt sorry for Andrews, falling for her stories of abuse when she was a young child. The couple began living together, and Andrews was determined to make Cressman her husband. By this time, unbeknown to Cressman, Andrews was already receiving medication including Prozac for depression (Andrews blamed her depressed state for losing her job with the Duchess in 1997).

As time passed by, Andrews never heard the proposal of marriage she yearned for so much from Cressman. She invested all her hopes in the wealthy businessman, but her desperate adoration of Cressman went unrequited, only serving to fuel her obsessive intent. A few years earlier, Andrews had stalked one of her former lovers demonstrating even then her compulsive and obsessive nature. Another lover claimed that when he split up with Andrews she had sent him an impassioned plea that she was pregnant and that they should marry – these all turned out to be lies from Andrews.

Andrews gave the reluctant Cressman an ultimatum to marry her within six months. A friend of Cressman later said: 'Jane was an intense character, intent on getting married, intent on catching Tommy, but Tommy was not yet ready. He was having second thoughts.'

On holiday in Cannes, shortly before the fateful night, Andrews believed her lover would at last pop the question, but the proposal of marriage never came. Cressman instead attempted to persuade Andrews to leave the relationship of her own volition, not wanting to be the initiator of a split; Andrews had previously threatened suicide and Cressman certainly did not want a repeat performance. Little did he know that the resulting death would be his own.

The police were not alerted to the murder scene until the following day. It was only when Cressman failed to show up at work on the Monday that police were called to his house, where they discovered the remains of a passionate and bloody murder.

In the early hours of the day before, Sunday 17 September 2000, Andrews battered Cressman with a cricket bat before gruesomely stabbing him in the chest with a 19cm kitchen knife. She claimed that Cressman had attacked and anally raped her and that she had lashed out in self-defence, frightened of what else he would do. Yet the crime scene provided some vital clues to contradict this. Diluted blood was found in the bathroom sink adjacent to the bedroom where Cressman was found, and a bloodstained towel was found on the floor above, demonstrating that Andrews had not been as frightened as she claimed and had not fled the house immediately.

Andrews claimed she thought she had hurt Cressman but not killed him, yet two notes addressed to her parents indicate that she knew exactly what she had done. The first read: 'My dearest parents, I am so sorry. No more hurt inside me anymore.' The second read: 'Tom hurt me so much. He was so cruel to me.'

Andrews went on the run following the murder until she was tracked down by police, hiding under blankets in her VW Polo car, in Cornwall on 20 September, having overdosed on 30–40 painkillers. In the few days between the murder and being found by the police, Andrews sent a number of dramatic text messages on her mobile phone to friends and family, claiming not to understand why Cressman had not been in touch and why her face was plastered over national newspapers.

The trial at the Old Bailey found Andrews guilty of murder by a verdict from the jury of 11 to 1. The overwhelming evidence from the crime scene and from acquaintances of both Andrews and Cressman gave the court little doubt that Andrews had committed an impassioned and brutal murder. Friends and family of Cressman were appalled by Andrews's attempts to destroy Tommy Cressman's character; her sordid allegations that he was a violent sexual deviant were attributed to her vindictive, deceitful and troubled mind.

The society girl who had gone from rags to riches brought about her own downfall through her obsessive and intense nature. Her desire to marry a wealthy husband and to live happily ever after was never going to be a fairytale-come-true. Instead Jane Andrews lied, cheated and killed without remorse.

A Tale of Two Sisters

Chronic alcoholism is a deep-rooted problem in the French countryside. Wine is cheap and the hard routines of farming life can be monotonous. To escape them, many a working man daily stupefies his senses with the bottle. M. Bouvier of Saint-Macaire came from a long line of hereditary alcoholics. His special drink was not wine, as it happens, but a crude cider alcohol distilled in the region of western France where he lived. Bouvier used to get violently drunk and regularly threatened to murder his wife and two daughters. From an early age, the girls learned to help their mother with the almost nightly ordeal of strapping him down to the bed. Someone would then run for the doctor. The doctor would give him the injections that brought a fragile calm to the household.

This is the story of those two sisters. Georgette, the older one, plays only a peripheral role in the drama. Yet it was to be intensely significant in the life of Léone, the younger girl.

The village of Saint-Macaire lies near the town of Cholet in the Maine-et-Loire departement. And, at the local school, Georgette showed considerable intelligence. At the age of 18 she managed to escape the household by entering a convent at Angers. Forsaking the hell of her family life, she submitted to the pious disciplines of a nun's existence and there, for a while, we must leave her.

Léone Bouvier, two years younger, cried for a week when her sister abandoned the household. She was alone now with the wreck of her father and a mother who had also taken to drinking. Léone was not bright; in fact, her school years had left her practically illiterate. The meagre salary she earned at a local shoe factory was absorbed by the family's needs. But her mother showed no gratitude. She mocked Léone for being worthless and dull-witted. And, rejected by all those closest to her, Léone looked for love elsewhere. She turned, in particular, to men.

She was not a pretty girl. Her eyes were wide-set, her nose was large and a ragged shank of dark hair fell across her low brow. A generous heart only made her an easier prey for the local lads.

Léone lost her virginity to a fellow factory worker at a hurried coupling in the corner of a field. She saw him the next day, laughing about the episode with his mates in the factory yard. Other sad encounters were to follow until she struck up with a decent-hearted young man in the Air Force. Fate never gave Léone a break, though; not long after they arranged to be married, the youth was killed in an accident.

It was in the bleak period following the incident that Léone met Emile Clenet, a 22-year-old garage mechanic from Nantes. Their first brief encounter was at a dance in Cholet, and they made a rendezvous for the following afternoon. Misfortune was Léone's constant companion, and while cycling to the meeting she had to stop to fix a puncture. By the time she arrived, he was gone.

Six months later, however, they met again at the Lent carnival in Cholet. 'You're six months late,' joked Emile. 'But never mind, we've found each other again.' They enjoyed all the fun of the fair together and, afterwards, Emile took her to a hotel room. She had never been treated to clean sheets before. She learned to love him then.

The couple fell into a set pattern of meetings. To reverse the lyrics of the popular song, it was 'Only on a Sunday' for Emile and Léone. He was a hard worker and reserved only the seventh day for his pleasures. Every Sunday, Léone would cycle to a particular spot near Cholet, and Emile would pick her up on his motorbike. After picnicking and perhaps some evening dancing, they would retire to a cheap hotel.

There was talk of marriage, and Emile took her home to meet his parents, who rather liked their son's strange little girlfriend. It is hard to determine exactly what went wrong. Perhaps Emile never seriously intended marriage. Once, there was an accident with his motorbike and Léone took a knock on the head. She suffered headaches and bouts of depression after that.

Emile could be cruel, too. Once, snapped by a street photographer, the couple went to pick up the picture. Emile took one look and said he didn't want it. When Léone asked why, he said: 'Just look at that face and you'll understand.' She hurried off to cry alone. Since meeting Emile, Léone had been taking care of her appearance, indulging in all the feminine vanities. Words like those must have wounded deeply.

The real blow came when she found she was pregnant and Emile told her to get rid of the unborn child. She did so – but the headaches and depressions grew worse after that. Then, in January 1952, she lost her job. There was a furious row in her home that night: her mother raged at her and her drunken father tried to give her a thrashing. Léone fled the household. It took her all night to cycle the 30-odd miles to Nantes where Emile worked. But, when she got there in the morning, Emile was annoyed. Their arrangement was only for Sundays, he said. It was a weekday. She must leave.

Utterly abandoned, Léone spent two weeks as an outcast in Nantes, wandering the cold, winter streets. A second attempt to see Emile resulted in another rebuff. He said he was too busy to see her for the next couple of Sundays. Her money ran out. She had nowhere to sleep. And, though she was never very clear about what happened during that blank fortnight, it seems she slipped into prostitution.

During the days, Léone took to standing outside gun-shop windows, gazing dazedly in at the gleaming butts and barrels. Later, she was to say that she did not quite know why she did so, perhaps suicide had been in her mind. But she remembered one incident very clearly. As she stood there, shivering in the rain, a strange young man had appeared at her side. 'Don't,' said the figure. 'He is too young. He has the right to live.' Then he disappeared.

Hallucination? Léone had been a victim all her life, and perhaps her conscious mind was moving towards thoughts of self-destruction. But perhaps, too, some last instinct to survive and strike outward was prompting from within. The impulse was to murder her lover. And, to redress the balance, her conscience invented the phantasmagoric young man who seemed to know her thoughts.

Whatever the truth, that voice seems to have earned Emile a reprieve. For she did not yet buy a gun. Instead, physically and emotionally exhausted, she returned to her village. Nothing had changed there. On arrival, her father was in one of his frenzies. Mechanically, she helped her mother strap him to the bed.

She had come back from one hell to another, and only thoughts of Emile sustained her. Fifteenth February 1952 was Léone's 23rd birthday. Would her lover remember? Last year he bought her a bicycle lamp – the only present of her adult life. She summoned up her courage, took the last of her savings, and boarded the coach back to Nantes. Humbly and apologetically she approached him at the garage and asked if they could meet on Sunday at the usual place. He showed no sign of remembering her birthday. But – to her intense joy – he agreed to meet at the rendezvous.

When he came, he brought no birthday present. Emile made love brusquely that Sunday and he did not stay the night as usual. It was on the following day that Léone went into Nantes and sought out one of the gun shops. There she bought a .22 automatic. The pistol had recently been declared a 'sporting weapon'. Léone, who could barely sign her name, did not need a licence.

She lived now only for their Sundays. Léone hung around in Nantes waiting for the next meeting, living from day to day in the dockside area by taking men into hotel bedrooms. When the grey haze of waiting hours was over she hastened to their rendezvous at Cholet. Emile was not there. She scoured the town and eventually found his motorbike parked outside a cinema. When the film was over she ran to meet him, but he brushed her off. He had flu, he said. He was going straight home. She must wait for the coming Lent carnival.

Fate, which had dogged Léone all her life, had reserved its completing irony for this meeting. It was at Cholet's Lent carnival that the couple had enjoyed their first night together two years earlier. It was at the Lent carnival too, with its hurdy-gurdy gaiety, that Léone Bouvier was to kill her lover.

Yet it started so well. Emile roared up on his motorbike at their rendezvous and she mounted pillion on the back just as in the old days. She kissed him as they rode into the town centre to mingle with the carnival crowds. They moved gaily among the stalls, the streamers and the balloons. Emile stopped by a shooting range to demonstrate his prowess. The weapon (fate again) was a .22 automatic. And above the staccato crackle of gunshot he told her he was leaving to work in North Africa. He was going, he said, for good.

'But what about me?' We were going to get married...'

'So what?'

'You don't want to marry me any more, then?'

'C'est la vie.' Emile shrugged and mumbled platitudes, telling her she would find someone better than him. Léone was incredulous. She asked again. Again he said no, he would never marry her.

Emile drove her back to her bicycle, locked up at their rendezvous. There she implored him: 'Emile, you aren't going off and leaving me like this?'

Emile said nothing, but returned to his motorcycle and climbed on, preparing to leave. Léone took the gun from her handbag and slipped it under her coat. She came up behind him. 'Emile,' she whispered, 'kiss me for the last time . . .'

He did not respond. She put her left arm around his neck and pulled him tenderly towards her. Gently, she kissed his cheek. And as she did so she withdrew the pistol and placed the barrel-end against his neck. Then she pulled the trigger.

There was only one shot.

Afterwards she mounted her bicycle and fled, pedalling blindly to the only place she knew that offered sanctuary. It was to Angers that she cycled, to her sister's convent. She arrived there in distress, without explaining what had happened. Georgette gave her coffee and put her to bed – the poor, ruined child come like a ghost from her past.

The police came the following afternoon. Léone was arrested in the convent, but such are the procedures of French law that it was not until December 1953 that she was brought before the Assizes of Maine-et-Loire. French courts are traditionally flexible in the handling of a *crime passionnel*. Léone's misfortune was to face an unusually aggressive prosecutor and a hostile judge.

Judges play a more active role in the French courts than their English equivalents do. They may examine and cross-question a defendant at some length. And, at

Léone's trial in Angers, the judge showed himself entirely lacking in the subtlety associated with the French legal mind. What he had in abundance was the stubborn hypocrisy of the French provincial bourgeois.

He simply could not see that Léone's blighted childhood or her lover's callous rebuffs made one jot of difference to the case. Why did she not stay at her parents' hearth instead of wandering the dockside at Nantes? The answer should have been evident when Léone's father was brought to the witness box, sweating and shaking under the ordeal of a morning without a drink. The experts declared him a hereditary alcoholic. The mother, too, frankly admitted that they had all lived in mortal fear of his violence. But she explained that she'd done the best she could, adding the fateful reflection that her other daughter was a nun.

The judge pounced.

'You see!' he called, rounding on Léone: 'There was no need for you to go wrong. Why did you go wrong?' It is hard to exaggerate the part played by this circumstance. It seemed to nullify every mitigating factor of Léone's background. The writer Derrick Goodman has made the point eloquently: they did not come down hard on Léone because she had murdered her lover. It was because her sister was a nun.

The judge continued with his tirade, dwelling on the fact that Léone had killed Emile as she kissed him. This was a detail that seemed to him an incomprehensible outrage: '*Atroce*!' he fumed, '*atroce*!'

Léone stood quietly in the dock, her head bowed low.

'Why did you kill him?' demanded the judge.

Tears were streaming down her cheeks as Léone raised her head.

'I loved him,' she said simply.

The prosecution had called for the death penalty on the charge of premeditated murder. For reasons stated in the case of Pauline Dubuisson, there was no likelihood of

Léone being executed. In fact, the defence had every right to expect a lenient judgement. What was Léone's crime if not a crime passionnel? Middle-class ladies had walked scot-free in cases of this nature.

The jury was out for only a quarter of an hour. And it would seem that they arrived at the same formula as in the case of Pauline Dubuisson. They avoided the charge of premeditated murder, for that carried an automatic death penalty, and found her guilty of murder – but without premeditation.

The foreman complacently suggested that the prisoner be given the maximum penalty of penal servitude for life – a minimum of 20 years. The judge readily agreed. And so, with the afflictions of a simple mind and a warm heart, a horrific childhood and a succession of rejections, Léone Bouvier fell victim to the full weight of French law.

Kittie Byron

When 23-year-old Kittie Byron stabbed her lover to death on the steps of a London post office, the charge really had to be murder. And murder in 1902 was a hanging offence. It made no difference that, when the flood of her fury was spent, she collapsed sobbing on his crumpled body, calling pitifully: 'Reggie . . . Dear Reggie . . . Let me kiss my Reggie . . .'

The crime was committed in broad daylight before a dozen witnesses. She had stabbed him twice: once through the back and once through the breast. The second blow was probably the one that killed him. He died almost instantly.

Yet everyone's sympathy was with the frail, dark-haired girl who had wielded the knife. The coroner's jury, for example, brought in a verdict of manslaughter. The officials were incredulous, and the coroner himself asked: 'Do you mean unlawful killing without malice?'

'Yes,' insisted the foreman, 'killing on the impulse of the moment. We do not believe she went there with the intention of killing him.'

In fact, all the evidence suggested that Kittie Byron went there with precisely that intention. And, when she was brought for trial the following month, it was on a charge of murder.

For some months before the fatal episode, Kittie Byron had been living with Arthur Reginald Baker in rooms at 18 Duke Street, off Oxford Street, in the West End. Baker was a married man and a member of the Stock Exchange. But that did not prevent him from presenting himself and his mistress to the landlady as 'Mr and Mrs Baker'. He drank heavily, often knocked Kittie about, and on one occasion half-strangled her. But Kittie was loyal. She never touched liquor herself, and tried to shield her lover from the consequences of his actions.

Events came to a head on the night of Friday 7 November 1902, when the landlady heard a furious row erupt in the bed-sitting room. She went up and entered; bedclothes had been thrown all about and lay in chaos on the floor; in one corner was a hat which had been ripped into shreds. The landlady confronted the drunken Baker, but Kittie interceded. 'Oh, there's nothing the matter,' she said: 'We've been playing milliner.'

Not long after the landlady left the room, the quarrel broke out again. It went on all evening, and at 1.15am the householder went back again to try to stop it. She found Kittie in the corridor, shivering in her nightdress. She was plainly terrified – yet still she insisted that nothing was the matter.

The next morning the landlady gave the couple notice to leave the premises. A weekend of calm followed, and on Monday morning Baker even took Kittie a cup of tea before leaving for the office. She kissed him goodbye – a domestic scene – nothing hinted at the coming drama. The date was 10 November 1902, the day of the fatal stabbing.

The whole sequence of events emerged clearly at the trial. Just before he left the house, Baker asked the landlady for a private word. He requested that they be allowed to stay in the house after all. The landlady, however, insisted that they must leave. It was then that Baker informed her that Kittie was not his wife. The girl was the cause of the trouble, he said. She was 'no class' and would leave tomorrow.

The conversation was overhead by a housemaid who immediately told Kittie that Baker was going to cast her aside. 'Will he?' fumed the enraged girl. 'I'll kill him before the day is out!' She made her own preparations for going out, and confessed to the landlady about the phoney marriage. 'Then why don't you leave him?' asked the landlady, who had assumed that only wedlock kept the couple together. 'I can't,' said Kittie, 'because I love him so.'

She went to a shop in Oxford Street and asked a cutler for a long, sharp knife. He showed her a large item with a sprung blade that fitted into the hasp. She seemed too slight a girl to handle it, and the cutler suggested alternatives. No, said Kittie, she had a strong grip, and she proved it by operating the spring action several times. Having bought the knife she slipped it into her coat and made her way to a post office in Lombard Street. The building stood in the heart of the City where Baker worked. It was Lord Mayor's Day. The crowds were out in the streets.

From the post office, Kittie sent Baker an express letter bearing the words: 'Dear Reg. Want you immediate importantly, Kittie.' But the messenger boy could not reach Baker at the Stock Exchange and returned to Lombard Street with the note. Kittie insisted that he go back again. The boy did so – and this time located Baker who returned with him to the post office.

Staff at the post office had noticed the girl's excited state. And they also noticed an absurdly trivial dispute which arose when Baker arrived. An extra charge of two pence had to be paid for the messenger boy's time. Baker flatly refused to hand the sum over; Kittie insisted that it be paid and offered her lover a florin. Somehow, the incident speaks volumes about the relative characters of the couple. Baker was still refusing to pay as he left the post office, with Kittie rushing after him. The staff noticed something flash in her hand as she made her exit.

She caught him on the steps. The two blows were swift, and bystanders noticed no blood. In fact, the several witnesses at first thought she was striking him with her muff. Baker may well have been dead before a workman grabbed Kittie's hand and the knife fell with a clatter to the pavement. The trance of her fury was shattered, and it was then that Kittie fell sobbing on her lover's body: 'Let me kiss my Reggie . . . Let me kiss my husband. . .'

Kittie Byron made two different statements to the police shortly after her arrest. In the first she said: 'I killed him wilfully, and he deserved it, and the sooner I am killed the better.' In the second: 'I bought the knife to hit him; I didn't know I was killing him.' At the trial which followed she only managed to whisper 'not guilty' as her plea to the indictment.

She made a pitiable figure in the dock, a pale and delicate girl whose dark eyes wandered dazedly around the court. She wore a blue serge suit and a shirt whose white linen collar was high about her throat, fastened with a black tie. The court heard that her real name was Emma Byron, but it was not hard to see why she had earned the diminutive of 'Kittie'. Sir Travers Humphreys, then a junior brief for her defence, later recalled how she clung to the wardress who brought her into the dock: 'It seemed as if she would break down at the very outset.'

Some 20 witnesses were called by the prosecution, and Kittie did break down. It happened as a surgeon was indicating on his own body the position of her lover's stab wounds. A stifled wail was heard. All eyes turned to the dock where Kittie was racked with violent sobs.

The defence called no witnesses – not even Kittie herself. Her counsel was Henry ('Harry') Dickens, son of the great Victorian novelist, and a man who had inherited his father's genius for stirring the emotions. Dickens tried to make out a case for Kittie having intended to commit suicide rather than murder. It was an improbable thesis which ran contrary to the evidence. He was on safer ground in pointing to the plight and character of the injured girl, and in touching the hearts of the jurors.

The judge, in his summing-up, was candid about his own emotions: 'Gentlemen of the jury, if I had consulted my own feelings I should probably have stopped this case at the outset.' But he was equally candid in dismissing manslaughter as an appropriate verdict. The jury was out for ten minutes. They found her guilty of murder – but with a strong recommendation for mercy.

The form had to be observed. The black cap was brought forth, and the dread sentence was passed. Kittie, weakly professing herself innocent of wilful murder, was to hang by the neck until dead. But she never did. Great waves of public sympathy had gone out to the frail and mistreated girl. A huge petition was quickly raised asking for a reprieve and no fewer than 15,000 signatures were obtained in a single morning. Three thousand signatures were raised from among the clerks at the Stock Exchange itself. In the event, the petition was never formally presented to the authorities, for the Home Secretary granted the reprieve before receiving the document.

Kittie Byron's sentence was commuted to penal servitude for life. In 1907, her sentence was reduced, and she was released the following year.